KT-403-831

Tramping in New Zealand
a Lonely Planet walking guide

Jim DuFresne
Jeff Williams

Tramping in New Zealand

3rd edition

Published by
Lonely Planet Publications
Head Office: PO Box 617, Hawthorn, Vic 3122, Australia
Branches: 155 Filbert St, Suite 251, Oakland, CA 94607, USA
               10 Barley Mow Passage, Chiswick, London W4 4PH, UK
               71 bis rue du Cardinal Lemoine, 75005 Paris, France

Printed by
Singapore National Printers Ltd, Singapore

Photographs by
Vicki Beale (VB), Department of Conservation (DOC), Jim DuFresne (JD), Nancy Keller (NK),
New Zealand Tourist Bureau (NZTB), Tony Wheeler (TW) and Jeff Williams (JW).

Front cover: Looking north from Mt Owen, Murchison, Nelson Region (Andris Apse,
             The Photo Library – Sydney)
Title page: Crossing Copland Pass, Southern Alps (JW)

First Published
November 1982

This Edition
January 1995

**Although the authors and publisher have tried to make the information as
accurate as possible, they accept no responsibility for any loss, injury or
inconvenience sustained by any person using this book.**

National Library of Australia Cataloguing in Publication Data

DuFresne, Jim
     Tramping in New Zealand.

     3rd ed.
     Includes index.
     ISBN 0 86442 253 9.

     1. New Zealand – Guidebooks. I. Williams, Jeff, 1954 Dec.
     I5- . II. Title. (Series : Lonely Planet walking guide).

919.310437

Jim DuFresne

A former sports and outdoors editor for the *Juneau Empire*, Jim was the first Alaskan sportswriter to win a national award from Associated Press. He is presently a freelance writer based in Clarkston, Michigan and author of 12 outdoor and wilderness/travel books, including Lonely Planet's *Alaska* and *Trekking in Alaska* guidebooks.

Jeff Williams

Since Jeff started working for Lonely Planet, he has divided his time between writing, chasing his two-year-old son, Callum, and wishing for a rest. He has languished in New Zealand and Western Australia researching and updating this book, and contributed to *New Zealand*, *Outback Australia* and *Australia*. He has just completed Lonely Planet's *Western Australia* guidebook.

From Jeff

First, thanks to Jim DuFresne for trusting me to go to New Zealand to do this update. Most importantly, however, my thanks go to the Kiwis, especially to those people who look after the tracks, maintaining both their sense of humour and pride in what they are doing. Those deserving souls who went out of their way are:

Diana Parr of the Department of Conservation (DOC) in Wellington (temporarily located at the Stewart Island field centre) is deservedly first in this list; Pearl Hewson, information officer for DOC, also in Wellington; Mary Anne Webber, who wanted the Queen Charlotte Walkway in the book and made it easy for us to walk it; 'Rat' of Auckland for being the sort of vermin that should be preserved not exterminated; Tim and Paula de Jong of Dreamers & East-Capers for hospitality in Opotiki; Dwayne Gray (not Zane Grey) from England who walked the new walks with me; Carla Rauer for giving me a new dimension on a writer's drinking consumption; Myra, Linda and Winston of Greymouth for the whitebait; Athol and Gill Forrest for reintroducing me to the contemplative David Lyon; the owners of Awaroa Lodge on the Abel Tasman Coast Walk for letting us sleep on the verandah – you don't understand how appreciated that sort of gesture is; the DOC staff in Christchurch; the staff of Buller Adventures for an unforgettable night on Westport's Rugby Park; Ray Hirama Tamihana for

unlocking the secret of Papaitonga and the key to longevity; and Alison and Callum at home.

Since the last edition, microeconomic reform and privatisation have plunged New Zealand into administrative turmoil. This economic tsunami has effected everything except the tracks themselves. Sure, the odd flood and landslide have altered them slightly, a hut here and there has disappeared in conflagration, and Mt Cook shed a 10-metre thickness of its East Face, but the routes remain much as they were.

This book

This is the third edition of *Tramping in New Zealand*. The first two editions were written by Jim DuFresne; this edition was updated by Jeff Williams, co-author of Lonely Planet's *New Zealand* guidebook. This edition has been reorganised to respond more effectively to trampers' needs. It also includes a number of new tramping regions and walks.

From the Publisher

This edition of *Tramping in New Zealand* was edited by Alison White and proofed by David Collins. The maps were drawn by Andrew Smith and Sandra Smythe. Tamsin Wilson was responsible for layout and the cover was designed by Jane Hart.

Warning & Request

Things change – prices go up, schedules change, good places go bad and bad places go bankrupt – nothing stays the same. So if you find things better or worse, recently opened or long since closed, please write and tell us and help make the next edition better.

Your letters will be used to help update future editions and, where possible, important changes will be included in a Stop Press section in reprints.

We greatly appreciate all information that is sent to us by travellers. Back at Lonely Planet, we employ a hard-working readers' letters team to sort through the many letters we receive. The best ones will be rewarded with a free copy of the next edition or another Lonely Planet guide if you prefer. We give away lots of books, but, unfortunately, not every letter/postcard receives one.

Contents

Map Legend

BOUNDARIES

～～～～～～～～ .... International Boundary

～～～～～～～～ .... Provincial Boundary

— — — — — — — — — .... Marine Park Boundary

ROUTES ....

──────────────── .... Freeway

──────────────── .... Highway

──────────────── .... Major Road

— — — — — — — — — .... Unsealed Road or Track

════════════════ .... City Road

════════════════ .... City Street

+++++++++++++++ .... Railway

.... Underground Railway

— — — — — — — — — .... Walking Track

•••••••••••••••••• .... Walking Tour

— — — — — — — — — .... Ferry Route

-H-H-H-H-H-H-H-H- .... Cable Car or Chairlift

AREA FEATURES

.... Park, Gardens

.... National Park

.... Forest

.... Built-Up Area

.... Pedestrian Mall

.... Market

\+   \+   \+   \+ .... Cemetery

.... Beach or Desert

.... Glacier

HYDROGRAPHIC FEATURES

.... Coastline

.... River, Creek

.... Intermittent River or Creek

.... Lake, Intermittent Lake

.... Canal

.... Swamp

SYMBOLS

◎ **CAPITAL**	.... National Capital		✚	★	.... Hospital, Police Station
◉ **Capital**	.... Provincial Capital		✈	✝	.... Airport, Airfield
▒ **CITY**	.... Major City		◪	✿	.... Swimming Pool, Gardens
● **City**	.... City		❖	🐘	.... Shopping Centre, Zoo
● Town	.... Town		↑	⊤	.... Golf Course, Picnic Site
● Village	.... Village		←	A25	One Way Street, Route Number
■	.... Place to Stay			∴	...... Archaeological Site or Ruins
▼	.... Place to Eat		⋒	♟	.... Stately Home, Monument
♟	.... Pub, Bar		ㅤ	◼	.... Castle, Tomb
✉	☎	.... Post Office, Telephone	∩	⌂	.... Cave, Hut or Shelter
❶	❾	.... Tourist Information, Bank	▲	☀	.... Mountain or Hill, Lookout
◓	ℙ	.... Transport, Parking	🚻	⊻	.... Lighthouse, Shipwreck
⬫	🛈	.... Museum, Youth Hostel	)(	⌖	.... Pass, Spring
⌸	⚘	Caravan Park, Camping Ground	■─────	.... Ancient or City Wall
✝	▱	✝ .... Church, Cathedral	──»»──	»──	.... Rapids, Waterfalls
☪	✡	.... Mosque, Synagogue	┉┉⟹	⟸	.... Cliff or Escarpment, Tunnel
⊥	⚏	Buddhist Temple, Hindu Temple	+++++++	.... Railway Station

Note: not all symbols displayed above appear in this book

Introduction

A tramping holiday is the best way to explore the New Zealand bush and the only way to see much of the country's unique flora & fauna. This guide is both an aid to the Kiwi who wants to progress from day hikes to overnight outings, and an invaluable tool for overseas travellers who are choosing the tracks to walk during their stay in New Zealand

Nearly 50 tracks are featured (see map on page 50), and each track description has an accompanying map. All these tracks are walks of two or more days, and all but three (Inland Pack Track, Te Paki Reserves and Nydia Track) have huts along them.

The track descriptions encompass tramps from Cape Reinga in the far north of the North Island to two tramps on Stewart Island, off the south coast of the South Island. Tracks in all 13 national parks, nine of the 20 forest parks and two of the three maritime parks are included, and most of the interesting geological features of New Zealand are passed along the way.

The tracks present a good cross-section of the country's tramping opportunities, from easy walking in the Abel Tasman National Park to wilderness treks in the Raukumaras and the technical and highly challenging alpine crossings of the Copland Pass and Cascade Saddle in the Southern Alps.

The book covers the popular Milford

Track in Fiordland and the Routeburn Track in Aspiring and Fiordland national parks. It also covers often-overlooked areas such as the Wilkin-Young valleys in Aspiring, and the Whirinaki Track in Whirinaki Forest Park. At the end of each section, there are brief descriptions of additional nearby tracks.

The tracks in this book cover a range of difficulties, lengths and landscapes, providing all kinds of trampers with the best possible selection of New Zealand's natural wonders and scenery.

Facts about the Country

HISTORY
Pre-European History

The original inhabitants of New Zealand were known until fairly recently as Morioris, or moa hunters. Recent evidence indicates that Polynesians arrived in New Zealand in a series of migrations and that the people known as Morioris were in fact an early wave of Polynesians, not a separate race from the Maoris who came later. It is estimated that the first Polynesians arrived in New Zealand at least 1000 years ago.

It was these early settlers who hunted the moa – a huge, flightless bird – both for food and for its feathers, until it became extinct. Today, the name Moriori refers to the original settlers of the Chatham Islands (770 km east of Christchurch) who migrated there from New Zealand.

Before the arrival of Europeans, the Maoris did not have writing. Instead, as in many parts of the world, their history was preserved in intricate and very specific chants and songs. A priestly class, the tohungas, was charged with keeping the genealogy, stories and spiritual matters of the tribe, like living libraries.

In addition to this rich mythology, the Maoris also kept quite accurate history, though not always in the precisely dated and geographically specific ways that modern historians do. However, there seems to be much factual truth in their account of how New Zealand was discovered by Kupe around 950 AD and how it came to be populated by Polynesians.

Kupe, a brilliant Polynesian navigator, is said to have set sail from Hawaiki, the Polynesian homeland, in the 10th century for the 'great southern land, uninhabited and covered with mists'. Despite the similar names, Hawaiki is not Hawaii; experts believe it is more likely to have been an island in the Marquesas, possibly Raiatea, in what is now French Polynesia, though no-one knows for sure exactly where Hawaiki was.

It is said that when Kupe sighted New Zealand, a huge land mass relative to most Polynesian islands, it had a white cloud stretching as far as the eye could see. Kupe named the land Aotearoa – Land of the Long White Cloud – and Aotearoa is still the Maori name for New Zealand. Kupe stayed at least several months, making explorations of the coast and, in some places (such as the Whanganui River in the North Island), exploring inland. He then returned to Hawaiki with stories about the land he had discovered.

Centuries later, when things weren't going so well in Hawaiki – overpopulation, shortages of food and all those other familiar problems – the decision was made to follow Kupe's navigational instructions and head south. According to legends, 10 great canoes sailed to Aotearoa around 1350 AD, stopping at Rarotonga along the way; some historians believe the Great Migration may have occurred even earlier. The names of all the canoes are remembered, as are their landing points, crews and histories. They were very large canoes, lashed together to form double-hulled vessels, and the people who came on them brought their domestic animals (dogs and rats) and various agricultural plants (including taro, yam and kumara, or sweet potato). Today, all Maoris trace their lineage back to one of the 10 canoes of the Great Migration.

When the canoes reached Aotearoa, the country was not devoid of human beings; there were small groups of moa hunters who had arrived in earlier, smaller migrations. The new immigrants soon established themselves in their adopted home, displacing or assimilating with the previous residents.

Maori culture developed without interference from other cultures for hundreds of years, with each canoe group establishing itself in its own territory. Being warriors, however, they engaged in numerous tribal battles, mainly over territory, and the losers often became slaves or food. Eating an enemy was a way not only to deliver the ultimate insult but also to take on the enemy's life force, *mana* or power.

Although they remained a Stone Age culture – it would have been difficult to get beyond that stage in New Zealand, since there are few metals apart from gold – the Maoris evolved a culture sustained by agriculture and hunting. They had a complex social structure of tribes, subtribes and clans, and a stratified society which included a royal class, a priestly class and a class of experts in various fields, all the way down to a slave class.

Genealogy *(Whakapapa)* was extremely important, since it told who was who in the tribe. Land was held communally and, as in other parts of Polynesia, each tribe and subtribe had a *marae*, a place of high spiritual significance where the mana and the tribe's ancestral spirits resided. Tribes often lived in *pa* or fortified villages.

They made clothing from flax, dog hair, feathers and other materials; fur cloaks decorated with feathers can still be seen in some New Zealand museums. They also made *poumamu* (greenstone) ornaments and war clubs, beautifully carved war canoes and a variety of household items. Expeditions were mounted to the South Island to find poumamu, but most of the tribes stayed in the much warmer North Island.

European Exploration

In 1642, Dutch explorer Abel Tasman sailed from Batavia (modern-day Jakarta, Indonesia) around Australia and up the west coast of Aotearoa. He didn't stay long in Aotearoa after his only attempt at landing resulted in several of his crew being killed and eaten. His visit, however, meant that the Europeans knew of Aotearoa's existence, and in those days of colonialism it also meant that they would eventually want it. Another result of his visit was a new name – he christened the land New Zealand, naming it after the Netherlands' province of Zeeland. He also named Tasmania and the Tasman Sea, the

body of water between New Zealand and Australia.

The Dutch, after this first uncomfortable look, were none too keen on the place, and it was left alone until British navigator and explorer Captain James Cook sailed around New Zealand in the *Endeavour* in 1769.

Since Tasman had only sailed up the west coast, there had been speculation that this could be the west coast of a large southern continent. In the logical European cosmology, it was thought there must be a balance to everything and that a large southern continent must exist to offset the large land masses in the northern hemisphere.

Cook sailed right around the coast of New Zealand, mapping as he went, and many places in New Zealand still bear the names that he gave them as he literally 'put them on the map'. Having concluded his sail around the coasts of both the North and South Islands, and realising that this was not the large southern continent, Cook claimed the entire land for the British Crown and then took off for Australia. In 1777, when he published the account of his voyage, Europe learned about the idyllic lands to the south.

Another European, the French explorer Jules Sébastien César Dumont d'Urville, was sailing around New Zealand at the same time as Cook, but the two never met. They came very close – even passing on one occasion in a very thick fog, with neither suspecting the other was there.

When the British started their antipodean colonising, they opted for the larger and even more lightly populated Australia. New Zealand's first European settlers were temporary ones – sealers (who soon reduced the seal population to next to nothing) and then whalers (who did the same with the whales). They introduced diseases and prostitution, and created such a demand for preserved heads that Maori chiefs started decapitating their slaves to order (previously they'd only preserved the heads of warriors who had died in battle).

Worst of all, the Europeans brought firearms, and when the Maoris exchanged poumamu *meres* (war clubs) for muskets, they soon embarked on wholesale slaughter of one another. Equally devastating were the diseases brought by Europeans, such as smallpox, measles, mumps, influenza, syphilis and gonorrhoea. By 1830, the Maori population had dwindled dramatically.

European Settlement

In 1814, the arrival of Samuel Marsden, the first missionary, brought Christianity to New Zealand. He was soon followed by Anglican, Wesleyan Methodist and Roman Catholic missionaries. The Bible was translated into Maori, and for the first time the Maori language was written down. By the middle of the 19th century, warfare had been reduced, cannibalism fairly well stamped out and the raging impact of European diseases curbed. But the Maori people then found themselves spiritually assaulted and much of their tradition and culture irrevocably altered. Despite the missionary influence, their numbers continued to decline.

During the early 19th century, European settlers were arriving in New Zealand, some on settlement campaigns organised from Britain. There were plenty of challenges in settling a new land, and although the land they settled on was 'purchased' by the New Zealand Association, relations with the Maoris did not always go smoothly, especially as the Maori and Pakeha (European) concepts of land ownership were quite different.

The new settlers began to demand British protection from the Maoris and from other less savoury settlers. The British were not keen on further colonisation – what with burning their fingers in America, fighting in Canada and worrying about Australia – but the threat of a French colonising effort stirred them to dispatch James Busby to be the British Resident in 1833. His efforts to protect the settlers and keep law and order were made somewhat difficult by his lack of forces, arms and authority. He was soon dubbed 'the man of war without guns'.

The Treaty of Waitangi

In 1840, the British sent Captain William Hobson to replace Busby. Hobson was instructed to persuade the Maori chiefs to relinquish their sovereignty to the British Crown. A treaty was drawn up to specify the positions, the rights and duties, and a mutually agreed method of land sales between the two sides.

On 5 February, over 400 Maoris gathered in front of Busby's residence at Waitangi in the Bay of Islands to hear the treaty read. The Maori chiefs had some objections, the treaty was amended, and they withdrew across the river to debate the issue throughout the night. The following day, the treaty was signed by Hobson and 45 Maori chiefs, mostly from the Bay of Islands region. Over the next seven months, the treaty was carried throughout New Zealand by missionaries and officials, eventually being signed by over 500 Maori chiefs. Busby's house is now known as the Treaty House and the anniversary of 6 February 1840 is considered the birthday of modern New Zealand.

Though the treaty was short and seemed to be simple, it was a controversial document then and has continued to be controversial ever since. Basically, the treaty said that the chiefs ceded the sovereignty over their land to the Queen of England, in exchange for the Queen's protection in the unqualified exercise of their chieftainship over their lands, their people, their villages and all their possessions. The treaty granted to Maori people all the same rights, privileges and duties of citizenship enjoyed by the citizens of England. The treaty also established a policy for land sales, stipulating that the Maoris were guaranteed the full, exclusive and undisturbed possession of all their lands and fisheries for as long as they wanted, but that if and when they wanted to sell land, the Queen's agent had the exclusive right to buy it, at a price mutually agreed upon by both parties. The Queen's agent would then sell the land to the settlers in an orderly and fair fashion.

When settlers arrived and needed land and the Maoris didn't want to sell, conflict inevitably resulted. The admirable idea that the government should act as a go-between in all

Maori-Pakeha deals to ensure fairness on both sides fell apart when the government was too tightfisted to pay the price.

The first visible revolt came when Hone Heke, the first chief to sign the Treaty of Waitangi, chopped down the British flagpole at Kororareka. Despite new poles and more and more guards, Hone Heke or his followers managed to chop the pole down four times; it was eventually covered with iron to foil further attempts. After his final destruction of the pole, in 1845, Hone Heke burnt down the town of Kororareka for good measure. In the skirmishes that followed, the British governor put a £100 reward on Hone Heke's head, to which he responded by offering a matching £100 for the governor's head.

This was only one in a long series of skirmishes, battles, conflicts and disputes between the Maoris and Pakehas. The original benign intent of the Treaty of Waitangi began to ebb under the pressure of ever-increasing numbers of European settlers. The Maoris became alarmed at the effect the

Chief of the Ngati Kahunguna Tribe

European settlers were having on the land and on their own society. The Pakehas, in turn, began to disregard the principles of fairness outlined in the treaty, particularly after the administration of New Zealand passed to a settler government under the Constitution Act of 1852. Pressures between the Maoris and Pakehas finally escalated into full-scale wars between 1860 and 1865, which were known collectively as the Maori Wars.

Although the Maoris were brilliant warriors, they were outnumbered and lacked equipment. Following the Maori Wars, with the Maori people defeated and relatively powerless, the Pakeha government confiscated much Maori land. The Treaty of Waitangi was disregarded and, in 1877, Chief Justice Prendergast ruled that the treaty was 'a simple nullity'.

Late 19th Century

The Maori Wars were the last time there was widespread armed conflict within the country. Things calmed down, European settlement and influence grew, and New Zealand became an efficient agricultural country. Sheep farming, that backbone of modern New Zealand, took hold as refrigerated ships made it possible to sell New Zealand meat in Europe. New Zealand became Britain's 'efficient offshore farm', exporting agricultural products – especially mutton, wool, sheepskins and dairy products – and importing manufactured goods. Still, remote as it was, New Zealand had to take care of its own needs to a large extent, and became known as a rugged, independent country.

Towards the end of the 19th century, New Zealand went through a phase of sweeping social change that took it to the forefront of the world. Women were given the vote in 1893, 25 years earlier than Britain or the USA, and more like 75 years ahead of Switzerland. An eminent leader at this time was Richard John 'King Dick' Seddon who, together with the Liberal Party, was responsible for many of the reforms. The range of far-sighted social reforms and pioneering legislation included old-age pensions, minimum wage structures, the establishment of arbitration courts and the introduction of child health services.

Modern Times

New Zealand became a self-governing British colony in 1856, and a dominion in 1907. By the 1920s, it controlled most of its own affairs, but it took until 1947 to become a fully independent country.

New Zealand's economy prospered after WW II but, along with much of the rest of the world's, it took a nosedive in the 1970s and 1980s. The closure of its traditional European market for agricultural products, combined with the oil crisis, and price hikes of many of its mineral and manufactured imports, did not help the country's economic situation at all.

Despite the economic climate, things finally began to turn around for the Maoris, largely due to various Maori leaders who kept pressing for justice and refused to give up until their cause had been heard.

In 1975, the Treaty of Waitangi, which in 1877 had been ruled 'a simple nullity', was reconsidered. In 1985, the act was amended to order the examination of claims dating back to the original signing of the treaty in 1840. Financial reparations were made to a number of Maori tribes whose lands were found to have been unjustly confiscated, allowing them to buy land, invest in education and do other things to uplift their people. Today, the Maori population is increasing faster than the Pakeha – they now number about 330,000, or 9.6% of the population.

New Zealanders are proud of their record of racial harmony, despite past difficulties – there has never been any racial segregation and intermarriage is common. In recent years, there has been a growing interest in *Maoritanga* (Maori culture), and Maori language, literature, arts and culture are experiencing a renaissance.

Internationally, New Zealand has become one of the most interesting and important countries in the South Pacific region. New Zealand's antinuclear stance introduced a sour note to relations with the USA. Although it remains one of New Zealand's principal trading partners, the USA decided to suspend its obligations to New Zealand within the ANZUS defence pact after New Zealand established a policy of not allowing nuclear vessels to use its harbours.

New Zealand led opposition to nuclear testing by the French at Moruroa Atoll in French Polynesia. In 1985, the French sent several agents to New Zealand to sink the Greenpeace ship *Rainbow Warrior* while it was docked in Auckland Harbour preparing to lead a flotilla to French Polynesia to protest against French nuclear testing. A Greenpeace photographer, Fernando Pereira, was killed in the bombing. Two French agents were caught, tried, found guilty and sentenced to 10-year terms but they were repatriated by France, with honours, well before their time was served.

In 1983, Australia and New Zealand signed a Closer Economic Relations Trade Agreement, permitting free and unrestricted trade between the two countries. In 1987, the New Zealand government began to privatise government-operated enterprises and diminish the welfare state.

Increasing pressures on the economy, and conflicting policies on what should be done, caused havoc in the government in the late 1980s. In the general election of October 1990, the overwhelming victory by the National Party saw Jim Bolger become prime minister.

In the November 1993 elections, no decisive result was achieved, leaving the whole New Zealand political system in limbo. The economy responded accordingly, with the dollar sliding on world markets. Things stabilised when a National Party government, again led by Bolger, was hastily formed. In 1994, there were hints that New Zealand, like its neighbour Australia, was contemplating the formation of a republic by the year 2000.

GEOGRAPHY

New Zealand stretches 1600 km from north to south. The country consists of two large islands, a number of smaller scattered islands nearby, plus a few islands hundreds of km away: New Zealand's territorial jurisdiction extends to the islands of Chatham, Kermadec, Tokelau, Auckland, Antipodes, Snares, Solander and Bounty (most of them uninhabited) and to the Ross Dependency in Antarctica.

The North Island (115,000 sq km) and the South Island (151,000 sq km) are the two major land masses. Stewart Island, with an area of 1700 sq km, lies directly south of the South Island. The country is 10,400 km south-west of the USA, 1700 km south of Fiji and 2250 km east of Australia, its nearest large neighbour. Its western coastline faces the Tasman Sea, the part of the Pacific Ocean which separates New Zealand and Australia.

With a land mass of 268,000 sq km, New Zealand's total area is greater than that of the UK (244,800 sq km), smaller than that of Japan (377,800 sq km), and just a little smaller than that of Colorado in the USA (270,000 sq km). New Zealand has only 3,435,000 people and almost 70% of them live in the five major cities, which leaves a lot of wide open spaces. The coastline, with many bays, harbours and fiords, is very long relative to the land mass of the country.

Both the North Island and South Island have high mountains, formed by two distinct geological processes, both associated with the westward movement of the Pacific tectonic plate.

When one tectonic plate slides underneath another, it forms a subduction zone. Geologists say that the North Island of New Zealand is on the southern reaches of the subduction zone where the oceanic Pacific plate is sliding underneath the continental plate, resulting in volcanic activity which has created a number of large volcanoes and thermal areas, and some equally impressive volcanic depressions.

A rough 'line' of volcanoes, some of which are still active, extends from the steaming Whakaari (White) Island in the Bay of Plenty, south past Mt Putauaki (Edgecumbe) and the highly active thermal areas in and around Rotorua and Lake Taupo.

South of Lake Taupo are the North Island's spectacular volcanoes – Tongariro, Ruapehu, Ngauruhoe and the smaller Pihanga. Continuing south-west, there's the lone volcanic cone of Mt Egmont/Taranaki. It is said that Port Nicholson, the bay on which Wellington is located, is a flooded volcanic crater. Other parts of the North Island also have evidence of volcanic activity; in Auckland, for example, there are over 50 volcanic cones, including most of the famous 'hills' (One Tree Hill, Mt Eden) that rise from the flatlands.

The North Island has ranges of hills and mountains produced by folding and uplift, notably the Tararua and Ruahine ranges in the southern part of the North Island. In general, though, most of the high places of the North Island were formed by volcanic activity.

In the South Island, the geological process is different. Here, the two tectonic plates are smashing into each other, resulting in a process called 'crustal shortening'. This has caused the Southern Alps to rise as a spine extending along virtually the entire length of the South Island. Thrust faulting, folding, and vertical slips all combine to create a rapid uplift of the Southern Alps – as much as 10 mm per year – and though the Southern Alps receive a lot of rainfall and hence a lot of erosion, they are continuing to rise.

Most of the east side of the South Island is a large plain known as the Canterbury Plains. Banks Peninsula, south-east of Christchurch, was formed by volcanic activity, and joined to the mainland by alluvial deposits washed down from the Southern Alps.

Another notable feature of New Zealand's geography is the country's great number of rivers. There's a lot of rainfall in New Zealand and all that rain has to go somewhere. The 425-km Waikato River, in the North Island, is New Zealand's longest river. The Whanganui River, also in the North Island, is the country's longest navigable river and it remains an important waterway. New Zealand also has a number of spectacular lakes; lakes Waikaremoana and Wanaka are two of the most beautiful. New Zealand's largest lake, Lake Taupo, was formed by a gigantic volcanic explosion in 186 AD, and still has thermal areas nearby.

CLIMATE

This is an important travel factor of great interest to trampers. Located between 34°S and 47°S, New Zealand lies squarely in the 'roaring forties' latitude, meaning it has a year-round prevailing wind blowing from west to east. This wind ranges from a gentle breeze to occasional raging gales in winter.

The usual weather pattern in New Zealand is a cycle of high-pressure system (anti-cyclones or ridges) followed by low-pressure system (troughs or depressions), travelling from west to east. The anticy-clones normally pass the northern portions of the country at intervals of three to seven days, bringing fine weather with light or moderate winds. In between them are depressions of rain, strong winds and cooler temperatures.

One early sign of approaching bad weather is an increase in wind speed and the appearance of high cloud sheets. These sheets, which look as if they are stacked on top of each other, are known as 'hog's back'

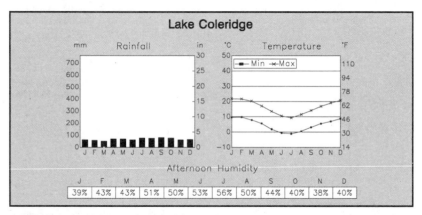

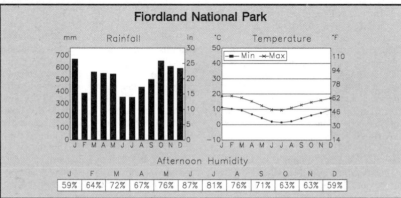

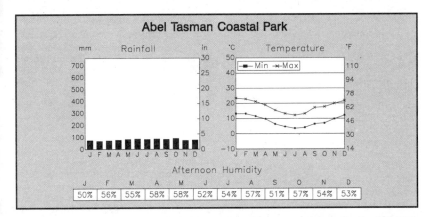

Abel Tasman Coastal Park

Afternoon Humidity

J	F	M	A	M	J	J	A	S	O	N	D
50%	56%	55%	58%	58%	52%	54%	57%	51%	57%	54%	53%

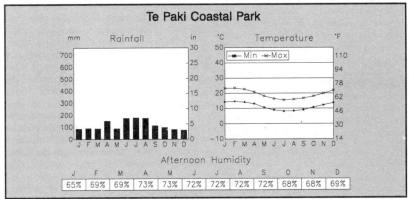

Te Paki Coastal Park

Afternoon Humidity

J	F	M	A	M	J	J	A	S	O	N	D
65%	69%	69%	73%	73%	72%	72%	72%	72%	68%	68%	69%

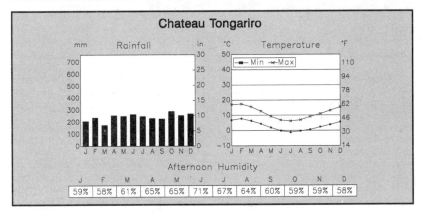

Chateau Tongariro

Afternoon Humidity

J	F	M	A	M	J	J	A	S	O	N	D
59%	58%	61%	65%	65%	71%	67%	64%	60%	59%	59%	58%

and are the outriders of north-west storms. As the depression moves on, the wind changes direction, often quite suddenly, and a change in weather results.

The wind is the key to reading the weather out in the bush. As a general rule, north-westerlies bring wet weather and storms, while southerlies are a sign of a cool frontal change, often followed by clearer conditions. North-easterlies are also a sign of good weather approaching; south-westerlies are cool, rain-laden winds.

Most important, however, is to keep in mind that weather in New Zealand changes quickly and is highly unpredictable beyond a day or two. Because most mountain ranges run roughly north to south, they make their own weather. It is not uncommon to have rain on the windward or western side of a range, fine weather on the lee side and miserable conditions of heavy wind and rain along the ridges on top.

Snow falls mostly in the mountains, though there can be falls even at sea level in the South Island, particularly in the extreme south. Some of the plains and higher plateaus also receive snow in winter, notably the Canterbury Plains in the South Island and the high plateau around the Tongariro National Park in the North Island, especially on the 'desert' (east) side.

Almost all Department of Conservation (DOC) offices and national park headquarters and visitor centres receive weather forecasts at around 9 am and again in the evening. It is a wise practice to stop in at one of these offices before any tramp to check the weather and outline your intentions.

If heavy storms move in once you are out on the track, the best idea is to stay in a hut and take a day off, especially if you are in an alpine area. Be patient and don't worry about missing a bus or train at the end of the walk. Pressing deadlines and time limitations are one of the main causes of mishaps in the bush. An excellent brochure to pick up is *Weather Wisdom In New Zealand Mountains*, published by the New Zealand Mountain Safety Council and available at most park centres.

POPULATION & PEOPLE

The 1991 census showed New Zealand to have a population of around 3,435,000. Ethnically, 78.8% were New Zealand Pakeha, 9.6% were New Zealand Maori, 3.9% were Pacific Island Polynesian, 1.1% were Chinese, 0.8% were Indian and 5% were 'Other'. All groups except Pakehas had increased the proportion of the population they accounted for.

FLORA & FAUNA

Like most other Pacific islands, New Zealand's native flora & fauna are, for the most part, not found anywhere else in the world. And, like other Pacific islands, New Zealand's native ecosystem has been dramatically affected and changed by plants and animals brought by settlers, mostly in the last 200 years. Wild pigs, goats, possums, wallabies, rabbits, foxes, dogs, cats and deer have all made their mark on the native wildlife, and blackberries, gorse, broom and the usual crop of agricultural weeds have infested huge areas of land.

Much of New Zealand's unique flora & fauna has survived, but today over 150 native plants – 10% of the total number of native species – and many native birds are threatened with extinction.

Flora

In the 1800s, when the first European settlers arrived, about 70% of New Zealand was covered in native forest. Much of it was cleared for timber or farmland. Nevertheless, New Zealand still has some magnificent areas of native forest and bush. About 10% to 15% of the total land area of the country, or around six million hectares, is native flora, much of it in protected national parks and reserves.

The variety of vegetation in New Zealand is enormous. In the North Island, there are giant kauri forests; luxuriant lowland kohekohe forests; rainforests dominated by rimu, beeches, tawa, matai and rata and tree ferns; podocarp and hardwood forests; summer-flowering alpine and subalpine herb fields; and windswept scrub on the smaller islands.

In the South Island, the vegetation changes dramatically as you climb into the mountains. The lowland supplejacks give way to rimu, miro, and then tree ferns at about 800 metres. Above 1000 metres, the totara, wineberry, fuschias, rata and kaikomako are gradually left behind, to be replaced by subalpine scrub. At about 1200 metres, the scrub gives way to the tussock grasses and alpine herb fields, and at the extreme heights only some hardy lichens cling to the rock, ice and snowbound peaks.

The northern rata is a tall tree that begins life high in another tree, sending down aerial roots that join horizontally and gradually enclose the host in a hollow trunk. It's found throughout the North Island and along the north-western coast of the South Island. The kahikatea, or white pine, dominates the lowland forests all over New Zealand, from North Cape to Bluff, often having massive buttress roots to support a 60-metre-high trunk.

New Zealand has hundreds of species of ferns, including several types of tree ferns. Probably the best-known tree fern is the silver fern, so named because of the silver colour on the underside of its fronds; the silver fern is New Zealand's national plant.

One of the more noticeable plants is the pohutukawa, known as the New Zealand Christmas tree, which explodes with brilliant red flowers around December, peppering the forests with colour. Another Kiwi favourite is the yellow-flowered kowhai.

Like the Australian species, most of the 72 New Zealand orchids are not large or brilliantly coloured; one exception is the beautiful *Earina autumnalis*, which produces heavily perfumed cream flowers at Easter.

Two plants to be wary of are the tutu and the ongaonga, or tree nettle, both tall shrubs or small trees. Every part of the tutu is poisonous, but particularly the black berries that hang invitingly in clusters. Unless you are an expert on edible native plants, leave all of them alone. The leaves of the ongaonga are covered in brittle stinging spines. If you

Sun Orchid

brush against them they'll break off and stick to your skin, releasing a poison that makes you groggy and uncoordinated for several days. It's extremely painful and can be fatal.

The matagouri, or wild Irishman, is a thorny bush of the South Island lowlands. Its incredibly hard thorns were used by the Maoris for tattooing in pre-European times, when bones were in short supply.

Another plant that was important to the Maoris in pre-European times was harakeke, or flax, which they used to make rope, baskets, mats, fishing nets and clothing; the traditional Maori 'skirts' are still made of flax today.

Three species of trees which fascinate most trampers are mamuku or the black fern tree, which grows to heights of 15 metres; the nikau, which is New Zealand's only native member of the palm family and is found along the warmer coastal areas of the country; and the ti or cabbage tree, which can grow to 20 metres in height and is recognised by its distinctive grouping of narrow leaves.

Fauna

Overseas visitors will be surprised that there are virtually no native mammals in New Zealand. The first Maori settlers brought some rats and the now-extinct Maori dog with them, but the only indigenous mammals were bats. You can imagine how surprised the Maoris were when the Europeans turned

Takahe

up with sheep, cows, pigs and everything else the farm could offer.

New Zealand's birds thrived on the absence of predatory animals. Some birds, however, did not survive the introduction of predatory species and seven species of native birds are now on the list of endangered species. The worst affected were the flightless birds like the kakapo and takahe, which were easy prey.

Other species have been affected by modern human activities. The rare brown teal's wetland environment has been affected by drainage and reclamation of swamps and by the modification of rivers for irrigation and hydroelectricity.

Common birds found all over the country include the morepork (mopoke), a small spotted owl whose call you will often hear at night; the tui, a large black bird with a white crop under its throat and a pure call; and the little fantail, which will often flit around as you're tramping through bush. This habit has given the fantail the reputation of being very 'friendly', but it really flies along beside you to snatch insects that fly out of the bush as you pass.

The raucous kea lives in the high country of the South Island. Keas have a reputation for killing sheep, which makes them unpopular with farmers, but they may become just as unpopular with you, because they like to hang around humans, tipping over rubbish bins and sliding noisily down roofs at night. Yet the mountains would be far poorer if the birds were not there to greet you with their strident call 'kee-aa' when you tramp into their domain. Keep a close eye on your gear when they're around – they have incredibly strong beaks, will peck at anything, and can rip sleeping bags and tents.

Another amusing bird is the duck-like weka, which hangs around camp sites and rushes over to steal things when you turn your back. The weka will purloin anything it can carry in its bill, particularly shiny objects, so don't leave rings lying around.

There are plenty of birds around the coasts too, such as seagulls, albatross, and a number of species of penguin, including the yellow-eyed penguin, which is the rarest of all penguins.

The New Zealand bird you *won't* see is the famous moa, a sort of oversized ostrich. Originally, there were numerous types and sizes, but the largest of them – the huge giant moas – were as high as four metres. They had been extinct for several centuries by the time Europeans arrived, but you can see moa skeletons and reconstructions in many New Zealand museums.

Tuatara

Surprisingly not extinct is the tuatara, the sole survivor of a group of ancient reptiles somewhat akin to the dinosaurs. Sometimes mistakenly referred to as a lizard, it is now found only on a few islands and is protected.

New Zealand has no snakes, and only one spider that is dangerous to humans: the rare katipo, which is a close relative of the North American black widow and the Australian redback.

New Zealand is renowned as an angler's paradise, largely due to the introduction of rainbow and brown trout, perch, carp, Atlantic salmon and quinnat salmon to its rivers and estuaries. Native fish include the tenacious kahawai and the moki, hapuku, John Dory, gurnard and tarakihi.

The country's location gives it a number of areas attractive to marine mammals. In particular, the waters off Kaikoura, on the north-east coast of the South Island, have a combination of warm and cold currents and a continental shelf that results in abundant nutrients being swept up from the sea floor, attracting fish, squid and a number of marine mammals, including dolphins, whales and seals.

If you hear something croaking during the night in New Zealand, you can be sure it's not one of the three species of Kiwi frogs – they lack a vocal sac, and can only produce a high-pitched squeak. They're also remarkable in not having a free-swimming tadpole stage, instead they undergo metamorphosis in a capsule. One frog species is restricted to the high parts of the Coromandel Peninsula, and another to the summit of Stephens Island and remnant rainforest around Marlborough Sounds.

LANGUAGE

New Zealand has two official languages: English and Maori. English is the language you will usually hear spoken. The Maori language, long on the decline, is now making a comeback. Trampers will encounter many Maori place names in their travels, and there are many Maori terms in everyday use.

Facts for the Tramper

VISAS & EMBASSIES
Everyone needs a passport to enter New Zealand. If you enter on an Australian or New Zealand passport, or any other passport containing an Australian or New Zealand residence visa, your passport must be valid on arrival. All other passports must be valid for at least three months beyond the time you intend to stay in New Zealand, or one month beyond the intended stay if the issuing government has an embassy or consulate in New Zealand that is able to issue and renew passports.

Australian citizens or holders of current Australian resident return visas do not need a visa or permit to enter New Zealand, and they can stay in New Zealand as long as they like. There is no need for Australians to have a work permit to work in New Zealand.

Citizens of the UK, and other British passport holders who have evidence of the right to live permanently in the UK, do not need a visa, and upon arrival in New Zealand they are issued with a permit to stay in the country for up to six months.

Citizens of Austria, Belgium, Brunei, Canada, Denmark, Finland, France, Germany, Greece, Iceland, Indonesia, Ireland, Italy, Japan, Kiribati, Liechtenstein, Luxembourg, Malaysia, Malta, Monaco, Nauru, the Netherlands, Norway, Portugal, Singapore, South Korea, Spain, Sweden, Switzerland, Thailand, Tuvalu or the USA do not need a visa, and upon arrival in New Zealand are issued with a permit for a stay of up to three months.

Citizens of all other countries require a visa to enter New Zealand, available from any New Zealand embassy or consular agency. Visas are normally valid for a stay of up to three months. To qualify for a visitor's permit on arrival, or to qualify for a visa if you need one, you must be able to show:

- Your passport, valid for three months beyond the time of your intended stay in New Zealand.

- Evidence of sufficient funds to support yourself in New Zealand for the time of your intended stay, without working. This is calculated to be NZ$1000 per month (NZ$400 per month if your accommodation has been prepaid) and can be in the form of cash, travellers' cheques, bank drafts, or an American Express, Bankcard, Diners Club, MasterCard or Visa card.
- Onward tickets to a country to which you can show you have right of entry, with firm bookings if travelling on discount airfares.

New Zealand Embassies & Consulates
New Zealand embassies and consulates in other countries include:

Australia
> High Commission, Commonwealth Ave, Canberra, ACT 2600 (☎ (06) 270 4211; fax 273 3194)

Canada
> High Commission, Suite 801, Metropolitan House, 99 Bank St, Ottawa, Ont K1P 6G3 (☎ (613) 238 5991; fax 238 5707)

Germany
> Embassy, Bundeskanzlerplatz 2-10, 5300 Bonn 1 (☎ (228) 22 8070; fax 22 1687)

Ireland
> Consulate-General, 46 Upper Mount St, Dublin 2 (☎ (01) 76 2464; fax 76 2489)

Netherlands
> Embassy, Mauritskade 25, 2514 HD The Hague (☎ (70) 346 9324; fax 363 2983)

Switzerland
> Consulate-General, 28A Chemin du Petit Saconnex, CH-1209 Geneva (PO Box 334, CH-1211, Geneva 19) (☎ (22) 734 9530; fax 734 3062)

UK
> High Commission, New Zealand House, The Haymarket, London SW1Y 4TQ (☎ (0171) 973 0366/63; fax 973 0370)

USA
> Embassy, 37 Observatory Circle NW, Washington DC (☎ (202) 328 4848; fax 667 5227)

DOCUMENTS
No special documents (other than your passport) are required in New Zealand.

CUSTOMS
Customs allowances are 200 cigarettes (or

50 cigars or 250 grams of tobacco), 4.5 litres of wine or beer and one 1125 ml (40 oz) bottle of spirits or liqueur. Don't even think about importing illegal drugs.

MONEY

The currencies of Australia, the UK, the USA, Canada, Germany and Japan are all easily changed in New Zealand.

American Express, Visa, MasterCard and Thomas Cook travellers' cheques are all widely recognised. Visa, MasterCard, Australian Bankcard, American Express and Diners Club credit cards are the most widely recognised. Banks will give cash advances on Visa and MasterCard, but for American Express card transactions you must go to an American Express office.

Unless otherwise noted, all prices quoted in this book are in New Zealand dollars.

Currency

New Zealand's currency comes in dollars and cents. There are five, 10, 20, 50 and 100 dollar notes and five, 10, 20, 50 cent, $1 and $2 coins. You can bring in as much of any currency as you like and unused foreign currency or travellers' cheques which you brought in with you may be exported without limitations. Unused New Zealand currency can be changed to foreign currency before you leave the country. Banks are open from 9.30 am to 4 pm Monday to Friday.

Exchange Rates

A$1	=	NZ$1.23
C$1	=	NZ$1.22
DM1	=	NZ$1.05
S$1	=	NZ$1.11
UK£1	=	NZ$2.55
US$1	=	NZ$1.66
¥100	=	NZ$1.66

Costs

It's possible to travel quite economically in New Zealand, although there's also plenty of opportunities to spend up. If you stay in hostels, the cost will usually be around $12 to $16 per person per night. Eating out can cost from $5 for a simple takeaway meal to

around $50 for dinner for two at most medium-priced restaurants. The average long-distance (three to five-hour) bus ride might cost around $30 (half that with a discount card).

Tipping is not a widespread or traditional custom in New Zealand; if you feel you have received exceptional service, the tip would be about 5% of the bill.

Consumer Taxes

Goods and services tax (GST) adds 12½% to the price of just about everything in New Zealand. Most prices are quoted inclusive of GST, but beware of small print announcing GST exclusive – you'll be hit for the extra 12½% on top of the stated cost.

WHEN TO GO

Most national parks and state forests experience their largest influx of trampers during the Christmas school holidays (roughly the third week of December to the end of January). Most tracks, including those in this book, can be undertaken any time from mid-November to early April, although snow may be encountered in the alpine areas in November or March. June, July and August are New Zealand's winter months – tramping at this time requires special skills and equipment to combat the cold temperatures, snow and strong winds.

For overseas travellers, the best time to explore the country's wilderness may be February and March. This is the driest time of the year, the kids are in school, mums and dads are back at work and on most tracks you can usually count on getting a bunk in the next hut. If you do plan on tramping around Christmas, choose a track that lies off the beaten path.

WHAT TO BRING

New Zealand may be a small country but it has very changeable weather, so be prepared for widely varying climatic conditions. Waterproof rain gear and a warm sleeping bag will make your stay in New Zealand much more pleasant at any time of the year.

Special equipment for tramping is covered

in the Tramping Information section in this chapter.

TOURIST OFFICES
There are local tourist information centres in nearly every city or town. They are united by the Visitor Information Network (VIN), which strives to ensure that each of its members provides top-quality information and service.

USEFUL ORGANISATIONS
There are a number of useful organisations in New Zealand that assist travellers. Perhaps the most useful for the tramper is the Department of Conservation (DOC) – Te Papa Atawai. This government organisation is covered in the Tramping Information section in this chapter.

Also of use are members of the Federated Mountain Clubs, such as the New Zealand Alpine Club and the various tramping groups (see the list in Tramping & Outdoor Clubs in the Tramping Information section in this chapter).

BUSINESS HOURS
Office hours are generally 9 am to 5 pm Monday to Friday. Most government offices are open Monday to Friday from around 8 am to 4 or 4.30 pm. Shops are usually open Monday to Friday from 9 am to 5 pm, and on Saturday mornings, with 'late-night shopping' to 8 or 9 pm one night of the week

---

Conservation Volunteer Programme
The DOC enables volunteers to participate in conservation projects such as counting birds, protecting nesting areas, and track maintenance. You don't get paid but you do get to go to some out-of-the-way places and get hands-on conservation experience. You can volunteer for any length of time. South Island locations include Mt Cook National Park, Queen Charlotte Sound and the Catlins. North Island locations include Whirinaki Forest Park, the Whanganui River and Kawau Island in Hauraki Gulf. ■

(usually Thursday or Friday). Many small convenience stores (called 'dairies' in New Zealand) stay open much longer hours.

POST & TELECOMMUNICATIONS
Postal Rates
Ordinary mail within New Zealand costs 40 cents, and delivery takes two days between major centres and a bit longer for rural areas. Post offices are open from 9 am to 5 pm on weekdays. You can have mail addressed to you 'c/o Poste Restante, CPO' in any town. CPO stands for Chief Post Office. Mail is usually held for 30 days.

Telephones
Most payphones in New Zealand have now been converted to the card-operated type. The few coin phones still remaining are usually in remote areas.

The card phones accept $5, $10, $20 or $50 cards, which you can buy from any shop displaying the lime-green 'phone cards available here' sign.

For emergencies in the major centres, ☎ 111 and ask for police, ambulance or fire brigade. Emergency calls are free.

STD Codes
City codes, called area codes in many countries, are called STD codes in New Zealand. The entire South Island and Stewart Island are on the (03) STD code. The North Island has various regional STD codes: (09) in Auckland and the Northland, (07) in the Coromandel Peninsula, Bay of Plenty and central North Island, (06) in the East Coast, lower-central North Island and Taranaki regions, and (04) in and around Wellington. In this book, the STD codes are not listed for telephone numbers in the South or Stewart Island but are included for numbers in the North Island.

TIME
Being close to the international date line, New Zealand is one of the first places in the world to start a new day. New Zealand is 12 hours ahead of Greenwich Mean Time (GMT) and Universal Time Coordinated

(UTC) and two hours ahead of Australian Eastern Standard Time.

In summer, New Zealand observes Daylight Saving Time, an advance of one hour, which comes into effect on the last Sunday in October and lasts to the first Sunday of the following March.

ELECTRICITY
Electricity is 240V AC, 50 cycle, as in Europe and Australia, and Australian-type three-prong plugs are used.

WEIGHTS & MEASURES
New Zealand uses the metric system for all weights, measures and distances. Heights are in metres, and scales on maps are in km in this guide.

HEALTH
There are no vaccination requirements to enter New Zealand. New Zealand is largely a clean, healthy, disease-free country and medical attention is of high quality and reasonably priced, but you should still have medical insurance. Care in what you eat and drink is the most important health rule – stomach upsets are the most likely travel health problem, though most will be relatively minor.

The information included here is for trampers and is intended to supplement information widely available in guidebooks.

Medical Kit
A small medical kit is a wise thing to carry. A possible kit list includes:

- Antibiotics – useful if you're travelling well off the beaten track, but they must be prescribed and you should carry the prescription with you
- Antihistamine (such as Benadryl) – useful as a decongestant for colds, allergies, to ease the itch from insect bites or stings and to help prevent motion sickness
- Antiseptic, mercurochrome and antibiotic powder or similar 'dry' spray – for cuts and grazes
- Aspirin or Panadol – for pain or fever
- Bandages and Band-aids – for minor injuries
- Calamine lotion or anti-itch cream – to ease irritation from bites or stings

- Insect repellent (DEET), sunscreen, suntan lotion, chapstick
- Kaolin preparation (Pepto-Bismol), Imodium or Lomotil – for stomach upsets
- Rehydration mixture – for treatment of severe diarrhoea (particularly important if travelling with children)
- Scissors, tweezers and a thermometer (note that mercury thermometers are prohibited by airlines)
- Water-purification tablets or other water-purification system, if you'll be camping in the bush

Water
Tap water is clean, delicious and fine to drink in New Zealand. Water in lakes, rivers and streams will look clean and could be OK, but since the parasite *Giardia protozoa* has been found in many New Zealand lakes, rivers and streams, water from these sources should be purified before drinking. The simplest way to purify water is to boil it for more than three minutes. Filtering is acceptable only if you use *Giardia*-rated filters, available from some outdoor equipment retailers.

If you cannot boil water it should be treated chemically. Iodine is very effective and is available in tablet form (such as Potable Aqua), but follow the directions carefully and remember that too much iodine can be harmful. Before buying, check the manufacturer's specifications on the packet to ensure that the tablets will kill the *Giardia* parasite.

If you can't find tablets, tincture of iodine (2%) or iodine crystals can be used. Two drops of tincture of iodine per litre of clear water is the recommended dosage; the treated water should be left to stand for half an hour before drinking. Iodine crystals can also be used to purify water, but this is a more complicated process because you have to first prepare a saturated iodine solution. Iodine loses its effectiveness if exposed to air or damp, so keep it in a tightly sealed container. Flavoured powder will disguise the taste of treated water, and is a good idea if you are travelling with children.

Giardia This intestinal parasite has been found in water supplies in New Zealand, so it's important to know about it if you're in the bush. Your chances of getting giardiasis are remote, and in just about every bush area in New Zealand you can still drink water from lakes, rivers and streams.

Giardiasis can be spread by any mammal, including possums, rats and mice, and humans. Drinking contaminated water is the most common way to catch giardiasis, but it can also occur as a result of poor personal hygiene or unhygienic food handling.

The symptoms are stomach cramps, nausea, a bloated stomach, watery, foul-smelling diarrhoea and frequent gas. Giardiasis can appear several weeks after you have been exposed to the parasite. The symptoms may disappear for a few days and then return; this can go on for several weeks. As long as you are carrying the parasite, you risk spreading it to the environment and to other people.

Metronidazole (known as Flagyl) is the recommended drug, but should only be taken under medical supervision. Treatment is simple and acts quickly. You might want to carry Flagyl in your first-aid kit if you plan to be in the bush for a while. Antibiotics are of no use. If you suspect you have giardiasis, see a doctor as soon as practical.

Amoebic Meningitis This very serious disease can be a danger if you bathe in natural, hot, thermal pools. Fortunately, it's very easy not to catch the disease – just keep your head out of the water!

Climatic & Geographical Considerations
Sunburn You can get sunburnt surprisingly quickly, even through cloud, on the beach, in the snow or at high altitudes. The sun is particularly dangerous in New Zealand because the ozone layer is said to be considerably thinner than in other parts of the world. Use a sunscreen and take extra care to cover areas which aren't normally exposed to the sun – such as your feet. A hat provides added protection, and you can use zinc cream for your nose, lips and ears. Calamine lotion is good for mild sunburn.

Cold Too much cold can be dangerous, and can lead to hypothermia, a real danger in New Zealand due to the country's extremely changeable weather. A number of visitors die from hypothermia every year because they have gone out walking without adequate preparation. Always be prepared for cold, wet or windy conditions even if you're just out walking or hitching; this is especially important if you're tramping out in the bush, away from civilisation.

Hypothermia occurs when the body loses heat faster than it can produce it and the core temperature of the body falls. It is surprisingly easy to progress from very cold to dangerously cold due to a combination of wind, wet clothing, fatigue and hunger, even if the air temperature is above freezing. It is best to dress in layers – silk, wool and some of the new artificial fibres are all good insulating materials. A hat is important because a lot of heat is lost through the head. A strong, waterproof outer layer is essential, since keeping dry is vital. Carry basic supplies, including food containing simple sugars to generate heat quickly, and lots of fluid to drink.

Symptoms of hypothermia are exhaustion, numb skin (particularly fingers and toes), shivering, slurred speech, irrational or violent behaviour, lethargy, stumbling, dizzy spells, muscle cramps and violent bursts of energy. Irrationality may take the form of sufferers claiming they are warm and trying to take off their clothes.

To treat hypothermia, get the patient out of the wind and rain and replace wet clothing with dry, warm clothing. Give them hot liquids – not alcohol – and some high-kilojoule, easily-digestible food. This should be enough for the early stages of hypothermia, but if it has gone further it may be necessary to place the victim in a warm sleeping bag and get in with them. Do not rub the patient, place them near a fire, or remove their wet clothes in the wind. If possible, place a sufferer in a warm (not hot) bath.

Get a copy of the New Zealand Mountain Safety Council pamphlet No 8, *Outdoor Safety: Hypothermia*.

Toxic Shellfish Though it doesn't happen often, certain algae or other substances in sea water can cause shellfish that are normally safe to eat to become dangerous. Seek local advice before you eat any type of shellfish.

Cuts, Bites & Stings
Cuts & Scratches Skin punctures can easily become infected while travelling and may take time to heal. Treat any cut with an antiseptic solution and mercurochrome. Whenever possible, avoid bandages and Band-aids, which can keep wounds wet; if you have to keep a bandage on during the day to protect the wound from dirt, take it off at night while you sleep to let it get air.

Bee & Wasp Stings Wasps are a problem in some places in New Zealand, especially in late summer. They are attracted to food (eg, at picnic sites) and are especially numerous in beech forests, where they are attracted to the honey dew. Calamine lotion will give relief; ammonia is also an effective remedy.

Mosquitoes & Sandflies Mosquitoes appear after dusk. Avoid bites by covering bare skin and using an insect repellent. Insect screens on windows and mosquito nets on beds offer protection, as does burning a mosquito coil or spraying with a pyrethrum-based insect spray. Mosquitoes may be attracted by perfume, aftershave or certain colours. They can bite you through thin fabrics, or on any small part of skin not covered by repellent.

Another New Zealand insect that can drive you wild is the sandfly. This tiny black creature is found in inland areas as well as around the coasts, where it lives in bushes, trees or grasses. Wearing shoes, thick socks and plenty of insect repellent is not only advisable but practically a necessity where sandflies are present.

The most effective insect repellent is called DEET; it is an ingredient in many commercially available insect repellents. Look for a repellent with at least a 28% concentration of DEET. Other good insect repellents include Off! and Repel, which comes in a stick or a spray and will not eat through plastic the way DEET-containing repellents do.

Spiders The only poisonous spider in New Zealand is the retiring, little katipo spider, *Latrodectus katipo*. Its bite can be fatal, but antivenom is available from most hospitals.

Jellyfish Local advice is the best way of avoiding contact with these sea creatures and their stinging tentacles. The most effective folk remedy for jellyfish stings, used all over the world, is to apply fresh urine to the stings as soon as possible.

WOMEN TRAVELLERS
There are few hassles awaiting women travellers in New Zealand. Women should, however, exercise the same degree of caution they would in most other countries. You should observe the normal safety precautions (such as not walking through isolated urban areas alone in the middle of the night) and avoid hitchhiking alone.

DANGERS & ANNOYANCES
Violent crime is not very common in New Zealand, but with high unemployment and an economy that has seen better days, theft is a worsening problem. Theft from cars is a particular problem for trampers. Where there is secure car storage near tracks, it has been mentioned.

FILM & PHOTOGRAPHY
Photographic supplies, equipment and maintenance are all readily available in New Zealand. You can probably find any kind of camera or equipment you're looking for, though it may cost more here than elsewhere.

Note that if you're taking photographs in the bush, the native vegetation is quite dense and may be darker than you think, photographically speaking. If you intend to take many photographs in dense bush, carry a couple of rolls of ISO (ASA) 400 film.

ACCOMMODATION
This guide covers budget accommodation

close to the beginning and end of tracks (Places to Stay), camping grounds and camp sites both on and near tracks, and huts on or close to tracks.

To find your way around New Zealand's motor camps, hotels, motels and so on, pick up a copy of the *Accommodation Guides* published by the Automobile Association (AA) – there's one for the North Island and another for the South Island.

Information about camping and huts is included in the Tramping Information section.

Backpackers

The numerous backpackers' (private or independent) hostels have basically the same facilities and prices as YHA hostels – fully equipped communal kitchens, common areas, laundry facilities and so on. Most backpackers charge extra if you need to hire bedding, so it's best to travel with your own sleeping bag.

A couple of handy brochures are useful for the latest listings of backpackers' accommodation, which is springing up all around the country. The *New Zealand Budget Backpackers' Accommodation* pamphlet, com- monly known as the 'Blue Brochure', is an excellent publication, with details and prices on many backpacker facilities, some of which are close to the tracks.

Tramping Information

Tramping, or bushwalking as it is often called, is the best way of coming to grips with New Zealand's natural beauty. It gives the traveller the satisfaction of being a participant rather than just a spectator.

The country has thousands of km of tracks, many well marked, some only a line on the maps. Tramping is especially attractive because the hundreds of huts available enable trampers to avoid the weight of tents. Many tracks are graded; some are easily covered by those with only moderate fitness and little or no experience, while others are more rewarding for experienced, fit walkers. Many travellers, having tried a track, then gear the rest of their trip in New Zealand to travelling from one track to another, with side trips to see other sights. Before attempting any track, consult the appropriate authority for the latest information.

The most popular tracks in New Zealand are the Abel Tasman Coastal Track, which 20,000 people walked in 1990/91, the Milford Track (10,000), the Routeburn Track (8360), the Kepler Track (6700), the Lake Waikaremoana Track (6500) and the Tongariro Crossing (5000).

If you like tramping but want to avoid crowds, it's worth asking at DOC offices and park headquarters for details on lesser-known tracks – they will be happy to help you plan some enjoyable walks. DOC offices in every city and in dozens of towns give free information about tramping in their areas. Every national park, forest park and maritime park has its own DOC headquarters, and they all have information on a number of long and short walks. There are also council, farm and regional parks, all of which have walking possibilities.

Once on the track, be careful. In good weather, most of the tracks are safer than walking around town, but what really makes them dangerous is New Zealand's contrary weather. A glorious walk in perfect conditions can suddenly become a fight for survival in a blizzard. An easy two-hour walk to the next hut can turn into a grim struggle against wind, wet and cold over a washed-out track and swollen rivers. Hopefully this won't happen, but such unexpected and abrupt changes are common, so be prepared and be careful. Weather forecasts should be watched but taken with a grain of salt. New Zealand's prevailing weather comes from the south-west, an area which has no inhabited land and very little sea or air traffic, making accurate reporting difficult. In Fiordland, forecast weather tends to hit the area a day before it is forecast to do so.

For an enjoyable tramp, the primary considerations are your feet and shoulders. Make sure your footwear is adequate and that your pack is not too heavy. Having adequate, waterproof rain gear is also important, especially on the West Coast of the South Island, where you can get drenched to the skin in minutes if your protective clothing is not up to the challenge.

Above all else, *toitu te whenua* – leave the earth undisturbed.

INFORMATION CENTRES

When you arrive in New Zealand, spend an afternoon gathering the latest information on parks, walks and transportation, and buying any gear that was left behind at the last minute. Travellers arriving without the basic tramping needs (sleeping bag, pack and stove) would do well to check the bulletin boards at hostels.

Auckland

The best information centre for trampers is the DOC information centre, which is in the same building as the Auckland Conservancy (☎ (09) 307 9279; fax 377 2919), on the corner of Liverpool St and Karangahape Rd. The centre is open all year from 8.30 am to 5.30 pm Monday to Friday; from December to February it is also open on Saturday, from 10 am to 1 pm. It sells brochures, maps and books for most tracks and parks in the North Island and for the popular ones in the South Island.

All maps, including topographicals, can be obtained from the Department of Survey & Land Information (DOSLI) office (☎ (09) 377 1899; fax 307 1025), 99 Albert St, on the corner of Albert and Victoria Sts. The DOSLI centre is open on weekdays from 8 am to 4.30 pm. They also have an outlet in the same building as the DOC information centre.

Christchurch

Tramping information can be obtained in Christchurch at the DOC Canterbury Conservancy (☎ 379 9758; fax 371 3770) in Forestry House, 133 Victoria St. It is open on weekdays from 9 am to 4.30 pm.

 Department of Conservation
Te Papa Atawbai

North Island

Trampers can obtain information, brochures and, often, books and maps from the following North Island DOC regional and district offices:

Head Office
59 Boulcott St, Wellington (☎ (04) 471 0726)

Northland
Northland Conservancy, 149-151 Bank St, Whangerei (☎ (09) 438 0299)
Whangerei Field Centre, 12 Kaka St, Whangerei (☎ (09) 438 0299)
Russell Field Centre, Bay of Islands Maritime & Historic Park, Russell (☎ (09) 403 7685)
Kerikeri Field Centre, Landing Rd, Kerikeri (☎ (09) 407 8474)
Waipoua Field Centre, Waipoua Forest Park (☎ (09) 439 0605)
Te Paki Reserves, Private Bag 2007, Kaitaia (☎ (09) 409 7521)
Kaitaia Field Centre, Pukepoto Rd, Kaitaia (☎ (09) 408 2100)

Auckland
Auckland Conservancy, Auckland North Field Centre & Auckland South Field Centre, cnr Karangahape Rd & Liverpool St, Auckland (☎ (09) 307 9279)
Great Barrier Field Centre, Headquarters, Port Fitzroy (☎ (09) 429 0044)

Waikato
Waikato Conservancy, Level 1, BDO House, 18 London St, Hamilton (☎ (07) 838 3363)
Hamilton Field Centre, Northwat St, Te Rapa, Hamilton (☎ (07) 838 3363)
Pureora Field Centre, Pureora Forest Park (☎ (07) 878 4773)
Kauaeranga Field Centre, Kauaeranga Valley (☎ (07) 868 6381)
Coromandel Field Centre, Kapanga Rd, Coromandel (☎ (07) 866 6869)

Tongariro/Taupo
Tongariro/Taupo Conservancy & Turangi Field Centre, Turanga Place, Turangi (☎ (07) 386 8607)

Taupo Field Centre, Centennial Drive, Taupo (☎ (07) 378 3885)

Whakapapa Field Centre, Tongariro National Park Headquarters (☎ (07) 892 3729)

Ohakune Field Centre, Ohakune Mountain Rd, Ohakune (☎ (07) 385 8578)

Bay of Plenty

Bay of Plenty Conservancy, 48-50 Amohau St, Rotorua (☎ (07) 347 9179)

Rotorua Lakes Field Centre, 14 Scott St, Rotorua (☎ (07) 346 1155)

Whakatane Field Centre, 28 Commerce St, Whakatane (☎ (07) 308 7213)

Te Ikawhenua Field Centre, Main Rd, Murupara (☎ (07) 366 5641) – handles queries for Whirinaki Forest Park

East Coast

East Coast Conservancy & Gisborne Field Centre, 63 Carnarvon St, Gisborne (☎ (06) 867 8531)

Aniwaniwa Field Centre, State Highway 38, Aniwaniwa (☎ (06) 837 3803)

Opotiki Field Centre, cnr Elliot & St John Sts, Opotiki (☎ (07) 315 6103)

Wanganui

Wanganui Conservancy & Whanganui Field Centre, Ingestre Chambers, 74 Ingestre St, Wanganui (☎ (06) 345 2402)

Taumaranui Field Centre, Cherry Grove, Taumaranui (☎ (06) 895 8201)

New Plymouth Field Centre, 220 Devon St West, New Plymouth (☎ (06) 758 0433)

North Egmont Visitor Centre, Egmont Rd, via Inglewood (☎ (06) 756 8710)

Stratford Field Centre, Pembroke Rd, Stratford (☎ (06) 765 5144)

Dawson Falls Display Centre, Upper Manaia Rd, via Hawera (☎ (025) 43 0248)

Palmerston North Field Centre, 717 Tremaine Ave, Palmerston North (☎ (06) 358 9004)

Hawkes Bay

Hawkes Bay Conservancy & Napier Field Centre, The Old Courthouse, 59 Marine Parade, Napier (☎ (06) 835 0415)

Wellington

Wellington Conservancy, Bowen State Bldg, Bowen St, Wellington (☎ (04) 472 5821)

Masterton Field Centre, Departmental Bldg, Chapel St, Masterton (☎ (06) 378 2061)

Te Kopa Field Centre, Haurangi Forest Park (☎ (06) 307 8230)

South Island

Trampers can obtain information, from the following South Island DOC offices:

Nelson/Marlborough

Nelson/Marlborough Conservancy, Munro State Bldg, Nelson (☎ (03) 546 9335)

Takaka Field Centre, 1 Commercial St, Takaka (☎ (03) 525 8026)

Motueka Field Centre, cnr King Edward & High Sts, Motueka (☎ (03) 528 9117)

Havelock Field Centre, 13 Mahakipawa Rd, Havelock (☎ (03) 574 2019)

Picton Field Centre, Auckland St, Picton Foreshore, Picton (☎ (03) 573 7582)

Blenheim Field Centre, Gee St, Renwick, Blenheim (☎ (03) 572 9100)

Kaikoura Field Centre, Ludstone Rd, Kaikoura (☎ (03) 319 5714)

St Arnaud Field Centre, View Rd, St Arnaud (☎ (03) 521 1806)

West Coast

West Coast Conservancy & Arahura Field Centre, Sewell St, Hokitika (☎ (03) 755 8301)

Fox Glacier Field Centre, Main Rd, Fox Glacier (☎ (03) 751 0807)

Franz Josef Field Centre, Main Rd, Franz Josef (☎ (03) 752 0796)

Haast Field Centre, cnr State Highway 6 & Jackson Bay Rd, Haast (☎ (03) 750 0809)

Karamea Field Centre, Main Rd, Karamea (☎ (03) 782 6852)

Punakaiki Field Centre, Main Rd, Punakaiki (☎ (03) 731 1893)

Westport Field Centre, Palmerston St, Westport (☎ (03) 789 7742)

Canterbury

Canterbury Conservancy & Christchurch Field Centre, Forestry House, 1st floor, 133 Victoria St, Christchurch (☎ (03) 379 9758; fax 371 3770)

Akaroa Field Base, Old Coach Rd, Akaroa (☎ (03) 304 7334)

Waimakariri Field Centre, Arthur's Pass Township, State Highway 73 (☎ (03) 318 9211)

Hanmer Springs Field Centre, Jollies Pass Rd, Hanmer Springs (☎ (03) 315 7264)

Twizel Field Centre, Wairepo Rd, Twizel (☎ (03) 435 0802)

Mt Cook Field Centre, Mt Cook Village, Mt Cook (☎ (03) 435 1819)

Raukapuka Field Centre, North Terrace, Geraldine (☎ (03) 693 9994)

Otago

Otago Conservancy, Conservation House, 77 Stuart St, Dunedin (☎ (03) 477 0677)

Dunedin Field Centre, 77 Stuart St, Dunedin (☎ (03) 477 0677)

Glenorchy Field Centre, cnr Mull & Oban Sts, Glenorchy (☎ (03) 442 9937; fax 442 9938)

Makarora Field Centre, Haast Pass Highway (☎ /fax (03) 443 8365)

Owaka Field Centre (Catlins), cnr Campbell & Ryley Sts, Owaka (☎ /fax (03) 415 8341)

Queenstown Field Centre, 37 Shotover St, Queenstown (☎ 442 7933; fax (03) 442 7932)

Wanaka Field Centre, Ardmore St, Wanaka (☎ /fax (03) 443 7660)

Southland

Southland Conservancy, State Insurance Bldg, Don St, Invercargill (☎ (03) 214 4589)

Te Anau Field Centre & Milford Track Bookings, Visitor Centre, Lakefront Drive, Te Anau (☎ (03) 249 7921; bookings ☎ 249 8514)

Tuatapere Field Centre, 21 Orawia Rd, Tuatapere (☎ (03) 226 6607)

Queenstown Field Centre, 37 Shotover St, Queenstown (☎ (03) 442 7933)

Halfmoon Bay Field Centre, Main Rd, Halfmoon Bay, Stewart Island (☎ (03) 219 1130).

Parks & Park Authorities

In April 1987, the newly created DOC replaced the Lands & Survey Department and the New Zealand Forest Service, and took on the functions of several other government agencies. This unprecedented reorganisation of the country's Crown lands and natural resources affected every national park, forest park, maritime park and scenic reserve. Practically all of New Zealand's tracks now fall under the jurisdiction of the DOC – or as one national park ranger put it, 'we all work for the DOC now'.

Also under the management of the DOC are the welfare of the country's flora & fauna and the promotion and development of recreational policies. Described in one brochure as a 'voice for conservation', the DOC is responsible for conserving New Zealand's natural resources, and it has staff in 14 conservancies carrying out that task.

Changes have already rippled down to those eager to tramp in New Zealand's bush. Trampers now search out a DOC office, whether it's a regional or district centre, when seeking information. Having found one, many trampers then painfully discover another policy the new department has instituted: 'user pays'. This means that if you want a brochure on the Hollyford Track or a Mt Aspiring National Park pamphlet, it's going to cost you about $1. User pays is being applied to most visitor services, from the summer nature programmes presented in national parks to the country's hut system.

In the early 1980s, trampers were only charged for using huts along the Routeburn and Milford tracks; now all national parks charge hut fees. Eventually, even huts in forest parks and other obscure preserves will be charging fees in an effort to recover their construction and maintenance costs.

Tramping & Outdoor Clubs

Because Kiwis love the outdoors, there are a great number of tramping and outdoor clubs. Overseas visitors could contact these clubs to see which walks they are undertaking, because it could be a good way to get out and see a part of the bush you may not otherwise visit. The clubs are listed in a pamphlet put out by the Federated Mountain Clubs of New Zealand – *Join a Club: Tramping, Climbing, Skiing*, available from DOC offices. The addresses and phone numbers of some of the clubs follow:

North Island

Whangarei Tramping Club, Box 346, Whangarei (☎ (09) 435 1166)

Auckland Tramping Club, PO Box 2358, Auckland (☎ (09) 815 1598)

Auckland University Tramping Club, Private Bag, Auckland 1 (☎ (09) 309 0789)

New Zealand Alpine Club (Auckland Section), PO Box 3036, Auckland (☎ (09) 445 1501)

Hamilton Tramping Club, PO Box 776, Hamilton (☎ (07) 849 4447)

Waikato Tramping Club, c/o Recreation Centre, Private Bag, Hamilton (☎ (07) 829 3883)

Rotorua Tramping & Ski Club, PO Box 337, Rotorua (☎ (07) 345 3794)

Tauranga Tramping Club, PO Box 2294, Tauranga (☎ (07) 575 5909)

Taupo Tramping Club, PO Box 650, Taupo (☎ (07) 378 2732)

Gisborne Canoe & Tramping Club, PO Box 289, Gisborne (☎ (06) 868 4741)

Napier Tramping Club, PO Box 992, Napier (☎ (07) 843 9696)

New Plymouth Tramping Club, PO Box 861, New Plymouth (☎ (06) 753 4389)

Palmerston North Tramping & Mountaineering Club, PO Box 1217, Palmerston North (☎ (06) 358 3467)

Ruahine Tramping Club, PO Box 300, Dannevirke (☎ (06) 374 6630)

New Zealand Alpine Club (Wellington Section), PO Box 1628, Wellington (☎ (04) 384 4413)

Tararua Tramping Club, PO Box 1008, Wellington (☎ (04) 567 3240)

Victoria University Tramping Club, Private Bag, Wellington (☎ (04) 475 3091)

Wellington Tramping & Mountaineering Club, PO Box 5068, Wellington (☎ (04) 477 0218).

South Island

Marlborough Tramping Club, PO Box 787, Blenheim (☎ (03) 578 2938)

Nelson Tramping Club, 114 Vanguard St, Nelson (☎ (03) 546 4239)

West Coast Alpine Club, PO Box 136, Greymouth (☎ (03) 732 3749)

Canterbury University Tramping Club, c/o Students Association, Private Bag, Christchurch (☎ (03) 377 2551)

Christchurch Tramping Club, PO Box 527, Christchurch (☎ (03) 351 9811)

New Zealand Alpine Club (Canterbury-Westland Section), PO Box 1700, Christchurch (☎ (03) 384 4413)

Otago Tramping & Mountaineering Club, PO Box 1120, Dunedin (☎ (03) 464 0325)

Otago University Tramping Club, Otago University, Dunedin (☎ (03) 477 7961)

Waka Tramping & Mountaineering Club, PO Box 137, Queenstown (☎ (03) 442 9321)

Fiordland Tramping Club, PO Box 125, Te Anau (☎ (03) 249 7385)

Southland Tramping Club, PO Box 11, Invercargill (☎ (03) 230 4166).

RESERVES & NATIONAL PARKS

In 1887, Te Heuheu Tukino IV, paramount chief of the Tuwharetoa Maori tribe, was worried about the future of his people's sacred ancestral mountains, the North Island's Central Plateau. Rival Maori tribes were eyeing the peaks, so were European settlers, who saw the tussock lands around the volcanoes as potential grazing country. With remarkable foresight, the native chief offered the land to the New Zealand Government as a gift to all the people, with one stipulation: it had to be kept *tapu* (sacred) and protected. The area became Tongariro National Park, New Zealand's first park and the start of the world's fourth national park system, following those of the USA, Australia and Canada.

With the creation of Kahurangi National Park in 1994, there are now 13 within the country – four in the North Island and nine in the South Island – each preserving a distinct area of the country, ranging from volcanoes, glaciers and the Southern Alps to coastal beaches, native forests and the longest navigable river. They are under the jurisdiction of the DOC, but each park is administered by a chief ranger from its headquarters, usually located within the town or city that serves as the major access point.

Park headquarters and visitor centres are good places to visit before tramping off into the bush or mountains. They can provide the latest weather report as well as information on track and hut conditions. They sell maps, brochures and park handbooks that explain the natural and historical significance of the area. Most have visitor centres that contain a series of interesting displays, along with a small theatre where a video presentation on the park is shown on request. These are also the best places to register your intentions and pay hut fees. The walks included in this guide are listed in italics after the park.

North Island

Te Urewera The visitor centre is at Aniwaniwa, on the eastern arm of Lake Waikaremoana. The postal address is Aniwaniwa Field Centre, Te Urewera National Park, Private Bag 213, Wairoa (*Lake Waikaremoana Track, Whakatane River Track*).

Tongariro The headquarters and visitor centre are at Whakapapa Village. The postal address is Whakapapa Field Centre, Tongariro National Park, c/o Post Office, Mt Ruapehu (*Tongariro Northern Circuit*).

Egmont The headquarters is in New Plymouth but the visitor centre is at North Egmont, within the park. The postal address is North Egmont Visitor Centre, Egmont National Park, RD 6, Inglewood (*Mt Taranaki Round-the Mountain Track, Pouakai Track*).

New Zealand's National Parks

0   100   200 km

Approximate Scale

Whangarei

Auckland

Thames

Hamilton

Tauranga

TE UREWERA

Rotorua

Gisborne

WHANGANUI

Taupo

New Plymouth

Turangi

MT EGMONT

TONGARIRO
WORLD
HERITAGE

Napier

Wanganui

Palmerston
North

ABEL TASMAN

KAHURANGI

Nelson

WELLINGTON

PAPAROA

NELSON LAKES

Greymouth

Hokitika

ARTHUR'S PASS

WESTLAND

Christchurch

TE WAHIPOUNAMU
WORLD HERITAGE
AREA

MT COOK

FIORDLAND

MT ASPIRING

Queenstown

Dunedin

National Parks

World Heritage Area

Invercargill

Stewart Island (Rakiura)

Wanganui The headquarters is at the DOC office in Wanganui, while a visitor centre and river museum are at Pipiriki. The postal address is Whanganui Field Centre, Whanganui National Park, Private Bag 3016, Wanganui *(Matemateonga Walkway)*.

South Island

Abel Tasman The headquarters is on Commercial St in Takaka. The postal address is Takaka Field Centre, Abel Tasman National Park, PO Box 53, Takaka *(Abel Tasman Coast Track)*.

Kahurangi This is the most recently established national park, formerly called North West Nelson Forest Park. The headquarters and visitor centre of the park have not been finalised, so direct enquiries to the DOC, Private Bag 5, Nelson (☎ (03) 546 9335) *(Heaphy Track, Wangapeka Track, Leslie-Karamea Track)*.

Nelson Lakes The headquarters and visitor centre are in the small village of St Arnaud. The postal address is St Arnaud Field Centre, Nelson Lakes National Park, Private Bag, St Arnaud *(Travers-Sabine Circuit, D'Urville Valley Track)*.

Arthur's Pass The headquarters and visitor centre are in the alpine village of Arthur's Pass. The postal address is Waimakariri Field Centre, Arthur's Pass National Park, PO Box 8, Arthur's Pass *(Goat Pass Track, Waimakariri-Harman Pass Route, Harper Pass)*.

Paparoa There is a DOC office in Punakaiki and a visitor centre one km south, at the Pancake Rocks. The postal address is Punakaiki Field Centre, PO Box 1, Punakaiki *(Inland Pack Track)*.

Westland The headquarters and a visitor centre are at Franz Josef. There is another visitor centre at Fox Glacier. The postal address is Franz Josef Field Centre, Westland National Park, PO Box 14, Franz Josef *(Copland Pass)*.

Mt Cook The headquarters and visitor centre are in the village of Mt Cook, and there are plans to build a mountaineering museum there as well. The postal address is Mt Cook Field Centre, PO Box 5, Mt Cook *(Copland Pass, Mueller Hut)*.

Mt Aspiring The headquarters and a visitor centre are located in Wanaka. The postal address is Wanaka Field Centre, Mt Aspiring National Park, PO Box 93, Wanaka *(Routeburn Track, Greenstone Track, Caples Track, Rees-Dart Track, Cascade Saddle Track, Wilkin-Young Valleys Circuit)*.

Fiordland The headquarters and an impressive visitor centre are in Te Anau, on the southern shore of Lake Te Anau. The postal address is Te Anau Field Centre, Fiordland National Park, PO Box 29, Te Anau *(Milford Track, Routeburn Track, Hollyford Track, Kepler Track, Dusky Track)*.

Te Wahipounamu World Heritage Region The headquarters of the World Heritage area, which encompasses four national parks – Mt Aspiring, Westland, Mt Cook and Fiordland – is located at Haast, in Westland. The postal address is World Heritage Visitor Centre, PO Box 50, Haast.

Forest Parks

Additional bush and wilderness areas are preserved in New Zealand's forest park system, with 14 parks in the North Island and six in the South Island. Forest parks fall under the jurisdiction of the DOC.

While the theme of national parks is to preserve 'an area in its natural state', forest parks follow a multiple-use concept. In a national park, everything is secondary to preservation, tramping included. But forest parks are managed to sustain a balance of land uses, which might include timber production, deer harvesting to provide stock for farms, possum hunting for the fur industry and, of course, recreational activities.

The main recreational activity in most forest parks is tramping; all forest parks have huts and a variety of tracks. A number of the tracks described in this guide lie in forest parks, ranging from the easy two-day Whirinaki Track near Te Urewera National Park to the challenging alpine treks found in the Tararuas north of Wellington.

The North Island forest parks are Northland, Coromandel *(Coromandel Forest Walk)*, Kaimai-Mamaku, Pirongia, Raukumara *(East-West Traverse)*, Pureora, Whakawerawera, Whirinaki *(Whirinaki Track)*, Kaweka, Kaimanawa *(Te Iringa-Oamaru Circuit)*, Ruahine, Rimutaka, Haurangi and Tararua *(Holdsworth Circuit, Totara Flats Track)*.

In the South Island, the forest parks are Mt Richmond *(Pelorus River Track)*, Victoria, Hanmer, Lake Sumner *(Harper Pass)*,

**New Zealand's
Forest Parks**

0   100   200 km

Approximate Scale

NORTHLAND

Whangarei

COROMANDEL

Auckland

Thames

RAUKUMARA

KAIMAI-MAMAKU

Hamilton

Tauranga

PIRONGIA

Rotorua

WHAKAWERAWERA

PUREORA

Taupo

Gisborne

WHIRINAKI

New Plymouth

Turangi

Napier

KAIMANAWA

KAWEKA

Wanganui

RUAHINE

Palmerston
North

TARARUA

RIMUTAKA

HAURANGI

Nelson

WELLINGTON

LEWIS PASS
NATIONAL RESERVE

VICTORIA

MT RICHMOND

Greymouth

Hokitika

HANMER

LAKE SUMNER

Christchurch

CRAIGIEBURN

Queenstown

Dunedin

Invercargill

CATLINS

STEWART ISLAND (RAKIURA)

Craigieburn *(Cass-Lagoon Saddles Track)* and Catlins.

Maritime & Historic Parks

There are three maritime parks in New Zealand: Bay of Islands (also an historic park), Hauraki Gulf and Marlborough Sounds. These popular summer holiday spots combine great scenery, historical significance, venues for water sports and, very often, tramping tracks.

All three parks are included in this guidebook, with three walks described in detail – Great Barrier Island in the Hauraki Gulf, and the Queen Charlotte Walkway and Nydia Track in the Marlborough Sounds. The Bay of Islands is of exceptional historical interest, and the Cape Brett Walk is described briefly in this guide. One special area, the Otago Goldfields Park, is not a park as such but consists of many small sites scattered across Otago.

Forests & Scenic Reserves

Other types of preserved land in New Zealand includes forests in DOC stewardship land, which contain networks of tracks and huts. Forests included in this book are Urutawa Forest *(The Pakihi Stock Route)*, DOC stewardship land south of Paparoa National Park *(Croesus Track)* and Stewart Island *(Rakiura Track and North-West Circuit)*.

Trampers will also find walking opportunities in many of the scenic reserves, most notably in the Lewis Pass National Reserve, which contains a portion of the St James Walkway. Another walk in this guide is the Mt Somers Subalpine Walkway, in the Mt Somers Recreation & Conservation area, another example of DOC stewardship land. In the North Island there is the Ninety Mile Beach-Cape Reinga Walkway, in the Te Paki Reserves, once set aside as farmland.

Private land is also being opened up for walking, and a good example is the very scenic Banks Peninsula Walk. For up-to-date information on forests, conservation and scenic reserves, and private walks, contact the nearest DOC regional or district office.

WALKING STANDARDS

Each track is rated according to difficulty – see The Track subsection for each walk.

Easy tracks are those that are well maintained and frequently used, with planking over most wet areas, swing bridges over major streams, and directional signs. These tracks can be attempted by trampers with just day-hiking experience.

Those rated as *medium* are tracks that are well cut and usually well marked with small metal tags but are more strenuous than easy tracks, with numerous stream crossings. They require a greater degree of physical stamina and better map-reading skills.

Walkways

The idea of a national walkway – a path from one end of New Zealand to the other – captured the enthusiasm of Kiwis in the 1970s, and by 1975 the country's legislators passed the Walkways Act, which set up the framework for this immense project. Under the direction of the New Zealand Walkways Commission, the ultimate goal was a network of interconnecting tracks to provide a path from Cape Reinga (at the north end of the country) to Bluff (at the south end).

Initially, the main emphasis was on providing access for short family walks into the countryside from major urban areas. But there are now walkways all over the country, varying in difficulty and terrain. However, the idea that the walkway should continue all the way from Cape Reinga to Bluff seems to have been shelved for the time being.

Several of the walkways lend themselves to tramps lasting several days, including some described in this book – the St James, Mt Somers Subalpine and Queen Charlotte walkways in the South Island and the Matemateaonga and Ninety Mile-Cape Reinga walkways in the North Island. For more information on New Zealand Walkways, write to The Secretary, New Zealand Walkway Commission, c/o DOC, Private Bag, Wellington. ∎

Difficult tracks are often not tracks at all but routes marked only by rock cairns (and snow poles in alpine areas), or they may not be marked at all (such as a route along a river valley). These trips should be attempted only by experienced trampers with the right equipment and a good knowledge of New Zealand's bush and weather patterns.

Keep in mind that no matter what the track is rated, even easy walks will probably involve some climbing and descending of ridges or passes. It's almost impossible to find a completely flat walk in New Zealand – it's just the nature of the country.

Approximate walking times are also provided, usually from one hut to the next. It is important to remember these are only average tramping times based on the average tramper covering one km of well-marked and somewhat level track in 20 to 25 minutes. Your hiking time will probably be different. What one person thinks is a back-breaking trudge will be judged as a pleasant stroll. Determine your own endurance and speed and then adjust the times in this book accordingly.

The times do not include major rest periods, lunchbreaks or afternoon teas. They are also based on good weather conditions. Swollen streams or muddy tracks will slow you down.

The distances given within the text are approximate only. This is especially true of routes where there is no exact track, such as up a river bed or over an alpine ridge. On these routes, the path followed and the distances covered will differ from one party to the next.

Track Classification

Tracks are classified according to their difficulty, and many other features – how they are marked, degree of steepness etc. Although the track classification system is relatively new, you will often hear the classifications used. They are:

- **Path** Easy and well-formed, these allow for wheelchair access (or 'shoe' standard). Paths are suitable for people of all ages and fitness levels

- **Walking Track** Easy and well-formed, walking tracks are constructed to 'shoe' standard and are suitable for people of most ages and fitness levels
- **Tramping Track** These require skill and experience. Constructed to 'boot' standard, they're suitable for people of average physical fitness
- **Route** Requiring a high degree of skill, experience and route-finding ability, routes are suitable only for well-equipped trampers.

Great Walks

Several of New Zealand's most famous tracks have been designated 'Great Walks'. They are:

- Lake Waikaremoana Track, Te Urewera National Park (North Island)
- Tongariro Northern Circuit, Tongariro National Park (North Island)
- Abel Tasman Coast Track, Abel Tasman National Park (South Island)
- Heaphy Track, Kahurangi National Park (South Island)
- Routeburn Track, Mt Aspiring and Fiordland National Parks (South Island)
- Milford Track, Fiordland National Park (South Island)
- Kepler Track, Fiordland National Park (South Island)
- Rakiura Track (Stewart Island)
- The canoe trip down the Whanganui River in Whanganui National Park in the North Island is obviously not a walk – they call it the Whanganui Journey – but it, too, is part of the Great Walks system.

TRAMPING ACCOMMODATION
DOC Camping Grounds

The DOC operates over 120 camping

DOC Camp Site Logo

grounds (conservation camping areas) in New Zealand. There are DOC camp sites in reserves and in national, maritime, forest and farm parks.

DOC camping grounds are of three types. Serviced camping grounds have flush toilets, hot showers, tap water, kitchen and laundry areas, outdoor lighting, picnic tables and rubbish collection, and usually have powered as well as nonpowered sites. They may also have barbecue and fireplace facilities, a shop and a campervan waste disposal point. Nightly fees are around $6 to $9 per adult.

Standard camping areas are more basic, with minimal facilities, including cold running water, toilets, fireplaces and not much else, but they also have minimal charges: around $2 to $6 per adult.

Children aged five to 16 are charged half-price at both types of sites; it's free for children under the age of five.

The third type – informal camping areas – are free. They have limited facilities, usually just a cold-water tap and places to pitch tents. Sometimes the access to these types of sites is difficult – you may have to walk rather than drive – but they are worth it if you're geared for camping.

The DOC publishes a useful brochure, *Conservation Camp Sites*, which gives details of all the DOC camping grounds throughout New Zealand. You can pick it up at any DOC office, or write for it to the DOC, PO Box 10420, Wellington.

You can check with local DOC offices for details on facilities, what you need to take with you and whether you should book in advance. Bookings can be made for all serviced camping grounds; contact the DOC office nearest the camping ground.

Standard camping areas and informal camping areas operate on a first-come, first-served basis, and fees are paid according to a self-registration system. Since all fees are used for the maintenance of the camping grounds, and are kept as low as possible, it's important to pay them (usually into an 'honesty box'), even when there's no warden present.

Back-Country Huts

The DOC has a network of back-country huts in the national, maritime and forest parks. Hut fees range from $4 to a maximum of $20 per night for adults, paid with tickets purchased in advance at any DOC office or park visitors' centre. The tickets cost $4 each (you can buy them in booklets) and are valid for 15 months. Children 11 years and older are charged half-price and use a special 'youth ticket'. Children under 11 years of age can use all huts free of charge.

Huts fall into four categories, and depending on the category, a night's accommodation may require one or two tickets, except on Great Walks, where Great Walks passes are required. On arrival at a hut, you simply date the tickets and deposit them in the box provided. Hut accommodation is on a first-come, first-served basis.

The best (Category One) huts have cookers and fuel, bunks or sleeping platforms with mattresses, toilet and washing facilities, and a water supply. They may also have lighting, heating, radio communications, drying facilities, and a hut warden on duty. Category One huts are found on the Great Walks, where Great Walks passes are required (see the following section). The cost in Great Walks huts ranges from $6 to $20 per night (youths half-price).

Category Two huts have bunks or sleeping platforms with mattresses, as well as toilet and washing facilities and a water supply. They may also include cooking and heating facilities, but you may have to provide your

own cooker and fuel. The cost is $8 (two tickets) per night.

Category Three huts are more basic, with bunks or sleeping platforms (but no mattresses), toilet and water supply only. You provide your own cooker and fuel. These huts are $4 (one ticket) per night.

There is no fee for Category Four facilities, which are usually just simple shelters for getting out of the rain – no bunks or other amenities. You will probably end up in one or two at some time, however, if you tramp for long enough in New Zealand.

On some tracks – the Tongariro Northern Circuit and the Whanganui Journey, for example – Great Walks passes are necessary only at certain times of year, when the tracks are busiest. During the times of year when Great Walks passes are not required on these tracks, ordinary back-country hut tickets and Annual Hut Passes are accepted.

Huts – Popular Tracks
The following notes on huts and wardens apply only to the popular 'tourist' tracks. If you venture onto any other tracks, things will be quite different. For example it may take you an hour to cover one km, huts may be eight hours or so apart, there won't be any wardens and you will have to be much better prepared.

Keep these factors in mind:

* When walking, allow about four km per hour on easy ground
* Huts are usually located three to four hours apart
* Huts usually cater for 24, and beds are thick foam mattresses on bunks
* Huts on the more popular tracks usually have wood stoves with gas burners
* There is a two-night limit on huts, if they are full.

Camping is allowed on all tracks except the Milford Track. On Great Walks tracks, where the huts can fill up, camping areas are provided beside all the huts for overflow. On the Milford Track, numbers are regulated so that the huts don't get overloaded.

The New Zealand Environmental Care Code (obtainable from any DOC office; see the Environmental Care Code section) gives guidelines for camping. Always leave firewood in huts for the next group, in case they arrive in heavy rain or after dark.

In the last decade or so, there has been an amazing improvement in the conditions of tracks and huts. Tracks are administered by conservation officers and wardens; the former are permanent staff, well trained and very knowledgeable. The wardens are temporary, usually employed for the summer season to keep an eye on and maintain the huts, provide track information and first aid, collect hut fees and generally be helpful to trampers.

Wardens in the national parks collect hut fees when they're on duty (from November to April). Whether a warden is present or not, it's important to pay your hut fees because all huts require maintenance and this is how it is paid for. Most DOC offices in the regional centres near the start of tracks sell back-country hut tickets. Check with wardens or DOC staff in the regional offices for weather forecasts and information about the track.

Annual Hut Pass
If you plan to do much tramping, consider getting an Annual Hut Pass. The pass allows you to stay overnight at all Category Two and Three huts (on a first-come, first-served basis) and to camp outside all Category One huts, where this is allowed. (A list of all huts and their categories is available at any DOC office.) The pass costs $58 (children $29), and is valid for one year from the date of purchase. It does not apply to the Great Walks – the Milford Track operates on its own system.

ENVIRONMENTAL CARE CODE
It is traditional in New Zealand to dig rubbish pits next to huts, but in recent years there has been a concerted effort to do away with them. There is now a campaign to encourage trampers to carry out the rubbish they create, with signs in most huts urging trampers and hunters to 'pack it in and pack it out'. Still, the volume of rubbish left in many huts is disturbing.

NEW ZEALAND

ENVIRONMENTAL CARE CODE

A number of organisations (Federated Mountain Clubs, Environment & Conservation Organisations, New Zealand Mountain Safety Council, New Zealand Institute of Park & Recreation Administration, Royal Forest & Bird Protection Society of New Zealand and the DOC) provide copies of the Environmental Care Code, which lists 10 points to remember: protect plants and animals; remove rubbish; bury toilet waste; keep streams and lakes clean; take care with fires; camp carefully; keep to the track; consider others; respect cultural heritage; and enjoy your visit.

Remember: 'The land is the property of a great family, some of whom are living, a few of whom are dead, most of whom have yet to come'.

TRAMPING BOOKS

The national parks produce very good books with detailed information on the parks' flora & fauna, geology and history. The DOC has leaflets available on hundreds of walking tracks throughout the country, and the local DOC office is usually the best source of information on specific tracks. In addition to the books listed below, there are magazines such as *NZ Adventure, Forest & Bird, New Zealand Geographic* and *FMC Journal* which periodically have interesting articles on tramping.

General

There are a number of useful publications which describe the skills needed to tramp

successfully. Two of the best are *Bushcraft* (New Zealand Mountain Safety Council Manual 12, Wellington, 1983) and *Mountaincraft*, by Lindsay Main (New Zealand Mountain Safety Council Manual 20, Wellington, 1980). Other general books are *The New Zealand Trampers Handbook*, by Grant Hunter (Reed, Auckland, 1989), and *Safety in the Mountains* (FMC, Wellington, 9th edition, 1992).

Tramping gets more than a casual mention in two compendiums of the zany adventures that New Zealanders and their guests get up to. The first, *Classic New Zealand Adventures*, by Jonathan Kennett et al (GP Publications, Wellington, 1992), is a favourite. The other is an annual production: *The New Zealand Adventure 1993 Annual & Directory*, by John Woods (First Light Media, Gisborne, 1992), tells you who to contact for information about all sorts of outdoor activities.

Even though it's getting a bit dated now, the glossy *Wild New Zealand* (Reader's Digest, Surry Hills, 1981) is a joy to read, with well-written text accompanied by photographs that do not date.

Guidebooks

There are plenty of guidebooks about tramping in New Zealand. The paperback *New Zealand's Top Ten Tracks*, by Mark Pickering (Heinemann Reed, Auckland, 1990), contains many of the obvious ones (Milford, Routeburn etc). *101 Great Tramps*, by Mark Pickering & Rodney Smith (Reed, Auckland, 1991, paperback), has 101 suggestions for two to six-day tramps around the country. There is also *A Tramper's Guide to New Zealand National Parks*, by R Burton & M Atkinson (Reed Methuen, Auckland, 1987).

Tramping in North Island Forest Parks, by Euan & Jennie Nicol (Reed, Auckland, 1991, paperback), and *Tramping in South Island Forest Parks*, by Joanna Wright (Reed, Auckland, 1990, paperback), are good for walking and tramping possibilities in forest parks, with suggestions for everything from half-hour walks to tramps taking several days.

The Forest & Bird Book of Nature Walks, by David Collingwood & E V Sale, revised by Joanna Wright (Reed, Auckland, 1992, paperback), has good suggestions for short walks (half an hour to several hours in length).

BP (Penguin) publishes a series of pocket-size paperback guides to several of New Zealand's most popular walking tracks. There's also a series of *Shell Guides* on the more popular tracks.

Moir's Trampers' Guide to the Southern Lakes & Fiordland, by the New Zealand Alpine Club, is the definitive work on tracks in the south of the South Island. It comes in two volumes: *Northern Section: Lake Wakatipu to the Ohau Watershed* (1984) and *Southern Section: Hollyford Valley South* (1986), both in paperback.

Regional Guides

The DOC (or its predecessors) have produced an excellent series, *The Story of ...*, which covers the following parks: Bay of Islands Maritime & Historic, Hauraki Gulf Maritime, Tongariro, Te Urewera, Egmont, the Wanganui River, Marlborough Sounds Maritime, Abel Tasman, Mt Cook, Nelson Lakes, Arthur's Pass, Westland and Fiordland. These guides are slowly going out of print and, unfortunately, may not be reprinted. They are good collectors' items.

There are a number of useful regional guides, specific to either a national or a forest park; enquire at DOC offices. Some examples are *Ruahine Forest Park: A Guide to Family Walks*, by Kathy Ombler (Craig Potton Publishing, Nelson, 1993), *Tararua Forest Park Route Guide* (2nd edition), by J N Jennings (New Zealand Forest Service, Wellington, 1981), and *The Paparoas Guide*, by Andy Dennis (NFAC, Nelson, 1981).

Natural History

There's a wide choice of literature on the flora & fauna of New Zealand. The following are just some of the titles available.

Flora *Eagle's Trees & Shrubs of New Zealand*, by A Eagle (Collins, Auckland,

1986, revised paperback edition); *A Field Guide to the Native Trees of New Zealand*, by J T Salmon (Reed Methuen, Auckland, 1986); *Collins Guide to the Alpine Plants of New Zealand*, by J T Salmon (Collins, Auckland, 1985, revised edition); and *The Greening of Gondwana*, by M White (Reed, Sydney, 1986).

Fauna *A Field Guide to New Zealand Birds*, by Geoff Moon (Octopus, Auckland, 1992); *Birds of New Zealand: Locality Guide*, by Stuart Chambers (Arun Books, Hamilton, 1989); *Collins Guide to the Birds of New Zealand*, by R A Falla et al (Collins, 1986); *The New Zealand Birdwatchers' Book*, by B A Ellis (Reed Methuen, Auckland, 1987); *Whales & Dolphins of New Zealand & Australia: An Identification Guide*, by Alan N Baker (Victoria University Press, Wellington, 1990); and *Whales & Dolphins of Kaikoura, New Zealand*, by Barbara Todd (Potton Publishing, Nelson, 1991).

MAPS

There is no substitute for a good map. The maps in this edition do not contain contour lines – this is our strongest suggestion to trampers that these maps have value for planning only. The best maps are the locally produced topographical quads, and we won't try to emulate them.

There are two types of maps commonly used by trampers: the topographical sheets (also called quads), and the specific maps of national parks, forest parks and tracks.

Topographical maps are best, and can be purchased from the DOSLI InfoMap Topomaps 260 series in a scale of 1:50,000 (one cm to 500 metres). Some areas have not been mapped in this series, so obtain one of the NZMS 1, the original series with a scale of 1:63,360 (one inch to one mile). These topographical quads do not indicate tracks. Topomaps cost $12.50 each.

The InfoMap Parkmaps cover the majority of forest and national parks in the North and South islands. Scales range from 1:25,000 *(Whakarewarewa)* to 1:250,000 *(Fiordland)*, but most are around 1:80,000 to

1:100,000. While these maps provide less detail, they are still suitable for most well-marked tracks. Many also contain track notes, walking times and information on the park's natural history; these maps are usually the ones posted in huts. They do not have contour intervals, relying on hill shading to show relief.

Some of the areas in this book are covered in the Holidaymaker series. These maps concentrate on areas popular with visitors. Great Barrier Island (1:50,000), Lake Waikaremoana (1:40,000), Marlborough Sounds (1:100,000), Banks Peninsula (1:100,000) and Stewart Island (1:100,000) are covered in this series; the cost of these maps is $11.

Topographical maps with a larger scale (such as 1:250,000) are of little use to trampers because they do not have enough detail.

There are seven Trackmaps which cover the more popular walking and tramping tracks. Those referred to in this book are the Hollyford, Milford, Routeburn, Kepler and Heaphy.

Most maps are produced by DOSLI, the government's Department of Survey & Land Information, and are sold at InfoMap centres throughout the country as well as at DOC offices and park visitor centres. DOSLI map sales offices in the North Island are in Auckland, Gisborne, Hamilton, Napier, New Plymouth, Palmerston North, Rotorua, Wellington and Whangarei; in the South Island you'll find them in Blenheim, Christchurch, Dunedin, Hokitika, Invercargill, Nelson and Timaru. DOC offices often sell a selection of DOSLI maps of tracks in their immediate area.

If you are unsure about your map-reading skills, pick up an *Information for Map Users* pamphlet at any InfoMap centre.

TRACK SAFETY

It's *very important* that you learn and follow some basic rules of safety if you're tramping in New Zealand. Thousands of Kiwis and overseas visitors tramp in New Zealand every year without incident, but every year a few die in the mountains. Most fatalities would not have happened if the victims had observed simple safety rules.

The main thing to be aware of when tramping in New Zealand is the extremely changeable climate. New Zealand has a maritime climate, not a continental climate – which means that if you come from any of the large land masses (Australia, North America, Europe or wherever), the climate holds surprises.

Always remember that the weather can change extremely quickly. Heavy rain, snow and high winds can hit mountain areas at any time, and this can happen in a matter of minutes, even on a warm, sunny day. Always be mentally and physically prepared for all kinds of weather. Take along warm enough clothes, waterproof rain gear (raincoat and overtrousers) and a waterproof pack liner. If you find your clothing and footwear inadequate for the conditions, it's best to turn back.

Hypothermia is the main health hazard for trampers in New Zealand. Be aware of what causes it so you can avoid it, and know what to do about it if it does occur. (Hypothermia is covered in the Health section of this chapter.)

Getting lost is another very real danger, so stick to the tracks. Getting lost in the bush is more of a danger in New Zealand than in many other places. The native bush is very dense and people have become hopelessly lost on a simple 15-minute walk, being found many days later (or not at all). It sounds so strange it's almost comical, but if you spend any length of time in New Zealand and keep up with the news, you'll start to notice that people go missing in the bush quite frequently. And it's not always overseas visitors

Where Am I?
Track descriptions in this book refer to the 'true left' and 'true right' sides of rivers. What exactly does this mean? If you are looking downstream in the direction of the water flow, the true left is the left bank and true right is obviously the other side of the river. Sometimes, more information is given in brackets, eg '...the true left (west) side of the river'. ∎

either – it's often experienced trampers who know the areas they're tramping in.

Always make sure that someone responsible knows where you're going, what route you intend to take and when you expect to come out, so that they can notify police if you go missing. Then remember to let them know when you've come out safely!

Fill out an intentions and/or help form at the DOC office, national park headquarters or visitor centre at the start of the trip, and write in the logbooks of huts along the way, giving the names of the members of your party and details about when you were there and where you are going when you leave. Do this even if you don't stay in the huts – it will make it far easier to find you if you should go missing.

Other safety rules include:

- Choose a track that suits your level of fitness and experience
- Find out what to expect on the track. Always seek local advice about current track and weather conditions – from the local DOC office, national park headquarters, etc – before you set out
- Go with at least one other person, and stay on the track
- Purify river or lake water before drinking it
- Take a first-aid kit and everything else you're supposed to – water purifier, warm clothes etc
- If you meet heavy rain, and rivers in your path have risen, stay where you are until the rivers go down, retrace your tracks, or take another route. Don't cross a flooding river unless you are absolutely certain you can get across safely.

The New Zealand Mountain Safety Council has published a number of pamphlets with good information for trampers, with titles like *Bushcraft, Mountaincraft, Outdoor First Aid, Hypothermia, Survival* etc. They are widely available at information centres and hostels. The DOC also gives excellent safety advice, and it's worth talking to them about it.

Going with tramping clubs can be a great way to tramp in New Zealand, because you will be with like-minded people who know about the bush. Federated Mountain Clubs (PO Box 1604, Wellington) has information on local clubs throughout New Zealand (see Tramping & Outdoor Clubs in this chapter).

Crossing Rivers

At many rivers and major streams you'll find either swing bridges, wires or even cableways to ensure a safe crossing. Smaller streams require only a quick wade through to reach the track on the other side, but any crossing must be carefully considered – take time to choose a good spot to ford and remember that a strong current in water that reaches higher than your knees is often too hard to cross without the mutual support of several people with a pole between them.

During and immediately after heavy rains is a particular dangerous time to ford. It doesn't take long – sometimes less than an hour of hard rain – to turn a mountain creek into an impassable thunder of white water. If this is the case, search for a bridge or wire nearby, or camp and wait, rather than attempt a crossing. Remember that streams and rivers rise quickly but return to their normal levels almost as fast. If you wait a day, or even an afternoon, the water will often lower enough for you to ford safely.

EQUIPMENT

Mishaps in the bush begin with people being unprepared or with people underestimating the difficulty of a track or the changeability of New Zealand's erratic weather. Tramping in this mountainous country, regardless of which track you choose to walk, should not be taken lightly. If you arrive without the proper gear, then either rent it or look into joining a guided trip where the outfitter supplies the necessary equipment.

Overseas travellers should plan on bringing all their own gear, or at least major items such as boots, packs, sleeping bags and stoves.

- **Alternative footwear** Carry thongs (jandals)/sandals or running/tennis shoes for strolling around the huts or if your boots become too painful to wear.

- **Backpack** The popular choice is an internal-frame pack. If you plan to do a considerable amount of tramping, bring a good backpack, not a piece of luggage, and a pack cover to keep everything dry inside.
- **Boots** Light to medium boots are recommended. They should be broken in, unless you want painful blisters. Cover your heels with moleskin before you start if you think there is any chance of blisters. Feet are the greatest source of discomfort on a track, and you should therefore take the greatest care of them.
- **Camera, binoculars** See the Film & Photography section in this chapter.
- **Camping stove** Take one along even if you intend to stay in huts. Many huts don't have cookers, and on popular tracks competition for a spot on the hut stove can be fierce. Overseas trampers who use white gas in their stoves need to ask for white spirits, which can be purchased at most petrol stations and hardware stores.
- **Candle** Calculate on half to one candle per day, depending on how many people are sharing the hut. Some huts have lanterns supplied.
- **First-aid kit** See the Health section earlier in this chapter.
- **Fishing rod** Take a rod if you want to make the most of New Zealand's excellent trout fishing.
- **Knife, fork & spoon** Pack a cup, plate and soup bowl as well. You can cut this back to knife, spoon and bowl – a bowl is multipurpose: you can eat or drink out of it, and mix things in it.
- **Map and compass** See the Maps section in this chapter.
- **Matches/lighter** You'll need these for cooking and lighting candles. Matches are a bit of a bind because it is difficult to keep them dry.
- **Pack of cards** Brush up on Crib, 500 and Euchre.
- **Pans** Two pans 15 cm across and five cm deep are big enough. The pans are adequate for two to three-course meals for two people. Preferably they should fit into each other, and be made of aluminium for lightness.
- **Pen/pencil and paper**
- **Pot/billy** A capacity of 1½ to two litres is sufficient.
- **Pot scrubber and tea towel** Washing up is usually done in cold water, making pot cleaning difficult.

- **Shorts, light shirt** Remember clothes for everyday wear and swimsuits for the modest.
- **Sleeping bag** A warm down or Hollofill, light to medium weight, including a light stuff bag for rapid and easy packing is the best choice.
- **Sleeping mat** This will only be necessary when camping, because most huts have mattresses. However, in the popular huts it will be useful because you may end up on the floor without a mattress.
- **Socks** Three heavy polypropylene or woollen pairs are a good idea – wear two at once to reduce the chance of blisters. Frequent changes of socks during the day can also reduce blisters, but isn't too practical.
- **Sun protectors** A hat, sunscreen and sunglasses are essential.
- **Tent** This allows you to get away from the overflowing huts, but on most tracks it will be a bulky and unnecessary item to carry. There are places where it will be useful, such as in the Raukumara Range and on the tracks that have no huts.
- **Toilet paper, Band-aids, insect repellent** Advice on insect repellents is given in the Health section in this chapter.
- **Towel** Choose a small one that will dry quickly.
- **Torch/flashlight** This is essential for nocturnal toilet visits and late arrivals at huts.
- **Useful books** Books on bird-watching and plant identification may be worth carrying (paperbacks are lighter).
- **Waterproof clothing** Take a raincoat and overtrousers. A combination of wet and cold can be fatal.
- **Water purifier** See the Health Section in this chapter.
- **Woollen clothing** Take a woollen sweater/jersey, and woollen trousers These are essential in case of cold weather. Some of the modern synthetics, such as polypropylene and polar fleece, are just as good as wool.

FOOD

The food you eat on a tramp should be nourishing, tasty and lightweight.

Breakfast is the most important meal of the day, and could include muesli/porridge or bacon & eggs (vacuum packed bacon lasts for days). Bread, butter/margarine, Vegemite/honey, tea/coffee, sugar and instant milk are the other staples.

Lunch is normally eaten between huts and should therefore not require too much preparation. Bread/crackers, butter/margarine and tasty cheese are about all you need. There are some nice wholemeal crackers available, but 'Cabin Bread' is larger and stronger and so will stand up better to being crammed into a pack.

Dinner must be hot and substantial. Instant soups help to counter the biggest appetites. Fresh meat is good for the first two days of a tramp, after that you will have to rely on dehydrated food (Alliance is excellent, Vesta is OK), instant mashed potatoes or rice. Check the preparation time of packaged food; 20 minutes is the limit.

Easy to cook, quick desserts such as tapioca, custard or instant puddings are a treat.

It's important to maintain energy levels while tramping, so snacks are important. Chocolate (100 grams per person per day), raisins, sultanas and dried fruit are all good sources of energy. Glucose – in the form of barley sugar, glucose tablets or powder from chemists gives almost instant energy.

Biscuits are great both while you are walking and before bed with tea. Get a recipe for 'Tararuas', an indestructible, calorie-packed life saver.

Other useful items are cordial concentrate powder (a great thirst quencher which adds flavour to purified water) and instant noodles.

All rubbish should be carried out, so ensure that everything is in suitable containers. Extra lightweight metal and plastic containers are available from supermarkets. Don't carry glass – transfer foods into light containers.

This list of equipment is by no means complete for a long trek, but it should get you through the first tramp without suffering from withdrawal symptoms. For a three-day tramp, one loaf of bread, 200 to 300 grams of butter/margarine and 200 grams of instant dried milk per person are sufficient amounts of the basics. Many dishes require milk, so don't underestimate your requirements.

Everything should be kept in plastic bags (preferably two), to protect them from the elements. Clothes must be kept dry under all circumstances. Plastic pack liners ('survival bags'), made by the New Zealand Mountain Safety Council, are sold in outdoors shops for about $4 and are an excellent investment.

Made of thick plastic that will not tear, a survival bag is large enough for you to climb into it for survival if need be, or you can split it and make a shelter. Put it all into a lightweight, waterproof backpack. The total weight should not exceed 14 kg for a three-day tramp.

ACTIVITIES
Fishing
The one introduced creature to have made a hit with everybody in New Zealand is the trout. Before the Europeans arrived, there were only a few species of freshwater fish and eel. The English, being English, imported the brown trout, via Tasmania, in 1867, and in 1883 imported and stocked the rivers with the California rainbow trout. The superb water of the lakes and rivers soon led to a thriving species that easily exceeded its ancestors in size. Today, New Zealand is renowned for its fly fishing.

Those interested in combining fishing with tramping should plan to bring either a lightweight spinning outfit or fly-fishing gear. You'll also need to look into seasons and limits, and purchase a fishing licence, which is sold as a one-day, one week or season-long permit. Freshwater game fish are protected, and under the control of 24 Acclimatisation Societies throughout the country, who stock rivers, issue licences and patrol their region. A licence purchased from one society is good for the entire country, with the exception of the Rotorua and Taupo districts, where special permits are needed.

Overseas anglers find it best to bring a selection of their favourite spinners and spoons or flies (wet flies and nymphs being the most widely used) and then purchase a few local varieties once they arrive. Any good bookshop will carry a number of trout guides for serious anglers.

Canoeing & Kayaking
An open two-person canoe, called simply a canoe or an Indian canoe in other parts of the world, is called a 'Canadian canoe' in New Zealand. A kayak, a smaller, narrower one-person craft, which is covered except for the

paddler's cockpit, is often called a kayak in New Zealand but it can also be called a canoe. It's a good idea to specify whether you mean a 'Canadian canoe' or a 'kayak' when talking about river trips in this country.

Many companies offer canoeing and kayaking trips on rivers which are popular with rafters. You can go for a few hours of quiet paddling or white-water excitement in hired canoes or kayaks without a guide, or take longer solo or guided camping trips with fishing and other activities thrown in.

Canoeing is especially popular on the Whanganui River, in the North Island, where you can hire a canoe for days at a time; there are many other possibilities. Canoeing is also popular on lakes, notably Lake Taupo, and on lakes not far from Christchurch.

Kayaking is a very popular sport. Commercial trips (for those without their own equipment) are offered on a number of rivers and lakes in the North and South Island. One of the best is with Down to Earth Adventures on the Matukituki and Makarora rivers near Wanaka.

Sea Kayaking Sea kayaking is one of the fastest-growing water sports in New Zealand. Popular North Island sea kayaking areas are the Bay of Islands (with trips departing from Paihia) and Coromandel. In the South Island, try the Marlborough Sounds or the coast of the Abel Tasman National Park, where sea kayaking has become a viable alternative to walking on the Coast Track.

Fiordland has become a popular destination for those wishing to hone their sea-kayaking skills. There are tour operators in Te Anau and Manapouri who can arrange trips on the lakes and fiords.

Bird-Watching
New Zealand is a bird-watcher's paradise – in this small country there are many endemic species, a number of interesting residents and wave upon wave of visitors. New Zealand is as famous for extinct and point-of-extinction birds as it is for existing species, but visiting bird-watchers will not be disappointed by the more accessible species. The kiwi is probably the most sought-after, and you are guaranteed to see the Stewart Island subspecies at all times of the year.

Other birds prized by ornithologists are the southern royal albatross (found in a mainland colony on the Otago Peninsula), white heron or kotuku (found near Okarito in Westland), cheeky kea (which ranges throughout the Southern Alps), blue duck or whio (found in mountain streams on both islands), yellowhead or mohua (seen in the remote Catlins), Fiordland crested penguin, yellow-eyed penguin (seen in colonies along the south-eastern coast of the South Island), Australasian gannet (at Farewell Spit, Muriwai and Cape Kidnappers), wrybill, oystercatcher and, in the forests, the kereru or New Zealand pigeon, rifleman, tui, kaka and saddleback.

There are a number of field guides to bird-watching in New Zealand (see the Books section, in this chapter).

THE TRACKS
(GW denotes Great Walk)
Ninety Mile Beach-Cape Reinga Walkway (easy). This tramp can be a 50-km, three-day walk from the northern end of Ninety Mile Beach to Spirits Bay, or up to a 133-km walk if the long beach is followed from its southern end at Ahipara. The best part is the scenic Cape Reinga area, which has a sweeping coastline and the semitropical sands of Te Werahi Beach and Tapotupotu Bay. There is plenty of camping, but no huts.

Great Barrier Island Trek (moderate). The heart of the largest offshore island in Hauraki Gulf is an 80-sq-km regenerating kauri forest with a 100-km network of tracks and two huts. Spend two to four days on the island and take in the native forest, the interesting remains of kauri dams, the hot springs and the opportunities for camping, swimming and saltwater fishing.

Coromandel Forest Park Walk (easy to medium). A three-day tramp takes you up and around the Kauaeranga Valley, the most popular area of the forest park because of the large number of logging and gold-mining relics that can be seen. The track is well cut and easy to follow in most places.

Pakihi Stock Route (medium). This is a two-day walk in the Urutawa Forest, at the base of East Cape. The track follows an old benched stock route near the Motu Coach Rd for half of its length, before following the Pakihi Stream to the Pakihi Rd south of Opotiki. The walk is an introduction to the rugged beauty of the forests and river valleys of this region.

East-West Traverse of the Raukumara Range (extremely difficult). This is for experienced trampers only, because it will test all navigational and bush skills. A five-day tramp using routes through river valleys, across bush-clad saddles and on historic Maori paths. It starts in the south-west of the Raukumara Forest Park and ends near the sacred summit of Hikurangi in the north-east of the park. The forest is untouched in many places and the tramp typifies the goal of many Kiwi trampers.

Lake Waikaremoana Track *(GW;* easy to medium). One of the most popular tramps in the North Island, this track circles most of the shore of Waikaremoana, the largest lake in Te Urewera National Park. Highlights of the three to four-day, 40-km walk are the spectacular views from the Panekiri Range, fine beaches and excellent trout fishing.

Whakatane-Waikare River Loop Track (medium). This four to five-day circular route begins from Ruatahuna in Te Urewera National Park and includes an all-weather track along the Whakatane River and two days following the banks of the Waikare River, with numerous fords. Both rivers offer excellent trout fishing.

Whirinaki Track (easy). This is an all-weather track that runs 27 km from Minginui to an access road off State Highway 5. It's an easy two-day tramp along the scenic Whirinaki River. Trampers with more time, however, can combine it with other more challenging tracks to make a circular five to six-day route in the Whirinaki Forest Park, located just west of Te Urewera National Park.

Tongariro Northern Circuit *(GW;* medium). This is a four-day walk which circles the perfect cone of Mt Ngauruhoe in the Tongariro World Heritage area. The tracks are well cut and sections of the route are well marked with snow poles. A popular walk that includes highlights such as hot springs and active volcanic areas.

Te Iringa-Oamaru Circuit (medium). A five to six-day tramp which takes you through the forests of Kaimanawa Forest Park east of Tongariro National Park. Although there are a number of ridges and passes to climb, much of the walk is along rivers that are favourite spots for trout fishing.

Mt Taranaki Round-the-Mountain Track (medium). This popular 55-km track goes around the cone of Mt Taranaki in Egmont National Park. The full tramp takes four days, though many people tackle only a portion of it. Although there are excellent views of Taranaki and opportunities to climb it, much of the track is in dense beech forest.

Pouakai Track (medium). A shorter, alternative loop to the Taranaki Round-the-Mountain Track, this track requires only two to three days' walking but still provides excellent views of the national park from lofty perches above the bush-line.

Matemateaonga Walkway (medium). The four-day, 42-km track is located in an isolated section of Whanganui National Park, north of Wanganui. It provides trampers with one of the few true wilderness experiences in the North Island. One end of the track can only be reached by boat up the Wanganui River.

Mt Holdsworth Circuit (medium to difficult). This two to three-day alpine walk through Tararua Forest Park is in a favourite area of Wellington tramping clubs. The circuit includes nights at two scenic huts above the bush-line and a day following alpine ridges.

Totara Flats Track (medium) Also located in the rugged Tararua Range, this walk is considerably easier, with no open alpine crossings. The 38-km, three-day tramp follows river valleys much of the way.

Queen Charlotte Walkway (medium). This is a four-day walk around the bays and along the ridges between Queen Charlotte and Kenepuru sounds in the Marlborough Sounds. The 67-km walk is from Ship Cove (in the north) to Anakiwa (near Havelock, in the south). It combines fascinating history, beautiful scenery and vestiges of native forest. Accommodation is at camp sites, and in private lodges such as Furneaux Lodge, The Portage and Te Punga.

Nydia Track (easy). A two-day walk takes you from Pelorus Sound, in the south of the Marlborough Sounds, to Tennyson Inlet. The track crosses two low saddles (Kaiuma and Nydia), skirts bays and passes through coastal and beech forests.

Pelorus River Track (medium). This popular three-day tramp is in Mt Richmond Forest Park (with a choice of finishes, 27 km south of Nelson or almost in the city itself). The river is famous for its trout,

WALK STANDARDS & SEASONS

Island	Track	Rating	Days
N	Ninety Mile Beach-Cape Reinga Walkway	Easy	3
N	Great Barrier Island Trek	Medium	2-4
N	Coromandel Forest Park Walk	Easy to Medium	3
N	Pakihi Stock Route	Medium	2
N	East-West Traverse	Extremely Difficult	5
N	Waikaremoana Lake Track	Easy to Medium	3-4
N	Whakatane-Waikare River Loop Track	Medium	4-5
N	Whirinaki Track	Easy	2
N	Tongariro Northern Circuit	Medium	4
N	Te Iringa-Oamaru Circuit	Medium	5-6
N	Mt Taranaki Round-the-Mountain Track	Medium	4
N	Pouakai Track	Medium	2-3
N	Matemateaonga Walkway	Medium	4
N	Mt Holdsworth Circuit	Medium to Difficult	2-3
N	Totara Flats Track	Medium	3
S	Queen Charlotte Walkway	Medium	4
S	Nydia Track	Easy	2
S	Pelorus River Track	Medium	3
S	Abel Tasman Coast Track	Easy	3-4
S	Heaphy Track	Easy to Medium	4-5
S	Wangapeka Track	Medium	5
S	Leslie-Karamea Track	Medium to Difficult	5-7
S	Travers-Sabine Circuit	Medium to Difficult	5
S	D'Urville Valley Track	Medium to Difficult	5
S	Banks Peninsula Track	Easy to Medium	4
S	Mt Somers Subalpine Walkway	Medium	2-3
S	St James Walkway	Easy to Medium	6
S	Goat Pass	Medium to Difficult	2
S	Waimakariri-Harman Pass Route	Difficult	4-5
S	Harper Pass	Medium	4-5
S	Cass-Lagoon Saddles Track	Medium	2-3
S	Inland Pack Track	Medium	2-3
S	Croesus Track	Medium	2
S	Copland Pass	Extremely Difficult	4
S	Mueller Hut	Difficult	2
S	Routeburn Track	Medium	3
S	Greenstone Track	Easy	2
S	Caples Track	Medium	2
S	Rees-Dart Track	Medium	4-5
S	Cascade Saddle Route	Difficult	4-5
S	Wilkin-Young Valleys Circuit	Difficult	3
S	Milford Track	Easy	4
S	Hollyford Track	Medium	4-5
S	Kepler Track	Difficult	4
S	Dusky Track	Difficult	4-7
St	Rakiura Track	Medium	3
St	North-West Circuit	Difficult	10

N – North Island
S – South Island
St – Stewart Island

WALK STANDARDS & SEASONS

Transport	Summer	Autumn	Winter	Spring	Features
Bus	E	E	E	E	Beach, rugged coast
Boat, Plane	E	E	P	E	Kauri dams, hot pools
Bus	E	E	P	E	Kauri dams, forest
Bus, Private	E	E	F	F	Wilderness, river valley
Private	E	E	F	F	Isolation, challenge, untouched bush
Boat, Bus	E	E	P	E	Lake, trout fishing
Bus, Taxi	E	E	P	E	River, trout fishing
Bus, Taxi	E	E	P	E	River, caves, gorge
Bus	E	F	NA	F	Hot pools, volcanoes
Private	E	F	P	P	River valleys, fishing
Bus, Taxi	E	F	NA	F	Volcano, forest
Private, Taxi	E	F	NA	F	Alpine views
Boat, Taxi	E	E	F	E	Wilderness, isolation
Private	E	P	NA	P	Alpine scenery, peaks
Private	E	F	P	F	River, grassy flats
Boat, Bus	E	E	F	E	Sunken river valleys, bays
Boat, Bus	E	E	F	E	Saddles, bays
Bus, Private	F	P	P	F	Rivers
Boat, Bus	E	E	F	E	Coastal Beaches
Taxi, Plane	E	E	P	E	Forest, beach
Taxi, Private	E	F	P	F	Rivers, passes
Private	E	F	P	F	Gold-mining history
Bus, Boat	E	F	NA	F	Alpine passes, peaks
Bus, Boat	E	F	NA	F	Alpine pass, peaks
Bus	E	E	F	E	Private track, seascapes, forest, wildlife
Bus, Private	E	F	P	F	Alpine pass, coal-mining/pastoral history
Bus	E	F	P	F	Rivers, alpine views
Bus	E	F	NA	F	Alpine pass
Bus	E	P	NA	P	Alpine peaks, remote valley
Bus, Train	E	F	NA	F	Rivers, alpine scenery
Bus, Train	E	F	NA	F	Alpine passes
Bus	E	F	P	F	Granite cliffs, caves
Bus, private	E	F	NA	F	Subalpine scenery, gold-mining history
Bus, Plane	E	NA	NA	NA	Peaks, glaciers
Bus, Plane	E	NA	NA	NA	Peaks, glacier
Bus	E	F	NA	F	Alpine scenery
Bus	E	F	P	F	River, fishing
Bus	E	F	P	P	Rivers, fishing
Bus, Taxi	E	P	NA	F	Alpine pass, river
Taxi	E	NA	NA	NA	Peaks, glaciers
Bus, Boat	E	P	NA	P	Pass, rivers
Bus, Boat	E	NA	F	P	Waterfalls, pass
Plane, Boat	E	F	P	F	Rugged coast, wildlife
Private	E	P	NA	P	Alpine scenery, peaks
Boat, Plane	E	P	NA	P	Lakes, fiords
Boat, Plane	E	F	P	F	Rugged coast, forest
Boat, Plane	E	P	P	P	Rugged coast, wildlife

Season: E – Excellent   P – Poor
F – Fair   NA – Do Not Attempt

New Zealand Tramps

0   100   200 km

Approximate Scale

NINETY MILE BEACH-CAPE REINGA WALKWAY

Whangarei

GREAT BARRIER ISLAND TREK

COROMANDEL FOREST
PARK WALK

WHAKATANE-WAIKARE
RIVER LOOP

PAKIHI STOCK ROUTE

Auckland

Thames

Hamilton

Tauranga

RAUKUMARA
EAST-WEST TRAVERSE

MATEMATEONGA
WALKWAY

Rotorua

Taupo

Gisborne

LAKE
WAIKAREMOANA
TRACK

New Plymouth

Turangi

Napier

WHIRINAKI TRACK

POUAKAI TRACK
MT TARANAKI
ROUND-THE-MOUNTAIN TRACK

Wanganui

TE IRINGA-OAMARU
CIRCUIT

QUEEN CHARLOTTE WALKWAY

NYDIA TRACK

ABEL TASMAN
COAST TRACK

HEAPHY TRACK

LESLIE-KARAMEA TRACK

WANGAPEKA TRACK

Palmerston
North

TONGARIRO NORTHERN
CIRCUIT

WELLINGTON

MT HOLDSWORTH CIRCUIT

TOTARA FLATS TRACK

Nelson

D'URVILLE VALLEY TRACK

INLAND PACK TRACK

CROESUS TRACK

Greymouth

PELORUS TRACK

TRAVERS-SABINE CIRCUIT

ST JAMES WALKWAY

Hokitika

WAIMAKARIRI-HARMAN PASS
ROUTE

ACROSS HARPER PASS

GOAT PASS TRACK

CASS-LAGOON SADDLES TRACK

Christchurch

COPLAND PASS

MUELLER HUT

BANKS PENINSULA TRACK

CASCADE SADDLE
ROUTE

HOLLYFORD
VALLEY TRACK

MT SOMERS SUBALPINE WALKWAY

WILKIN-YOUNG VALLEYS CIRCUIT

MILFORD
TRACK

Queenstown

REES-DART TRACK

ROUTEBURN TRACK

CAPLES TRACK

GREENSTONE TRACK

KEPLER TRACK

Dunedin

DUSKY TRACK

Invercargill

NORTH-WEST CIRCUIT

RAKIURA TRACK

Stewart Island (Rakiura)

though the track doesn't always offer easy access to the deep, green pools where the fish are found.

Abel Tasman Coast Track *(GW*; easy). This three to four-day trip follows the shoreline of the Abel Tasman National Park. It is one of the best coastal tracks in New Zealand but is, unfortunately, also one of the most popular. Despite the number of trampers and boaters in this area, the beaches, beautiful bays and tidal areas are unmatched anywhere else in the country.

Heaphy Track *(GW*; easy to medium). The Heaphy Track is a popular 76-km tramp in Kahurangi National Park (formerly North West Nelson Forest Park). The scenery ranges from hilly beech forest to a palm-lined beach.

Wangapeka Track (medium). Lying in the same national park as the Heaphy, but not nearly as popular, this 65-km, five-day walk is a pleasant alternative. A more challenging trip overall, the track begins at Rolling River and ends 25 km south of Karamea; it's often walked after the Heaphy to return to Nelson.

Leslie-Karamea Track (medium to difficult). Even more remote and unknown, this trip traverses the Leslie and upper Karamea River valleys in the heart of Kahurangi National Park. Access to the route is via Wangapeka Track (in the south) or the Tablelands (to the north), and all together the 85-km tramp requires five to seven days.

Travers-Sabine Circuit (medium to difficult). Grassy river flats, beech forests and two alpine saddles are features of this circular walk through Nelson Lakes National Park. The six-day tramp includes excellent alpine scenery and two huts above the bush-line.

D'Urville Valley Track (medium to difficult). A more remote tramp which includes the alpine crossing of Moss Pass and a night at scenic Blue Lake Hut. The D'Urville and Sabine valleys can be combined for a five-day circular walk beginning at the south end of Lake Rotoroa, in the Nelson Lakes area. (Add two more days if you walk in from Rotoroa or St Arnaud rather than taking a water-taxi.

Banks Peninsula Track (easy to medium). This was the first of the private walks established in New Zealand. The suggested walking time for the 30-km track is four days, which is very generous and places it in the easy category. There is also an option to walk it in two days which makes it medium. Excellent accommodation, especially at Stony Bay, is included in the booking fee. The walk takes in spectacular coastal scenery which abounds with wildlife, remnant

tracts of native forest and, for overseas visitors who haven't experienced it, farmland.

Mt Somers Subalpine Walkway (medium). This 17-km track in the Canterbury foothills at the top of the Ashburton River can be walked in two or three days, depending on time constraints. It passes through a challenging canyon, then crosses a high saddle before circuiting alpine Mt Somers. The track is only deemed difficult if the Canyon Route is taken on the first day.

St James Walkway (easy to medium). The 66-km St James was the first walkway to be established in subalpine terrain. The five-day trip passes through Lewis Pass Scenic Reserve, beginning and ending at State Highway 7, where there are good public bus services.

Goat Pass Track (medium to difficult). A popular overnight tramp of 25 km takes you over Goat Pass in Arthur's Pass National Park. Much of the tramp is along rivers and is easy to follow, with the highlight a night spent at the alpine hut on Goat Pass.

Waimakariri-Harman Pass Route (difficult). A much more challenging route in Arthur's Pass, this four to five-day tramp involves ascending two alpine passes and following the upper reaches of the Taipo River, renowned for its trout fishing. Good transportation is available at both ends of the trip, on State Highway 73.

Harper Pass (medium). The four to five-day tramp begins in Lake Sumner Forest Park, crosses the historic Harper Pass and ends in Arthur's Pass National Park. The pass is low and much of the route is through beech forest and along wide river flats.

Cass-Lagoon Saddles Track (medium). Located in Craigieburn Forest Park just south of Arthur's Pass, the two to three-day walk is along a well-marked track and is considerably easier than most of the trips in the national park north of it. There are spectacular views from two alpine passes.

Inland Pack Track (medium). This historic track, carved out by gold miners who wanted to avoid the rugged West Coast, is located in Paparoas National Park. The walk features an unusual landscape of steep limestone gorges, caves and towering bluffs. There are no huts, but trampers can get away without a tent on the 21-km track by staying at the Ballroom, one of the largest rock bivvies (shelters) in New Zealand.

Croesus Track (medium). This is another historic goldfields route which links the Grey River Valley with the West Coast at Barrytown. It passes through bush and then the tussocky 'tops' of the Paparoas before dipping steeply to the coast. The tramp can be completed in a long day but would be far more enjoyable with a one-night stopover at the hut situated above the tree line. It is in DOC stewardship land.

Copland Pass (extremely challenging). A highly technical trip from Mt Cook National Park to Westland National Park, the track crosses the Southern Alps via the famous Copland Pass. It is not to be taken lightly – read all the warnings that go with the track description.

Mueller Hut (difficult). This is the only track on which you have to return the way you came. It is included because the climb to Mueller Hut allows trampers to overnight in the Southern Alps at Mt Cook National Park without undertaking the extremely challenging Copland Pass.

Routeburn Track *(GW;* medium). New Zealand's renowned alpine crossing, it lies in both Mt Aspiring and Fiordland national parks. The three-day walk includes rainforest, subalpine scrub, and spectacular views from ridges, peaks and saddles. It is immensely popular and thus very crowded.

Greenstone Track (easy). The two-day walk is an easy tramp along the Greenstone River, noted among anglers for its trout fishing. The tramp passes through grassy river flats and beech forest and is often combined with the Routeburn to form a circular trip.

Caples Track (medium). A little more difficult than the Greenstone, this two-day track is another way to return from the Routeburn to the car park on Lake Wakatipu. Or for those who want to skip the mass of humanity on the Routeburn, the Caples and Greenstone can be combined for a pleasant and less crowded four-day loop.

Rees-Dart Track (medium). A classic four to five-day round trip from Glenorchy, this track has a variety of scenery, including forests, grassy river flats and mountain vistas. Most of the trip lies in Mt Aspiring National Park.

Cascade Saddle Route (difficult). A steep and difficult climb, this alpine crossing can, in good weather, be one of the most scenic in the country.

Superb views of Mt Aspiring and the Dart Glacier are enjoyed before the route joins the Rees-Dart Track.

Wilkin-Young Valleys Circuit (difficult). The three-day trip, part of it in the Mt Aspiring National Park, involves bush tracks, grassed valleys and the 1490-metre Gillespie Pass. The alpine scenery on the walk is exceptional and the area does not suffer from the heavy overuse found elsewhere in the park.

Milford Track *(GW;* easy). Undoubtedly the best-known track in New Zealand, the Milford is so popular that reservations are needed to enjoy the four-day walk. It runs from Lake Te Anau to the Milford Sound, in Fiordland National Park, and includes a wide variety of rainforest, alpine meadows and spectacular waterfalls.

Hollyford Track (medium). This is a tramp through thick rainforest, past Lake McKerrow and out to isolated Martins Bay on the west coast. The track lies in Fiordland National Park and features excellent trout and coastal fishing, good mountain scenery and interesting seal and penguin colonies.

Kepler Track *(GW;* difficult). The Kepler was finished in 1988 in an effort to reduce the number of trampers using the Routeburn and Milford. The four-day loop begins and ends near Te Anau. It includes a longer alpine crossing, and is thus more difficult than its two famous counterparts to the north.

Dusky Track (difficult). At the other end of Fiordland National Park, this rugged, exceptionally scenic track offers the isolation and wilderness experience the Milford or Routeburn cannot. Special transport arrangements have to be made, as the tramp begins and ends on remote lake or coastal shores.

Rakiura Track *(GW;* medium) This latest addition to Stewart Island's network of track is a tramper's delight. The route connects the beginning and end of the North-West Circuit to form a shorter, three-day tramp.

North-West Circuit (difficult). This is the classic 10-day tramp around the northern portion of Stewart Island. The famous mud and bogs of the island make it difficult, but for those trampers with the time and energy, the isolated beaches and the birdlife make it worthwhile.

Getting There & Away

ARRIVING IN NEW ZEALAND
See the Visas & Embassies section in the Facts for the Tramper chapter for information on what you will need when you arrive in New Zealand.

TRAVEL INSURANCE
Trampers should be covered for the worst possible scenario, such as an accident which requires hospital treatment and a flight home.

AIR
The overwhelming majority of visitors to New Zealand arrive by air. There are three airports which handle international flights – Auckland, Wellington and Christchurch. All North American flights arrive in Auckland; Wellington and Christchurch predominantly handle trans-Tasman traffic.

Special Tickets
Circle Pacific Tickets These tickets use a combination of airlines to circle the Pacific, offering stopovers in Australia, New Zealand, North America and Asia. You can start and finish the circle at any point; the circle goes from the US west coast via various Pacific islands to New Zealand and Australia, onto Asia and back to the US west coast. Circle Pacific fares cost around A$2750 or US$2250.

Round-the-World (RTW) Tickets RTW tickets have become very popular in the last few years, and they can be useful to visit New Zealand in combination with other destinations. Airline RTW tickets are often bargains, and can work out no more expensive or even cheaper than an ordinary return ticket. Prices start at about £850, A$1800 or US$1300.

To/From Australia
The number of air routes between Australia and New Zealand has proliferated in the last few years. New Zealand cities with flights to/from Australia are Auckland, Christchurch and Wellington. Australian cities with flights to/from New Zealand are Adelaide, Brisbane, Cairns, Canberra, Coolangatta (Gold Coast), Hobart, Melbourne, Perth and Sydney.

Examples of one-way/return economy fares are Sydney-Auckland A$520/650, Melbourne-Auckland A$600/720; flying into Christchurch or Wellington can cost from A$50 to A$150 more. Fares rise about A$200 during the Christmas high season.

It's much cheaper to take an Advance Purchase Excursion (Apex) fare, which can get you to New Zealand and back for little more than a regular one-way fare. In Australia, STA and Flight Centres are major dealers in cheap airfares. They have branches in all major cities.

To/From the USA
Most flights between the USA and New Zealand are to/from the US west coast. Most go through Los Angeles but some fly via San Francisco.

Several airlines offer excursion (round-trip) fares. The lower-priced fares have more restrictions and advance-purchase requirements, and have a shorter term of validity; a one-year ticket for example will cost more than a ticket good for only a month or two. Cheaper excursion fares are about US$1170 in the low season, US$1470 in the high season. The more expensive excursion fares are around US$1500 and US$1800. If you continue to Australia after New Zealand add another US$100. Cheaper 'short life' fares are frequently offered, for limited periods.

Two of the most reputable discount travel agencies in the USA are STA and CIEE/Council Travel Services:

STA Travel
  5900 Wilshire Blvd, Suite 2110, Los Angeles, CA 90036 (☎ (213) 937 1150; fax 937 2739; telephone sales: (800) 777 0112, (212) 986 9643)
CIEE/Council Travel Services
  205 East 42nd St, New York, NY 10017 (☎ (212) 661 1414; fax 972 3231)

The magazine *Travel Unlimited* (PO Box 1058, Allston, MA 02134) publishes details of cheap airfares and courier possibilities from the USA to destinations worldwide.

The Coral Route Air New Zealand operates a special 'Coral Route' through the Pacific which departs from Los Angeles and has excellent stopover options. The airline's direct LA-Auckland-LA return fare is US$798, but for an extra US$100 you can include a stopover, and you can add more stopovers for US$100 each.

To/From Canada

Travel CUTS is a Canadian student and discount travel agent which has 35 offices. You don't have to be a student to use their services. Their primary offices in the west and east will give you the address of the office nearest you:

Travel CUTS
    602 West Hastings, No 501, Vancouver, BC V6B 1P2 (☎ (604) 681 9136; fax 683 3567)
    187 College St, Toronto, Ontario M5T 1P7 (☎ (416) 979 2406; fax 979 8167)

The *Vancouver Sun* and the *Toronto Globe & Mail* carry travel agents' ads. The magazine *Great Expectations* (PO Box 8000-411, Abbotsford BC V2S 6H1) is useful.

Most flights coming from Canada will have at least one stopover on the way to New Zealand. See the USA section; much of the same advice applies.

To/From the UK

London-Auckland return tickets can be found in London bucket shops for around £950. Some stopovers are permitted on this sort of ticket but the options will vary according to which airlines you fly with. You may fly to New Zealand across Asia or across the USA. If you're flying via Asia, you can often stopover in India, Bangkok, Singapore and Australia; coming across the USA, stopover possibilities include New York, Los Angeles, Honolulu or a variety of Pacific islands.

New Zealand's location makes RTW

tickets from the UK hardly more expensive than return fares. RTW tickets that go through the South Pacific generally cost around £1930, but agents can organise an RTW route from £850.

Look in the listings magazines *Time Out* and *City Limits*, and scan the Sunday papers and *Exchange & Mart* for ads. Two good, reliable low-fare specialists are Trailfinders (in west London) and STA:

Trailfinders
    46 Earls Court Rd, London W8 (☎ (0171) 938 3366)
STA
    74 Old Brompton Rd, London SW7 (☎ (0171) 581 4132; fax 581 3351)
    117 Euston Rd, London NW1 (☎ (0171) 465 0484; fax 388 0944).

To/From Europe

Frankfurt is the major arrival and departure point for flights to/from New Zealand; it has good connections to other European centres.

There are plenty of bucket shops in continental Europe and STA and Council Travel have a number of offices, including:

STA
    c/o Srid Reisen, Berger Strasse 118, 6000 Frankfurt 1, Germany (☎ (69) 43 0191; fax 43 9858)
    c/o SSR Reisen, Leon Hardstrasse 10, 8001 Zurich, Switzerland (☎ (1) 242 3000)
    c/o Voyages Decouvertes, 21 Rue Cambon, 75001 Paris, France (☎ (1) 4296 1680; fax 4261 0001)
Council Travel
    18 Graf Adolf St, 4000 Dusseldorf 1, Germany (☎ (211) 32 9088; fax 32 0475)
    31 Rue St Augustin, 75002 Paris, France (☎ (1) 4266 2087), (☎ (/fax 4495 9575)

To/From Asia

Flights between New Zealand and Asia have increased dramatically in the past few years. Direct flights to Auckland operate from Tokyo, Nagoya, Taipei, Hong Kong, Singapore and Denpasar/Bali, and there are connecting flights from Sapporo, Fukuoka, Seoul, Bangkok and Kuala Lumpur. Most of the connecting flights have stopovers in Australia. There are also a few direct flights to/from Christchurch, including flights to/from Tokyo and Singapore.

Ticket discounting is widespread in Asia, particularly in Hong Kong, Singapore and Bangkok. You can get return fares from Hong Kong for around HK$10,200 in the high season, HK$8400 in the low season; from Singapore for around S$2625; and from Malaysia for around M$2925.

SEA

Apart from cruise ships, there are no longer regular passenger ships sailing to New Zealand. Tramp steamers are also a thing of the past.

LEAVING NEW ZEALAND

STA and Flight Centres have discount fares from New Zealand. They both have offices throughout the country. There's a $20 departure tax at the airport.

WARNING

This chapter is particularly vulnerable to change – prices for international travel are volatile, routes are introduced and cancelled, schedules change, rules are amended, special deals come and go. The details given in this chapter should be regarded only as pointers and cannot be any substitute for your own careful, up-to-date research.

Getting Around

AIR

New Zealand has two major domestic airlines: Air New Zealand and Ansett New Zealand. Several smaller airlines – Mt Cook Airline, Eagle Air and Air Nelson – are partly owned by Air New Zealand, and have been grouped together as 'Air New Zealand Link' to complement Air New Zealand's services.

Discounts

Air New Zealand has regular economy fares, but it also has discounts which make it unnecessary to ever pay the full fare. If you purchase your tickets before you arrive in New Zealand, you can save 12.5% off the full fare because you do not have to pay GST tax. However, some fares, such as the Air New Zealand Visit New Zealand fare, are GST-exempt for visitors.

If you purchase tickets in New Zealand, you can sometimes save up to 50% off the regular fare. Both Air New Zealand and Ansett New Zealand offer good deals if you have an International Student Identity Card (ISIC), a Youth Hostel (YHA) card or a VIP Backpackers card, giving you a 50% discount on standby flights.

Local Air Services

Apart from the major operators, there are also a host of local and feeder airlines. Services that may interest trampers include Southern Air's economic service between Invercargill and Stewart Island (cheaper than the ferry), flights to Great Barrier Island off Auckland, or flights to the remote parts of Fiordland, such as the Hollyford Track or Supper Cove. You can also fly from Wellington to Picton for little more than the ferry fare, putting you in a good position to do some of the walks in Marlborough Sounds.

BUS

New Zealand has an extensive bus network. The main operator is InterCity, which operates in both the North and South islands. Until mid-1993, when the New Zealand Rail and Interislander ferry services were sold, InterCity operated all three systems; it's still uncertain what the effects of the sale will be on the country's transport network.

The two other major bus operators are Newmans (in the North Island) and Mt Cook Landline (in the South Island). Although these companies have less extensive networks, they have interests in other areas of tourism, such as local tours. There are also a number of local operators.

For details of buses which pass near track entrances and exits, see the Access section for each of the walks.

Discounts

Although fares do vary from company to company, they are generally fairly close. Due to competition, however, all the major bus lines offer discounts. If you are travelling by bus in New Zealand, knowing which discounts are being offered by which companies can cut your travel costs by up to 50%. The major bus lines also offer discount travel passes. For more information on all aspects of Getting Around, get a copy of Lonely Planet's *New Zealand a travel survival kit*.

Shuttle Buses

A number of small shuttle-bus companies offer useful services. These services are typically cheaper and friendlier than the services offered by the larger companies. In the North Island, there are shuttles around the East Cape, around Coromandel Peninsula, and up into Northland. In the South Island, there are shuttles between Christchurch and Akaroa, Nelson and the Nelson Lakes, Queenstown and Te Anau/ Milford, and Westport and Karamea. Check the Access section for each walk.

North Island
- Kiwi Safaris – 'Mud & Worm Loop' circle trip passes through Auckland, Waitomo, Rotorua, Te Aroha and Thames, with great entertainment on board and a free pick-up and drop-off service (it makes the loop in both directions)
- Alpine Scenic Tours – between Turangi and the Tongariro National Park, with stops at various spots in the park that are useful for trampers, and extension services to Taupo and Rotorua
- C Tours – shuttle from New Plymouth to Rotorua, with a one-hour stop at Waitomo; this gets you there faster than the major bus lines

South Island
- Kiwi Backpacker Track Special – from Queenstown to the Routeburn Track and Milford Sound
- Skyline Connections' Abel Tasman Bus Services – Abel Tasman Track
- Nelson Lakes Transport – between Nelson and St Arnaud (for the Nelson Lakes National Park)
- Leisuretime Activities – between Tekapo and Mt Cook via Twizel and Glentanner
- Coast to Coast Shuttle and Alpine Coach & Courier – both cross the South Island between Christchurch and Greymouth
- New Zealand Shuttles – from Picton down the east coast as far as Oamaru
- Skyline Connections – between Picton and Motueka (via Nelson) along the scenic Queen Charlotte Drive

TRAIN
About the only train route useful for trampers is the TranzAlpine (Greymouth to Christchurch via Arthur's Pass). The nationwide Central Reservations Centre (☎ (0800) 80 2802) is open daily from 7 am to 9 pm.

CAR & MOTORBIKE
New Zealanders drive on the left side of the road. The roads are good and well signposted, traffic is light and distances are short. Petrol (gasoline) is expensive – around $1 a litre (about US$2.30 for a US gallon).

If you intend to drive in New Zealand, pick up a copy of *The Road Code* (Wellington: GP Publications, 1992, paperback), which will tell you all you need to know. Although it costs around $15, it's well worth the investment.

Car Rental
The major operators – Avis, Budget, Hertz – have extensive fleets of cars in New Zealand, and offices in almost every town. Smaller operators often offer lower rates, but they may have more restrictions on use, and one-way rentals may not be possible.

Buying a Car
If you're travelling in a group or planning a long stay in New Zealand, buying a car and selling it at the end of your stay can be a cheap, enjoyable and efficient way to reach tramping routes. It is a particularly good option for trampers thinking of hiring a car, because you're not paying days of unused rental while you're on the track. For more information, see Lonely Planet's *New Zealand a travel survival kit*.

BOAT
Inter-Island Ferries
The Interislander ferry service shuttles back and forth between Wellington and Picton, a three-hour crossing. The ferries, the *Aratika* and the newer *Arahura*, usually provide a total of four services daily in each direction.

The fares vary with the seasons; normal fares are $28 during off-peak times, $36 during standard times. At peak periods, you must make reservations in advance – the ferries can be booked solid at popular holiday times. You can book up to six months in advance, either by phone (☎ (04) 498 3999, (0800) 80 2802) or at railway stations, AA travel centres, or most travel agencies and information centres.

There are also scheduled ferry services to the islands off Auckland (see the Great Barrier Island Walk in the Far North chapter) and between Stewart Island and Bluff (see the Stewart Island chapter for details).

Other Water Transport
There are several places where water transport is more convenient than travelling on land, especially in the Marlborough Sounds area, where a number of places to stay are only accessible by water. Regular launch and water-taxi services operate along the coast of the Abel Tasman Coast Track, departing

from Nelson and Golden Bay. Water transport is necessary to access tracks in the Marlborough Sounds, at Glenorchy, Lake Te Anau, Doubtful Sound, Lake Hauroko and Lake Waikaremoana.

BICYCLE

In recent years, there has been a marked increase in the number of cyclists touring New Zealand. It is not really an option for trampers, unless there is secure storage available at the start or finish of the track. Some of the trampers' shuttle services will store your bike (see the Mt Somers Subalpine Walkway in the Canterbury chapter).

Pick up a copy of *Cycle Touring in New Zealand* by Bruce Ringer (Auckland:

Hodder & Stoughton, 1989, paperback) – it's full of useful information for cyclists.

HITCHING

Hitching is never entirely safe in any country, and we don't recommend it. Trampers who decide to hitch should understand that they are taking a small but potentially serious risk.

Having said that, New Zealand is a good place for hitching, although you will undoubtedly get stuck somewhere for an uncomfortably long period of time. Unfortunately, trampers seem to carry more gear than other travellers, and at the end of a track often look dirty and bedraggled. It's easier hitching alone if you are male, but women should always hitch with a partner.

North Island

Far North

Many overseas travellers who arrive in Auckland think they have to head south to go tramping in New Zealand. Not so. The rugged Cape Reinga, where the Tasman Sea meets the Pacific Ocean, boasts New Zealand's most northern trek, a shoreline walk from Ninety Mile Beach to Spirits Bay. There's a 100-km network of tracks plus hot springs, native forest and mountains on Great Barrier Island, in the Hauraki Gulf. And the Coromandel Forest Park, on the Coromandel Peninsula, north-east of Auckland, includes the popular tramping area of Kauaeranga Valley.

You'll encounter fascinating artefacts in these areas from the days of logging and mining, and there are steep climbs that rival any in the North Island. About the only thing lacking is huts – there are none along the Ninety Mile Beach-Cape Reinga Walkway, only two on Great Barrier Island and, until Moss Creek Hut is replaced, just one in the Kauaeranga Valley. A tent is therefore a handy piece of gear to carry.

Cape Maria van Diemen, a point south-west of Cape Reinga.

CLIMATE
There is good tramping in the Far North, but it means packing the sunscreen lotion and mosquito net. One of the nicest features of the region is the long spells of dry weather during summer, with temperatures that are warm enough at times to be considered almost tropical.

NATURAL HISTORY
Te Paki is one of New Zealand's most outstanding wildlife habitats. The wide variety of rare species living here includes a native land snail, *Acostylus ambagiosus*, found only in the pockets of broadleaf forest remaining in the North Cape region. There are also impressive stands of native bush, such as giant kauri and pohutukawa trees. The wildlife most trampers will encounter, however, are coastal birds such as oystercatchers, New Zealand dotterel, pied

Te Paki Reserves

The Ninety Mile Beach-Cape Reinga walk described in this section lies entirely in the Te Paki reserves. The 24,300-hectare reserves contain dramatic coastal landscapes, two coastal camp sites and many km of walkways. The reserves and facilities are managed by the DOC, although part is leased as a shop and a cattle station.

HISTORY
The Maoris were already well established in New Zealand's far north by the time the Europeans arrived, and Cape Reinga had long been regarded in Maori legend as the departure point of spirits. In 1642, Dutch explorer Abel Tasman sailed by and named

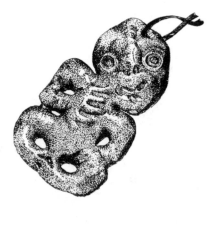

Tiki

stilt, terns, gulls and the occasional white-faced heron.

NINETY MILE BEACH-
CAPE REINGA WALKWAY
Once described as a 'desert coast', Ninety Mile Beach is almost concrete-hard below the high-tide line, and is bordered much of the way by sand dunes six km wide and rising in places to 143 metres in height. The walkway follows the beach 83 km south to Ahipara; trampers will find the 32-km portion from Hukatere to Bluff (a famous spot for surf fishing) ruler straight. Walking the entire beach requires at least three days. However, you can enter it at Waipapakauri (69 km south of Te Paki Stream), at Hukatere (51 km from the stream) or at Bluff (19 km from the stream). The walk described here is a three-day walk from Te Paki Stream, at the northern end of Ninety Mile Beach, to Kapowairua, at the eastern end of Spirits Bay.

Information
For additional information, contact the DOC regional office (☎ (09) 438 0299) in Whangarei, 149-151 Bank St. Other sources of information are the Kaitaia field centre (☎ (09) 408 2100), on Puketopo Rd, and the Cape Reinga field base (☎ (09) 409 7540), at the Cape Reinga shop. Get a copy of the informative 1986 pamphlet *Te Paki: Northland, New Zealand*.

Maps
The walk from Te Paki Stream to just west of Spirits Bay is covered by the 1:50,000 Topomaps 260 quad M02 *(North Cape)*, although to cover the entire route you would also need to purchase quad N02 (also *North Cape)*. If you are walking from Ahipara up Ninety Mile Beach, quads N03 *(Houhora)* and N04 *(Ahipara)* complete the coverage.

Huts
There are no huts on this walk, so make sure you bring a tent.

Equipment
This trip requires a tent with insect netting. Take sunscreen lotion, a wide-brimmed hat, a long-sleeved shirt and trousers of light material (not wool). You should also have a one-litre water bottle per person, and be aware of where water is going to be available. Because of the extreme fire risk in summer, take a safe liquid-gas cooker.

Access
You can enter the walkway at a number of points by vehicle, or you can walk the entire 83 km from the town of Ahipara at the southern end of the walkway to Spirits Bay (a six to seven-day journey). Keep in mind, however, that cars and tour buses will be encountered daily on Ninety Mile Beach until you pass Te Paki Stream.

The main departure point for the tramp is Kaitaia, near the northern end of State Highway 1 – but it can also be arranged from Whangaroa or the Bay of Islands. All three places have youth/backpackers' hostels and are serviced daily by regular buses. There is no regular bus transport beyond Kaitaia, but a number of companies run tours up to Cape Reinga and trampers can usually arrange to be dropped off and picked up by them.

Most tours begin in Kaitaia and swing onto Ninety Mile Beach, leaving it at Te Paki Stream for Cape Reinga. Once at the cape, they turn around and head south through the middle of the long peninsula. Ask first, but what most companies will do for the price of a tour is drop you off somewhere along Ninety Mile Beach (Te Paki Stream is the most common spot) and then pick you up three or four days later at Waitiki Landing – site of a tearoom, store and petrol station. The only hassle is getting from Kapowairua, near the camping ground at the eastern end of Spirits Bay, to Waitiki Landing, a road trip of about 16 km. Without a vehicle, hitching or walking is the only way.

To Kaitaia Several daily buses go between Kaitaia and Auckland via Doubtless Bay, the Bay of Islands and Whangarei. Travel time is half an hour to Doubtless Bay, 2½ hours

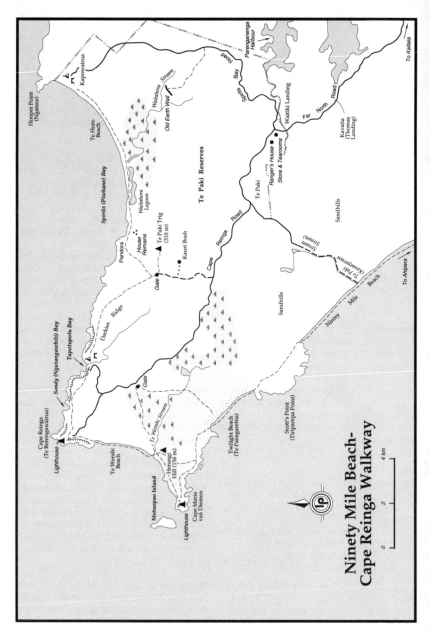

Ninety Mile Beach–
Cape Reinga Walkway

Pupuharakeke (Snail Trail)
Although not part of the Ninety Mile Beach-Cape Reinga Walkway, the Pupuharakeke Trail is a logical extension of it. The name derives from the occurrence of the pupuharaheke (flax snail) in the region. This is the only trail which gets you to North Cape, and because it passes through Maori land, you have to go there on an organised tour with the Ngati Kuri people, the traditional owners.

On this walk, in the company of knowledgeable Maori guides, you will see a part of New Zealand that many people don't see. Apart from the pupurareheke, you will see the kurahaupo rock where that waka (canoe) was tied when the Great Migration reached New Zealand's shores; the white silica sands of Te Kokota spit; the foreshores of Te Parengarenga harbour, home for hundreds of years to the Ngati Kuri; and the one and only money tree.

If you are in a small group, the four-day trip will cost you $55 per person; meals, refreshments, accommodation and transport to and from Kaitaia are included. Book with Tall Tale Travel 'n' Tours (π(09) 408 0870; fax 408 1100), 123b Commerce St, Kaitaia. ■

to Paihia, 3½ hours to Whangarei and seven hours all the way to Auckland. The Cape Reinga tours leave from the visitor information centre, or will pick you up from your accommodation.

To the Track Several small, locally owned tour operators run from Kaitaia and Doubtless Bay up to Cape Reinga. Sand Safaris (π (09) 408 1778), 27 South Rd, Kaitaia, has small buses which carry between 12 and 19 people. They will take trampers if there are seats available; ask about the cost to your particular destination.

Nor-East Coachlines (π (09) 406 0244) is a good, local company operating from Mangonui. Another small-group operation is Tall Tales Travels 'n' Tours, based at Kaitaia's Main Street Hostel, but with an office at 123b Commerce St (π (09) 408 0870) as well.

Places to Stay
Camp Sites If you do plan to stay on the cape, there are several DOC camp sites in the Cape Reinga area: Spirits Bay has cold water and limited toilet facilities, Tapotupotu Bay has toilets and showers – neither has electricity, so you should bring a cooker with you because fires are prohibited.

There's a sheltered DOC camp site at Rarawa Beach, three km north of Ngataki, which has water, cold showers and toilet facilities only. No prior bookings can be

made and no open fires are permitted. Cooking is confined to gas cookers because of the fire risk.

Camp site fees for Rarawa and Tapotupotu are $5 per person per night; at Spirits Bay (Kapowairua) you pay $4. Remember to take all rubbish out, at least as far as the transfer station at Houhora.

Budget Accommodation The *Pukenui Lodge Motel & Backpackers Hostel* (π (09) 409 8837), overlooking Pukenui Harbour, has dormitory beds at $12.50 per person. Follow Lamb Rd west about 500 metres to reach the *Pukenui Motor Camp* (π (09) 409 8803). *Northwind Backpackers* (π (09) 409 8515), at Henderson Bay, will pick you up from Pukenui; beds cost $12.50 per person per night.

Kaitaia There are two excellent hostels in Kaitaia. The *Kaitaia YHA Hostel* (π (09) 408 1840) is on the main drag, at 160 Commerce St. It charges $13 a night. In the next block north, at 235 Commerce St, is *Main Street Backpackers* (π (09) 408 1275). It's privately run and a great place to stay; a bed costs $13 to $15.

The Track
The trip can be walked in either direction, but for those depending on tour buses for transport, it is easier to begin at Ninety Mile Beach and then return to the bus at Waitiki

Landing. The trip described is a 50-km tramp from Te Paki Stream (at the northern end of Ninety Mile Beach) to the eastern side of Spirits Bay. It's an 18-hour walk that most people cover in three days – camping at Te Werahi Beach and the camping grounds at Tapotupotu and Spirits (Kapowairua) bays. For those with time, the trip can be extended by hiking a portion of Ninety Mile Beach, which is really only 103 km long. The tramp is rated easy.

Stage 1: Te Paki Stream to Te Werahi Beach
Walking Time: 4½ hours via Herangi Hill; five hours via Cape Maria van Diemen
Accommodation: There are no huts or developed camping grounds

Te Paki (Kauaparaoa) Stream marks the southern border of the coastal park of the same name, but is more famous for being a 'quicksand stream'. Tour buses depart from Ninety Mile Beach at this point; trampers continue north along the Tasman Sea coast.

Within an hour, you cross Waitapu Stream and the marked track moves inland to ascend Scott's Point. The trail over the point is an old vehicle track – it's well marked but should still be carefully followed. It takes about 1½ hours to cross the point and descend onto Twilight Beach (Te Paengarehia).

Trampers will find themselves hiking along a sandy shoreline devoid of tourists. Plan on an hour to reach the northern end of the beach (if the sun and sand don't delay you for an afternoon), where there's a small stream and a signposted route to the Cape Reinga Rd, a 1½-hour walk. The walkway continues towards Cape Maria van Diemen, where a lighthouse was built after the one on nearby Motuopao Island closed in 1941.

After moving inland, the track comes to a signposted junction where a high-level trail climbs 156 metres over Herangi Hill and descends to Te Werahi Stream at the southern end of Te Werahi Beach. The other track, which has excellent coastal views, follows the cape to the lighthouse, before swinging

east and joining the main track. At the southern end of Te Werahi Beach, where the walkway descends from a ridge to Te Werahi Stream, there is another signposted route back to the road (one hour). It's an hour's walk along the main track over Herangi Hill and a 1½ to two-hour tramp via Cape Maria van Diemen.

Stage 2: Te Werahi Beach to Tapotupotu Bay
Walking Time: 3½ to four hours
Accommodation: DOC camping ground

It takes 45 minutes to an hour to walk along the sweeping beach from Te Werahi Stream to Tarawamaomao Point at the beach's northern end, where the track begins to climb sharply. The track continues along cliff tops, and on clear days you are rewarded with spectacular views of sandy beaches, Cape Maria van Diemen and Motuopao Island. Within an hour of the ascent from Te Werahi Beach, the walkway emerges at Cape Reinga, a short distance from the lighthouse.

The cape is a scenic spot and often appears on travel brochures. It's also a good place to witness that often violent meeting of the Pacific Ocean and the Tasman Sea. Keep an eye out for the many pods of dolphins which round the cape in feeding forays. If you're at the cape during 'shop hours', you can get a limited number of supplies.

In the Maori language, Reinga means the 'place of leaping'. According to legend, spirits travelled to the pohutukawa tree on the headland of Cape Reinga and descended to the underworld by sliding down a root into the sea. They emerged on Ohaua, highest point of the Three Kings Islands, to bid their ancestors farewell before returning to the Polynesian homeland of their ancestors.

The walkway resumes in the car park, sidles the hill, then follows a ridge of scrub before descending steeply to Sandy (Ngatangawhiti) Bay – a very pleasant spot with a nice beach, freshwater stream and grassy flats beneath pohutukawa trees. On the other side of the small bay, the track begins an equally steep climb up a coastal

Top: Lake Mackenzie, Routeburn Track (VB)
Middle: Lake Wakatipu, Otago (VB)
Bottom: Mutton Cove, Abel Tasman National Park (VB)

Top Left: Hot springs on Great Barrier Island (JD)
Top Right: Tramping to the hot springs, Great Barrier Island (JD)
Bottom: Lake Waikaremoana, Te Urewera National Park (JW)

ridge, turns inland for a spell, then returns to the cliff tops, from which it descends sharply towards Tapotupotu Bay – a two-hour walk from Cape Reinga.

Tapotupotu is one of the most scenic beaches in the far north. It's a horseshoe bay of white sand and light green seas, enclosed by forested cliffs. There's a freshwater stream here, and a DOC camping ground which offers cold showers, toilets and fresh water, thanks to the gravel road which enables access from the Cape Reinga Rd.

Stage 3: Tapotupotu Bay to Kapowairua (Spirits Bay)
Walking Time: eight to nine hours
Accommodation: DOC camping ground

To reach Spirits Bay, cross the stream past the kitchen block in Tapotupotu Bay (easiest at low tide) and follow the track as it ascends sharply along the coastal ridge. After an hour, the walkway heads inland along Darkies Ridge and joins the Pandora Track, eventually reaching a gate at the end of a partially metalled road.

At the gate, there is a 15-minute side track which continues up to Te Paki Trig, 310 metres above sea level; here you'll encounter the remains of a wartime radar station and enjoy a spectacular panorama of the coastline.

From the gate, a rough vehicle track heads south to the main road. Heading north of the gate is Pandora Track, which soon swings north-east and leads down to Pandora Beach, where you'll find the remains of a house and gardens. If you hit the beach at low tide, you can reach Spirits Bay by the seaward route, around the rocks. Otherwise, follow the route above the rocks.

Once on the bay, either follow Te Horo Beach or trek through the sand dunes to Kapowairua at the eastern end of the beach. You pass Waitahora Lagoon on the way, which is a good swimming spot. You'll find the Spirits Bay camping ground near a smaller lagoon at the eastern end of the beach. This DOC facility has fresh water, toilets and cold showers. Spirits Bay Rd leads south from the camping ground towards Waitiki Landing. Plan on 3½ hours to walk from Tapotupotu Bay to the Te Paki Trig, and five hours from the Trig to the camping ground.

Great Barrier Forest

Great Barrier Island, situated 88 km north of Auckland, features many long, white, sandy beaches on the eastern side and sheltered inlets with deep water on the western side. In the middle is a rugged area of steep ridges rising to a peak of 621 metres at Hirakimata (Mt Hobson), the highest point on the island.

The 80,000-hectare preserve is a state forest recreation area under the management of the DOC. A network of tracks through rugged bush combine with old logging roads and tramways (the rails have long since rotted) to provide numerous tramping opportunities. Natural hot springs, towering kauri trees and the relics of kauri dams are the most interesting features of the recreation area; the island's relaxing, 'get away from it all' aura is a bonus.

HISTORY
The Hauraki Gulf was one of the first places settled by Polynesians who travelled south across the Pacific. Captain Cook sighted and named Great Barrier Island (it seemed to bar the entrance to the Hauraki Gulf) in 1769. Like the Far North region, it was the rich resources that led Europeans to settle on Great Barrier Island. The first settlement was a whaling station in Whangaparapara Harbour, but it was the kauri tree and its natural by-product, gum, that was the most sought after and longest-lasting resource.

By the 1930s, logging had devastated the land. Timber drives with kauri dams had been especially destructive, quickly eroding valleys and stream beds and leaving a broad silt flat at river mouths. In 1955, the New Zealand Forest Service began a programme to rehabilitate the Great Barrier Forest, and in 1973 it was declared a forest recreation

Kauri Dams

The key to retrieving timber from the rugged areas of Great Barrier Island were the kauri dams. These massive wooden structures were built across the upper portions of streams to trap water. For three months, trees were cut and positioned in the creek bed either above or below the dam catchment. When the water was high enough, a loose-plank gate in the middle of the dam was tripped, and the sudden flood swept the timber through the steep and difficult terrain to navigable rivers below. ■

reserve. In 1987, when the DOC was established, it took over administration of the area.

CLIMATE

Summers on Great Barrier Island are hot and dry, sometimes as much as 3° or 4° C warmer than in Auckland, and it's not unusual for the temperature to top 28° or 30° C. The average annual rainfall at Port Fitzroy, in the northern half of the island, is 1852 mm; the southern half is drier. Tramping takes place all year round, though the wet winters can quickly turn the tracks into a sea of mud.

NATURAL HISTORY

Great Barrier Island is predominantly volcanic rock. The heart of the island is a regenerating kauri forest of 80 sq km.

GREAT BARRIER ISLAND TREK

There are three communities on Great Barrier Island which serve as arrival and departure points, but most trampers arrive at Port Fitzroy. Not only does is it have a scenic harbour, rugged coastline and fiord-like bays, you can also hike to the first hut on the track before nightfall even if you arrive late in the afternoon. Port Fitzroy has lodges, a store that sells limited supplies, and an information hut where transportation can be arranged. The other potential arrival and departure points are Claris, on the eastern side, and Tryphena, in the south-western corner of the island.

The peak season for tramping is mid-December to mid-January. However, because of the cost of getting to Great Barrier Island, the tracks and huts, though busy, are not overrun like those in Coromandel Forest Park or Tongariro National Park. Visitors begin thinning out after January, and many believe the best time of the year to explore this island is March to May, when temperatures are still warm, but the rainy season has yet to set in.

Information

The Hauraki Gulf Islands are administered by the DOC, so the DOC information centre in Auckland is one of the best places for information. It produces leaflets on several of the islands and can advise you on natural features, walkways and camping.

On the island, the main DOC field centre (☎ (09) 429 0044) is in Port Fitzroy, a 15-minute walk from the ferry landing. It has information and maps on the island, collects camping fees and sells hut tickets, and operates a good camping ground. The field centre is open Monday to Friday from 8 am to 4.30 pm, and on weekends during the height of summer. There's another DOC field centre in Whangaparapara, but it has irregular hours.

The Outdoor Adventure Company (☎ (09) 358 5868), in the Ferry Building on Quay St in Auckland, also has plenty of information on Great Barrier Island. The New Zealand Adventure Centre (☎ (09) 309 9192) in the Downtown Shopping Centre, in Auckland's QE II Square, offers package tours to the island. The Auckland Central Backpackers' Travel Centre (☎ (09) 358 4874) at the Auckland Central Backpackers Hostel, 9 Fort St, just off Queen St, also has plenty of information.

In Tryphena, Safari Tours & Travel runs a Great Barrier Island Information & Travel Office at the Stonewall Store (☎ (09) 429 0448). They also operate bus tours, arrange transport, and offer rental cars, mountain bikes and kayaks.

There's no power on the island, and no street lights, so bring a torch (flashlight). Most people on the island generate their own power by using solar, wind or diesel energy. Food is available, but is more expensive than on the mainland.

Maps

Maps can be obtained from the Port Fitzroy DOC field centre and information centre. The 1:50,000 Topomaps 260 quad SO8, *Barrier* ($12.50), covers most of the tracks, but the Great Barrier and Little Barrier Islands recreation map, the 1:50,000 Holidaymaker No 239 *Great Barrier Island*, is just as good, and cheaper ($11). The *Great Barrier Island Track Information* pamphlet, available from the DOC, is useful.

Huts

Camping is not allowed outside the designated camping grounds without a permit from the DOC. There's an $8 hut fee for Kaiarara and Whangaparapara huts, a $4 camp site fee for Akapoua (where barbecues are supplied) and a $3 camping ground fee at the other six camping grounds, payable at the DOC Great Barrier field centre (☎ (09) 429 0044) just outside Port Fitzroy, on the road to Kaiarara Hut.

The Kaiarara and Whangaparapara huts are in bush settings, both an hour's walk from the nearest wharf. Each hut sleeps up to 24 people in two bunkrooms; facilities include cold water, pit toilets and a kitchen with a wood stove. The huts are very busy from November to January, and accommodation is on a first come, first served basis – so the early birds get the bunks!

Access

Air Great Barrier Airlines (☎ (09) 275 9120) flies twice daily from Air New Zealand's Domestic Terminal at Auckland Airport to Claris (and also to Okiwi in summer). The flight from Auckland takes half an hour and costs $89/170 one-way/return on weekdays ($119 return on weekends), or there's a fly-boat combination flying one way and catching the boat the other for $119 any day. The airline operates a free transfer bus from Claris to Tryphena and from Okiwi to Port Fitzroy.

Boat Fullers Cruises (☎ (09) 377 1771) operates ferries between Auckland and Great Barrier Island several times weekly, stopping first at Tryphena and then at Port Fitzroy. The voyage takes two hours and costs $99 (children $49). Fullers also makes a day-trip cruise to the island, departing from the Auckland Ferry Building at 9 am and returning by 6 pm; the cost is $50 (children $25), with an optional $17 bus tour.

Most of the Fullers ferries depart from Auckland in the morning, but there is also a Friday night ferry. This one does not always continue to Port Fitzroy, so if you're heading there, make sure you check in advance.

A 22-foot (7.3-metre), open, rigid-hulled, inflatable boat (the same kind used for whale-watching) operates between Fletcher Bay, on the Coromandel Peninsula, and Tryphena. You must book ahead for this service, because it operates on demand (weather permitting) rather than to schedule. The crossing takes about half an hour (15 minutes in fine weather) and costs $35. Phone the Sunkist Lodge in Thames (☎ (07) 868 8808) to book a trip. Sunkist also offers a discount option which involves travelling on its boat from Fletcher Bay to Tryphena, then joining the Fullers cruise to Auckland – all for $70 (a $20 discount on normal prices).

The 1909 schooner *Te Aroha* also sails to Great Barrier Island; it leaves from the Captain Cook Wharf in central Auckland every few days, but doesn't always go to Great Barrier Island. You can sleep in two-person cabins or on deck under the stars.

On the Island Roads on the island are rough and ready. The trip from Tryphena (in the south) to Port Fitzroy (in the north) is about 47 km by gravel road, or 40 km via Whangaparapara using the walking tracks. The roads are so bad that walking is a good option!

A bus operates from Tryphena to Port Fitzroy and back (via Claris and Okiwi) once a day. Its timetable coincides with ferry arrivals and departures. You can arrange to send your luggage on ahead on this bus if you like; a convenient service for trampers and

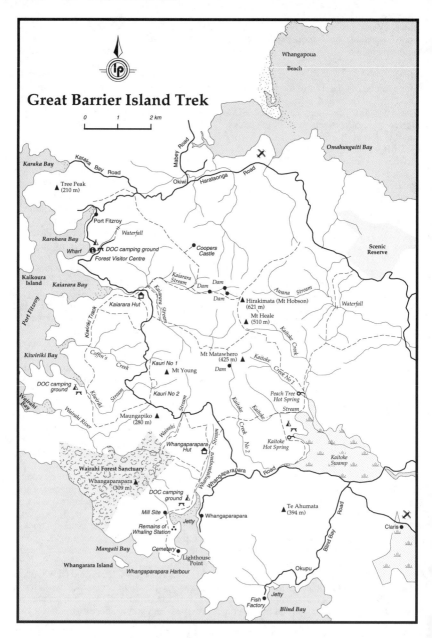

Great Barrier Island Trek

0   1   2 km

Whangapoua
Beach

Omahungaiti Bay

Karaka Bay

Karaka Bay Road

Tree Peak
(210 m)

Mabey Road

Okiwi

Harataonga Road

Scenic
Reserve

Port Fitzroy

Waterfall

Rarohara Bay

Wharf

DOC camping ground

Forest Visitor Centre

Coopers
Castle

Kaikoura
Island

Kaiarara Bay

Kaiarara
Stream

Dam   Dam

Dam

Awana Stream

Hirakimata (Mt Hobson)
(621 m)

Waterfall

Port Fitzroy

Kaiarara Hut

Kaiarara Stream

Kiwiriki Track

Mt Heale
(510 m)

Kaitoke Creek

Kiwiriki Bay

Coffin's Creek

Kauri No 1
Mt Young

Mt Matawhero
(425 m)

Kaitoke

Kaitoke Creek No 1

DOC camping
ground

Kiwiriki Stream

Kauri No 2

Dam

Peach Tree
Hot Spring

Waitahi Bay

Waitahi River

Maungapiko
(280 m)

Waitahi Stream

Kaitoke Creek No 2

Kaitoke Stream

Stream

Kaitoke
Hot Spring

Kaitoke
Swamp

Whangaparapara Hut

Wairahi Forest Sanctuary

Whangaparapara
(309 m)

Whangaparapara Stream

Whangaparapara Road

DOC camping
ground

Te Ahumata
(394 m)

Mill Site

Jetty

Whangaparapara

Blind Bay Road

Claris

Remains of
Whaling Station

Mangati Bay

Cemetery

Lighthouse
Point

Whangarara Island

Whangaparapara Harbour

Okupu

Fish
Factory

Jetty

Blind Bay

cyclists. If the place you're staying knows you're coming, and they're not on a bus route, they will come to pick you up.

Safari Tours & Travel (☎ (09) 429 0448), at the Stonewall Store in Tryphena, provides hire cars, mountain bikes and kayaks. There are a handful of taxis on the island, but they aren't cheap.

Places to Stay

DOC Camping Grounds & Huts The DOC operates camping grounds at Port Fitzroy (Akapoua), Harataonga Bay, Medlands Beach, Awana Beach and Whangaparapara – all with basic facilities (including water and pit toilets). Fires are permitted on the island only in the designated fireplaces.

Hostels Three places at Tryphena offer hostel-style accommodation. *Pohutukawa Lodge* (☎ (09) 429 0211), on the Tryphena beachfront, charges $13 per night. The *Shoal Bay Holiday Park* (☎ (09) 429 0485), on Cape Barrier Rd, costs $16 for two. The *Sunset Beach Motel* (☎ (09) 429 0568) – the only motel listed on the island – has cheap beds ($15). The *Fitzroy Hostel* (☎ (09) 429 0055), at Port Fitzroy, has beds for $12.

Cabins & Holiday Homes The *Shoal Bay Holiday Park* (☎ (09) 429 0485) at Shoal Bay, near Tryphena, has cabins sleeping four for $16 per person. Holiday bachs (holiday huts/homes) and caravans, all privately owned and maintained, are often available to visitors – Safari Tours & Travel (☎ 429 0448) keeps a list.

The Track

The described trek is a four-day loop from Port Fitzroy, including travel to and from the island. The trip can easily be adjusted to start from Tryphena or Claris, although some transportation or hitching would be involved; with a tent, the tramp can be extended considerably. Camping is allowed around both DOC huts on the track and at a number of designated camping grounds (but definitely not in the forest). Camping anywhere other than at designated camping

grounds must be approved through a permit system.

Stage 1: Port Fitzroy to Kaiarara Hut
Walking Time: 1½ hours
Accommodation: camping ground at DOC information office; Kaiarara Hut (24 bunks)

Take the Kaiarara Rd south past the wharf and follow the signposts to 'Mt Hobson Track'. For the next 1.2 km, the road climbs a high coastline bluff, with views of Rarohara Bay and the boats that often fill the harbour. The DOC information office and camping ground, a pleasant grassy area with water and toilets, is 20 minutes from the wharf.

Past the DOC information office, the road resumes climbing, crosses the head between Rarohara Bay and Kaiarara Bay, then swings south-east and follows the coastal ridge above Kaiarara Bay. A locked gate across the road is the border of the DOC forest area, closed to all vehicle traffic. The road drops quickly, passes Blairs Landing, a popular spot for boaters, and finally reaches Kaiarara Stream, a good hour's walk from the camping ground. After fording the stream (prone to flooding), you arrive at an information sign. The road fords the stream two more times, passing good swimming pools along the way, and then arrives at the hut.

Even if you are not contemplating the entire circuit over Hirakimata (Mt Hobson), you should still consider a side trip up to the first kauri dam on the north fork of the Kaiarara Stream. The 1½ to two-hour walk (steadily uphill) to the massive structure is well worth it, because the dam is one of the biggest and best-preserved in the country.

Stage 2: Kaiarara Hut to
Whangaparapara Hut via Kiwiriki Track
Walking Time: five to six hours
Accommodation: Whangaparapara Hut (24 bunks)

Return to the information sign and map, and follow the Kiwiriki Track. The first one km is level, then climbs slightly to the spur track to Bush's Beach. The recreation area on

Stage 2A: Whangaparapara Harbour

From the hut, the track continues towards the bay, crossing bridges over a stream several times, passing the junction to Whithey's Track and the Mt Whangaparapara Track (a 2½-hour round trip) before arriving at a field. Step over the fence and cross the swing bridge to reach the village of Whangaparapara; you'll quickly spot the DOC field base on a small hill to the left. Information and brochures can be obtained here, and there is a payphone at Whangaparapara Wharf. The road continues towards the harbour, passing Great Barrier Lodge, where there is a small store.

If you continue past the swing bridge in the cow pasture, you will quickly pick up a track which leads to the western side of the harbour. It's about a km to the DOC camping ground (cooking shelter, toilets), and then another 15 to 20-minute walk over two ridges to reach the site of the Kauri Timber Company sawmill, the largest in the southern hemisphere in 1910. Today, all that remains are the concrete foundations and some pilings.

From the mill site, the track climbs two ridges (the first quite steep) and descends into Mangati Bay, a 1½-hour walk from the swing bridge. The rugged Whangarara (Cliff) Island shelters the entrance to the secluded bay, providing calm water that's ideal for swimming, snorkelling and shore fishing. ∎

Kaiarara Bay is a pleasant spot, which has barbecues, a small, sandy beach and grassy areas for picnicking. The main track departs from the spur track and quickly reaches a second junction. Line W Track heads east (left) to the Forest Rd across the Kaiarara Plateau (half an hour's walk), while the main track (right) makes a steady descent to Coffin's Creek.

The creek is one to 1½ hours from the hut, and marks the point where trampers will begin to do some serious climbing on their way to Whangaparapara. The track begins a steep ascent, climbing 160 metres in a km, before topping out on the crest of the ridge that separates Coffin's Creek from Kiwiriki Bay. The climb is steady but the views are good. Once on top, the track reverses and sharply descends to the bay. Near the bottom is a spur track to the water. The track heads south from here and quickly arrives at a DOC camping ground.

The camping ground is an hour's walk from Coffin's Creek. It's situated in a grassy area on the edge of the forest, and has a toilet and a table. However, it's not that close to the bay, and can be a haven for insects. The track follows the nearby creek for a while and then begins another steep climb, rising 100 metres in less than a km. Once near the top of the ridge, the views back to Kiwiriki Bay are excellent. The track follows the crest, working up and over two knobs and then

ascending slightly at the end, to emerge at the Forest Rd, 1½ hours from the camping ground.

The track is signposted from the road, as is the short spur track which climbs steeply to Maungapiko Lookout, a 280-metre knob offering good views to the south. Follow the road, which is badly eroded in places, as it descends two km to Wairahi Stream. A couple of hundred metres before the creek, the Pack Track is signposted – it does not begin after the stream, as shown on many maps. The track, which provides a short cut to the Whangaparapara Hut, drops steeply to Wairahi Stream and then climbs up and over another ridge to emerge at the tramline track. The hut is just down the old tramline, a 45-minute walk along the Pack Track from the Forest Rd.

Stage 3: Whangaparapara Hut to Kaiarara Hut via Hirakimata

Walking Time: seven to nine hours
Accommodation: Kaiarara Hut (24 bunks)

This trek passes two hot springs before ascending Hirakimata. Trampers should think twice, however, about soaking in the springs and then climbing the island's highest point. The springs are best enjoyed as a side trip from Whangaparapara Hut without having to endure a long tramp with a backpack afterwards.

From the hut, follow the tramline track as it climbs steeply for about a km to the Forest Rd. Head north on the road for a short way until you reach the signposted track to the east, which was once a logger's tramway to the sawmill. The wide track drops steeply through the rugged terrain to Kaitoke Creek No 2, ascends on the other side, and then descends again to a tributary of Kaitoke Stream (this is unnamed on most maps). It follows the stream, gradually dropping towards the eastern side of the island until it arrives at a major junction.

The junction is signposted and points the way south to Kaitoke Hot Spring. The track immediately crosses Kaitoke Stream and then steadily climbs uphill for a km to an open spot with an excellent view of Kaitoke Swamp, the surrounding ridges and the crashing surf of Kaitoke Beach, on the eastern side of the island.

The track then swings west and drops sharply to the thermal stream below. The first dammed pool is rather muddy and uninviting, but hike upstream and you will encounter others, half-hidden in a canopy of trees, which are much more delightful. From the springs, a track continues south to Whangaparapara Rd (45 minutes).

Back at the junction, near Kaitoke Stream, trampers heading for Hirakimata continue east along the track as it follows Kaitoke Stream, swings north around a corner of extensive swamp and in 45 minutes reaches Peach Tree Hot Spring. This area was an old Kauri Timber Company camp site, and the thermal pool was dug out by loggers. It is smaller and hotter, but many think it a more pleasant setting than Kaitoke Hot Spring.

The track leaves the hot-spring area and crosses Kaitoke Creek No 1 to a signposted junction. The track to the north (the right fork) leads to the Fitzroy-Harataonga Rd (1½ hours). Trampers with their eye on Hirakimata should follow the track to the left (north-west) which steeply climbs 200 metres, levels out as it crosses a branch of upper Kaitoke Creek, climbs again for

another 240 metres and then sidles around to the west of Mt Heale.

Halfway up the second ascent, 1½ hours from Peach Tree Hot Springs, you pass a junction with an old bridle track that heads west along Central Ridge and hits the Forest Rd a km south of Kaiarara Hut. It's a two to three-hour walk to the hut.

The final leg to the peak of Hirakimata (621 metres) is a steep ascent of 180 metres. The walk from Peach Tree Hot Springs to the summit takes 2½ to 3½ hours, but from the top you're rewarded with excellent views of both sides of Great Barrier Island, as well as of the outer islands in the Hauraki Gulf.

Take the left fork at the junction near the peak to descend to the northern branch of the Kaiarara Stream. In 30 to 40 minutes you pass one of the upper dams. In another 30 to 40 minutes, the recently upgraded track drops to the impressive lower dam, which is reached by a short side track to the left.

The dam is a massive, wooden structure held in place across the gorge by huge kauri logs. The dams were built in 1926, and loggers then proceeded to cut trees and skid them above and below the lower dam. When sufficient water was stored, the upper dams were tripped, sending a blast of river and logs rushing towards the lower one. The lower dam would be tripped at the right moment, resulting in a force of water that sent the timber all the way to Kaiarara Bay, where it was gathered into huge booms and floated to sawmills in Auckland. The most unbelievable aspect of the dams is that, after all the work to build them, they were used for only three years.

The descent towards the hut is steep in places. The track levels out at a stream, where a signpost declares that the hut is only half an hour away. The stream is crossed again and you climb over another ridge before the track becomes a very pleasant stroll, gradually dropping through the valley, and crossing the northern branch of Kaiarara Stream four times before emerging at an old bridle track. The hut is a short walk away at this point.

Those tramping to Kaiarara Hut from

Hirakimata should plan on a walk of two to 2½ hours, depending on how much time is spent at the dams. Heading in the other direction, it's an uphill climb and closer to a three to four-hour hike to reach the island's high point.

Coromandel Forest Park

The 740 sq km of rugged, forested hills which make up the reserves of the Coromandel Forest Park are situated northeast of Thames on the Coromandel Peninsula. The highest point in the park is Mt Moehau (892 metres), located near the northern tip of the peninsula; Table Mountain (836 metres) is the highest point in Kauaeranga Valley.

HISTORY
It is thought that the crews of the *Arawa* and *Tainui* canoes of the Great Fleet rested on the peninsula during their epic journey. Tamatekapua, one of the captains, is believed to be buried near sacred Mt Moehau. In 1769, Captain Cook sailed into a rugged, little inlet on the eastern shore of the Coromandel Peninsula. He raised the British flag over New Zealand for the first time and, after the planet appeared that night, labelled the spot Mercury Bay. The peninsula, however, takes its name from the HMS *Coromandel*, which visited in 1820, bringing with it the missionary Samuel Marsden.

Full-scale kauri logging began in the mid-1800s, and by the 1880s there were timber millers within the Kauaeranga Valley. It was the gold rush at Thames which gave impetus to the logging efforts in the Kauaeranga Valley, because of the sudden demand for building materials in the boom towns. The first trees cut were near the sea or from country where bullock teams could easily haul the logs out, but eventually the loggers relied on kauri dams to flush the logs to accessible locations (see the aside in the Great Barrier Island section of this chapter).

The Coromandel Peninsula was declared a state forest in 1938 and a programme to re-establish the native bush began. In 1971, the status of the Coromandel area was upgraded to that of a forest park.

CLIMATE
Although not as warm as Great Barrier Island or Cape Reinga, the climate of the forest park is still mild, with long dry periods in the summer and an average temperature of around 23° C. Winters are moist, but frosts are rare. The area averages an annual 1255 mm of rain in the valleys and 2500 mm in the ranges.

NATURAL HISTORY
Before it was logged, the peninsula had a variety of rich forest flora unmatched by any other area of comparable size in the country. Now much of the park is regenerating native bush, including kauri and rata, the latter noted for its brilliant orange-red flowers. The Kauaeranga Valley and surrounding ridges are covered with podocarps and hardwoods, a few scattered pockets of kauri, and areas of bracken, fern and scrub. The predominant species are rimu and tawa, and there are also miro, matai and kahikatea. The wildlife consists of the usual native birds of New Zealand – tuis, bellbirds, kereru (wood pigeons) and fantails – and introduced mammals – pigs, possums, goats, cats and ferrets.

There are various kinds of jaspers, petrified wood, rhodonite and agate in or near most streams, which makes the place an excellent source of rare rocks and gemstones. Interested rock collectors need to pick up a permit from the field centre in the Kauaeranga Valley, and can use only a geological hammer to assist in removing surface material.

COROMANDEL FOREST PARK WALK
The forest park is only a two-hour drive from Auckland, so it can be busy in early summer and on weekends, when school and scout groups frequent the area. If at all possible, go elsewhere during the Christmas holidays or plan your walk for the middle of the week to avoid crowded huts.

A logging boom took place in the Coromandel Range during the late 19th century, when the stands of massive kauri were extracted. Today, like Great Barrier Island, dams, pack-horse trails and tramway clearings are silent, deteriorating reminders of yesterday's feast.

There are over 30 walks and tramps through Coromandel Forest Park, covering the area from the Karangahake Gorge (near Paeroa) to Cape Colville; the most popular region is the Kauaeranga Valley, which cuts into the Coromandel Range behind Thames. There are many old kauri dams in the valley, including the Tarawaere, Waterfalls, Dancing Camp, Kauaeranga Main, Moss Creek and Waterfalls Creek dams. You are requested not to climb on them.

Information

The DOC visitor information centre (☎ (07) 868 6381), formerly the Coromandel Forest Park headquarters, is in the Kauaeranga Valley about 15 km from Thames. It is open daily from 8 am to 4 pm. Inside, there are two rooms of exhibits and displays on the park. Sunkist Lodge in Thames also has lots of walking information.

Maps

All the walks are outlined in the excellent DOC pamphlet *Coromandel Recreation: A Forest & Coastal Experience*, available from DOC offices and visitor information centres for $1. The alternatives are the 1:50,000 quads T11 *(Whitianga)* and T12 *(Thames)* of the Topomaps 260 series, and the 1:150,000 Parkmaps No 274-01 *(Coromandel Forest Park)*.

Huts

There is only one hut on this track at present (the Moss Creek Hut burnt down and has not yet been replaced). Fees for the solitary Pinnacles Hut are $8 per person per night. The big plans afoot for this walk include the upgrading of Pinnacles Hut and the rebuilding of Moss Creek Hut, both in the style of gum-diggers' camps. When the improve-

ments have been completed, the walk will probably attain Great Walk status.

Access

The departure point for trips into the Kauaeranga Valley is Thames, the first town most people pass through when touring the Coromandel Peninsula. The DOC visitor centre is now located in the Kauaeranga Valley, not in Thames. The road to the valley begins at the southern edge of town; it's 14 km to the visitor centre and another 10 km to the end of the road, where the track begins.

Thames Sunkist Bus Services (☎ (07) 868 8808) operates daily buses between Auckland, Thames and Whitianga. It's a 1½-hour trip from Auckland to Thames and another 1½ hours to Whitianga; the ticket ($65) is valid for three months. For an extra $20, the trip can include the peninsula loop (and Fletcher Bay).

Connections can be made to Rotorua with Kiwi Safaris Hot Mud Safaris (☎ (0800) 80 0616), who do an Auckland-Thames-Te Aroha-Rotorua loop. Similarly, there is an Auckland-Thames-Tauranga loop with Bayline Coaches (☎ (07) 578 2825). Get a copy of the *Coromandel Peninsula Bus Services* pamphlet.

To the Tracks Once in Thames, a good bus network enables you to reach the far-flung parts of the peninsula. Murphy's (☎ (09) 867 6829) travels between Thames, Coromandel, Whitianga and Tairua and back to Thames every day except Saturday; the loop costs $35. If you wish to go further afield, such as the Kauaeranga Valley or to Fletcher Bay, the Sunkist Lodge (☎ (07) 868 8808) can arrange transport. The lodge offers transport to the Kauaeranga Valley at 1.30 pm daily, and trips go to Fletcher Bay daily in the peak season (on Monday, Wednesday and Friday from May to October). You can combine trips to the Kauaeranga Valley and Fletcher Bay with Sunkist's Auckland-Thames fare (listed above) for $82.

Coromandel Forest Park Walk

Places to Stay

The *Sunkist Lodge* (☎ (07) 868 8808; fax 868 7426), 506 Brown St, Thames, is a pleasantly relaxed hostel; dorm/twin beds are $13/17. The Sunkist Lodge operates the *Fletcher Bay Backpackers* (☎ 866 8989), a comfortable 16-bed place overlooking the beach; the cost is $14 per night.

There are DOC camping grounds at various places throughout the Coromandel Forest Park. You'll find them on the west coast and northern tip of the peninsula at Fantail Bay, Port Jackson and Fletcher Bay, and at Stony Bay and Waikawau Bay on the east coast. All have only a nominal fee, and you don't have to book.

Eight of the camping places are up the Kauaeranga Valley ($4/2 for adults/children), as is the only DOC hut on the peninsula ($8 per night).

In Coromandel, *Tui Lodge* (☎ (07) 866 8237), at 600 Whangapoua Rd, charges $14 per person in twin/double rooms. It's a 10-minute walk from town, 500 metres past the spot where State Highway 25 heads east. The *White House Backpackers* (☎ (07) 866 8468) is on the corner of Frederick St and Ring's Rd; dorm beds are $10. *Tidewater*

Tourist Park (☎ (07) 866 8888) is on Tiki Rd; modern backpackers' cabins cost $12 per person.

The Track
The described three-day tramp is a popular walk in the Kauaeranga Valley, rated easy to medium. The track is well cut, marked and posted with directional signs, but it does involve a certain amount of climbing (as does just about every walk in New Zealand). It includes a possible side trip to Mt Rowe (794 metres), which has good views of the valley.

The track starts and finishes at the end of Kauaeranga Valley Rd. It can be walked in either direction, with one night spent in a hut and the other night spent camping. The trek described here involves ascending to the site of Moss Creek Hut on the first day. A slightly easier climb, however, is to hike to Pinnacles Hut for the first night.

Stage 1: Road's End to Former Moss Creek Hut Site
Walking Time: three to four hours
Accommodation: camping only (Moss Creek Hut is being replaced)

The tramp begins at the end of Kauaeranga Valley Rd (about 10 km past the visitor centre), where there is a large cairn offering directions. Follow the track towards Table Mountain and Moss Creek; it immediately crosses the Kauaeranga River by way of a suspended footbridge. Just after crossing the river, there is a signposted junction to Billy Goat Track and Hydro Camp (to the south), an alternative way of reaching Pinnacles Hut.

The main track then follows a boardwalk north for 15 to 20 minutes along the true left bank of the river, going through an impressive forest of rata, tree ferns and nikau palms. Just before Webb Creek, there is another signposted junction. The track to the north (the left fork) is the main one. The other fork (east) leads to Hydro Camp and then to the northern part of the Billy Goat Track.

Cross Webb Creek, and continue up the

Kauaeranga Valley until the track crosses the Kauaeranga River a second time, a 1½-hour walk from the road's end. The track continues along the river's true right side for a short time and then arrives at the old junction to Mt Rowe by way of Table Mountain Plateau. Trampers can no longer head to Mt Rowe via this route, because it has been closed for ecological reasons. Similarly, the path across to Table Mountain, to the south-west of Mt Rowe, has been closed.

Bypass the old track to Table Mountain Plateau and continue along the true right side of the Kauaeranga River. The track soon swings north-east and ascends directly towards the former Moss Creek Hut site. From the road's end, this route involves a three to four-hour walk to the hut.

There is a side track to the summit of Mt Rowe (794 metres) which offers scenic views of the valley. The track is about one km south-west of the site of the former Moss Creek Hut. Nearby are the deteriorating remains of two kauri dams, including Moss Creek Dam, 50 metres before the former hut site.

Moss Creek Hut burnt down in December 1993 and its rebuilding is a high priority. The rebuilt hut is expected to reflect the historic traditions of a gum-diggers' camp, have 60 bunks and a water supply, and be equipped with gas and mattresses.

Stage 2: Former Moss Creek Hut Site to Pinnacles Hut
Walking Time: 3½ to four hours
Accommodation: Pinnacles Hut (60 bunks)

The track continues to head east through bush and an occasional scrubby clearing, passing a kauri dam (or what remains of it). Within 1½ to two hours you arrive at a junction with a pack-horse track leading north to Rangihau Rd and eventually to Coroglen. The southern fork, which heads towards the Pinnacles, runs alongside a power transmission line and eventually arrives at the upper reaches of the Kauaeranga River, which it crosses.

When the river is low, it's possible to hike

down to the Kauaeranga Gorge by departing from the track and heading past the Main Dam, 10 to 15 minutes downstream. Built in 1912, this was the largest dam constructed in the valley, but all that remains today is the floor and a few supporting beams. Travel in the gorge should never be attempted when the river is swollen, and even at normal water levels will involve walking through waist-deep pools. There are good swimming pools near the dam.

The main track continues south, dropping slightly through scrub until it reaches a signposted junction 45 minutes from the river crossing. The fork to the south-west, follows the transmission line towards the Webb Creek-Billy Goat Loop, and returns to the valley road. The other fork leads east towards the Pinnacles, but in 10 minutes comes to the short spur track to Pinnacles Hut. The hut is in a scenic location, and its verandah overlooks the headwater gullies of the Kauaeranga River. The hut is scheduled to be upgraded, with 60 bunks, gas rings and a water supply planned. It, too, will reflect the style of an early gum-diggers' camp.

In a stream directly below the hut is one of the better-preserved kauri dams, the Dancing Camp Dam, which was built in 1924 and was the second largest in the valley.

From the junction near the hut, a track swings south-east and in 20 minutes reaches the Pinnacle Peaks (759 metres). The route to the Pinnacles can be steep in places, but the track is cut and well signposted and the views at the end are among the best in the valley.

Stage 3: Pinnacles Hut to Kauaeranga Valley Rd

Walking Time: three hours via Webb Creek; four hours via Billy Goat Track

The pack-horse track continues south-west from Pinnacles Hut, passing close to the Tauranikau Dam (only structural timber remains) towards Webb Creek. Along this stretch, there are good views of the Pinnacles' steep-faced ridges and deep chasms, but most of the vegetation is low scrub, due

to bushfires in the 1920s. The track skirts the side of Tauranikau Peak and descends to Hydro Camp, an hour's walk from the hut.

Hydro Camp is a clearing built in the 1970s by workers erecting the power lines from Thames to Whitianga. It is also the site of a major junction for those heading back to the valley road. The track that heads west (the right-hand fork) follows Webb Creek to its confluence with the Kauaeranga River, descending sharply most of the way and crossing the creek several times. Just before reaching the river, the track passes over a deeply worn pack-horse staircase that was cut by gum diggers on their way to Coroglen (known as Gumtown). Once at the river, you backtrack along the track on which you started, reaching the road 1½ to two hours from Hydro Camp.

The other fork (south) is Billy Goat Track. It's a longer walk, but most trampers think it's far more interesting. The track heads south and immediately crosses Webb Creek, where 200 metres upstream it's possible to see the remains of Webb Creek Dam. Most of the walk is downhill, and in 1½ hours the track reaches the junction with the Long Trestle spur track; it's a short walk to view the collapsed girders.

The main track swings north-west and follows the route of the Billy Goat Tramline down past the falls and the remains of Short Trestle. It ends with a steep descent to the Kauaeranga River, crossing Atuatumoe Stream and merging into the track you started on at the first bridge across the river. From Hydro Camp, the walk back to the road takes three hours.

OTHER TRACKS
Mt Moehau

You can get to Mt Moehau from two places – Te Hope and Stony Bay. You need to be fit to make the four-hour climb to the sacred summit, which at 892 metres is Coromandel's highest point; the walk should not be attempted in rain or low cloud. From the top, you get great views of the Hauraki Gulf and its islands, and the Coromandel.

This is the northernmost limit of New Zealand's subalpine flora.

Coromandel Walkway

This walk takes three hours one-way from Stony Bay to Fletcher Bay. Transport from both ends is provided by the Sunkist Lodge, Thames. It's possible to combine the Moehau ascent and the Coromandel Walkway, making for a varied two-day walk.

Central North Island

The Central North Island includes the following areas to the south of Auckland and the Coromandel: the rugged Raukumara Forest Park and the Urutawa Forest of the East Cape; beautiful Lake Waikaremoana, the Whakatane River and Whirinaki Forest in the Te Urewera region; the northern part of Tongariro National Park; and the remote, little-explored Kaimanawa Range.

As a tramping area, it rivals some of its more illustrious cousins in the South Island, such as Arthur's Pass and the Nelson region. The East Cape, in particular, waits moodily to surprise the capable tramper.

East Cape

The East Cape of the North Island is one of New Zealand's most exciting tramping locations. It includes the rugged Raukumara Forest Park (115,103 hectares) and the Urutawa Forest (21,750 hectares). The incredible terrain and virgin rainforests of Raukumara are a protected wilderness area.

There are only four huts in Raukumara Forest Park, all of them situated along the East-West Traverse of the range, from the Tapuaeroa River to the Motu River.

If you're looking for good descriptions of staged walks, this area is not for you. It's for the more adventurous tramper, equipped with good navigational skills, proper gear and a strong measure of individuality. The walks are usually through wilderness, with few benched paths, multiple river crossings and a wall of thick, virgin bush.

All the areas covered elsewhere in this book have careful track descriptions – the East Cape doesn't. If you feel capable of undertaking such a rugged tramp, some ideas are offered here. Remember, these descriptions are to whet your appetite only; they are not meant to be followed religiously. Once in the area, you will see that you need more than someone else's brief description to get you through.

The East-West Traverse would best be walked with locals who know where they are going, while the Hikurangi climb should be done with the blessing or assistance of the Gisborne Canoe & Tramping Club.

If your stay in the area is limited, there is full coverage of a medium two-day walk down the Pakihi Stock Route; two other walks in the Raukumara Forest Park are highlighted.

HISTORY

This area is deeply rooted in Maori folklore, and the mighty Hikurangi (1752 metres) is one of the legendary focal points. The Great Fleet had an important role in the settlement of the East Cape. The *waka* (canoe) *Tainui* landed 24 km from Opotiki and the daughter of Hoturoa, the captain, left the canoe. Her name was Torere, and she is remembered in the bay of the same name.

Captain James Cook sailed along the coast in early November 1769, naming Cape Runaway, White Island and Mt Edgecumbe as he passed. Cook commented in his journals on the large number of people in the area.

The first European to make it as far as Opotiki was the Reverend John Wilson, in December 1839. For the next 20 years, missionaries operated in the region, but little is known about them. Along the coast, traders were active, and whaling was pursued at Te Kaha and Waihau Bay.

During this period, the first Europeans penetrated the Raukumara Range. Bishop Selwyn and others were guided across the range by local Maoris in December 1842. Undoubtedly, many of the tracks had been used by the Ngati Porou raiding parties who attacked the Te Whanau-a-Apanui people in the Te Kaha region. The missionary and botanist William Colenso visited the area in

1843 and had a local Maori climb above the bush-line to collect alpine plants.

Essentially, though, the ranges repulsed most newcomers, and what we see today are forests much as they were before the arrival of the Pakeha. This 'untouched' quality led to the ranges being gazetted as a forest park in 1979 and to it subsequently being declared a wilderness area.

CLIMATE

The climate is generally mild, with moderate to heavy snow in winter at altitudes above 750 metres. Annual rainfall varies from 2500 mm in the lowlands to 5000 mm at higher altitudes, and deluges often lead to flash flooding, especially along the Motu River.

The cape's location means it is subject to frequent easterly storms, making it wetter east of the ranges – a very unusual occurrence in the mountains of New Zealand. There is less rainfall in the north-west, towards the Bay of Plenty, because the Raukumaras act as a partial rain shadow.

NATURAL HISTORY

The rugged terrain of the Raukumara and Urutawa forests encloses large areas of pristine wilderness. It is deeply dissected by almost impenetrable river valleys and bush-choked catchments. On the western side, three main river systems flow into the Bay of Plenty – the Motu, Raukokore and Haparapara/Kereu rivers. On the eastern side, the Awatere to the north and the Waiapu to the south, drain into the Pacific Ocean. The mountains only rise above the thick bush at the peaks of Whanokao and Hikurangi.

The Raukumara Range, in its relatively untouched state, is an important resource for botanists. The diverse vegetation contains some unique forest types, including unusual combinations of alpine plants.

On the lower valley walls, the forest is predominantly podocarp/hardwood, but podocarp/beech is found in the upper valleys. On ridges above 1050 metres, there is mainly beech, and above the bush-line, silver beech. Between 1400 and 1500 metres, unique plant associations of subal-

pine and alpine vegetation are found. This is the northern limit of many of these species.

Wildlife enjoys the sanctuary of the wilderness, and there are fewer predators than elsewhere. Many rare and endangered species are still present in the park – it is possible that the kokako, a rare bird, is still found here, although it has not been recorded for some time. The whio (blue duck) is often seen, especially in the Pakihi Stream in the Urutawa Forest. Other interesting birds include parrots (kaka, red-crowned and yellow-crowned parakeets), the North Island brown kiwi and the New Zealand falcon.

One of the three native species of frog, the primitive *Leiopelma hochstetteri*, is also found in the park, as is the New Zealand land snail *(Schizoglossa novaezelandia)*.

Information

There are a number of DOC offices in the region. Probably the most useful is the Opotiki field centre (☎ (07) 315 6103), on the corner of Elliot and St John Sts. The visitor information centre is in the same building.

Across the road, on the corner, is Dreamers & East-Capers (☎ (07) 315 5557), whose staff give out loads of free advice on a range of adventure activities in the region. They have established a good transport system for trampers and will drop off and pick up at any of the track entrances and exits (obviously it works out far cheaper if there is a large group). They also provide free car storage. Because of the range of tramping options on the cape, telephone to find out the cost.

Maps

There is no Parkmaps sheet for either the Raukumara Forest Park or the Urutawa Forest. The 1:50,000 Topomaps 260 quads Y14 *(Cape Runaway)*, X15 *(Omaio)*, Y15 *(Hikurangi)*, X16 *(Motu)* and Y16 *(Tauwhareparae)* are useful for this region. There is also the small-scale 1:250,000 terrain maps No 5 *(East Cape)*.

The map to use for the Pakihi Stock Route is the 1:50,000 Topomaps 260 quad X16

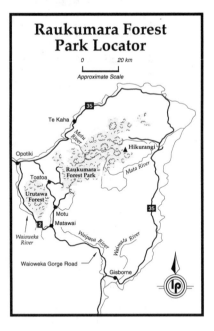

Raukumara Forest Park Locator

(Motu), and for Mt Hikurangi the 1:50,000 Topomaps 260 quad Y15 *(Hikurangi)*.

Huts

Strangely, one of the criteria for the establishment of a wilderness area is the absence of tracks and huts. Fortunately, a number of huts remain in the Raukumara Forest Park. There is one Category Three ($4) hut on the East-West Traverse of the Raukumaras – Oronui. The other huts are Mangakirikiri, one up a side stream on the Mangakirikiri, and Mangatutara; all are free.

On Mt Hikurangi, the Gisborne Canoe & Tramping Club (GC&TC) has a hut – the Hikurangi Hut (☎ (06) 868 4741) – and in the Urutawa Forest, there is one Category Three hut, Te Waiti. The GC&TC phone number may have changed, so check with the DOC in Gisborne or Opotiki. In 1994, it cost $2 per night to use the hut, but this may now be $4, in line with DOC hut fees.

In the Urutawa Forest, there are Category

Four bivouacs (Hastings, Lagoon, Pakihi Heads, Savlon and Tokenui) and three huts (Pakihi, Wahaatua and Manganuku).

Access

The East Cape is not that well serviced for visitors coming from major centres, such as Rotorua and Auckland, so many trampers arrive in their own vehicles. The two closest centres to the East Cape are Opotiki (in the west) and Gisborne (on the eastern side of the ranges). Opotiki and Gisborne can both be reached by InterCity bus. Once in either town, ask at the visitor information centres about how to access the walks.

If you have a conventional car, you will be limited in how close you can get to the start of many of the walks. Additional road walking will probably be necessary.

The Raukumaras can be accessed via Otipi Rd, a 4WD access road to the upper reaches of the Motu River, or via Motu Rd, off Waioeka Gorge Rd. Ruatoria and Tokomaru forests have vehicle access, but you need to obtain permits. Te Kumi-Waikura Rd, west from Hicks Bay, has vehicle access to the Waikura River; the park boundary is five km up, at Raukokore River.

To Opotiki The InterCity bus depot (☎ (07) 315 6450) is on Elliott St. Its buses link Opotiki with Whakatane (one hour), Tauranga (three hours), Rotorua (three hours) and Auckland (7½ hours via Rotorua).

InterCity runs a daily service between Opotiki, Gisborne and Rotorua via Waioeka Gorge (State Highway 2) for $34. It arrives in Opotiki at around 10 am.

At the time of writing, there was a courier bus running from Opotiki up the western coast to Hicks Bay, linking with another service down the eastern side of the cape to Gisborne. These may be useful if you exit a track close to State Highway 35. InterCity is about to trial a scheduled passenger bus around the East Cape, leaving from Opotiki for Gisborne one day, and returning on the same route the next ($68).

Around the Cape The whole of State

Highway 35 around the cape is connected by various local services; these may change, so contact the Opotiki visitor information centre or Dreamers & East-Capers for information.

Fastways (☎ (06) 867 9127) connects Gisborne to Hicks Bay; the cost is $25. From Hicks Bay/Te Araroa, there is a backpackers' special to Opotiki (☎ (07) 315 6350) for $26. The loop is completed by InterCity, which operates round Gisborne-Opotiki-Rotorua each day. This bus goes via Whakatane as well, and reaches Opotiki in time to connect with the service to Hicks Bay (Rotorua to Opotiki costs $39, Rotorua to Gisborne $68).

Hitching around the cape was once notoriously slow because of the lack of passing traffic, though many locals say the hitching situation really isn't that bad. There are regular transport services if you get stuck.

Places to Stay
Opotiki has a number of backpackers' places. Out at Waiotahi Beach, about five minutes west of the town centre, is the *Opotiki Backpackers Beach House* (☎ (07) 315 5117); the $12 beds are in a loft. *Eastland Backpackers* (☎ (07) 315 4870) is at the Waiotahi Estuary, which is well signposted off State Highway 2. It charges $13 per night. There are two places in the centre of town: the *Opotiki Hotel* (☎ (07) 315 6078) in Church St has backpackers' beds for $10; *Central Backpackers* (☎ (07) 315 5165), 30 King St, has beds for $12.

PAKIHI STOCK ROUTE
The 21,750-hectare Urutawa Forest is located 14 km south of Opotiki and five km east of the Waioeka Gorge (State Highway 2). The forest consists of the Pakihi, Te Waiti and Tutaetoke streams, which flow into the Otara River in the north, and the Manganuku Stream, which flows into the Waioeka River in the south. There are a number of interesting tramps in the Urutawa Forest, and these are briefly outlined in information pamphlets available from the DOC.

Access
To get to this walk from Opotiki, turn off onto State Highway 2 on the Waioeka Gorge Rd. From here, it is just over 72 km to Matawai. Just past the post office, take the first left turn, onto the Old Motu Rd. Proceed up the road for 15 km to Whitikau Scenic Reserve. The Pakihi Bench Track access sign is hard to spot, because it is low on the left of the road. There is a car park on the right. There's a ford two km past the access sign, so if you cross this, turn back; the access sign is obvious when you approach from this direction. It's best to set your trip meter from the turn-off to the Old Motu Rd.

If you're coming from Gisborne, take the right turn just before the Matawai post office. Matawai has a pub, a petrol station and basic food supplies.

For transport costs to/from various East Cape tramps, contact Dreamers & East-Capers (see Information and Access in this section).

The Track
This is a good tramp for those people with little time in the area. It's a medium two-day (or difficult one-day) 19-km walk from the drop-off point on the Motu Rd to the finish of the track on Pakihi Rd. The Pakihi Stock Route was once used to get cattle from the Motu region to Opotiki. For some of its length, the track follows the river bed.

Stage 1: Old Motu Road to Pakihi Hut
Walking Time: three hours (nine km)
Accommodation: Pakihi Hut (six bunks)

The benched track starts at the sign, and it is approximately nine km to the hut from this point. The track is not hard to follow because it eases down into the Pakihi Valley by circuiting around the tops of the creek valleys which feed into the main Pakihi Stream. The forest is lush, generally consisting of rimu, tawa and beech.

The first obvious sign indicates the Ashford Spur; this is just over a km from the start of the track. Take the right fork at this

To Opotiki

479 m

592 m

To Opotiki

Wairere Stream

Toatoa

Pakihi Road

Bridge

422 m

707 m

755 m

677 m

680 m

Maunganga
(739 m)

Toatoa
(792 m)

497 m

334 m

Meremere Hill
Scenic Reserve

722 m

Papamoa
(787 m)

600 m

737 m

749 m

Toatoa Scenic
Reserve

P No2
(659 m)

480 m

532 m

Pakihi

600 m

587 m

Whitikau

534 m

707 m

Te Waiti
Stream
Catchment

670 m

472 m

563 m

Stream

403 m

587 m

591 m

407 m

552 m

To Te Waiti
Stream

605 m

445 m

Pakihi
Hut

600 m

670 m

Ford

471 m

316 m

507 m

Motu

844 m

456 m

526 m

409 m

539 m

625 m

To Motu &
Matawai

570 m

612 m

Pakihi
(297 m)

Road

714 m

Waihaitua Stream

Urutawa
(797 m)

674 m

**Pakihi Stock Route:
Urutawa Forest**

318 m
Wahaatua Hut

0   1   2 km

point and continue to sidle around the tops of the valleys and contour around the spurs.

It is hard to get lost until a junction some 200 metres from the hut. Just before this junction, there is an old slip which offers glimpses of the river 100 metres below. From the slip, it is 10 minutes to a not-so-prominent fork in the path. Take the left fork, a zigzag track, and it's a short drop to the hut.

The hut is on the bench above the river and has bunk space, a pit toilet and adequate water. It is not clean, but there are plans to upgrade it because this route has become attractive to hard-core mountain bikers. The hut does, however, have an inspiring view down the Pakihi Stream, which is heavily forested on both banks. You are not required to pay any fees, because this is a Category Four hut. The small triangular huts scattered around are for deer-stalkers' dogs or desperate bed-less trampers.

Stage 2: Pakihi Hut to Pakihi Rd
Walking Time: three hours

The track down to Pakihi Stream is on the true right bank, close to the hut. When you reach the Pakihi, turn right and follow it downstream.

Pakihi Stream is usually a gentle, braided stream, but beware in rain because it can fill quickly and there are sections of the river walk that are enclosed by steep gorges. If the first incoming tributary of the stream is discoloured a muddy brown, reconsider going any further. If necessary, return to the Pakihi Hut and wait for the stream to subside, or head back up to the Motu Rd (about four hours uphill from the hut).

The river section takes about 1½ hours. Use the dry, shingle fans as much as possible, crossing the stream when the shingle banks (actually composed of Waioeka shale) peter out. Several tributary streams come in on both the right and the left.

There is a huge log jam just before a prominent bend in the river. Shortly after this, you round the corner to find a large slip on the true left-hand bank. Track work is still in progress on the bank, so in future you may be able to exit the river before the slip.

The track starts immediately after the slip. Climb up about five metres out of the river to reach the track. The dry, four-km amble to the track end is pleasant walking, and the track hugs the bank well above the river. Keep your eye on the stream on your right and you may see a brace of the rare whio (blue duck) or herds of not-so-rare feral goats.

The track ends at the Pakihi Rd, where a swing bridge crosses to a farm on the true right (east) bank. This is where you should have arranged to meet transport.

EAST-WEST TRAVERSE

The East-West Traverse, one of the most challenging traverses of any mountain range in New Zealand, requires impeccable navigational skills, good bush knowledge and a high sense of adventure. This extremely difficult five-day walk has been included to show you one of the hard tramping possibilities in this wilderness region. It would be foolhardy to do this tramp without adequate preparation, and it's essential to make use of local knowledge (going with locals who

Tattooed Maori

have done it before is a good idea). These route notes merely let you know what you are in for and should not be used as a guide.

The routes were used long before the coming of the Pakeha. The forest in the Raukumara is ancient, untouched and full of spiritual meaning. Warriors heading off to war left their mana in the care of huge rata trees, and it was collected on their return passage. If the warriors were killed, the trees took on significance as memorials to the fallen.

In 1993, the Ngati Porou and the Apanui, iwi of different coasts, traversed the Raukumara in a symbolic gesture of goodwill between once-deadly foes. Their journey was made without a compass – the ancient chants tell of the route through the apparently impenetrable bush.

Access

To get permission to use the Wainui Rd and Puketoetoe Track to reach the start of the route, contact the Maori owners of the land in writing (Torere Forestry Block 64 Inc, RD1 Omaramutu, Opotiki). Once the owners

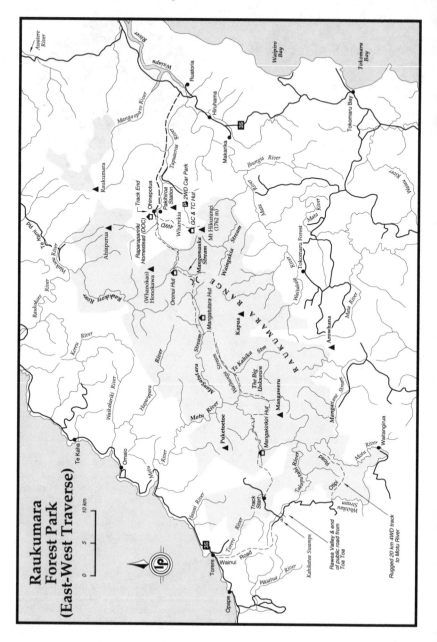

Raukumara
Forest Park
(East-West Traverse)

have given permission, you must approach PF Olsens Ltd (☎ (07) 315 7768), who manage the forestry blocks, to get a key for the gates. Dreamers & East-Capers can arrange permission for any trampers using its transport services or guides. If the owners refuse access (this is possible during peak hunting periods or during forestry operations), you can access the route via the 20-km 4WD track, the Otipi Rd.

Trampers will also need to ring the Pakihiroa Station (☎ (06) 864 0962), on the eastern side of the cape, to let the owners know that, at the eastern end of the traverse, you will be passing through their land.

The station is 130 km north of Gisborne via State Highway 35. Three km north of Ruatoria, there is a signposted turn-off to the station. Follow the gravel road past a turn-off to Raparapariki Homestead. Not far down the road (100 metres), turn south and cross the Tapuaeroa River to Pakihiroa Station. There are two fords along this road, so at times it may not be suitable for anything but 4WDs.

The Route

The East-West Traverse is probably about 60 km long, although no-one has been silly enough to take a pedometer in to measure it. It takes a good five days, but there are huts at three of the four overnight stops (assuming you find them). Trampers should allow for an extra day on the route, preferably at the scenic Mangakirikiri Hut, to allow for difficult weather or flooded rivers. The walk is rated extremely difficult because of the need for dead accurate navigation and because of the rugged terrain.

If you asked an experienced Kiwi tramper to describe one of his or her favourite tramps, it would be something like this. The route is no Milford or Routeburn, but it probably represents a 'tramp' in the truest sense of the word.

Stage 1: Opotiki to Mangakirikiri Hut

Walking Time: four to five hours
Accommodation: Mangakirikiri Hut

From Opotiki, head up the coast towards Torere Bay. Take the Wainui Forestry Rd (get the latest details from the DOC in Opotiki), which rises some 700 metres above the coast, providing spectacular views. Once inland, proceed along the Rawea Valley to Kahikatea Swamps.

Turn off this road and follow a bulldozed road (signposted by the forestry company) known as the Puketoetoe Track. This heads east, following a high ridge system; the coast and the headwaters of the Torere River are to the north and the Motu River is to the south. The drive to the start of the route takes about two to three hours.

The walk starts at a low (marked) saddle point on the Puketoetoe Track. Turn off to the south-west on a benched route that heads down into the Mangamate Stream. This is the start of a catchment which runs into the Mangakirikiri and, ultimately, all the way to the Motu River.

Mangakirikiri Stream is passable, although it has two gorges which you have to wade in waist-deep water. There are routes around both gorges, sparsely marked with red tape. At the Mangakirikiri-Motu River junction, you'll find a good ex-Forestry hut on a high bench, about 15 metres above the stream. This comfortable hut is used by river rafters and kayakers. It is also the site of Maori gardens and an old settlement.

There is another hut tucked up a side stream about halfway down the Mangakirikiri Stream, but you would have to be a magician to find it.

Stage 2: Mangakirikiri Hut to Te Kahika

Walking Time: seven to nine hours
Accommodation: camping only, Irishmens Flat

On the second day, you have to travel about seven km down the Motu River itself. Fortunately, at this central part of the Motu, it is a broad river with big bends, wide, spread-out river crossings and timbered banks.

Tramp down the Motu, crossing it a dozen or so times, until it plunges into the first of the gorges. Immediately before the gorge, a stream comes in from the south on the true right side of the river. It is a small stream choked in toetoe and flax; leave the Motu River and travel up this stream for about an hour.

If the weather permits, you will see a small dip ahead, an obvious saddle heading east. Climb over this to the other side; in front of you is an enormous, eroded slip. Climb down the slip into a stream at the bottom called, appropriately, the Big Unknown. Follow the Big Unknown downstream until you strike Te Kahika Stream, coming in on the true left side.

Turn up Te Kahika Stream and follow it for about half an hour. It opens into a large valley edged with flax, toetoe and kanuka. Head to the forks; the Te Kahika comes in from the south-west and the Waihunga Stream continues straight ahead (north-west). There was once a hut at these forks, an area known as Irishmens Flat, but it was destroyed by a landslide. Expect to spend a good day getting to this point.

Stage 3: Te Kahika to Mangatutara Hut
Walking Time: six to seven hours
Accommodation: Mangatutara Hut

Enter Waihunga Stream and follow it upstream for at least half a day. Eventually the stream starts to close in and gets choked with boulders. At one point, you have to sidle around a small lake which has been formed by a slip. If weather permits, search out the low dip on the skyline – you have to get through this to drop down to a tributary of Mangatutara Stream on the other side.

There is an old Maori trail here, a half-metre-wide, worn path about 30 cm deep which drops into the stream at the right point. Look ahead when you're in the stream, because there are white sight markers on the trees; get to one marker, then look ahead to ascertain where the next one is.

Once in the Mangatutara catchment, the broken, rocky country of the Te Kahika is left behind and you enter large-tree country – matai, miro and enormous rata. The wide, open flats of the Mangatutara have popula-

tions of wild cattle; give these a wide berth. There are also deer, pigs and, if you're lucky, the rare whio (blue duck). You should be here by 3 or 4 pm on the third day of tramping.

The well set-up, six-bunk forestry hut has an open fireplace. It's situated on the true left-hand bank of the Mangatutara. Slightly above the hut, on the true right, is a stream which drains tiny Lake Mangatutara.

Stage 4: Mangatutara Hut to Oronui Hut
Walking Time: six to seven hours
Accommodation: Oronui Hut

Set off up Mangatutara Stream. The going is easy for the first two hours but progressively gets harder, though the beauty of the moss-covered rocks in the stream bed and the massive trees to each side compensates for the difficulty of the tramp.

Once in the headwaters of the Manga-tutara, about five hours from the hut, there is a marked spur route, via a 790-metre knob, to a saddle; it takes you over into the Mangamauku catchment, which drains via the Waiapu River to the eastern coast. All the rivers and streams prior to this, drain in a westerly direction to empty into the Bay of

Plenty. The spur route, a well-worn Maori trail, winds through forests of big trees.

To the north are huge rock-tipped peaks, devoid of vegetation – the slopes of Whanokao – reminiscent of those seen in the Coromandel. Drop down the Mangamauku Stream for between half and one hour, until you come to a major stream junction. Right at the junction, about 15 metres above the stream, is the Oronui Hut.

Stage 5: Oronui Hut to Pakihiroa Station
Walking Time: six to seven hours

The route follows the Oronui Gorge downstream. Once you would have been up to your neck in water, but the gorge has recently filled with shingle and is now waist deep. There is much boulder-hopping until you come to an open area, where, if you look straight ahead, you will see slopes rising towards Hikurangi.

You can climb Hikurangi from this point by continuing straight ahead. If you don't want to head for Hikurangi's summit, continue down the Oronui to where it meets the Tapuaeroa River. Keep following the river to Pakihiroa Station, which is on private, Maori land. Phone from there for transport; the owners are used to people coming through (you must, however, have informed them, prior to leaving Opotiki, that you will be passing through their station).

OTHER TRACKS
Mt Hikurangi Summit
Hikurangi (1752 metres) would be the most popular tramp in the Raukumara Forest Park. Access to this sacred peak is via State Highway 35 from Ruatoria, then through private Ngati Porou land (Pakihiroa Station, ☎ (06) 864 0962) from the Tapuaeroa Valley. The Gisborne Canoe & Tramping Club hut (☎ (06) 868 4741 for permission to use the hut) is about 3½ hours from the road, at 1200 metres. The final part of the climb to the hut is steep.

The walk from the hut to the summit takes about two hours, passing through grass-covered scree, silver beech forest and tussock slopes. The last part of the climb to the summit trig can be tricky, especially the small rocky chute and the final ridge crest. If you are in a group, stick together in the chute so that the chances of being hit by a rock are reduced. Be careful on the steep descent – the tussock slopes can be dangerous.

The summit of Hikurangi is the first place in New Zealand to feel the sun's rays, and if you happen to be on top early on the morning of 1 January, you will be among the first witnesses in the world to the New Year's sunrise ('among', because there will be many other witnesses as well).

Waioeka River Track
This is a medium to hard four-day tramp through the Waioeka Gorge Scenic Reserve, at the base of East Cape. The Waioeka Forest comprises about 40,000 hectares of the headwaters of the Waioweka River; the 1800-hectare scenic reserve is to the east of the forest. The track passes through river flats, gorges and bush, with good fly fishing along the way. There are three Category Three huts available but none has cooking facilities. The reserve is bisected by State Highway 2, which connects Poverty Bay to the Bay of Plenty; access is from State Highway 2 at Moanui or Matawai. For more information, contact the DOC Opotiki field centre (☎ (07) 315 6103).

Te Urewera National Park

Te Urewera National Park has rugged terrain, beautiful lakes and crystal-clear trout streams, but it is the trees and the magnificent forests in the park which set this wilderness apart and capture the imagination of those passing through.

The main access road through Te Urewera is State Highway 38, which connects Rotorua to Wairoa on the eastern coast. The predominantly metalled road curves and winds its way through the park's mountainous interior and then around the eastern shore of Lake Waikaremoana ('sea of rippling waters'), which is bordered to the south by the towering Panekiri Bluff.

Geologists believe the 55-sq-km lake was formed 2200 years ago when an earthquake caused a huge landslide to dam the Waikaretaheke River. Today, Waikaremoana is by far the most popular section of the national park, especially with boaters, and is the centrepiece for Te Urewera's most scenic and popular tramp, best known as the Lake Track. The four to five-day walk rings the shoreline, and begins and ends near State Highway 38.

The northern portion of the park, above State Highway 38, is much more remote and is characterised by the long valleys of the Whakatane, Waimana and Rangitaiki rivers, all of which flow into the Bay of Plenty. Bordering Te Urewera to the west is Whirinaki Forest Park, a 60,900-hectare preserve surrounding the Whirinaki River.

HISTORY

Maori legends say that human settlement in Te Urewera began when Hine-Pokohu-Rangi, the Mist Maiden, married Te Maunga, a mountain, producing 'the Children of Mist', the fierce Tuhoe tribe. Genealogical evidence points to the arrival of the Tuhoe in 1350 AD, when the epic Maori migration landed on the North Island. One canoe, the *Mataatua*, arrived at the mouth of the Whakatane River, and its occupants quickly moved up into the hinterlands. The Tuhoe tribe evolved into fierce warriors, hardened by a difficult life, and they resisted European invasion and influence long after other areas of the country were settled and tamed.

The Tuhoe settled the rugged interior of Te Urewera, but not Lake Waikaremoana. That was home to another coastal tribe, Ngati Ruapani, who believed the lake was formed when one of their ancestors, Mahu, became enraged by his daughter's refusal to fetch some water from a sacred well. The father grabbed the girl and held her in a spring until she drowned. But only her body died; her spirit was turned into a *taniwha* (water monster) that desperately tried to escape.

First the taniwha thrust north and formed the Whanganui Arm, before the Huiarau Range stopped her. Then she formed the Whanganui-o-Parua Arm, before attempting to escape from the lake's mouth near Onepoto. Time ran out when dawn arrived, and the sunlight – fatal to all taniwhas – turned her to stone. The Ngati Ruapani identified her as a rock near the outlet of the lake.

The Tuhoe closely guarded Te Urewera's isolation, clinging to a natural suspicion of Europeans. Missionaries became the first Pakehas to explore the area when Reverend William Williams travelled through the region in November 1840 and came across Lake Waikaremoana. But the Tuhoe continued to resist any intrusion, eventually joining several other tribes in the 1860s to war against government troops.

They had just suffered a severe defeat when, in 1868, Tuhoe destiny took a strange turn. In that year, Te Kooti, the charismatic Maori leader, escaped from a Chatham Island prison and sought refuge in Te Urewera. Te Kooti and the tribe formed a pact that led to a running battle with government troops for more than three years. The soldiers applied a scorched earth policy in an effort to eliminate Tuhoe food supplies and flush the tribe from the woods.

Te Kooti used his unique military manoeuvres to score victories and to stage successful raids on towns, including Rotorua. But the Tuhoe, with their limited resources, were no match for the government troops. Te Kooti escaped narrowly several times, helped once by a premature gunshot that warned him off. By 1871, disease and starvation had overtaken the tribe and eroded its morale. The Tuhoe finally ended their involvement in the Land War by agreeing to swear allegiance to the Crown. Te Kooti, however, refused, and the rebel leader escaped once more to King Country.

The Tuhoe continued to distrust Pakeha, and in the early 1900s turned to another self-acclaimed prophet, Rua Kenana, who founded the isolated farming settlement of Maungapohatu. The tribe met the government surveyors and construction workers who were trying to build a road through Te Urewera with open hostility. The massive undertaking continued only after the Tuhoe were convinced that such a road would bring trade and agricultural benefits to them. Troops were still needed to protect government workers, and the road was not completed until 1930.

The idea of preserving the forest as a watershed was first promoted in 1925. After WW II, support for turning the area into a national park grew rapidly. In early 1954, the Tuhoe approved the name Urewera National Park at a meeting in Ruatahuna, and the new park was officially gazetted later that year.

CLIMATE

Because of the mountainous nature of the area, trampers can expect a considerably higher rainfall than in either the Rotorua or Gisborne regions, to the west and east. The yearly rainfall of 2500 mm is brought on north-westerly and southerly winds, and in winter can turn to snow in the higher altitudes. Fog and early morning mist are common characteristics of the area in the lower valleys, but usually burn off by midday. During the summer, trampers can generally expect regular spells of fine, dry weather, with temperatures rising to 21°C or even higher during February, the warmest month.

NATURAL HISTORY

The 212,672-hectare Te Urewera National Park is the fourth largest national park in New Zealand and the largest untouched native forest in the North Island. It is a rugged land which rises up to 1400 metres, and it forms part of the mountainous spine that stretches from the East Cape to Wellington. The forests of Te Urewera form a thick blanket over the mountains, so there are hardly any open peaks or ridges.

The lake was formed by a landslide which dammed the Waikaretaheke River about 2200 years ago. The lake filled up behind the landslide to a maximum depth of 248 metres. It was lowered five metres in 1946 by a hydroelectric development.

There is a diverse selection of trees in the forests of the park, ranging from the tall and lush podocarp and tawa forest in the river valleys to the stunted, moss-covered beech in the higher ranges. The major change in forest composition occurs at 800 metres, when the bush of rimu, northern rata and tawa is replaced by beech and rimu. Above 900 metres, only beech species are usually found. It is estimated that there are 650 types of native plant present in the park.

Te Urewera's rivers and lakes offer some of New Zealand's finest rainbow trout fishing. There is good fly fishing for brown trout from the shore on the Lake Track. Fishing with both fly and spinning gear is allowed in most areas, but you must have a licence for the Rotorua Fishing District.

LAKE WAIKAREMOANA TRACK

Built in 1962 as a volunteer project by boys from 14 secondary schools, the 46-km Lake Waikaremoana Track is one of the most popular walks in the North Island. Highlights include spectacular views from Panekiri Bluff, numerous beaches and swimming holes, excellent trout fishing and opportunities to hire sea kayaks.

All this makes for a popular and sometimes crowded walk at Easter and during the period from mid-December to the end of January. It's not a bad idea to carry a tent, if you have access to one, during these perods. A DOC report indicates that 4500 trampers tackled this track in 1992.

Information

Te Urewera National Park has two field centres. There's one near Murupara (Te Ikawhenua) and another within the park itself, at Waikaremoana, on the shores of the lake at Aniwaniwa (☎ (06) 837 3803). The latter is the park headquarters and visitor information centre. It has information on walking tracks, camp sites and huts in the park, and has interesting displays. It's open during the summer from 8 am until noon and from 1 to 5 pm daily.

If you are travelling from Rotorua, you can stop at the Te Ikawhenua field centre

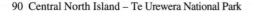

(☎ (07) 366 5641), two km east of Murupara on State Highway 38. The centre is open from 8 am to 5 pm daily in summer and at the same times on weekdays throughout the rest of the year. The field centre in Gisborne also has information on the park.

Maps

The best and cheapest map to use is the Parkmaps 1:100,000 No 170 (Urewera); it sells for $11. Otherwise, you will need to purchase Topomaps 260 quads W17 (Urewera) and W18 (Waikaremoana) to cover the walk. These cost $12.50 each.

Huts

Hut fees ($6 per night) and camping fees (also $6 per night) on this Great Walk are payable at the park headquarters at Aniwaniwa, or you can post them to Te Urewera National Park, Private Bag 213, Wairoa. The Marauti, Panekiri, Te Puna, Waiopaoa and Whanganui huts are all on the Great Walk; all other huts are Category Three ($4) or are free; there are over 40 of them.

Access

Both ends of the track are within easy walking distance of State Highway 38. The northern end is near Hopuruahine Landing, 15 km north-west of the park headquarters at Aniwaniwa. The southern end is at Onepoto, nine km south of the park headquarters.

InterCity buses make the five-hour trip between Rotorua and Wairoa on Monday, Wednesday and Friday, departing from the Waikaremoana Camp store for Rotorua at 9.05 am, and for Wairoa at 5.30 pm. The Waikaremoana Shuttle service (☎ (06) 837 3836) operates from Tuai, stopping at Twin Lakes store, Onepoto, the motor camp, the visitor information centre, Mokau landing, and Hopuruahine camp and bridge – twice daily except Wednesday and Thursday (on Thursday it runs in the morning only, because it does a return run to Wairoa). The cost from Tuai to Wairoa is $10, from Wairoa to Hopuruahine Bridge $20, from Tuai to the bridge $10 and from Tuai to the visitor information centre $9.

In the summer months, a launch ferry service runs from the Waikaremoana Motor Camp and will take you to any point along the track. It operates on a demand basis and costs $15.

Most of the 120-km stretch of State Highway 38 through the park, between the Onuka Rd (past Frasertown) and the town of Murupara, is on unsealed, winding, extremely scenic and beautiful road, so it's very time consuming. There is very little traffic on this route, making it a slow go for hitching. If you're taking the bus out of the park, it's a good idea to show up at least 15 to 20 minutes early, because the schedule is not always rigidly adhered to.

Car parking is available at Onepoto and Home Bay; there is a small fee at the latter. Be warned, however, that the DOC takes no responsibility for damage to cars in these parks.

Places to Stay

There are various camps and cabins spaced along State Highway 38, including a camp, cabins and motel 67 km inland from the Wairoa turn-off. There are several huts along the walking tracks, costing $6 per night ($3 for children). The DOC also maintains a

Great Walks Ticket

number of minimal-facility camp sites around Lake Waikaremoana; it costs only $2 to camp at these.

On the shore of Lake Waikaremoana, the *Waikaremoana Motor Camp* (☎ (06) 837 3826) has camp sites ($6.50 per person) and 12 cabins ($27 for two). At Tuai, just outside the southern entrance to the park, there is the *Tuai Lodge* and a *motor camp*.

The Track

The Lake Waikaremoana Track is 46 km long and is rated easy – the only difficult section is the climb over Panekiri Ridge. There are five huts spaced along the route but most walkers take only three to four days to complete the trip. The track can be hiked in either direction, although by starting out from Onepoto (as described here), you put all the steep climbing behind you in the first few hours. Walking in the opposite direction, you'll need an extra hour from Waiopaoa Hut to Panekiri and will take less time from Panekiri to the end of the trail, at Onepoto.

Stage 1: Onepoto to Panekiri Hut
Walking Time: five hours
Accommodation: Panekiri Hut (36 bunks)

The beginning of the track is signposted half a km from State Highway 38, next to the day shelter (where there is track information). Before embarking on the walk, make sure you fill your water bottle, because there is no water available along this first leg of the journey. You can look around the former Armed Constabulary Redoubt and Lake Kiriopukae before starting the walk proper.

There is little time to warm up at this end of the track because it immediately begins a steep climb up the sandstone cliffs of Panekiri Bluff. Plan on 2½ to three hours to ascend 532 metres over four km to Pukenui Trig, one of the highest points of the trip, at 1180 metres. Once at the trig, you begin the second half of the day's walk, following the track along an undulating ridge of many knobs and knolls from which you get spectacular views of Lake Waikaremoana, some 600 metres below.

Continue along the ridge through mixed beech forest for almost four km, until you suddenly break out at a sheer rock bluff which seems to bar the way. Closer inspection reveals a staircase and wire up the bluff where the bush has been cleared.

Panekiri Hut is another 100 metres beyond, at Puketapu Trig. At an elevation of 1180 metres and only 10 metres from the edge of the bluff, this hut offers the park's best panoramas, which include most of the lake, Huiarau Range and, at times, the eastern coast town of Wairoa. A rainwater tank is the sole source of water at the hut. Gas stoves are provided; the wood stove is for heat only. Camping is prohibited atop Panekiri Bluff, due to the vulnerability of the vegetation.

Stage 2: Panekiri Hut to Waiopaoa Hut
Walking Time: three to four hours
Accommodation: Waiopaoa Hut (18 bunks)

Continue south-west and follow the main ridge for three km, gradually descending around bluffs and rock gullies until the track takes a sharp right-hand swing to the north-west. If the weather is good, there will be panoramas of the lake and forest. At this point, the gradual descent becomes a steep one – the track heads off the ridge towards the Wairaumoana Arm of the lake, and at one section drops 250 metres in about a km. Slippery tree roots can be a problem on this section.

On the way down, there is an interesting change in the vegetation as the forest moves from the beech of the high country to tawa and podocarp with a thick understorey of ferns. The grade becomes more gentle as you approach the lake, and eventually you arrive at the Waiopaoa Hut and camp site, situated near the shoreline. The hut has a wood stove and tank water and is a five-minute stroll from a sandy bay where there are good places for fishing and swimming.

Stage 3: Waiopaoa Hut to Te Puna Hut
Walking Time: four to five hours to Marauiti Bay; six to seven hours to Te Puna
Accommodation: Marauiti Hut (32 bunks); Te Puna Hut (18 bunks)

Start this day early because there are many places to linger and whittle away the afternoon. The track turns inland from Waiopaoa Hut to cross Waitehetehe Stream and then follows the lake shore across grassy flats and terraces of kanuka scrub. In the first hour, you'll encounter a number of unbridged streams which should be easy to ford at normal water levels. If the lake is high, however, you might have to hike up the creeks to cross them.

The signposted junction to Korokoro Falls is 2½ km from the hut, an hour's walk for most trampers, and makes for a scenic diversion. It's 15 minutes one-way to the falls, which drop 20 metres over a sheer rock face, one of the most impressive displays of cascading water in the park. There is a small camp site 200 metres past the swing bridge. The main track continues around the lake, climbing 50 metres above the shore and sidling along a number of small sheltered bays accessible only by bushwhacking.

The track rounds Te Kotoreotaunoa Point and then drops into Maraunui Bay, three km from the junction to Korokoro Falls. It's a 30 to 40-minute walk along the southern shore of the bay to Te Wharau Stream, a popular fishing spot which has a small camp site. Along the way, you pass a Maori reserve and private huts. From here, the track climbs over a low saddle and, in a km, dips to Marauiti Bay, passing the 200-metre side track to the hut on the lake shore.

Continuing around the lake, the track swings north-east, and half an hour from Marauiti Hut, you arrive at Te Kopua Bay, which has white, sandy beaches. This is one of the most isolated bays on the lake and its protected waters are favoured by anglers. There are plenty of camp sites for those carrying a tent,

The track leaves the bay and climbs away from the lake to cross Te Kopua headland, before returning to the lake shore. Halfway to Te Puna Hut, the track passes Patekaha Island, no longer a true island, and the shoreline is dotted with a number of small, sandy beaches. It's three km from the island to Te Puna Hut, but trampers often reduce that distance at the end of the stage by cutting straight across the mud and grassy flats in front of the hut. Campers can pitch a tent at Waiharuru Camp Site, about 1½ km before the hut.

Stage 4: Te Puna Hut to Hopuruahine Landing
Walking Time: four to five hours
Accommodation: Whanganui Hut (18 bunks)

The track leaves the back of the hut and climbs over a saddle to meet the lake shore again at Tapuaenui Inlet, in the lake's Whanganui Arm, an hour's walk from Te Puna. There's a small camp site here. For the next hour, you follow the shoreline (with a short diversion up Tapuaenui Stream), until it reaches the 18-bunk Whanganui Hut and camp site, situated on a grassy flat between two streams, a short way from a nice beach.

The last leg of the trip begins with a scenic walk around the lake shore and through a short section of bush to the Waihoroihika Stream bridge. Once across the bridge, the track continues up through the grassy flats

on the north-western side of the Hopuruahine River to a point opposite the access road. A signposted spot on the river shows where to ford. It's usually an easy crossing, but if the river is swollen, use the escape route up the true right (west) side of the river to the concrete road bridge at State Highway 38, an additional half-hour walk.

Camping is allowed along the access road, and there are usually a few tents and trailers among the grassy sites, because the Hopuruahine River and its mouth are popular fishing spots. It's a one-km walk up the gravel access road to reach State Highway 38, but the shuttle bus picks up from both the camp site and the bridge.

WHAKATANE-WAIKARE RIVER LOOP
The Whakatane River walk is a four to five-day trip from the end of an access road off State Highway 38, north of Ruatahuna, to another access road near Ruatoki. If you want to complete the loop, once you've walked the Whakatane River Track as far as Waikare Junction Hut, head south-east along the Waikare River to return to Tawhiwhi Hut, on the Whakatane River.

The traditional Whakatane River route, an historic one for the Maoris, is along – and often through – the river; there is almost no climbing. The DOC has built an all-weather track that sidles the Whakatane and allows trampers to avoid any dangerous fords. Climbing is only necessary to avoid sharp bends in the river, and the tramp is not a difficult one. The track is well cut and formed, with bridges crossing major streams.

There are six huts along the Whakatane-Waikare loop track outlined here. Although they are considerably smaller than those on the Lake Track, the walk is not nearly as popular, so obtaining a bed in these huts is often easier. Carry a cooker and some extra food in case a swollen Waikare River holds you up for a day.

Information
There is a DOC field base (☎ (07) 366 5392) in Ruatahuna, about 100 metres east of the

store, where you can register your intentions, pay the hut fees and receive the latest information on track and river conditions. The office is open from 8 am to 4.30 pm on weekdays.

Maps

The 1:50,000 Topomaps 260 quad W17 *(Urewera)* covers the loop trip; if you are hiking the traditional route through to Ruatoki, you will also need quad W16 *(Waimana)*. Many trampers, however, content themselves with the 1:100,000 Parkmaps No 170 *(Urewera National Park)*. The *Whakatane River Guide* (1980), though a little dated, contains heaps of track and river route notes.

Huts

There are seven huts on the walk – Waikare Junction, Ohane, Waikare Whenua, Takarua, Tawhiwhi, Ngahiramai and Hanamahihi. All the huts are Category Three ($4), but none has cooking facilities.

Access

Ruatahuna, the departure point for this trip, can be reached by InterCity bus from Wairoa, Murupara or Rotorua on Monday, Wednesday and Friday. On these days, the bus arrives in Ruatahuna from Wairoa at 10.20 am and from Rotorua at 4.05 pm. The bus stop is at Ruatahuna Motel Store, the heart of the small village. Food, gas and other supplies can be obtained here, and you can arrange transport to the track.

From the store and State Highway 38, it's an 11-km trip to the end of the access road, where the track begins. You can walk it in two hours, or arrange for a lift with a local for about $30 to $35 per vehicle load. Hitching along the road is tough, because there is very little traffic.

Trout fishing is a highlight along the Whakatane-Waikare Loop Track, especially on the Waikare River, but bring all your gear because there is none available in Ruatahuna.

The Track

The route can be hiked in either direction, but if you follow the Whakatane River first, you can avoid a night at Waikare Whenua Hut, a less-than-desirable place to stay. The section from the road's end to Waikare Junction is rated medium, and the following description applies only to the all-weather track, or 'walking track' as it is called on signposts along the way. If the water levels are normal, and you don't mind getting your boots wet, you can follow the river route and save a bit of time, but the walking track is not that much longer and the views from above the river are worth the extra climbing.

The stretch along the Waikare River back to Tawhiwhi Hut is rated medium to difficult because two days of this trip are along rivers and streams where there is no formed track.

Stage 1: Road End to Tawhiwhi Hut

Walking Time: five hours from State Highway 38; three hours from road's end
Accommodation: Tawhiwhi Hut (18 bunks)

The access road off State Highway 38 is marked with a large display of the Whakatane Track system and ends at a farm gate with a small 'track' sign on it. The track swings west and quickly emerges high above the Whakatane River. It sidles the valley for three km, until you come to a split in the track. A 'Walking Track' sign points the way to the all-weather route, while the other track leads down to the river route along the Whakatane near Paripari Flat.

After 20 minutes, the track descends quickly and crosses Te Mania Flat, then Mahakirua Stream. From here, it continues to follow the valley for the next four km above the river's true right (east) side, but occasionally drops close to the river, where it is joined by the river route. Keep an eye out for white metal tags when confronted with a choice of tracks. Along the way, you'll pass Ohaua, recognisable by the old Maori tribal house on the true left side of the river. You will see the meeting hall from the track, but to view it up close requires fording the

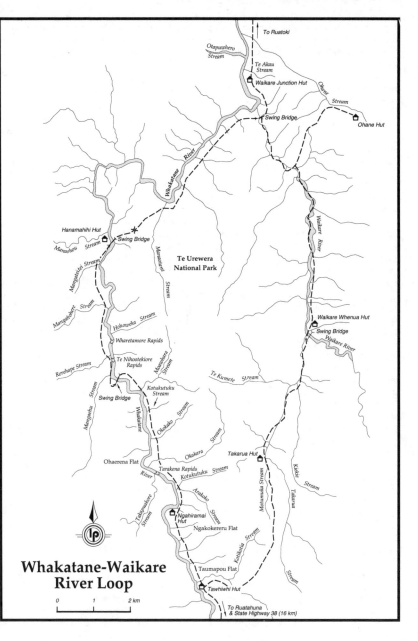

To Ruatoki

Otapuwhero Stream

Te Akau Stream

Waikare Junction Hut

Ohane Stream

Swing Bridge

Ohane Hut

Whakatane River

Hanamahihi Hut

Swing Bridge

Manaohou Stream

Mangatdehe Stream

Mamahare Stream

Te Urewera National Park

Mangakakere Stream

Hohoweka Stream

Waikare River

Wharetamore Rapids

Waikare Whenua Hut

Rerehape Stream

Te Nihootekiore Rapids

Swing Bridge

Moumouru Stream

Waikare River

Mangaehu Stream

Swing Bridge

Kotukutuku Stream

Whakatane

Okakako Stream

Te Kumete Stream

Okakara Stream

Ohaerena Flat

Tarakena Rapids

Takarua Hut

River

Kotukutuku Stream

Takapukore Stream

Arakoko Stream

Motumuka Stream

Kekie Stream

Ngahiramai Hut

Takarua

Ngakokereru Flat

Kotiharia Stream

Taumapou Flat

Stream

Tawhiwhi Hut

To Ruatahuna & State Highway 38 (16 km)

Whakatane-Waikare River Loop

0   1   2 km

river three to four km before reaching Tawhiwhi Hut.

At Manangatiuhi Stream, you pass the junction with a track heading south-east to the six-bunk Waiawa Hut (4½ hours); the main track crosses the stream on a wirewalk. From the stream, Tawhiwhi Hut is just half an hour away, in the middle of Taumapou Flat. It's a good place to spend the first night.

Stage 2: Tawhiwhi Hut to Hanamahihi Hut
Walking Time: one hour to Ngahiramai; 3½ to four hours to Hanamahihi
Accommodation: Ngahiramai Hut (eight bunks); Hanamahihi Hut (eight bunks)

Once across Taumapou Flat and Mangatawhero Stream, the track re-enters the forest, and in 10 to 15 minutes you actually enter Te Urewera National Park for the first time, although there is no signposted border. Up to this point, the track has been crossing private Maori land, with restrictions on camping and hunting. The track remains level and in 45 minutes to an hour breaks out into the small clearing where Ngahiramai Hut (eight bunks) is located.

From the one-room hut, the track continues to follow the true right bank of the river, and there are often good views of the Whakatane below. The Tarakena Rapids are passed half an hour beyond Ngahiramai Hut, just before the track descends into Ohaerena Flat. Beyond the flats, the track crosses two major streams; the second is Moawhara Stream. From Moawhara Stream the track climbs to a swing bridge across the Whakatane River.

For the first time, the track follows the true left side of the river (west bank), and immediately drops to the river, once to cross Mangaehu Stream and a second time to cross Rerehape Stream. It then climbs a terrace and emerges at Hanamahihi Flats, re-entering Maori land.

It's six km from the swing bridge to Hanamahihi Hut, with the last two km an up-and-down walk in bush before you emerge at a small, grassy flat. The one-room hut has eight bunks and a wood-burning stove. It also has a verandah that overlooks a scenic bend in the Whakatane River.

Stage 3: Hanamahihi Hut to Waikare Junction Hut
Walking Time: three hours
Accommodation: Waikare Junction Hut (eight bunks)

To continue along the all-weather track, cross the swing bridge in front of the hut, then follow the track as it begins a steep climb towards a saddle. The ascent levels off briefly on top, and then descends rapidly on the other side. An hour or so from the hut, you should return to the Whakatane River.

Once on the river, the track follows the true right side for 4½ km, until it reaches the bridge over the Waikare River. The valley is steep in many places, so there is quite a bit of climbing to do. In some places, it cuts through grassy terraces, where it might be difficult to see the track, although the route is well marked with white metal tags.

If the weather is good and water levels are normal, an easier and more pleasant route is to drop to the Whakatane once you have crossed the saddle. By following and fording the river at appropriate places, you will avoid the bluffs and still arrive at the junction of the Whakatane and Waikare rivers, where a sign points the way back up the bank to the swing bridge.

Near the bridge is a sign explaining that the Waikare Junction Hut has been shifted and is now 25 minutes away on the all-weather track. The 25 minutes is a little misleading; in fact, it may be the most misleading track sign in New Zealand. Once over the swing bridge, you begin a very steep climb as the track ascends around the bluff at the confluence of the two rivers. This is a knee-bending, two-rest climb, and most people need 40 minutes to an hour to reach the hut. The only consolation is an immense view of the upper Whakatane Valley.

The track drops quickly from the top, crosses a terrace (do not drop back down to

Top: Nature Walk, West Coast, North Island (NZTB)
Middle: Trampers Hut, Onuku, Canterbury (JW)
Bottom: Cape Reinga, Northland (JW)

Top: Rainbow Trout caught along Kepler Track, Fiordland NP (JD)
Bottom Left: Pakihi Hut, Pakihi Stock Route (JW)
Bottom Right: Dog shelter, Pakihi Stock Route (JW)

the river), passes through a stand of bush and reaches the hut, situated in a clearing.

Waikare Junction Hut sits on a grassy terrace, 50 metres above the river bed, and from its verandah you can enjoy a superb panorama of the upper portion of the river, made even more spectacular by a sunset on a clear night.

Stage 4: Waikare Junction Hut to Takarua Hut

Walking Time: three to 3½ hours to Waikare Whenua; 4½ to 5½ hours to Takarua
Accommodation: Waikare Whenua Hut (six bunks); Takarua Hut (six bunks)

Trampers wishing to reach Ruatoki, the small town just north of the national park, should continue down the Whakatane River along the all-weather track. The track is well cut and bridged, and from the Waikare Junction Hut, it's a three-hour walk to Ohora (22 bunks) and then another three hours to the road's end, south of Ruatoria.

However, if you want to complete the river loop, you should return to the swing bridge at the confluence. Don't cross the bridge; instead, descend to the Waikare River and begin hiking upstream. For 4½ km (about the first 1½ hours) there is no track, so just follow the river bed, crossing when necessary. This part of the Waikare runs through a gorge and you will probably have to ford it often. Needless to say, when the river is swollen, the route will be impossible to follow.

An hour up the river, a signpost on the true right (east) side marks the start of the track to the six-bunk Ohane Hut (1½ hours). In another km, the river valley opens up and it's possible to locate a track along the true left side of the Waikare. This track continues for quite a distance, even marked occasionally by metal tags, until it is necessary to begin fording the river.

The Waikare Whenua Hut is reached 1½ hours (five km) past the Ohane junction, but is not visible from the river. The track that leads to it, on the true right (east) side of the Waikare, is also easy to miss. When you

round a bend and see a swing bridge across the river, backtrack 50 metres and look for a track that leads up the true right side of the river to the grassy terrace where the hut is located.

The hut is a sub-standard, one-room shelter with an open fireplace and resident mice. The only reason to stay here is to enjoy the excellent trout fishing in the Waikare River.

From the hut, the route swings up the Motumuka Stream, which empties into the Waikare River on its true left (west) side 50 metres downstream from the swing bridge (useful during flooded conditions). There is a small sign marking the stream's mouth, but no continuous track up the stream for the first three km, only short paths here and there. The walk involves fording the stream too often to think about trying to keep your boots dry – but it's not unpleasant on a warm day. Kiekie Stream is passed in three km, flowing into the true right side, but it's easy to miss. Trampers usually notice Te Kumete first, a few hundred metres upstream on the opposite bank.

Another km upstream, an obvious track appears, and climbs steeply to avoid a very narrow gorge in the stream. The gorge can be seen only by departing from the track for a short distance. Further upstream, the track veers off to avoid a thundering waterfall.

For the final two km to Takarua Hut, there is a well-worn track (even marked in a few places), mostly on the true right (east) bank, though occasionally it swings to the other side. Eventually, the track leaves the stream, and quickly climbs a grassy terrace to the hut. Takarua is a much more pleasant place to spend the night than Waikare Whenua.

Stage 5: Takarua Hut to State Highway 38

Walking Time: 1½ to two hours to Tawhiwhi Hut; 4½ to five hours to access road; six to seven hours to State Highway 38
Accommodation: Tawhiwhi Hut (18 bunks)

A cut and well-marked track begins behind the hut and immediately climbs the ridge.

The climb is steep for the next two km, and eventually brings you to the crest of the Te Wharau Ridge. The track follows the ridge for about a km, until it reaches Te Wharau (666 metres), where it begins a very steep descent.

The long walk down (2½ km) levels out at Mangatawhero Stream and then works its way west towards the Whakatane River, emerging from the bush above Taumapou Flat, where Tawhiwhi Hut is located. It is a 1½ to two-hour walk from Takarua Hut to Tawhiwhi, but heading in the other direction the hike is considerably harder, so the walking time should be increased to 2½ to three hours.

From Tawhiwhi Hut, backtrack along the all-weather track you started out on until you reach the end of the access road. Plan on 2½ to three hours to the start of the road and another 1½ to two hours to hike the access road – don't expect to hitch a ride.

OTHER TRACKS
Lake Waikareiti Track
The track begins along State Highway 38, 100 metres west of the Aniwaniwa visitor centre. It's an easy 3½ km to the secluded lake, where there's a day shelter. The track continues along the western side of Lake Waikareiti, and in three hours reaches Sandy Bay Hut (18 bunks). This is a pleasant overnight trip that is rated easy. It can be shortened by renting one of the rowing boats that the park maintains at the day shelter and rowing to Sandy Bay. Rent the boats at Aniwaniwa (the fee is $8 overnight).

Waihua-Mangamako Stream Route
There's a network of ridge and stream routes with small huts in the north-western section of Te Urewera National Park. From Murupara, the area is reached by following the road to Te Teko, just east of town, and watching out for a national park sign 300 metres past the Waihua Stream bridge. A road here takes you to the bush edge and the start of the track. It's 4½ hours to Waihua Hut (six bunks) from the bridge, or three hours if you drive up to the edge of the bush. The next

day, you follow Te Onepu Stream, often in it, to Casino Bivouac (three bunks), and then drop down to Mangahoanga Stream to Mangamako Hut (six bunks). It's a three-hour walk from Waihua to Mangamako and then 3½ hours back out to the Murupara-Te Teko Rd.

Whakataka Trig
This track is rated difficult and should only be considered by experienced trampers. The route is posted along State Highway 38 at Taupeupe Saddle, east of Ruatahuna. It's a 4½-hour walk via a slatted and undulating ridge track to the trig, from which there are superb views of the national park, including Lake Waikaremoana. There's a small hut (six bunks) nearby. From the hut, you can continue on the second day along a steep, rugged route for four hours to Hopuruahine Landing, at the northern end of the Lake (Waikaremoana) Track.

Manuoha Trig
This tramp takes you to the highest point in the park (1392 metres), where there's a small hut (six bunks) and excellent views. The track begins one km from the northern end of the Lake Waikaremoana Track, at Hopuruahine, and climbs along a ridge for six km to the summit – a seven-hour walk. Experienced parties can continue on the Pukepuke route to Lake Waikareiti, descending for six hours before reaching the hut at Sandy Bay. The third day is an easy hike along the Lake Waikareiti Track to State Highway 38. This trip is rated difficult and the Pukepuke route should be considered waterless.

Whirinaki Forest Park

The 60,900-hectare Whirinaki is the latest addition to New Zealand's forest park system. It shares a very similar climate and natural history to the adjacent Te Urewera National Park.

What sets Whirinaki apart from other forest parks is the sheer majesty and density of the trees. It has living examples of podocarps (rimu, matai, totara and kahikatea) that are similar to the forests that blanketed Gondwanaland in the Jurassic, over 150 million years ago. This world-recognised forest is so important that it had to be preserved at all costs. It survived after one of the most acrimonious of modern conservation debates. Today, about 88% of the forest consists of native trees.

HISTORY
From the beginning of their recorded history, the Ngatiwhare, a *hapu* (or clan) of the Tuhoe tribe, lived in harmony with the forest of Whirinaki, and there is still plenty of evidence of their occupation. Intense logging of the native bush in the area began in the 1930s, but in the 1970s the land became a battlefield, when conservation groups challenged government policy concerning the management of the forests.

One result of the bitter conflict was an effort to preserve the remaining native bush. The forest park was formed in 1984, though full protection for the Whirinaki forests was not achieved until 1987, when the DOC took complete responsibility for their administration.

WHIRINAKI TRACK
The Whirinaki Track is a surprisingly easy tramp, ideal for families, novice hikers or overseas travellers who want to ease into back-country tramping. While Whirinaki lacks dramatic natural features like towering Panekiri Bluff or sweeping views of Lake Waikaremoana, it is still an interesting walk, with highlights such as Te Whaiti-nui-a-toi Canyon, thundering Whirinaki River waterfall, and the caves near the southern end of the track. Trout fishing is very good in the lower reaches of the Whirinaki River, up to the waterfall; more challenging above.

Information
The park headquarters were once located in the sawmill village of Minginui, but its functions are currently being performed by the Te Ikawhenua field centre (☎ (07) 366 5641), Main Rd, Murupara.

Maps
The park is covered by the 1:50,000 Topomaps 260 quad V18 *(Whirinaki)*. There is no recreational map of the park, but the Te Ikawhenua field centre sells an old, informative booklet called *Tramping & Walking in Whirinaki Forest Park* (1986), which often has up-to-date information pasted inside the back cover.

Huts
All huts in the Whirinaki Forest Park are Category Three ($4); they are basic, with no cooking facilities. The huts are Central Te Hoe, Central Whirinaki, Mangakahika, Mangamate, Moerangi, Mid Okahu, Te Wairoa, Upper Te Hoe, Upper Whirinaki and Whangatawhia (Skips).

Access
To reach Minginui, head east on State Highway 38 to the Te Whaiti junction, site of a former sawmill town, 18 km from Murupara. Turn south and follow the road for eight km, until it ends at a car park. Hitching isn't that bad, and if you get into Minginui late, there's always the Ohu Camp.

The northern end of the track is seven km from the park headquarters, at the end of River Rd, which begins across from Ohu Camp. It's a 1½ to two-hour walk along River Rd, unless you hitch a ride. Hitching is possible at times because the most popular day walk, the waterfall loop, begins at the car park at the end. Park officials discourage trampers from leaving their cars here because of the possibility of them being vandalised while the owners are out on the track. Whirinaki Forest Holidays (☎ (07) 366 3235) runs guided trips into the area, but also offers a car-care and drop-off service.

The southern end is at the end of Plateau Rd, accessible either by forest roads from Minginui or from State Highway 5 (Napier-Taupo Rd), 2½ km south of Iwatahi. From State Highway 5, turn north onto Low Level Rd and follow it for 27 km, until it intersects

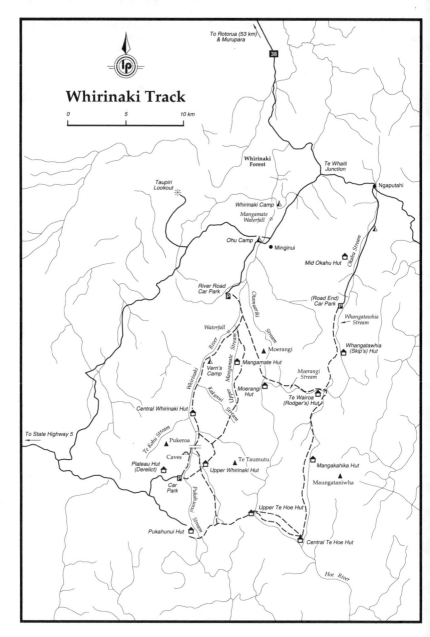

Whirinaki Track

0   5   10 km

Whirinaki
Forest

To Rotorua (53 km)
& Murupara

Te Whaiti
Junction

Ngaputahi

Taupiri
Lookout

Whirinaki Camp

Mangamate
Waterfall

Ohu Camp

Minginui

Mid Okahu Hut

Okahu Stream

River Road
Car Park

Ohumariki Stream

(Road End)
Car Park

Whangatawhia
Stream

Waterfall

Whirinaki River

Mangamate Stream

Moerangi

Mangamate Hut

Vern's
Camp

Moerangi
Hut

Upper Mangamate Stream

Kakanui Stream

Moerangi
Stream

Te Wairoa
(Rodger's) Hut

Central Whirinaki Hut

To State Highway 5

Te Kohu Stream

Pukeroa

Caves

Plateau Hut
(Derelict)

Car Park

Te Taumutu

Upper Whirinaki Hut

Pukahunui Stream

Mangakahika Hut

Maungataniwha

Upper Te Hoe Hut

Pukahunui Hut

Central Te Hoe Hut

Hoe River

with Arterial Rd. A sign for Whirinaki Forest Park South and Matea Lodge directs you to turn right. Once the lodge is reached, continue for another seven km, then turn right at the signposted intersection and follow the signs for 'Whirinaki Track'.

Places to Stay

The *Whirinaki Recreation Camp* (☎ (07) 366 3601) is just north of Minginui. In the town itself, there's the *Ohu Forest Users' Camp* ($5/2.50 for adults/children). There's also a basic camping area by the Whirinaki River, near Mangamate Waterfall; a site costs $5.

The Track

The 26-km track, rated easy, is a wide, well-cut path with no difficult fords. It is so level that it even uses a tunnel to get through a hill. The two-day tramp includes a night at Central Whirinaki Hut – a large, roomy facility near the river – but can also be extended into a four-day loop, a six-day loop or an even longer tramp. The other tracks in the forest park also have huts along them, but these tracks are more difficult than the Whirinaki Track.

The following description covers the Whirinaki Track from its northern end to its southern end, a two-day walk. At the end of this section are additional notes and times for those wanting to undertake a longer loop to return to Minginui.

Stage 1: River Rd Car Park to Central Whirinaki Hut

Walking Time: three hours to Vern's Camp; five hours to Central Whirinaki Hut
Accommodation: Central Whirinaki Hut (18 bunks)

The start of the track is signposted at the car park, and there's a map of the forest park here which shows walking times. The entire route to the hut is surprisingly level, considering how steep the banks and bluffs are along the river. The track immediately passes the return track of the waterfall loop, and in the next km comes to a bridge over an impress-

ive gorge known as Te Whaiti-nui-a-toi Canyon. From here, you follow the true right bank of the Whirinaki River for the rest of the day.

Half an hour from the car park, the track passes the junction with the track to the eight-bunk Moerangi Hut (4½ hours). In another half-hour it crosses Upper Mangamate Stream and passes the signposted junction to Mangamate Hut (2½ hours, eight bunks).

From here, it's a short distance to the side track to the Whirinaki River waterfall. The five-minute walk is well worth it. The cascading water is an impressive sight that can be viewed from all angles, as the track curves 180° around it to head back to the car park. It makes a great lunch spot, if it's that time of day.

The main track remains in view of the river, often sidling the steep bluffs above it. Three km from the junction with the waterfall track, it reaches Vern's Camp. This signposted grassy spot is about eight km from the car park. At one time, it was the site of a day shelter. The shelter is no longer there but the area is still an excellent camp site. In another three km, the track makes one of the few descents of the day, passes a noticeable camp site on the edge of the river and arrives at the signposted Kakanui Stream.

Once over the stream, the track stays just above the river for most of the next two hours. Along the way, it passes deep pools that will intrigue any angler (keep in mind, however, that the largest trout will be found in the first hour of the walk, below the waterfall). There is very little climbing at this point. Fifteen to 20 minutes before the hut, the track passes through a short and rather unusual tunnel. Central Whirinaki Hut is in a small, grassy clearing near the river, 16 km from the car park.

Stage 2: Central Whirinaki Hut to Plateau Rd

Walking Time: 2½ hours

A dated directional sign next to the hut points the way to the track heading south. The walk resumes along the bluffs above the river, and in half an hour arrives at Taumutu Stream and a junction with a track to Upper Whirinaki Hut (1½ hours, nine bunks). From the stream, it's a long but gradual ascent before the track descends back to the river. An hour from the hut, you reach a swing bridge across the Whirinaki River.

A major track junction is well signposted from the eastern side of the bridge. Cross the swing bridge to reach the end of Plateau Rd or to see the caves; trampers heading for Upper Whirinaki Hut or Upper Te Hoe Hut (eight bunks) should continue along the eastern bank of the river.

To reach the caves, turn south once you've crossed the bridge on the true left side and follow the track for about 70 metres. When the main track begins to ascend, look for a partially obscured track that continues along the river – it will quickly lead to the main cave. The huge cavern is interesting, and at night it is possible to see glow-worms. It's an hour's walk from Central Whirinaki Hut. The track is wide, and it's an easy night-time excursion if you take a torch.

The main track climbs the ridge along the river and then heads south-west to the car park at the end of Plateau Rd.

Loop Tramps

For trampers who want to return to Minginui, there are two possible loops, including a three-day trek.

Via Upper Mangamate Stream From the bridge (north of the caves) you need to continue south-east along the Whirinaki River for another hour, fording it perhaps a dozen times. A track, signposted on the true right side of the river, leads to Upper Whirinaki Hut (nine bunks), 20 minutes from the main track or two to 2½ hours from the caves.

The hut is located in a grassy flat, and a track departs from the north-western corner to follow Taumutu Stream to its confluence with Kakaiti Stream. Here, a directional sign points the way to the route to Mangamate Hut (eight bunks). This is a secondary track,

marked with metal tags, but not cut and bridged.

From Upper Whirinaki Hut, it is 3.3 km (an hour's walk) to the confluence of the two streams, and then another three hours over a low saddle to Mangamate Hut. The next day, it is a three-hour tramp out to the car park, the final hour backtracking along the northern end of the Whirinaki Track.

Via Pukahunui Ridge An even longer trek involves passing the junction to Upper Whirinaki Hut and hiking to Upper Te Hoe Hut (eight bunks). This involves a challenging tramp along the Pukahunui Ridge Track and takes six hours from Central Whirinaki Hut. The next day involves a five-hour walk along the ridge track to Central Te Hoe hut (20 bunks), followed by another five-hour walk on the fourth day to Te Wairoa (Rodger's) Hut (six bunks), a rustic but charming hut built in the 1950s.

The trip ends with an easy three-hour walk to Moerangi Hut (eight bunks), then a 5½-hour return to the car park, with the final 20 minutes on the Whirinaki Track. This option is much more demanding than the Whirinaki Track, and trampers should allow five to six days to complete this loop.

Tongariro National Park

The heart of the North Island, and the heart of New Zealand's national park system, is Tongariro. The park is a sacred, ancestral homeland to Maoris, and a beautiful volcanic walking region to trampers. The international significance of Tongariro has earned it World Heritage status.

The central region ranges from stands of giant red beech and rimu in Kaimanawa Forest Park to alpine gravel fields, glaciers and the only desert in New Zealand. The park's trademark, however, is volcanoes. Three of them – Ruapehu, Ngauruhoe and Tongariro – form the 'top of the roof' for the North Island.

Tongariro is the southern end of a volcanic

chain that extends north-west through the heart of the North Island, past Taupo and Rotorua, to finally reach Whakaari (White) Island. The volcanic nature of the region is responsible for Tongariro's hot springs, boiling mud pools, fumaroles and craters.

Despite these diverting attractions, it is the three volcanoes themselves which attract most of the attention. Ruapehu (2796 metres) is the highest mountain in the North Island, and its snowfields are the only legitimate ski area north of Wellington. Next to Ruapehu is the almost symmetrical cone of Ngauruhoe (2291 metres); the most continually active volcano on the mainland. Tongariro (1968 metres) is the smallest and northernmost of the three peaks. In summer, trampers are scrambling up these volcanic peaks; in winter, they are skiing down.

Since its establishment in 1887, the park's 78,761 hectares have been well developed for recreational use. The park contains the famous Chateau Grand Hotel (formerly the Chateau Tongariro), a golf course, various ski fields and a network of tracks and day walks. Most of the tracks lie in tussock or through areas left void of vegetation by eruptions, making Tongariro the best alpine tramping area in the North Island.

The variety of scenery and recreational activities has made Tongariro the most popular national park in New Zealand, with more than 850,000 visitors a year. The vast majority come to ski, but the summer season draws over 250,000 people, who arrive to tramp, to climb to Crater Lake or just to spend their holiday around park headquarters at Whakapapa. Although you cannot get away from the more commercial activities within the park, even on the longer treks, most trampers consider this a small price to pay for their view of the park's outstanding natural features.

HISTORY

To the Maoris, the three volcanoes of Tongariro – Ruapehu, Tongariro and Ngauruhoe – were *tapu*, and they sought to prevent anybody from climbing them. They believed Ngatoro-i-rangi, high priest of the

Maori Wood Carving

Tuwharetoa tribe of Lake Taupo, arrived in the Bay of Plenty in the *Arawa* canoe and travelled south to claim the volcanic plateau for his people. He climbed Mt Ngauruhoe to view the land, but upon reaching the top, suddenly found himself in the middle of a raging snowstorm. It was something the high priest had never experienced before, and he cried out to priestess sisters in the north to send him warmth.

The gods responded by sending fire from underneath; it burst out throughout the North

Island, including the craters of Ngauruhoe and Tongariro, thus saving Ngatoro-i-rangi. The high priest slew a female slave named Auruhoe, then climbed to the newly formed crater and tossed the body in, laying claim to the surrounding land for his people.

The volcanoes, especially Tongariro, have been sacred to the Maoris ever since. They often travelled to Ketetahi Hot Springs to bathe, but were forbidden to go any further. Europeans were also discouraged from the area. John Bidwill, a botanist and explorer, became the first European to scale Mt Ngauruhoe, in 1839.

For the next 12 years, the local tribe was successful in keeping intruders away from its sacred grounds. But in 1851, Mt Ruapehu fell to a climber's passion when Sir George Grey ascended one of the volcano's peaks and then hid from his Maori guides to avoid their discontent. In 1879, George Beetham and J P Maxwell became the first Europeans to scale Mt Ruapehu and see Crater Lake.

The Ngati Tuwharetoa clan could not keep other Maori tribes from claiming the land. After the Land Wars, during which Ngati Tuwharetoa chief Horonuku Te Heuheu Tukino IV aided the rebel Te Kooti, those tribes loyal to the Crown wanted the area redistributed. In 1886, at a schoolhouse in Taupo, the Native Land Court met to determine the ownership of land around Taupo.

Horonuku showed great concern, pleading passionately with the court to leave the area intact. At one point, he turned to the rival chiefs who were longing for the land and asked 'Where is your fire, your ahi ak? You cannot show me for it does not exist. Now I shall show you mine. Look yonder. Behold my fire, my mountain Tongariro!' The forcefulness of his speech dissuaded the Maoris from dividing up the sacred land, but Horonuku was equally worried about pakehas, who were eyeing the area's tussock grassland for grazing.

The chief saw only one solution that would ensure the land's everlasting preservation. Before the Native Land Court on 23 September 1887, Horonuku presented the area to the Crown for the purpose of a national park, the first in New Zealand and only the fourth in the world. With incredible vision for a man of his time, the chief realised that Tongariro's value lay in its priceless beauty and heritage, not as another sheep paddock.

An act of parliament created New Zealand's first national park in 1894, but the park's development was slow. The main trunk railroad reached the region in 1909. By then, there were huts at Waihohonu, in the east, with a track leading to them and to the Ketetahi Hot Springs. The railroad brought a large number of tourists to the western side and, by 1918, a track and hut were built at Mangatepopo for skiers on Mt Ngauruhoe.

Development of the park mushroomed in the 1950s and 1960s as roads were sealed, tracks cut and more huts built. By the early 1970s, annual visitors to Tongariro reached 400,000, and today the number tops 850,000; it is only a matter of time before this sacred region averages a million visitors a year.

CLIMATE
Because most of Tongariro is mountainous, it has its own unpredictable weather patterns. The western slopes of all three volcanoes experience sudden periods of bad weather, with heavy rain or perhaps snow on the peaks even as late as the start of summer. The winds, usually out of the west, can reach gale force on the ridges. At Whakapapa Village, rain falls 191 days a year on average. Average annual precipitation is 2743 mm.

It is usually drier on the eastern side of the mountains, where the Rangipo Desert nestles in the rain shadow of Ruapehu. Rangipo is a barren landscape of dark-reddish sand and ash, with small clumps of tussock. This unique area is the result of two million years of volcanic eruptions, especially the Taupo eruption 2000 years ago, which coated the land with thick deposits of pumice and destroyed all vegetation.

NATURAL HISTORY
Geologically speaking, the Tongariro volcanoes are relatively young. Ruapehu and

Tongariro were formed only two million years ago. They were shaped by a mixture of eruptions and glacial action, especially in the last ice age. At one time, glaciers extended down Mt Ruapehu to below the 1300 metres line, leaving polished rock far below their present snouts.

Mt Ngauruhoe is even younger. It began forming in an old crater of Mt Tongariro only 2500 years ago, when eruptions started building its 700-metre cone. Today, it is the most active volcano in New Zealand, tossing out steam and dark clouds of ash every few years. All three volcanoes, however, have a long history of eruptions.

One eruption of Mt Ruapehu began in March 1945 and continued for almost a year, spreading lava over Crater Lake and sending huge, dark clouds of ash as far away as Wellington. Ruapehu rumbled again in 1969 and 1973. However, the worst disaster Ruapehu caused was not the result of an eruption at all. On Christmas Eve 1953, an ice wall that held back a section of Crater Lake collapsed. An enormous mud and water flow swept down the mountainside and took everything in its path, including a railway bridge. Moments later, a crowded train plunged into the gorge and sent 151 people to their deaths; it was one of New Zealand's worst accidents.

A year later, Ngauruhoe staged a major eruption that lasted 11 months and disgorged six million cubic metres of lava. In 1975, a brief, one-day burst sent ash 14,000 metres into the sky.

TONGARIRO NORTHERN CIRCUIT

Technically, the usual Round-the-Mountain Track is the four to five-day walk around Ruapehu. Many trampers, however, include Mt Ngauruhoe as well, making it a six to seven-day journey.

The Tongariro Northern Circuit described here is one of New Zealand's Great Walks. It only circumnavigates Mt Ngauruhoe, but it was selected for a number of reasons. The route can easily be walked in four days from either Whakapapa or the car park near Ketetahi Springs, and both places are con-

nected to Turangi by public transport. The walk covers the most popular and interesting thermal areas of the park and, although it involves some climbing, follows a well-marked track. None of the stages are excessively long.

Information
Turangi, located north-east of the park, serves as an excellent place to organise the tramp. The Turangi Information Centre (☎ (07) 386 8999), opposite the Turangi Shopping Mall, just off State Highway 1, has a detailed model of the national park and lots of information on the area's many activities. The centre is open daily from 9 am to 5 pm.

The DOC Tongariro/Taupo Conservancy office (☎ (07) 386 8607), near the junction of State Highway 1 and Ohuanga Rd, is open the usual DOC hours: 8 am to 4.30 pm Monday to Friday.

In Whakapapa Village, the park headquarters is at the Whakapapa DOC field and visitor centre (☎ (07) 892 3729), behind the Grand Chateau Hotel, opposite the holiday park. It's open every day from 8 am to 5 pm. It can supply you with maps, and lots of information about walks, huts and current skiing, track and weather conditions.

The Ohakune DOC field centre (☎ (06) 385 8578) is on Ohakune Mountain Rd, on the northern side of town, across the railway tracks. It's open Monday to Friday from 8 am to 4.30 pm. At all of these DOC places, you can buy your Great Walks pass or pay your hut and camping fees (see Huts in this section).

Maps
The excellent 1:80,000 Parkmaps No 273-04 *(Tongariro National Park)* is well worth looking at or purchasing before you go off tramping. Tongariro is also covered by four 1:50,000 Topomaps quads: T19 *(Tongariro)*, T20 *(Ruapehu)*, S20 *(Ohakune)* and S19 *(Raurimu)*. A number of other leaflets are available from DOC centres, including *Turangi Walks, Whakapapa Walks, The Tongariro Northern Circuit* and *The Tongariro Crossing*; most pamphlets cost $1.

Huts

Nine huts are scattered around the park's tramping tracks; all of them accessible only on foot. The huts cost \$8; camping beside the huts costs \$4. Back-country hut tickets or annual hut passes are acceptable, but in the summer season (from the end of October to the end of May), a Great Walks pass is required for the four Tongariro Northern Circuit huts (Ketetahi, Mangatepopo, Waihohonu and Oturere); the cost is \$12 per night in huts, \$6 per night for camping. These huts have mattresses, gas heating, gas cookers, a water supply and toilet facilities.

For environmental reasons, camping is not permitted within 500 metres of the tracks. Camp sites have been established near each of the huts on the circuit.

Access

The circular route can be entered from four different points. The most popular points are Whakapapa Village, site of the national park visitor centre, and the car park near Ketetahi Hot Springs, off State Highway 47A, but the route can also be reached from access tracks to Mangatepopo Hut and New Waihohonu Hut. There is good public transport to both Whakapapa and Ketetahi.

The advantage of beginning at Ketetahi is that you will be able to enjoy a soak in the hot spring, the highlight of most treks here, on two nights instead of one. However, since more trampers arrive at the park headquarters in Whakapapa Village, the description in this section will begin there.

Taupo is about halfway between Auckland and Wellington. It's at the geographical centre of the island, so it's a hub for bus transport. Long-distance buses, including InterCity, Newmans, Magic Bus and Alpine Scenic Tours arrive at and depart from the Taupo Travel Centre (☎ (07) 378 9032), 17 Gascoigne St. InterCity and Newmans have several daily buses to Turangi (45 minutes). These buses stop at the Avis Rent-A-Car office on the corner of Ohuanga Rd and Ngawaka Place. The Avis office is open Monday to Friday from 8 am to 5 pm.

Alpine Scenic Tours (☎ (07) 378 6305)

operates a daily shuttle service between Taupo and Turangi, connecting with their other shuttle service from Turangi to National Park. This shuttle service runs several times daily between Turangi and National Park, stopping along the way in the Tongariro National Park – at the Ketetahi trail head, the Mangatepopo trail head, Whakapapa Village (the Chateau Grand) and, in winter, the Whakapapa Ski Area (Top of the Bruce). It's an excellent service for skiers and trampers. The cost from Turangi is \$15 per person one-way to Whakapapa Village; \$8 per person to Ketetahi car park. A lift from National Park, the nearest train station in the area, to the park headquarters is \$6 (minimum two persons).

From whichever direction you come, hitching to Whakapapa is never that easy because traffic is usually light. If you're coming south from Turangi, use the shorter saddle road, State Highway 47A – the locals no longer use the State Highway 1 to State Highway 47 route.

Places to Stay

Turangi *Turangi Holiday Park* (☎ (07) 386 8754) is on Ohuanga Rd, off State Highway 41; tent sites cost \$7.50 per person and cabins \$14.50. At Tokaanu, the *Oasis Motel & Caravan Park* (☎ (07) 386 8569) on State Highway 41 has camp sites/cabins at \$6.50/15 per person. The *River Rats Lodge* (☎ (07) 386 7492), on Ohuanga Rd, is right in the town centre; it costs \$14 per person, or \$7 per person for a tent site. The *Bellbird Lodge* (☎ 386 828), 3 Rangipoia Place, charges \$15 per person in twin, double or dormitory rooms.

Tongariro The choice at Tongariro is whether to stay in the national park or in one of the nearby small towns. Within the park, Whakapapa Village has an expensive hotel, a motel and a motor camp.

The popular *Whakapapa Holiday Park* (☎ /fax (07) 892 3897) is up the road from the Grand Chateau Hotel, opposite the Whakapapa visitor centre. Tent or powered sites cost \$9 per person and cabins are \$33

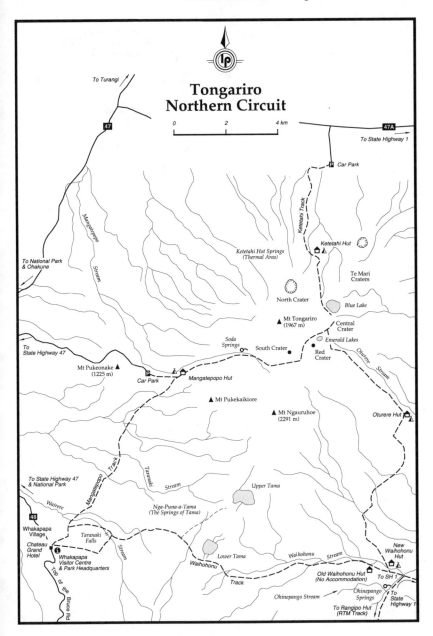

Tongariro Northern Circuit

To Turangi

47

To State Highway 1

47A

To National Park & Ohakune

To State Highway 47

Mangatepopo Stream

0   2   4 km

P Car Park

Ketetahi Track

Ketetahi Hut

Ketetahi Hot Springs (Thermal Area)

Te Mari Craters

North Crater

Blue Lake

Mt Tongariro (1967 m)

Central Crater

Soda Springs

South Crater

Emerald Lakes

Red Crater

Oturere Stream

Mt Pukeonake (1225 m)

Car Park

Mangatepopo Hut

Mt Pukekaikiore

Mt Ngauruhoe (2291 m)

Oturere Hut

To State Highway 47 & National Park

Mangatepopo Track

Taranaki Stream

Upper Tama

Waitere

Nga-Puna-a-Tama (The Springs of Tama)

48

Whakapapa Village

Chateau Grand Hotel

Top of the Bruce Rd

Whakapapa Visitor Centre & Park Headquarters

Taranaki Falls

Taranaki Stream

Lower Tama

Waihohonu

Waihohonu Stream

New Waihohonu Hut

To SH 1

Old Waihohonu Hut (No Accommodation)

Ohinepango Springs

To State Highway 1

Waihohonu Track

Ohinepango Stream

To Rangipo Hut (RTM Track)

for two. There are two basic DOC camping grounds in the park, both with cold water and pit toilets; they cost $2 (put your money in the honesty box). The *Mangahuia Campground* is on State Highway 47, between National Park and the State Highway 48 turn-off heading to Whakapapa. The *Mangawhero Campground* is near Ohakune, on the Ohakune Mountain Rd heading up to Mt Ruapehu.

Whakapapa The *Grand Chateau Hotel* in Whakapapa Village is indeed a grand hotel; it has been well preserved and is priced accordingly. Behind the Chateau is the *Skotel* (☎ (07) 892 3719) which offers hostel-style rooms for $20/36 for singles/doubles from the end of October to early July. There's a reasonable selection of food in the Whakapapa Store if you're preparing your own – but it's more expensive than most stores.

National Park Accommodation here gets very full during the ski season, so book ahead. The *Ski Haus* has tent sites at $7 per person. Tent sites at *Howard's Lodge* cost $8 per person. *Fletcher's Ski Lodge & Motel* also has tent sites.

The *Discovery Caravan Park* (☎ (07) 892 2744) is beside the Discovery Lodge on State Highway 47, 6½ km from National Park township and 6½ km from Whakapapa. Tent or powered sites cost $8 per person and cabins are $12.50 per person. The *Ski Haus* (☎ (07) 892 2854) is on Carroll St, about three blocks west of the highway. From November to June, rates are $12/15 per person in dorm/double rooms; in winter it's $15/20 per person. *Howard's Lodge* (☎ (07) 892 2827) is also on Carroll St, just a block from the highway. It charges $12/15 per person in dorm/double rooms; in winter it's $15/25.

Ohakune Finding a place to stay here is no problem in summer, and there are other places in Raetihi, 11 km west. The information centre has accommodation details and can make bookings.

The *Ohakune Motor Camp* (☎ (06) 385

Great Walks Ticket

8561) is at 5 Moore St; tent sites are $6.50 and cabins or on-site caravans cost $15. The *Raetihi Motor Camp* (☎ (06) 385 4176) in Raetihi, 11 km west of Ohakune, has tent sites ($7 for two) and cabins or on-site caravans ($10 to $12.50 per person). *High Country Cabins* (☎ (06) 385 8608), on Clyde St near the Big Carrot, has cabins for $10 per person in summer, rising to $20 in winter. The *Ohakune YHA Hostel* (☎ (06) 385 8724) is on Clyde St, near the post office and the information centre; beds cost $14 per night.

The Track
The Tongariro Northern Circuit is a four to five-day trip that can be walked in either direction. It's rated medium. The track is well marked and easy to follow but does involve a number of solid climbs. If you're beginning from Ketetahi car park instead of Whakapapa Village, plan on a 2½ to three-hour hike up to the hut and a 1½ to two-hour hike down to the car park.

Stage 1: Whakapapa Village to Mangatepopo Hut
Walking Time: 2½ to three hours
Accommodation: Mangatepopo Hut (24 bunks)

From the Whakapapa visitor centre, head up the road behind the Chateau Grand Hotel and follow it to the signposted Mangatepopo Track. The tramp begins along a well-maintained track that wanders through tussock grass and a few stands of beech for 1½ km. At Wairere Stream, it passes a signposted junction with a track that leads to Taranaki Falls and eventually to the Tama Lakes.

Mangatepopo Track, the left-hand fork, heads north-east, and at this point its condition deteriorates somewhat. It crosses tussock and dozens of small streams, which have eroded the track in places and make for sloppy conditions when it rains.

Nevertheless, the track is still well marked and easy to hike, and within three km of the start there are impressive views of the cones of the volcanoes, Mt Ngauruhoe and Mt Pukekaikiore to the north-east, and the scoria cone of Mt Pukeonake straight ahead. After a few more stream crossings, the track swings eastwards, and you quickly climb a ridge from which you can see the Mangatepopo Hut, two km in the distance.

The hut is in a pleasant spot, with good views of the climb to South Crater, the destination for many trampers the next day.

There is also a track that heads west from the hut and, in half an hour, reaches the end of the Mangatepopo Rd, which connects to State Highway 47. If you decide to walk out here, don't expect a lot of traffic on the metalled access road; although the Alpine Scenic Tours bus does drop off and pick up passengers here.

Stage 2: Mangatepopo Hut to Ketetahi Hut

Walking Time: five to six hours
Accommodation: Ketetahi Hut (24 bunks)

This section of the trip is on one of the most spectacular tracks in New Zealand. It's not unusual in foul weather for trampers to walk from one hut to the next in three hours, but if the weather is clear, plan on spending the whole day on the track rather than rushing off for a soak in Ketetahi Hot Springs.

The day begins with an easy trek up Mangatepopo Valley, along the stream of the same name, and over a succession of old lava flows. Within an hour, you pass the spur track to Soda Springs (a 15-minute round trip), which can be smelled long before they can be seen.

The main track continues up the valley and quickly begins a well-marked climb to the saddle between Mt Ngauruhoe and Mt Tongariro. The ascent among the lava rocks is steep, but well marked with poles, and in 45 minutes to an hour you reach the top and pass the signposted route to the summit of Mt Ngauruhoe (a three to four-hour round trip).

Follow the poles as they continue past the junction and cross South Crater, an eerie place when the clouds are hanging low, and a 'huge walled amphitheatre' when the weather is clear. The walk through the crater is flat, with the slopes of Mt Ngauruhoe to the right and the summit ridge to the left.

Once across the crater, the track, now more of a marked route, resumes climbing the ridge, and at the top, you can see Oturere Valley. The poles marking the track swing north here and follow the narrow crest of the ridge that separates the two craters, sidling around some huge rocks.

Eventually, the track reaches the signposted junction to the route up Mt Tongariro (a 1½ to two-hour round trip); to the right is steaming Red Crater, whose name comes from the dull, red colour of its sides. The side of the crater is the highest point reached on the track (1820 metres), and there are fantastic views from here that might even include Mt Taranaki, to the west, on a clear day.

The track begins its descent along the side of Red Crater, passes Emerald Lakes and then makes an even steeper drop along scoria-covered slopes into Central Crater. There's a signposted junction to Oturere Hut (two hours) here. To reach Ketetahi Hut, continue across the crater and climb its northern ridge to Blue Lake, another remarkable sight. After skirting the lake, the track descends along Tongariro's northern slopes below North Crater, reaching the hut two hours from the junction of the track to Oturere Hut.

The spectacular views from the front door of Ketetahi Hut include Lake Rotoaira, at the base of Pihanga, and Lake Taupo. The renowned hot springs are another 20 to 30 minutes along the track towards the car park. They are signposted on the northern side of the thermal stream (though the smell and greyish water are usually noticed first). A track begins up the true left side of the stream and it's about 100 metres to the first dammed pool.

Keep in mind that the further upstream you go, the hotter the water gets, until some pools are actually boiling. Also remember that half an hour in a pool usually leaves most trampers with only enough energy to climb back up to the hut.

The two stages just described (Whakapapa to Mangatepopo, Mangatepopo to Ketetahi Hot Springs) form the classic traverse known as the Tongariro Crossing, thought by many to be the best one-day walk in New Zealand (see Other Walks in this section).

Stage 3: Ketetahi Hut to New Waihohonu Hut
Walking Time: seven to 7½ hours
Accommodation: Oturere Hut (24 bunks); New Waihohonu Hut (24 bunks)

Return up the track towards North Crater, ascending 200 metres to the top in a series of switchbacks. Plan on two to 2½ hours to reach the junction to Oturere Hut, or even longer if the sights along the way make you pause to ponder their unusual features. At the junction, follow the signposted track to the south as it skirts the main Emerald Lake before working its way to the old lava flow that descends into Oturere Valley.

It's an hour from the junction to the valley floor, where the track follows Oturere Stream and passes clumps of tussock grass and piles of rocks and stones in a moonscape terrain. The walk is fairly level in the valley, until you begin a gentle descent to the hut. The Oturere Hut has 24 bunks, and a view of a small waterfall in the stream.

The track leaves the hut and swings south-west through open country as it skirts the eastern flanks of Mt Ngauruhoe. It descends straight towards Mt Ruapehu, working its way across numerous streams before reaching the bridge over Waihohonu Stream, 1½ to two hours from Oturere Hut. From the bridge, the walk becomes a gentle climb through stands of beech trees, descending only at the end, just before it reaches New Waihohonu Hut.

The hut sits in a clearing above the stream, with a nice view of Mt Ruapehu from the front door. Those heading back to Whakapapa Village can take a short side trip along the main track south to Ohinepango Springs, a 20-minute walk from the hut. The springs are cold and they bubble up from beneath an old lava flow. A huge volume of water discharges into the Ohinepango Stream.

Stage 4: New Waihohonu Hut to Whakapapa Village
Walking Time: 5½ to six hours

The day begins with the track descending from the hut and crossing a bridge over the upper branch of Waihohonu Stream. On the other side, there's a signposted junction; the Round-the-Mountain Track continues south along the slopes of Mt Ruapehu, and the Waihohonu Track (not part of the Tongariro Northern Circuit) heads east towards Desert Rd (1½ hours).

The track to Whakapapa Village heads west and in a km passes the corrugated-iron Old Waihohonu Hut, the oldest building in the park, which has an unusual display of log signs left by tramping parties. The hut is preserved by the Historic Places Trust and offers no accommodation. Next to the hut is a signposted side track to Ohinepango Springs.

The main track follows the upper branch of the Waihohonu Stream, dropping and climbing out of several streams that have eroded through the thin covering of tussock grass. The walking is tiresome at times, but beautiful if the weather is clear; Mt Ngauruhoe's perfect cone is on one side and Mt Ruapehu's snowcapped summit is to the south. Eventually, the track rises gently to the Tama Saddle between the two volcanoes and in another 1½ km arrives at a junction to Tama Lakes. The lower lake is a short trip up the side track, but it's a 45-minute walk along an exposed ridge to the upper lake.

The main track continues west, working down and out of another half-dozen streams until it descends to Taranaki Falls, three km from the junction with the Tama Lakes track. At the falls, the Wairere Stream spills over a 20-metre rock face into a boulder-ringed pool.

In the final stretch of the walk, the track passes an alternative route back to the park headquarters before making a steady descent to the Whakapapa Village, through tussock grass and then bush. It's a 30 to 45-minute walk from the falls to the village.

OTHER TRACKS
Tongariro Traverse
The five-day walk crosses Tongariro National Park, from its southern border near Ohakune, across the western slopes of Mt Ruapehu and Mt Ngauruhoe, to the car park on State Highway 47A. The trip includes the scenic section of craters and lakes between Ngauruhoe and Tongariro, and a night at Ketetahi Hot Springs.

Public transport is available from the car park at State Highway 47A using Alpine Scenic Tours, but getting to the top of Ohakune Mountain Rd can be tough at times in the summer. The best bet for hitching is to start early in the morning, when it's often possible to pick up a ride with ski-field workers. In addition to the mountain huts, there is accommodation in Ohakune, Whakapapa and Turangi.

Tongariro Crossing
Not to be confused with the full Tongariro Traverse, the classic Tongariro Crossing is arguably the best one-day walk in New Zealand. The crossing, from Whakapapa to Ketetahi Hot Springs and on to State Highway 47A, takes seven to eight hours (add an hour if you attempt it in the other

direction). One-day walkers should be prepared for all types of weather.

Usually, transport will have to be arranged at either end. The Ski Haus (☎ (07) 892 2854), Carroll St in National Park, provides round-trip transport, enabling you to do the Tongariro Crossing in one day; it departs daily at 8 am and costs $15.

Kaimanawa Forest Park

East of Tongariro National Park is Kaimanawa Forest Park, a 77,348-hectare reserve that is dominated by the Kaimanawa Range and the beech forest that covers much of the area. The park contains the upper catchments of four major rivers – the Mohaka, Rangitikei, Ngaruroro and Tongariro.

To trampers, Kaimanawa is a complete contrast to the Tongariro National Park: one is well known, well used and easily accessible, the other is little known, little used and difficult to reach on public transport. In Tongariro, tracks are benched and well marked, often with poles marking the route every 40 metres; in Kaimanawa, it is always challenging to pick the difference between the walking track and yet another hunter's trail.

HISTORY
There is little evidence of widespread Maori presence in Kaimanawa. Europeans arrived in the area by the 1880s, looking for gold and burning off the forest for farms. From the late 1930s to the 1970s, splitting took place in the northern sections of the park: splitting was a method of producing fence posts and other products from trees without the use of a sawmill.

In 1965, the Forest Amendment Act was passed to protect sections of forest as parks. Kaimanawa was gazetted in 1969, and by 1971, seven other forests had been turned into parks.

CLIMATE
Although the area receives an average of

3500 mm of precipitation a year, the summers are generally good, with long, dry spells and mild temperatures from December to April. In the southern, mountainous sections of the park, the weather can be unpredictable, with heavy rain, sleet or even snow developing quickly at high altitudes during early or late summer.

NATURAL HISTORY

Kaimanawa can be divided into two general regions. The central and southern portions of the park are mountainous and have forested valleys, extensive scrub lands and alpine grasslands. In contrast, the area to the north and east, and the Te Iringa Circuit, is less rugged and almost entirely forested – making it easier for tramping.

The walk touches the banks of four rivers famous for rainbow trout, so this walk is one of the best North Island tramps for anglers.

The park is also home to the famed sika (Japanese) deer, and the red deer; hunters make up a significant portion of park users during the roar (mating season) in late March and April.

The Kaimanawa is also known for its herd of over 1600 wild horses. Protected since 1981, their numbers have swelled enormously, and will have to be carefully managed to reduce their impact on the delicate ecosystem.

Common native birds in the park include the kereru (wood pigeon), fantail, bellbird, rifleman and whitehead. Less frequently seen are the blue duck, native falcon, fernbird and kiwi.

TE IRINGA-OAMARU CIRCUIT

This is a four to five-day walk in a secluded corner of the North Island's popular volcanic plateau region. There are no hot springs in this area, no steaming craters, no days above the bush-line and no Whakapapa Village. If trampers arrive outside the popular hunting time of mid-March to April, they'll find secluded tracks, uncrowded huts and great trout fishing along empty stretches of river.

The forest is interesting and there are some great views from the ridges, but above all else, this is an angler's adventure. Of the five days spent walking, anglers will pass productive rivers on three of them. If you're serious about catching some trout, plan an extra day at Oamaru Hut and, better still, Boyd Lodge. Stop at a sport shop in Taupo for advice on flies or spinners, and make sure you purchase a Taupo fishing licence for this portion of the park.

Information

Information and maps on the forest park can most easily be obtained from the Taupo information centre (☎ (07) 378 9000) on Tongariro St, near the corner of Heu Heu St. It's open daily from 8.30 am to 5 pm. If you need to see DOC personnel, the Taupo field centre (☎ (07) 378 3885) is in Centennial Drive. For the southern and western access to the forest park, you can get information from the Turangi field centre.

Maps

The most practical map for this trip is the 1:100,000 Parkmaps No 274-11 *(Guide to Kaimanawa State Forest Park)*, which covers the entire park. It has surprisingly good detail and includes contour lines. There is also the 1:50,000 Topomaps 260 quad U19 *(Kaimanawa)*.

Huts

There are five huts in the park and trampers pass four of them on this trip. Hut fees are $8 per night for Boyd Lodge, Waipakihi and Oamaru huts, and $4 for Cascade Hut. Te Iringa Hut, a Category Four hut, is free.

Access

Taupo is the nearest large centre to the Te Iringa-Oamaru Circuit and is usually the last town trampers pass through before entering the park, so stock up here on supplies or equipment.

Getting out to the track is a challenge if you don't have your own transport; vehicle owners have got it made. Head along State Highway 5 (Taupo-Napier Rd) for 27 km

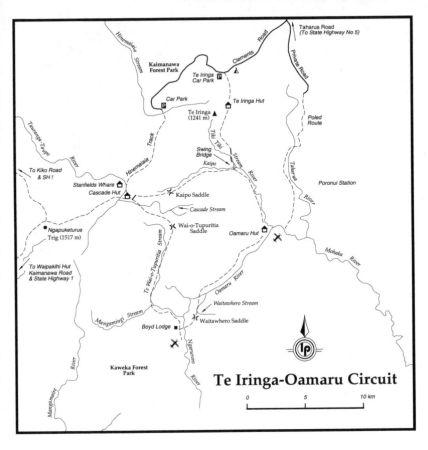

Te Iringa-Oamaru Circuit

0   5   10 km

east of Taupo. Turn right onto Taharua Rd. Hitching is pretty good, or you can make arrangements with the InterCity or Newmans bus driver to be let off at the corner on their run to Napier.

Once on Taharua Rd, head south for 11 km, then turn onto Clements Rd for another 3½ km to Te Iringa car park and camping ground. (Clements is an interesting forest road which continues for another 15 km into the park.) This portion is hard to hitch, because the only traffic on it is from a handful of sheep station families. They are very good about picking up trampers – it's

just that it may be some time before you see a car rumbling down the road in your direction.

Sometimes it's possible to contact the DOC Taupo field centre (☎ (07) 378 5450) and catch a ride out with a work crew. Of course, there is always one sure way of reaching the starting point – on foot. Plan on a four-hour walk, and spend the first night at Te Iringa Hut.

Places to Stay
In Taupo, the *Taupo Motor Camp* (☎ (07) 377 3080) is on Redoubt St, by the river; it

has tent sites for $8 per person. The *Taupo Associate YHA Hostel* (☎ (07) 378 3311), on the corner of Kaimanawa and Tamamutu Sts, charges $14 for a bed. *Rainbow Lodge* (☎ (07) 378 5754), 99 Titiraupenga St, is a busy and popular hostel. Beds cost $10 to $13 in bunkrooms, $15 in twin/double rooms. Nearby, *Burke's Backpackers* (☎ (07) 378 9292), 69 Spa Rd, costs about the same as Rainbow Lodge.

The Track

The following trip is a five-day loop that begins and ends at Clements Rd. Although there is some climbing along this track. The trip is rated medium to difficult because the track is not cut, benched and marked every 40 metres with a pole like much of Tongariro. There will be times in Kaimanawa when you'll have to retrace your steps to locate the main track, or stop and search for that reassuring white metal tag on a tree that tells you everything is OK.

You can cut two days off the trip by hiking to Oamaru Hut and following the poled route from the Mohaka River out to the end of Taharua Rd. Walking time is six to eight hours across the sheep and cattle paddocks. Trampers need to stay on the pole route and not cut over to the private road that parallels it part of the way.

Stage 1: Clements Rd to Te Iringa Hut

Walking Time: one to two hours
Accommodation: Te Iringa Hut (six bunks)

The trip begins at the Te Iringa car park and camping ground, approximately 15 km from State Highway 5. The area is signposted on Clements Rd and the track begins before you reach the grassy area for tents. The camping area is pleasantly situated; get water from the stream back along the road. In the first km, the track gently rises and then descends across a stream. At this point, the track begins a steady climb for 2½ km to a saddle. The climb is not hard, because the track is well graded.

Once over the saddle, the track sidles the ridge for a short way and it's possible to see

the roof of Te Iringa Hut just before the track descends to it. Te Iringa Hut has six bunks and an open fireplace, and though it is not new, it still provides good shelter.

If you wish to climb the 1241-metre summit of Te Iringa, there is a rough bush track to it from Te Iringa Hut. Carry on uphill for 40 minutes from the point where the main track leaves the ridge crest. From the top, on a clear day, you will see the Kawekas, Lake Taupo and the volcano summits of Tongariro National Park.

Stage 2: Te Iringa Hut to Oamaru Hut

Walking Time: four to five hours
Accommodation: Oamaru Hut (12 bunks)

The track departs from the back of the hut and makes a short climb, reaching a high point when it passes a signposted hunter's access route. There are good views of the park's rugged interior as the track descends the ridge.

Continue the descent for three km, until you reach a branch of Tiki Tiki Stream, where there is a popular camping area. The track crosses a tributary, and then follows the main stream along the true left (east) side for 1½ km, until it empties into the Kaipo River.

A swing bridge crosses the river, and the track resumes on the true right (west) bank. Most of the time it follows the edge of the forest, often climbing up ridges, where it can be easy to lose. It's a two-hour walk along the river, passing some tempting pools, until the track emerges onto the grassy flats along Oamaru River.

The hut sits on a terrace, with an excellent view of the surrounding hills and the flats below. This one, like Boyd Lodge, is very much a hunters' hut – there are gun racks in the bunkrooms. The nearby airstrip is busy on the weekends, when hunters and anglers are flown in. Anglers who spend an extra day here can pursue trout in the pools at the lower end of Kaipo River, or hike either up the Oamaru or down the Mohaka – all three rivers hold fish.

Stage 3: Oamaru Hut to Boyd Lodge

Walking Time: four to six hours
Accommodation: Boyd Lodge (16 bunks)

This stretch is a scenic forest walk that provides good views and access to the Oamaru River. Anglers will delight in the way the track follows much of the river bank, allowing them to search one pool after another for fish. The walk begins at the hut, where steps take you quickly down to the flats and a well-beaten path begins to cross in a south-westerly direction.

It's a three-km walk to the top of the flats. In places, the grass is so tall that the track is easy to lose. Just keep heading up the river and use the white bluff on the opposite side of the valley as a marker. As you approach the bluff, there's a 'Boyd Lodge' signpost pointing the way into the beech forest.

A well-cut track resumes here and climbs over several ridges to Ruatea Stream (Jap Creek), reached 3.4 km from the hut. Occasionally, a tramper will mistake the wide stream for the Oamaru River and continue up along a hunters' track until it ends in a km or so. The main track crosses the creek, and is

clearly marked with white metal tags on both sides. A level walk resumes along the river for the next six km, climbing only to avoid an occasional steep bank.

At the confluence of the Oamaru River and Waitawhero Stream, the track crosses the river and follows the stream up to the Waitawhero Saddle, a climb of a good hour or more. After crossing the stream several times, the track makes a final ascent to the saddle, where trampers are greeted with a view of Ngaruroro River. It's even possible to see the airstrip and windsock near Boyd Lodge.

The saddle is signposted where the track swings north for a short distance and begins its descent. It drops through beech forest at first and then onto a ridge of open tussock grassland before reaching the valley floor. The Ngaruroro River should be crossed north of the airstrip to avoid swampy ground. Climb up the terrace on the other side to locate an old pack track, which leads to the airstrip. The final climb of the day, via steps, takes you to the hut, 100 metres above.

Boyd Lodge is generally regarded as the best facility in the park. It's a large and roomy hut, equipped with gas cookers and mattresses, and from its verandah you can view the river below and the mountains in Kaweka Forest Park to the east.

The Ngaruroro River is renowned for its excellent trout fishing and has recently become a favourite with whitewater rafters.

Stage 4: Boyd Lodge to Cascade Hut

Walking Time: five to 6½ hours
Accommodation: Cascade Hut (six bunks)

Descend to the airstrip and follow the old pack track to the Ngaruroro River. Follow the true right (west) side of the river north into the upper valley, an area of river terraces, lower hill slopes, and flats of tussock grass and heath-like vegetation. The track is not cut but the route is clear as the Ngaruroro River gradually curves west around Tapuiomaruahine Peak towards its headwaters and the Mangamingi Stream. Fords should not be difficult at normal water levels as you cross Mangamingi near its confluence with Te Wai-o-Tupuritia Stream.

The route continues north through the tussock valley of Te Wai-o-Tupuritia Stream, and you ford the stream when necessary until the head of the valley is reached. A signpost points the way into the trees where a track ascends to Wai-o-Tupuritia Saddle. After the saddle, the track climbs steeply until the high point of the catchment ridge is reached, at almost 1250 metres.

After a sharp descent, the track levels out at Cascade Stream, then skirts a narrow gorge and a series of waterfalls before reaching Cascade Hut, situated on a terrace above the stream's confluence with the Tauranga-Taupo River. Halfway down to the hut, the track passes a signposted junction with the track to Kaipo Saddle, off to the east.

Stage 5: Cascade Hut to Clements Rd
Walking Time: four to six hours via Hinemaiaia Track

Cascade Hut is situated near a signposted junction that offers trampers three ways to leave the forest park. Heading off to the west is the Ngapuketurua Track, which crosses the summit of the same name and terminates at the end of Kiko Rd (six to eight hours).

For those with a car at Te Iringa camping ground, head east and return to the signposted junction to Kaipo Saddle. Cross Cascade Stream and then climb to Kaipo Saddle (945 metres). At the saddle, the track follows the Kaipo River, fording it often in the beginning, to the confluence with Tiki Tiki Stream, where it rejoins the track you started out on. It's a four to six-hour walk to the confluence and another four to five hours

over the flank of Te Iringa to the car park and camping ground on Clements Rd.

The shortest route out is the Hinemaiaia Track, which goes northwards from the hut and crosses the open flats of the Tauranga-Taupo River. Along the way, on the opposite shore to Cascade Hut, you pass a picturesque old shelter with a pumice chimney. This is Stanfields Whare, and it's open to the public. After a half-hour walk, the track ascends from the valley along a spur to the ridge top (1250 metres). It then drops steeply through the beech forest to the confluence of two streams, following the true left (west) bank of one of them and passing several scenic waterfalls on its way to the Hinemaiaia River.

The Hinemaiaia River is crossed below the confluence of its main tributaries, and from here it's a short distance through beech forest to the car park at the end of Clements Rd. The track at this end is well cut and signposted. For those without transport, the trip is far from over; it's about 18½ km to Taharua Rd and another 11 km to State Highway 5.

OTHER TRACKS
Waipakihi Valley Route
This is an overnight trip in the western side of Kaimanawa Forest Park. The first day is spent hiking over Umukarikari (1592 metres), ending at Waipakihi Hut (12 bunks). The trip is almost a complete loop, with both ends signposted off Kaimanawa Rd, 15 km south of Turangi on State Highway 1. Alpine Scenic Tours (☎ (07) 378 6305) can provide pick-up and drop-off services to the track from Turangi.

Southern North Island

The odd shape of the North Island, or Te Ika a Maui (the fish of Maui), makes any attempt at regionally classifying walks an arbitrary decision. This chapter includes walks in the south-west (Taranaki and Whanganui) and south (Tararuas) of the island. The walks described here are just a few of those available – the Rimutaka and Haurangi forest parks, for example, are mentioned only in passing, yet contain fascinating walks for trampers.

Mt Egmont National Park

Mt Taranaki (formerly called Mt Egmont) tantalised the Maoris, who made it a god. It fascinated Captain James Cook as well, when he sailed past in the *Endeavour* in 1770. Today, thousands make the pilgrimage to the summit of this lonely volcano which dominates the Taranaki region of the North Island. Snowcapped on a clear winter day, it is surely one of the country's most stunning sights.

The near-perfect symmetry of its cone makes Mt Taranaki a twin to Japan's Mt Fuji. The mountain was formed by a series of eruptions 16,000 years ago, and the only flaw in its symmetry is Fanthams Peak, on the southern slope.

The easy accessibility of its tracks and the magnificent views of patchwork dairy farms, the stormy Tasman Sea and the rugged Tongariro peaks make it a favourite with trampers; it is generally regarded as the most climbed summit in New Zealand.

The entire mountain, along with the Kaitake and Pouakai ranges, lies in Egmont National Park. The park includes 33,534 hectares of native forest and bush, more than 320 km of tracks and routes, and scattered huts and shelters. There are three main roads into the park and motorists can drive up to the 900-metre level, almost to the bush-line, on each one.

The easy accessibility allows inexperienced trampers to scale the 2518-metre summit. It's not a technical climb from Dawson Falls or the Stratford Plateau during good weather in the summer. The roads and the availability of accommodation also encourage families, school groups and novice trampers to tackle a number of day hikes and overnight tramps. All this means that the park is busy from the Christmas holidays to early February. In the winter, Mt Taranaki is a major North Island ski area.

The Round-the-Mountain Track is the traditional four to five-day tramp around Mt Taranaki; much of it is below the bush-line. To many, a shorter and more pleasant walk in Egmont National Park is the Pouakai Track. This two-day loop crosses the northern slopes of Taranaki and the rolling tops of the Pouakai Range, which offer excellent views of the volcano.

The heavy rain of Mt Taranaki is responsible for the numerous streams that flow down the volcano's slopes like the spokes of a wheel (radial drainage). The streams have carved numerous gorges and valleys, and there are several majestic waterfalls; particularly notable are Dawson Falls, with its drop of 18 metres, and Bell Falls, with a drop of 31 metres. But the gullies and gorges also make hiking tedious at times, because days are spent going in and out of unbridged stream beds.

HISTORY

According to Maori myth, the volcano was called Taranaki and was originally part of the central range of the North Island. Taranaki and Tongariro eventually came into conflict over the lovely maiden, Pihanga, and a battle ensued. Taranaki lost, and was exiled from the range. The volcano retreated west, carving out the Wanganui River and, while resting near Stratford, forming Te Ngaere Swamp. Finally, he settled on the coast, and when the Maoris saw the summit surrounded by mist, they felt the volcano was weeping.

Taranaki was a sacred place to the Maoris – a place where the bones of their chiefs were buried and a place to escape from the terrorism of other tribes. The legendary Tahurangi was said to be the first person to climb the summit, and when he lit a fire on it, he claimed the surrounding land for his tribe.

The first European to see Mt Taranaki was Cook, in 1770, and one of his ship's company later wrote that it was 'the noblest hill I have ever seen'. Two years after Cook's visit, Mt Taranaki was the first thing French explorer Marion du Fresne saw of New Zealand. Both Cook and du Fresne recorded seeing the fires of Maori settlers, but never made contact with them. Naturalist Ernest Dieffenbach did, however, in 1839. While working for the New Zealand Company, he told the local Maoris of his plans to climb the summit. The native tribes tried passionately to dissuade him, but Dieffenbach set off in early December. Although the first attempt was unsuccessful, the naturalist set out again on 23 December and, after bashing through thick bush, he finally reached the peak.

The volcano soon became a popular spot for trampers and adventurers. Fanny Fantham was the first woman to climb the parasite cone on the southern side of Mt Egmont, in 1887, and Panitahi was quickly renamed Fanthams Peak in her honour. A year later, the summit route from Stratford Plateau was developed. In 1901, Harry Skeet completed the task of surveying the area for the first topographical map.

Tourism boomed, and to protect the forest and watershed from settlers seeking to clear it for farmland, the Taranaki provincial government set aside an area extending roughly 9½ km in radius from the summit. The national park – only the second in New Zealand – was created in October 1900, when an act of parliament set up the first park board. In 1993, the park had over 360,000 visitors.

CLIMATE

Mt Taranaki has a maritime climate. Febru-ary is the warmest month, with an average reading of 18°C, while the temperature slides down to an average of 10°C in July. The air temperature drops 6°C for every 1000 metres you climb; the freezing level in winter is at 1750 metres. Snow is rare in the summer, but rain is not – Taranaki and surrounding mountains force the moist westerly winds from the Tasman Sea to rise, cool and release their moisture. The average rainfall at the 1000-metre level is 6500 mm a year, and at 2000 metres it is a soaking 8000 mm.

Mt Taranaki's high altitude means that trampers are exposed to strong winds, low temperatures and foul weather. The mountain is notorious for sudden changes from clear, fine weather to storms or squalls. Throw together the winds, possible freezing temperatures at night and heavy rains and you have the alpine dangers that have taken more than 40 lives.

NATURAL HISTORY

Volcanic activity began building Mt Taranaki some 70,000 years ago, and in about 30,000 years produced a 150-metre cone. Geologists believe the mountain then entered a dormant stage that ended a mere 3000 years ago with a series of eruptions. When they were over, Taranaki was left with the almost symmetrical cone you see today.

Activity continued with the Newall eruptions in 1500 AD, which destroyed much of the surrounding bush with gas-charged clouds. The most recent eruptions occurred in 1755, only 15 years before Cook sighted the summit. There is debate among geologists over whether Mt Taranaki is still active. Some point to dormant periods that have lasted for several thousand years and say the last eruption was too recent to be sure that it is inactive. Others believe its days of lava and streaming ash are over and that gradually, due to erosion by rain and ice, Egmont will wear down as Kaitake and Pouakai have.

The very high average rainfall and the isolation of Taranaki from the other mountainous regions of New Zealand have created a unique vegetation pattern. Species such as tussock grass, mountain daisy, harebell, koromiko and ourisia have developed local variations and about 100 of the common New Zealand mountain species are not found here. In particular, trampers will notice the complete absence of beech.

The lush rainforest that covers 90% of the park is predominantly made up of broadleaf podocarps. In the lower altitudes, you find many large rimu and rata. Further up, kamahi (often referred to as 'goblin forest' because of its tangled trunks and hanging moss) becomes dominant.

MT TARANAKI ROUND-THE-MOUNTAIN TRACK

The popular Round-the-Mountain (RTM) Track is a four-day, 55-km journey that takes the average tramper 20 hours to complete. It's a scenic walk but not, as many visitors imagine it to be, all above the bush-line. Much of the track drops into forested areas of the park and climbs across scree slopes and herb fields. More climbing will be encountered as you work around numerous bluffs, deep gorges and massive lava flows. The track is well cut and easy to follow.

In 1987, a low-level, all-weather Round-the-Mountain Track was completed, with (predominantly 18-bunk) huts placed a comfortable day's tramp apart. The new circuit takes about five days to walk and is almost entirely through bush. Although the two routes share many of the same tracks, the trip described here is the traditional high-level walk, with spectacular alpine scenery and the best views of Mt Taranaki.

Novices and experienced trampers should be aware of the dangers of Mt Taranaki before embarking on the RTM Track. The mountain often gives a false appearance of being safe. The high altitudes reached on the track mean that inexperienced people are within easy reach of icy slopes, and each year there are numerous accidents in the park – more so than in other alpine areas because of the sudden weather changes. Make sure you have enough warm clothing, preferably of wool, to avoid suffering from exposure.

Information

If you plan to tramp in Egmont National Park, get hold of local information about current track and weather conditions before you set off. The DOC operates a display centre and a visitor information centre on the mountain, offering maps and advice on weather and track conditions.

The North Egmont visitor centre (☎ (06) 756 8710) is the closest to New Plymouth. It's open from 9 am to 5 pm every day in summer (November to Easter), and from 9.30 am to 4.30 pm daily, except Friday, in winter (Easter to November). On the other side of the mountain, the Dawson Falls display centre (☎ (02) 543 0248) is open from 9 am to 5.30 pm Thursday to Monday.

Other places for maps and information on the mountain include the DOC's Stratford field centre (☎ (06) 765 5144), on Pembroke Rd coming up the mountain from Stratford, and the DOC field centre in New Plymouth (☎ (06) 758 0433).

If you want to climb or tramp with other people, there are various possibilities. Try the Stratford Tramping Club (☎ (06) 762 7822, 764 7028) and the Mt Egmont Alpine Club (☎ (06) 278 4460). The DOC can put you in contact with other tramping clubs in the area. Mountain Guides Mt Egmont (☎ (06) 758 8261, 762 4752) offers guided trips to the summit all year round.

Maps

The track is covered on the 1:50,000 Parkmaps No 273-9 *(Egmont National Park)*. In the 1:50,000 Topomaps 260 series, the park is covered on quads P20 *(Egmont)* and P19 *(New Plymouth)*.

Huts

Most huts in the park, including those on the RTM Track, cost $8 a night; Kahui Hut is $4. Arrange payment in advance at one of the visitor centres. You provide your own cooking, eating and sleeping gear, they provide bunks and mattresses. Bookings are not necessary.

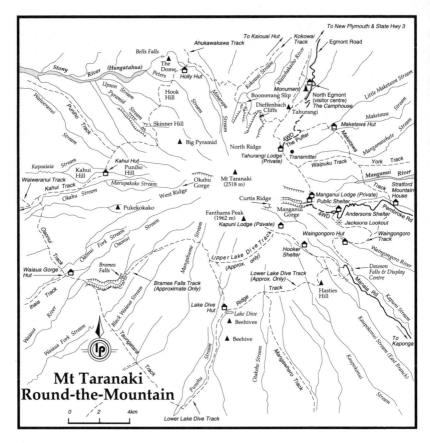

Mt Taranaki
Round-the-Mountain

0   2   4km

Access

New Plymouth is often the best departure point for trampers. The city can be reached from either Wellington or Auckland using InterCity or Newmans services.

There are more than 30 roads that go to or near the park, and from most of them a track leads into it. Three roads – Egmont, Pembroke and Manaia Rds – take you 900 metres up the mountain. These roads are the most common access points into the park; all three terminate near the RTM Track.

Most trampers access the park from Egmont Rd because it's the closest entrance

to New Plymouth. Egmont Rd departs from State Highway 3 some 13 km south-east of New Plymouth; it's then another 16 km to the North Egmont visitor centre. Pembroke Rd extends for 18 km from Stratford to Stratford Plateau (1140 metres), on the eastern side of the volcano. There's a field centre halfway up the road, and three km below the plateau is the Mountain House.

Manaia Rd is 15 km south-west of Stratford, and runs for eight km to Dawson Falls. There is a display centre at Dawson Falls, open daily, as well as backpackers' accommodation at Konini Lodge.

Those without transport will find it easy to hitch to Egmont Village, the turn-off to Egmont Rd on State Highway 3, but harder to get a ride to North Egmont.

Public buses don't go to Egmont National Park, but Tubby's Tours in New Plymouth (☎ (06) 753 6306) operates a daily door-to-door shuttle bus from New Plymouth to the mountain. The cost is $10/15 one-way/return. John Morton (☎ (06) 758 2315) operates an alternative shuttle service to the park from New Plymouth, going up early each morning and returning late in the afternoon.

Many trampers beginning at North Egmont will hike only as far as Stratford Plateau and then hitch down Pembroke Rd to State Highway 3, which cuts a day off the tramp. At Stratford, you can pick up an Inter-City bus to New Plymouth. This is a better alternative than ending the trip at Dawson Falls, because Manaia Rd can be very, very quiet, especially in the middle of the week.

Places to Stay

New Plymouth Most visitors stay in New Plymouth, the nearest large town to the park, from where there's a convenient daily door-to-door shuttle service to the mountain. Alternatively, you can stay in the park itself, or in other nearby towns around the mountain.

There are several camping grounds within easy reach of New Plymouth's centre. The *Belt Rd Seaside Motor Camp* (☎ (06) 758 0228) is at 2 Belt Rd, and the *Aaron Court Caravan Park* (☎ (06) 758 8712) is at 57 Junction Rd, on State Highway 3, three km south of the city centre.

The *Rotary Lodge II* (☎ (06) 753 5720), at 12 Clawton St, charges $13/14 in dorm/double rooms or $10 for tent sites.

Hostel 69 (☎ (06) 758 7153), at 69 Mill Rd, is 1½ km from the town centre; it charges $13. The *Inverness City Budget Lodge* (☎ (06) 758 0404), 48 Lemon St, is more central; it charges $13/15 in singles/doubles.

On the Mountain There are a number of

tramping huts scattered about the mountain which are administered by the DOC and accessible only by trails (see Huts in this section).

The Camphouse, a bunkhouse beside the North Egmont visitor centre (☎ (06) 756 8710), has bunks for $12. *Konini Lodge*, near the Dawson Falls display centre (☎ (025) 43 0248), costs $12 per person.

The Track

The trip can be hiked in either direction, and though a fair bit of climbing is involved, it is rated medium because the track is well cut and easy to follow. By heading anticlockwise, you spread the climbing fairly evenly over the four days.

Stage 1: North Egmont to Holly Hut
Walking Time: three hours
Accommodation: Holly Hut (30 bunks)

The trip begins on the Razorback or Holly Hut Track, near the Camphouse. The track climbs steadily for 240 metres, passing a monument on the way to Tahurangi Trig (1181 metres). It continues beyond the trig and up Razorback Ridge, ascending another 100 metres before reaching a junction with the RTM Track.

Head north-west (from now your direction is anticlockwise) on the well-marked RTM Track as it climbs around Waiwhakaiho River and along the base of Dieffenbach Cliffs, where there are excellent views of New Plymouth. You then descend slightly, cross a branch of Kokowai Stream and pass Boomerang Slip, which is signposted with warning signs. From the slip, the track works around the head of Kokowai Stream and then arrives at a junction with the Kokowai Track.

Head west, following the RTM Track as it crosses two streams and descends 244 metres over 2½ km to the junction with the Ahukawakawa Track. The RTM continues south and quickly crosses two branches and gullies of the Minarapa Stream before reaching Holly Hut. This is a popular place to spend a night in the park, and there are good views of the Pouakai Range from the verandah. From the hut, it's a two-km (half-hour) walk around the Dome to the spectacular, 31-metre Bells Falls. The map of the Pouakai Track in this section shows this part of the track in detail.

Stage 2: Holly Hut to Waiaua Gorge Hut
Walking Time: 5½ hours
Accommodation: Kahui Hut (six bunks); Waiaua Gorge Hut (18 bunks)

The RTM heads west across Holly Flats, passing the junction to Bells Falls, and then turns south into the gully of Peters Stream (named after Harry Peters, a well-known guide and Camphouse caretaker).

It climbs out the other side and then begins a steady ascent for the next two km, past Hook and Skinner hills, to the side of Pyramid Gorge. The erosion caused by Pyramid Stream has left the gorge so unstable that the track alongside it climbs to the tussock grassland above before crossing branches of the stream. Poles mark the route around the gorge; at one point, you climb to 1160 metres and are rewarded with excellent views of Stony River and the distant Pouakai Range.

The route descends from its high point through tussock and tall scrub, becomes a track again and passes the junction with Puniho Track. From here, it's one km to Kahui Hut (880 metres), one of the older huts in the park. This makes a good halfway point for lunch if you intend to spend the night at Waiaua Gorge.

The RTM becomes the Kahui Track as it makes a gentle descent through forest for two km until it reaches a major junction with Oaonui and Waiweranui tracks. The RTM continues to the south-east along the Oaonui Track, crossing numerous streams for the next 2½ km, until it fords the Oaonui Stream and arrives at the junction with the Ihaia Track at the site of the old Oaonui Hut; the Ihaia Track heads south-west for four km, ending at Ihaia Rd.

The RTM continues along Brames Falls Track, crosses a footbridge, and reaches Waiaua Gorge Hut. The new hut, built in 1984, is situated on the cliffs above the deep Waiaua Gorge, and provides excellent views of the western slopes of Taranaki.

Stage 3: Waiaua Gorge Hut to Lake Dive Hut
Walking Time: five to seven hours
Accommodation: Lake Dive Hut (18 bunks)

Choose carefully which track or route you hike from Waiaua Gorge to Lake Dive. The Mangahume Route to Lake Dive Hut is shorter, and much more scenic on a clear day, but involves a great deal more climbing, and should not even be considered during foul weather. The Taungatara Track, though it makes for a longer day, is an easier and safer walk.

From the Waiaua Gorge Hut, the Brames Falls Track immediately descends the gorge, via an aluminium ladder and steep track, to the Waiaua River and then climbs up the other side. It follows the steep edge of the gorge for 500 metres before arriving at the junction with the Taungatara Track. Trampers now have a choice of routes to Lake Dive Hut: through the forest or along an alpine route.

If you follow Taungatara Track to the south-east (the right fork), it will be a five-km walk or a three-hour stroll through thick forest, crossing eight streams, until you reach the junction with the Lower Lake Dive Track, one of the lowest points of the trip, at 535 metres.

The Lower Lake Dive Track continues north-east (the left fork) steadily climbing 400 metres over three km. It takes two hours to walk this stretch. Along the way, the track swings close to Punehu Canyon and has good views of the steep gorge. The track then sidles around the Beehive Hills and arrives at Lake Dive. The hut, built in 1980, is scenically situated at the far end of the lake; on a windless day a reflection of Fanthams Peak graces the water in front of it.

The alternative route is to continue from Waiaua Gorge on the Brames Falls Track, passing the falls, and emerging on tussock slopes, where a route of snow poles replaces the track. It's a climb of 700 metres from the junction with Taungatara Track to Manga-hume Stream, and along the way you sidle below bluffs before dropping to the stream bed and crossing it.

The route continues east and ascends sharply around the steep head of Punehu Gorge. From here, it drops just as quickly to a major junction. The track leading south (the right fork), quickly descends 1½ km to Lake Dive Hut.

Stage 4: Lake Dive Hut to North Egmont
Walking Time: six to seven hours via alpine route; seven to eight hours via low-level tracks
Accommodation: Konini Lodge (38 bunks); Waingongoro Hut (18 bunks); Maketawa Hut (18 bunks)

There are two ways to get from Lake Dive Hut to North Egmont. If you take the higher route, you begin the day by backtracking up towards Fanthams Peak. It's a steep ascent, made easier by numerous steps and 13 short wooden ladders. After passing the sign-posted Mangahume Route junction, the route sidles the slopes beneath Fanthams Peak for 30 to 40 minutes to reach the Kapuni Lodge Track.

To the north-west (the left fork) is the route to the peak; to the south-east (the right fork) are the infamous 'Egmont Steps', which descends 360 metres in just one km on the way to the three-sided Hooker Shelter (1140 metres). The steps continue to drop (240 metres in 1½ km) before reaching the Dawson Falls car park and the display centre. Plan on three hours for this leg of the journey.

If the weather is bad, take the low-level route, which departs from Lake Dive Hut and works its way through the forest before joining the Hasties Hill Track from Dawson Falls. This track ends at the display centre, a three to four-hour walk. If necessary, you could spend the night at Konini Lodge.

At Dawson Falls, you again have two choices. You can elect to take the popular, low-level Waingongoro Track via Waingongoro Hut (18 bunks) to Stratford

Mountain House (two hours), or a higher alpine route.

The alpine route follows the Wilkies Pool Track as it climbs away from the car park along an extremely well-benched and maintained track. The walk starts in a goblin forest, climbs into mountain totara and cedar, and emerges in subalpine scrub near a car park; you'll find Anderson Shelter and Jackson's lookout tower nearby. It's an hour or so from Dawson Falls to this point, where trampers again have a choice of following an alpine route or dropping down to a safer, low-level track.

The alpine route is much more scenic, but harder. Begin by strolling up the ski-field road, then follow the track down into and back out of Manganui Gorge to the public shelter facing the ski field. The track ascends the tussock slopes, passing the old lava flow known as Ngarara Bluff and Warwick Castle. In an hour, it reaches Tahurangi Lodge (locked) and the huge TV transmitter nearby. There's a 4WD track down to North Egmont, but there are better views if you continue along the poled route that descends beneath Humphries Castle to the top of Razorback Track. It is a half-hour descent on Razorback Track, mostly on steps and stairs, to the Camphouse.

The low-level track begins further down Pembroke Rd, across from the Stratford Mountain House. When descending to the Stratford Mountain House, you can enter the bush on the left side of the road and follow the Patea Track to the car park. From here, follow Curtis Falls Track to the Maketawa Hut, a walk of 1½ hours. From the hut, a track descends through the forest to North Egmont, which is a three to four hour walk from the Stratford Mountain House.

POUAKAI TRACK
For those who can't spare four or five days for the RTM trip, the Pouakai Track offers a shorter but equally scenic walk in Egmont National Park. The overnight trip includes spectacular views from the top of the Pouakai Range, which at one time was a volcano of similar size to Mt Taranaki.

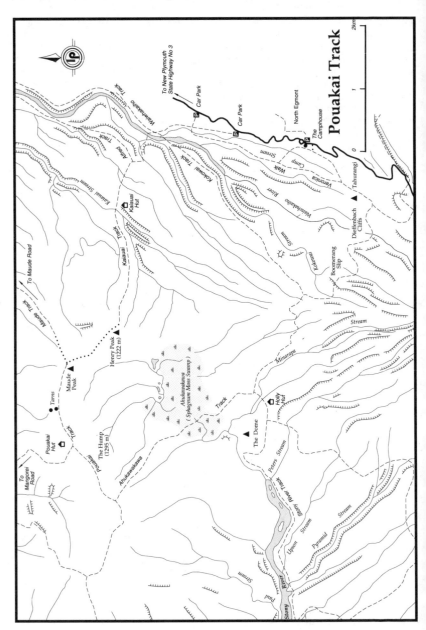

Pouakai Track

Natural erosion has since reduced it to a rugged area of high ridges and rolling hills of subalpine bush. The night can be spent at spacious Pouakai Hut, which has panoramic views of New Plymouth and the Tasman Sea from its verandah.

Information & Maps
See the Mt Taranaki Round-the-Mountain Track section for sources of information and recommended maps. The most commonly used map is the 1:50,000 Parkmaps No 273-9 *(Egmont National Park)*.

Huts
It is hard to believe that vandals wrecked Pouakai Hut in 1994 – perhaps they would like to be stranded on the side of this mountain with no shelter. The Pouakai and Holly huts cost $8, but are well worth the money because their subalpine locations and views are superb. The other hut on this route is Kaiauai, an older four-bunk facility that costs only $4 a night.

Access
The trip is best begun from North Egmont (see the Mt Taranaki Round-the-Mountain Track for transport) and walked as a two-day loop, ending back at the North Egmont visitor centre. You can also depart from Pouakai Hut and hike the Mangorei Track to Mangorei Rd. This will take you back to New Plymouth, but keep in mind that there is usually very little traffic on Mangorei Rd.

The Track
This walk is a two-day loop that follows the RTM Track for part of the way. The track is well marked and benched and is rated medium. It can be walked in either direction.

Stage 1: North Egmont to Pouakai Hut via Holly Hut
Walking Time: five to six hours
Accommodation: Pouakai Hut (16 bunks)

Begin at the Camphouse and hike the Razorback and RTM tracks to Holly Hut (see Stage 1 of the Mt Taranaki Round-the-Mountain

Track). Trampers getting an afternoon start from North Egmont should plan on staying at Holly Hut, a 2½ to three-hour walk from the visitor centre. In this case, take the left fork at the junction with the Ahukawakawa Track and ford Minarapa Stream to reach the 16-bunk facility, a short distance away.

Trampers hiking on to Pouakai Hut should follow the Ahukawakawa Track, which heads north (the right fork) just before the stream. A gentle descent through bush takes you to the south-western end of Ahukawakawa Swamp. The track crosses the open sphagnum swamp and then begins a long climb up a forested ridge. The 304-metre ascent to the junction with the Pouakai Track should take you a little over an hour.

Head north-east from the junction, following the track as it climbs gradually, sidles to the north of the Hump (1295 metres) and then makes a short descent to a saddle. Pouakai Hut, a 2½ to three-hour walk from Holly Hut, is located on the saddle five minutes down Mangorei Track, the western fork (left) of the junction.

If you're planning to return directly to New Plymouth along the Mangorei Track, it's a 2½-hour walk to the end of Mangorei Rd. Once you reach the road, you will probably have to continue walking, because there is little traffic this far up. However, it is mostly downhill to New Plymouth.

Stage 2: Pouakai Hut to Egmont Rd
Walking Time: four hours to Egmont Rd
Accommodation: Kaiauai Hut (four bunks)

Hope for clear weather as you traverse the backbone of the Pouakai Range because the views on this part of the trek are superb. Head north-east along the Pouakai Track as it descends 100 metres before levelling out at the Pouakai Plateau – marked by a pair of tarns, one km from the hut. The track, marked by snow poles, uses boardwalks to cross the fragile bog areas of the flat land. On a clear day, photographers will be able to capture reflections of Mt Taranaki in the tarns.

The track sidles Maude Peak (which can

be climbed in 10 to 15 minutes from the junction with the Maude Track), then drops south-east into a low saddle before steeply climbing 152 metres to the top of Henry Peak (1222 metres). There are more good views from the top, including ones of the ridges and plateaus of the Pouakai Range.

From the top of Henry Peak, the track begins a long, steady descent until it reaches and follows the gorge cut by Kaiauai Stream, 520-metres below the summit. The track eventually drops into the gully, then climbs back out. On the other (eastern) side sits Kaiauai Hut, which is only a little over an hour from Egmont Rd.

Kaiauai Track continues east and within a km reaches a junction with Alfred Track – the first of three tracks to Egmont Rd. From the signposted junction, the track drops off a terrace, crosses a stream a couple of times and arrives at a footbridge across the Waiwhakaiho River.

On the other side is the Waiwhakaiho Track. Head north (left) on this track and within a km you'll come to Mangaoraka Walk, a short track that leads to Egmont Rd, 4½ km from the visitor centre. Head south (the right fork) and the track leads to a car park that is two km from North Egmont. From here, you can also cross a branch of the Waiwhakaiho River and pick up the signposted Veronica Walk, which leads back to the Camphouse and the North Egmont visitor centre.

Whanganui National Park

The 74,231-hectare Whanganui National Park is a lowland forest which lies between Taranaki to the west and Tongariro to the east. The park's dominant feature is the 329-km Wanganui River, the second longest river in New Zealand and the longest navigable river in the country. Although access to the park is difficult, it attracts trampers keen to walk in remote wilderness.

Once a major route for travel between the sea and the interior of the North Island, first

by the Maori and then by the Pakeha, the Wanganui River was eventually superseded by rail and road. In recent years, however, recreational canoe, kayak and jet-boat enthusiasts have once again made the river a popular thoroughfare.

The Matemateaonga Walkway is a four-day walk along the crest of the Matemateaonga Range in Whanganui's remote interior – one end of the track can only be reached by boat. The walkway was opened in 1980 by the New Zealand Walkway Commission as the first major stage of a proposed walk from Cape Egmont to East Cape. It's extremely well graded and is rated easy to medium.

On each day's walk, there are vantage points that offer impressive views of the rugged countryside and glimpses of the peaks of Tongariro National Park. The main interest of this walk though is the lush bush and wilderness; the track itself and an occasional hut are the only artificial features.

HISTORY

The mighty Taranaki and Tongariro mountains battled over the *wahine* (maiden) Pihanga. When the fight ended, Taranaki was forced to flee toward the setting sun. As he plunged wildly westwards, he tore a long, deep gash in the earth. A stream of clear water from Tongariro's side gushed forth and healed this wound. Forests, echoing with the songs of birds, sprang up in the valley of this river, known from then on as Wanganui.

The river was settled early in New Zealand's history. The great Polynesian explorer Kupe explored some distance upriver in around 900 AD. Maoris began to settle along the river around 1350 AD, and flourished in pre-European days.

Food in the valley was plentiful – the Maoris cultivated sheltered terraces, and caught eels using sophisticated weirs on river channels. At each bend of the river, *kaitaki* (guardians) ensured preservation of the *mauri*, or life force, of the place.

Many *kaianga* (villages) were located in the rugged hill country. The many steep bluffs and ridges made suitable sites for pa (fortified villages), which were needed because intertribal warfare was common in this well-populated region (as it was around Mt Taranaki in the 1830s).

The Maori conflicts ceased only with the arrival of European missionaries in the 1840s. Reverend Richard Taylor of the Church of England may have been the most influential minister to travel up the Wanganui, but numerous other churches and missions were built along the banks of the river. At the Maoris' request, Taylor bestowed new names on many of their settlements. Hiru-harama (Jerusalem), Ranana (London), Koriniti (Corinth) and Atene (Athens) still survive today. The ministers persuaded the tribes to abandon their fortified pa and begin cultivating wheat, especially near the lower reaches of the river, where several flour mills were established.

By the early 1900s, there was a fleet of 12 boats plying the river; the largest one capable of carrying 400 passengers. Visitors to the region stayed at the Pipiriki House, a grand hotel with a worldwide reputation, which in 1905 registered a total of 12,000 guests.

In 1912, the Wanganui River Trust was established, and by 1980 it covered an area of 350 sq km. A national park assessment began in 1980, and Whanganui National Park, the country's 11th, was gazetted in December 1986. In 1993, the stretch of the river from Taumarunui south to Pipiriki (including an 87-km section of river between Whakahoro and Pipiriki which runs through an area untouched by roads) was added to the New Zealand Great Walks system and called the 'Whanganui Journey'.

CLIMATE

Whanganui has a mild climate, with few extremes. Annual rainfall ranges from 1000 mm near the coasts to 2500 mm on the high country inland. Frost and snow occur only occasionally on high ridges in winter. Early morning mist is common in summer and is usually the forerunner of a fine day.

NATURAL HISTORY

Whanganui is predominantly covered by a

Kiwi

broadleaf podocarp forest, but several species of beech are also present, including black beech, which often crowns the crests of ridges. The central area of the park, its most isolated section, is also a noted haven for birdlife. The more commonly seen species are the fantail, tui, North Island robin, tomtit and kereru (wood pigeon). Brown kiwis are present throughout the park and may be more numerous here than in any other region of the North Island.

MATEMATEAONGA WALKWAY

The 42-km Matemateaonga Walkway is one of two major tracks in Whanganui National Park. It's also one of the most isolated walks in the North Island. The walkway follows old Maori tracks and a settler's dray road across the broken and thickly forested crests of the Matemateaonga Range, at altitudes of 400 to 730 metres. Surprisingly, the walk is easier than the rugged nature of the countryside suggests, because the old graded road reduces the amount of steep climbing.

Total walking time is around 15 hours and the walk can easily be done in two days by experienced trampers. Most people, however, allow four days for the trip, because arranging transportation to and from the track is complicated, even if you have a vehicle.

Information

Maps, brochures and information about the park are available at the DOC offices in Wanganui (☎ (06) 345 2402), Pipiriki (☎ (06) 385 4631) and Taumarunui (☎ (07) 895 8201). Tourist information centres – at Wanganui, Raetihi, Ohakune and Taumarunui – have information on the park.

Maps

The 1:50,000 Topomaps 260 quad R20 *(Matemateaonga)* covers the entire Matemateaonga Walkway. In the Parkmaps series, there is the 1:160,000 No 273-06 *(Whanganui National Park)*.

For the Mangapurua/Kaiwhakauka Track, you will need the Topomaps 260 quads R20 *(Matemateaonga)*, S19 *(Raurimu)* and S20 *(Ohakune)*.

Huts

There are three huts along the upper section of the river between Whakahoro and Pipiriki: the Whakahoro, John Coull and Tieke (all $8). There are five huts along the Matemateaonga Walkway, but only three of them – the Puketotara, Pouri and Omaru huts – are good Category Two huts (Omaru is actually outside the park in Waitotara Forest). The other two, Humphries Hut and Otaraheke Hut, are much simpler huts ($4). On the lower part of the river, Downes Hut ($4) is on the west bank, opposite Atene. Two other huts, Ngapurua and Mangarau, are free.

During the summer season (1 October to 30 April), a Great Walks hut and camp site pass is required for boat trips on the river involving overnight stays in the park between Taumarunui and Pipiriki; the rule applies only to this stretch of the river. The pass is valid for six nights and seven days and allows you to stay overnight in the huts, in camp sites beside the huts or in other posted camp sites along the river. In order to minimise environmental damage, camping alongside the river is only permitted at designated camp sites in the park.

The Great Walks pass costs $25 if purchased in advance or $35 if purchased on the spot (children aged 11 and over pay half-price, children under 11 are free). Passes are available at all DOC offices and information centres in the region.

Note that back-country hut tickets and annual hut passes are not acceptable during the months that Great Walk passes are required (October-April). Great Walk passes are not required in the off season (1 May to 30 September), when the cost is $8 in huts, $4 for camping beside the huts (camping along the river at the designated camp sites is free); annual hut passes are also acceptable at this time.

Access

The eastern end of the walkway is at Tieke Reach, an isolated bend on the Wanganui River, 25 km upriver from Pipiriki. A half-hour ride on a commercial jet-boat is the only way to get to this end of the track. The western end of the track, at Kohi Saddle, is 60 km from Stratford. Take State Highway 43 to Strathmore and then head east on Brewer Rd to Mangaehu Rd.

Stratford is easily reached from either New Plymouth or Wanganui on an InterCity bus. There are also several private individuals who transport trampers to the end of Mangaehu Rd. Keep in mind these services may change; the best way to discover what is available is to call the DOC regional office in Wanganui.

Departing from Pipiriki, you can take a jet-boat to the start of the Matemateaonga Walkway at Tieke for about $45 per person (the return journey is about the same price). Jet-boat operators in Pipiriki include:

Bridge to Nowhere Jet-Boat Tours, PO Box 192, Raetihi ((☎ /fax (06) 385 4128)
Pipiriki Tours, PO Box 4182, Pipiriki (☎ /fax (06) 385 4733)

For an additional charge, Pipiriki Tours will arrange mini-van transport from Wanganui

Top: Gannets, Cape Kidnappers (NZTB)
Bottom: Mt Taranaki, Mt Egmont National Park (NK)

Top: View from the ridge, Queen Charlotte Walkway (JW)
Bottom: Tramper on Queen Charlotte Walkway (JW)

to Pipiriki. Wanganui is a good place to stage this trip, even if you plan to start from the western end of the track. All the jet-boat operators in Taumarunui and Whakahoro will provide transport to the river ends of the Matemateaonga Walkway and the Manga- purua Track.

There's road access to the river at Taumarunui, Ohinepa and Whakahoro. Whakahoro is a long drive through a remote area, along a road that is unsealed for much of its distance; roads leading to Whakahoro begin at Owhango or Raurimu, both on State Highway 4. There isn't any further road access to the river until you reach Pipiriki, 87 km downstream from Whakahoro. From Pipiriki, the Wanganui River Rd heads south 79 km to Wanganui and east 28 km to Raetihi.

The only way to reach the river by public transport is at Taumarunui, which is served by buses and trains, and at Pipiriki, where the mail-run bus makes a round trip from Wanganui on weekdays.

Places to Stay

There are camp sites, back-country huts and a lodge in the park. The *Bridge to Nowhere Lodge*, also called the *Ramanui Lodge* (☎ (06) 385 4128), has lodge accommoda- tion for $52 per person, meals included. It's quite remote, 21 km upriver from Pipiriki, near the Matemateaonga Walkway. The only way to get to the lodge is by river or on foot. The lodge will arrange for you to come in from Pipiriki by jet-boat.

The Track

The Matemateaonga Walkway can be hiked in either direction. Departure from either end must be carefully timed to coordinate with prearranged jet-boat pick up on the river or vehicle transport at Kohi Saddle. This trip, which is rated easy to medium, will be described from west to east. By walking in this direction, you leave the greatest physical feature of the park, the Wanganui River (and the jet-boat ride down it), as a highlight for the end.

Take good rain gear on this tramp. The

prevailing winds along the Matemateaonga Range are westerlies, and they often bring heavy rainstorms to this upland region of the park. The track can be walked year round, though snow may occasionally be encoun- tered in the winter and early spring.

Stage 1: Kohi Saddle to Omaru Hut
Walking Time: two hours
Accommodation: Omaru Hut (12 bunks)

Kohi Saddle and the walkway are well signposted from Brewer Rd. They're located at the end of Mangaehu Rd, 15 km east of Makahu. There is a large car park at the saddle and a large track sign that marks the beginning of the walkway. The track begins by climbing through regenerating bush along a spur towards the crest of the Matemateaonga Range. Within half an hour, however, you move into a thick forest of kamahi and tawa that will be the dominant feature for the rest of the trip.

The track eventually becomes a three- metre-wide trail as it follows the remains of the original dray road that was cut all the way to Pouri Hut. Sidle the narrow valley of Tanawapiti Stream and follow it to the signposted junction with the track which heads to Puniwhakau Road (three hours away), reached 1½ hours from the car park. Up until 1983, this track served as the western access to the walkway.

At the junction, the walkway has reached the crest of Matemateaonga Range. The track heads east (the left fork), then north, and descends steadily for half an hour. It levels out at a small saddle, where Omaru Hut is located in a clearing. The hut is sur- rounded by forest, but just behind it are ladders that can be used to scramble down to pools near the source of the Omaru Stream.

Stage 2: Omaru Hut to Pouri Hut
Walking Time: 4½ hours
Accommodation: Humphries Hut (two bunks); Pouri Hut (12 bunks)

The track heads south-east from the hut and continues in this direction for practically the

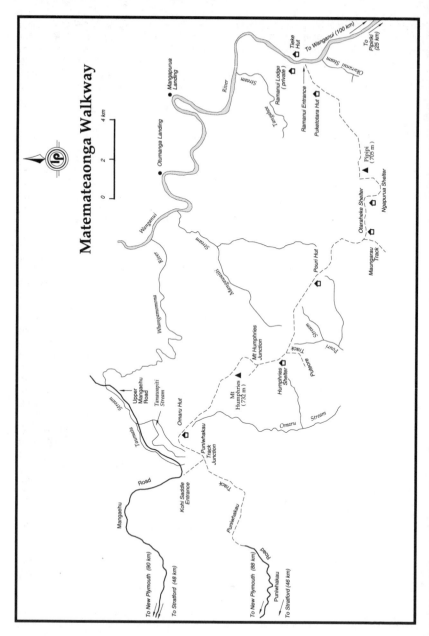

Matemateaonga Walkway

rest of this stage. It follows the south-western slopes of the Matemateaonga Range, but there are few views through the thick forest of mostly kamahi and rata.

After two hours, you cross over to the northern flank of the range; if the day is clear, there is an occasional glimpse of the Tongariro National Park volcanoes through the trees. The track, muddy in places, continues through the forest until it reaches the junction to Mt Humphries (Whakaihuwaka; 'made like the brow of a canoe'), 3½ hours from the hut. The signposted side track climbs 100 metres in a km until it reaches the 732-metres summit. The views are excellent, well worth the 1½-hour round trip to the peak; you can see the King Country to the north and Mt Taranaki to the west.

The walkway continues roughly south-east from the junction and, in 30 minutes or so, passes through Humphries Clearing, where there is a two-bunk shelter, a water tank and camp sites. Just beyond the clearing, the track arrives at the junction with the Puteore Track, a route that heads south-west into the Waitotara Forest. From the junction, it is just another hour to Pouri Hut, situated in a large clearing at the end of the dray road.

Stage 3: Pouri Hut to Puketotara Hut
Walking Time: seven hours
Accommodation: Otaraheke Shelter (two bunks); Ngapurua Shelter (two bunks); Puketotara Hut (12 bunks)

This is the longest leg of the trip, a distance of almost 20 km between huts, but it is an easy walk along a well-graded track which passes through the most pristine forest in the national park. Before taking off from Pouri Hut, make sure your water bottle is full because often the only water source along the ridge is the water tanks at Otaraheke and Ngapurua shelters.

For most of the day, the track remains on the crest of the ridge, at an altitude of about 640 metres, so there is very little climbing. Within three hours, you pass a junction with the Maungarau Track, which heads south. The walkway, however, continues south-east

and quickly descends to the clearing where Otaraheke Shelter is located. If you're not ready to break for tea, it's less than an hour to Ngapurua Shelter, also in a clearing.

Near Mt Pipipi, half an hour beyond Ngapurua Shelter, it's possible to see fossilised shells embedded in the track, and at this point the ridge begins a north-eastern swing. The track continues in this direction and, within 1½ hours, the final descent towards Puketotara Hut begins. It takes an hour to descend the 200 metres to the ridge-top clearing where the hut is located. This is a fitting place for a final night on the walkway – just beyond the hut there are sweeping views of the Wanganui River, while the volcanoes of Tongariro National Park crown the skyline to the east.

Stage 4: Puketotara Hut to Wanganui River
Walking Time: one hour

The final day is short. This is good if you are meeting a jet-boat for the trip back to civilisation, because you must make sure you reach the riverbank well before the jet-boat does. The track quickly drops 100 metres to a lookout along the crest of a spur and then descends steeply again for another 250 metres until you reach the large walkway sign above the sandy banks of the Wanganui River. It's a walk of about one hour down and 1½ hours up. Nearby is a private lodge, Ramanui, and across the river is the Tieke Hut.

OTHER TRACKS
Mangapurua-Kaiwhakauka Track
The Mangapurua Track is a 40-km track between Whakahoro and the Mangapurua Landing, both on the Wanganui River. The track runs along the Mangapurua and Kaiwhakauka streams (both tributaries of the Wanganui River), passing through the valleys of the same names.

Between these valleys, a side track leads to the Mangapurua Trig (663 metres). This is the highest point in the area, from where, on a clear day, you can see all the way to the volcanoes of the Tongariro and Egmont national parks. The route passes through land that was cleared by settlers earlier this century, but later abandoned. The famous Bridge to Nowhere, a large concrete structure built in 1936, is 40 minutes from the Mangapurua Landing end of the track.

The track takes 20 hours and is usually walked in three to four days. Apart from the Whakahoro Hut, at the Whakahoro end of the track, there are no huts. There are, however, many fine places for camping, with water available from numerous small streams. There is road access to the track at the Whakahoro end, and from a side track leading to the end of the Ruatiti Valley-Ohura Rd coming from Raetihi. Most trampers catch a jet-boat downriver from Mangapurua Landing to Pipiriki at the end of the track. This has to be arranged beforehand.

Tararua Forest Park

North of Wellington, there is a place where the wind whips along the sides of mountains and the fog creeps silently in the early morning. It's a place where gales blow through steep river gorges, snow falls lightly on sharp greywacke peaks and rain trickles down the sides of narrow ridges.

Tararua Forest Park and Wellington go hand and hand. For years the park was almost an exclusive weekend retreat for hikers and tramping clubs from the windy city. The park is only 50 km north of Wellington, so the Tararuas will always be a quick escape for those who live in the city. But today, trampers from around the country are attracted to the park's broken terrain and the sheerness of its features, which present a challenge to the most experienced walkers.

The park is centred on the Tararua Range, which stretches for 80 km north from Featherston to the Manawatu Gorge, a natural gap that separates it from the Ruahine Range. The tallest peak is Mitre (1571 metres), in the eastern central region, but there are many others close to that height throughout the park. Between the peaks, the ridges and spurs above the bush-line are renowned for being narrow, steep and exposed.

Tramping has a long history in the park, which has resulted in an extensive network of tracks and routes and more than 60 huts and shelters. Because of the capricious weather and the rugged terrain, trampers who undertake the longer treks into the heart of the park should be both experienced and well prepared. Keep in mind that tracks in this park are not as well formed as those in most other national parks, so it's easy to lose them – they are mostly of tramping and route standard. On the open ridge tops, there are rarely signposts or poles marking the routes, only the occasional cairn.

The trips described in this section are less demanding than most routes through Tararua, and are therefore undertaken by a greater number of trampers. The Mt Holdsworth Circuit is a two to three-day loop over the 1470-metre peak, beginning and ending at the Holdsworth Lodge, the eastern gateway to the park. The trip through Totara Flats also begins at the lodge, and is perhaps the best tramp for less experienced trampers, because it involves no open ridges or alpine areas at all. The three-day walk covers 40 km and involves climbing three low saddles.

HISTORY

Although the range was probably too rugged for any permanent Maori settlements, the local Maoris did establish several routes through the range to the western coast. It was Maori guides who led J C Crawford to the top of Mt Dennan in 1863, the first recorded ascent in the range by a European. From the 1860s to the late 1880s, prospectors struggled over the ridges and peaks in search of gold, but little was ever found.

The Tararua Tramping Club, New Zealand's first such club, was formed in 1919 by Wellington trampers who were keen to promote trips into the range. Independent trampers, however, had been visiting the range since the 1880s.

When the Forest Service was established in 1919, a move began to reserve a section of the Tararua Range, but it was not until 1952 that the government set aside the area as New Zealand's first state forest park. It was gazetted in 1967, and today covers 116,627 hectares. It is administered by the DOC.

CLIMATE

Wind, fog and rain are the park's trademarks. The entire park is exposed to westerly winds that funnel through the gap between the North and South islands. The range is often the first thing the airstreams hit, and they hit it with full force, smacking against the high ridges and peaks. At times, it's almost impossible to stand upright in the wind, especially with a pack on.

Calm afternoons and days of gentle breezes do occur during the summer, along with cloudless evenings that give way to glorious views of the sunset from the mountain tops. But on average, the summits and peaks are fogbound two days out of three.

Rainfall averages around 1500 mm in the lowlands, 2500 mm in the foothills and 5000 mm or more above the bush-line. Snow may lie above 1200 metres for three to four months of the year, and a snowstorm can be expected at any time in the alpine region.

It is the sudden storms – fierce and full of rain – that set the Tararuas apart from other parks in the country. They arrive with little warning and have dumped as much as 333 mm of rain in a single day. Trampers must be prepared to spend an extra day in the hut if such storms blow in, because they quickly reduce visibility in the uplands and cause rivers to flood dangerously in the lowlands.

NATURAL HISTORY

The sediments that would later form the Tararua Range were laid down in a deep sea basin some 200 million years ago. Earth movements along a series of faults that extended through the Upper Hutt Valley and the Wellington region resulted in a complicated uplifted mass of folded and faulted rock. This mass was subsequently eroded by wind, rain and ice, resulting in the rugged Tararua Range, which separates the rolling Wairarapa farm district from the western coast.

There is a good variety of flora in the park, and many plants reach their southern limits here. The forest is predominantly beech, with scattered rimu and northern rata in the lowlands. Silver beech is the species along the bush-line. Above 1200 metres, the forest gives way to open alpine vegetation of tussock and snow grass.

MT HOLDSWORTH CIRCUIT

The Mt Holdsworth recreation area is a beautiful spot to begin any trip in the forest park. Surrounded by rugged hills and graced by the rushing waters of Atiwhakatu Stream, this is a popular starting point for both trampers and day-users. There are no shops at Mt Holdsworth; any last-minute items must be picked up at Masterton, the last town before you turn off State Highway 2 into the park.

Information

There is a year-round caretaker (☎ (06) 377 0022) at Mt Holdsworth recreation area; the caretaker's office serves as an information centre. The caretaker also collects hut and camp site fees. There is a DOC field centre at Masterton (☎ (06) 378 2061) in the Departmental Building on Chapel St. It's open from 8 am to 4.30 pm Monday to Friday.

Maps

The walk is covered on the 1:50,000 Topomaps 260 quad S26 *(Carterton)*, and on the 1:100,000 Parkmaps No 274-02 *(Tararua Forest Park)*, which includes all the tracks and huts within the range.

Huts

The huts on this track include the Category Two Powell and Jumbo huts ($8) and the Category Three Atiwhakatu Hut ($4). At the start of the track is the Holdsworth Lodge (see Places to Stay in this section).

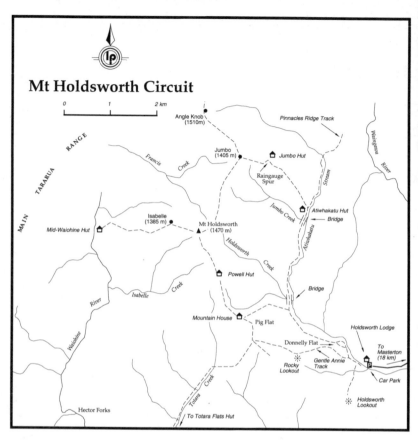

Mt Holdsworth Circuit

Access

You can reach the town of Masterton from Wellington by InterCity bus or on the Wellington-Masterton train.

If you don't have your own vehicle, getting from Masterton to Mt Holdsworth involves a taxi (which is expensive) or hitching.

The recreation area is reached from State Highway 2 by turning west onto Norfolk Rd, just south of Masterton. Norfolk Rd leads into Mt Holdsworth Rd, which ends at the recreation area, 15 km from State Highway 2. The roads aren't quite the hitchhiker's nightmare they appear on the map – there are a number of sheep stations along the way,

and between the farmers and the day visitors to the park, you can usually pick up a ride if you're patient.

Places to Stay

Plan on spending at least one night at Mt Holdsworth, either at the 32-bunk *Holdsworth Lodge* (☎ (06) 377 0022) or at a camp site ($8/4 for adults/children). Camping on the grassy flats around the lodge costs $4 (children $2).

The Track

This 20-km tramp, rated medium to difficult, can be walked in either direction, though

most people tend to hike up to Powell Hut
and return via Jumbo Hut.

Stage 1: Holdsworth Lodge to
Powell Hut
Walking Time: three to four hours
Accommodation: Mountain House (32
bunks); Powell Hut (40 bunks)

The track departs from the lodge on a wide,
gravel path, crosses Atiwhakatu Stream and
immediately passes a track to Holdsworth
Lookout (half an hour one-way). The junction with Gentle Annie Track (which heads
west) is a couple of hundred metres further.

Follow the well-graded Gentle Annie
Track, which climbs steadily on its way to
Mountain House. Approximately one hour
from the lodge, it reaches Rocky Lookout,
from which there are good views of Powell
Hut and, for those with sharp eyes, the trig
on Mt Holdsworth.

The track sidles around from Rocky
Lookout to the intersection with the Totara
Creek Track, approximately 45 minutes
from Rocky Lookout. The track continues
north (signposted) into Pig Flat, and crosses
to a track to Mountain House. Along the way,
you pass a side track that follows the ridge
to the same hut.

Mountain House, built by the Wellington
Tramping & Mountaineering Club, is a two-
hour walk from the lodge. It is listed as
capable of accommodating 20 people, but it
is badly run down, with no mattresses and a
shabby interior. Powell Hut is another one to
two hours' walk, and a much more pleasant
place to spend the night.

The track begins a steep climb to Powell
Hut but it is well cut and marked. It stays in
bush for most of the ascent, emerging from
the bush-line into subalpine scrub only in the
last 15 minutes. Powell Hut was built in 1981
to replace an older hut, constructed in 1939.
It sleeps 40 comfortably, and has gas rings,
mattresses and an excellent view of the surrounding mountains and valleys. If the night
is clear, you can watch the lights of
Masterton appear after sunset.

Stage 2: Powell Hut to Jumbo Hut
Walking Time: 3½ to four hours
Accommodation: Jumbo Hut (30 bunks)

The rest of the climb to Mt Holdsworth is
technically a route, with very few markers or
cairns. But the trip is so popular that a track
has been worn to the peak and most of the
way to Jumbo Hut. Before leaving Powell
Hut, fill your water bottle because there is
little water along the ridge.

The track begins next to the hut, then
climbs steeply for 15 to 20 minutes, until you
reach a small knob with a battered sign on
top. Below is Powell Hut; above, in good
weather, you can see the trig on Mt Holdsworth. It takes another 30 to 45 minutes to
follow the ridge that leads to the trig. The
1470-metre summit is a 210-metre climb
from the hut. It has excellent views of Mt
Hector, the main Tararua Range and the
small towns along State Highway 2.

Three ridges come together at Mt Holdsworth. The track from Powell Hut follows
one ridge, while another ridge is marked by
an obvious route that heads first north-west
then west towards Mid-Waiohine Hut (two
hours). Those heading to Jumbo Hut
(signposted) need to head directly east. You
almost have to backtrack a few steps from
the trig to pick up the partially worn track
that drops quickly to the ridge below.

Once on the ridge, it takes 1½ to two hours
to reach Jumbo Hut. The route climbs a
number of knobs: the first is marked with a
rock cairn near the top, the second involves
working around some rock outcrops on the
way up, and the third climb is towards Jumbo
Peak, which is really a pair of knobs with
several small tarns between them. The knob
to the south has a small cairn at one side; a
track which runs along the east-sloping ridge
begins here. By continuing on the main
ridge, you reach Angle Knob in about 40
minutes.

Within 15 to 20 minutes, the route to
Jumbo Hut comes to a spot on the ridge
where it's possible to spot the hut far below.
From Jumbo Peak, it's a steady half-hour
descent to the hut. Jumbo Hut was built in

1982, upgraded in 1993, and has excellent views from its verandah. At night you can view the town lights of Masterton, Carterton and Greytown, and if you get up early on a clear morning, the sunrise is spectacular.

It's less than a four-hour walk from one hut to the next, so an enjoyable afternoon can be spent exploring the ridges to the north and viewing prominent features such as Broken Axe Pinnacle or the Three Kings.

Stage 3: Jumbo Hut to Holdsworth Lodge

Walking Time: three to four hours
Accommodation: Atiwhakatu Hut (10 bunks)

The day begins with a steady descent to the Atiwhakatu Stream. Just south of Jumbo Hut, there is a new benched track. The route to the bush edge is marked, and this is the beginning of the descent of Raingauge Spur. The track is well marked, but steep and slippery, especially during wet weather. It should take about an hour to reach the valley. Atiwhakatu Hut is at the bottom of this track.

The hut, built in 1968, is clean and well maintained, though its location is less than inspiring. Just upstream are some shaded river flats, used occasionally for camp sites. It is planned in the near future to replace this hut with a Category Two hut about one hour upstream on the true left bank, where Atiwhakatu Stream swings west, at the bottom of the Pinnacle Ridge Track – ask at either the Wellington regional office or Holdsworth Lodge.

The track from the hut to Mt Holdsworth is well-defined and level. In the past, Jumbo Stream and Holdsworth Creek posed problems in wet weather; in fact they were downright dangerous. Now they are bridged, making the track negotiable in all weather. There's a junction not long after the bridge across Holdsworth Creek, and the trail to the west climbs steeply to Mountain House (one to 1½ hours).

The main track is well formed at this point and runs along the stream, past a small gorge, to Donnelly Flat, one km from the junction.

Donnelly Flat is a traditional camping area, and only a km from Holdsworth Lodge. There's a 15-minute loop track at the flat, which passes through tall stands of podocarp forest – rimu, matai and kahikatea. The walk from Donnelly Flat to Holdsworth Lodge backtracks along the starting route for part of the way. It's about 15 minutes to the lodge from the junction with Gentle Annie Track.

TOTARA FLATS TRACK

This is a three-day walk from Holdsworth Lodge down the Totara Flats in Lower Waiohine Valley and then along Tauherenikau Valley to the Kaitoke car park, 14 km north of Upper Hutt on State Highway 2. It's a good trip for less-experienced parties who may be unsure about crossing open, unmarked, alpine, ridge routes. The walk traverses open river flats and three low saddles, but never really climbs above the bush-line.

Information

There is a visitor centre at the Mt Holdsworth recreation area. The DOC district office (☎ (06) 378 2061) in Masterton is open from 8 am to 4.30 pm Monday to Friday.

Maps

The 1:100,000 Parkmaps No 274-02 *(Tararua Forest Park)* is fine for this walk. Alternatively, pick up the 1:50,000 Topo-maps 260 quad S26 *(Carterton)*.

Huts

The huts on this track include the Totara Flats and Tutuwai huts ($8), the Sayers and Cone huts ($4) and the Smith Creek Shelter.

Access

The northern end of the track is the Mt Holdsworth recreation area (see the Access section for the Mt Holdsworth Circuit). The southern end is the Kaitoke car park and day shelter, located on Marchant Rd, a 20-minute walk from State Highway 2. There's a youth hostel at the corner of Marchant Rd and the highway.

You can catch the Hutt Valley suburban

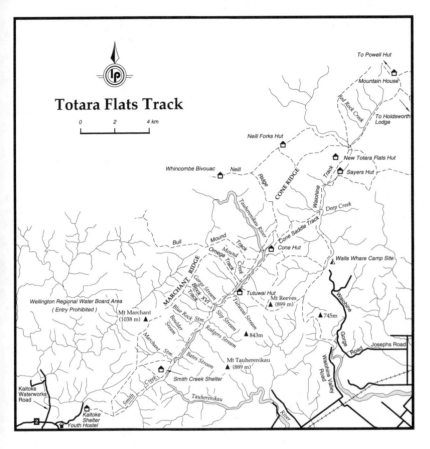

Totara Flats Track

0   2   4 km

train from Upper Hutt to Kaitoke; trains leave Upper Hutt about every half-hour on weekdays, a little less frequently on Saturday and Sunday.

Vandalism and theft are problems at the Kaitoke car park, so trampers with their own vehicles would probably be better off starting out from Holdsworth Lodge, where there is a safer car park.

Places to Stay
The *Kaitoke Youth Hostel* (☎ (06) 526 4626) is conveniently located at the corner of Marchant Rd and State Highway 2. It

charges $9 per night and is accessible via the Masterton bus. At Holdsworth recreation area, there's the Holdsworth Lodge and a camping ground (see Places to Stay for the Mt Holdsworth Circuit).

The Track
The three-day walk is described from Holdsworth Lodge to Kaitoke. The track crosses three low saddles and is rated medium.

Stage 1: Holdsworth Lodge to Totara Flats
Walking Time: four to five hours

Accommodation: New Totara Flats Hut (30 bunks)

The track begins by climbing from the Mt Holdsworth recreation area car park, past Rocky Lookout, to the signposted junction to Totara Flats. This is a 1½ to two-hour walk (see Stage 1 of the Mt Holdsworth Circuit for a description).

Take the fork that heads south, which begins with a steep descent along a well-worn track – so worn in places that it looks like a gully.

The track drops 400 metres in less than an hour before crossing Totara Creek; an easy ford most of the time. On the true right (west) side, the track becomes a level walk, only occasionally climbing to avoid a steep embankment. Keep an eye out for discs and rock cairns to help you stay on the track.

In 2½ km (about an hour's walk), the track reaches the confluence of Totara Creek and the bridged Waiohine River. Once on the other side, the track heads south, immediately coming to the site where the Old Totara Flats Hut once stood.

The track descends near the river and then emerges onto the grassy areas of Totara Flats. Across the flats and 20 minutes from the old hut site, the track leads around a stand of trees to the New Totara Flats Hut, situated at the edge of the bush-line. The hut is only a four to five-hour hike from the lodge, but is by far the most pleasant place to stay along the route. It has gas, mattresses, a warden (on weekends) and a sweeping view of the flats.

Stage 2: Totara Flats to Tutuwai Hut

Walking Time: 4½ to five hours
Accommodation: Cone Hut (12 bunks); Tutuwai Hut (20 bunks)

The flats are a scenic spot, and have a fine view of Mt Holdsworth to the north and the foothills you'll soon be climbing over to the south. For an interesting side trip, hike up the Waiohine River Gorge – best done in the water when the river is at a normal level. If the New Totara Flats Hut is too crowded, there is always Sayers Hut (eight bunks),

located on the opposite side of the river, halfway down the flats. It's an older hut with an interesting interior, but look carefully for it, because it's easy to miss.

Totara Flats are two km long and easily the largest clearing in the Tararuas. Cut across the grassy area to the bluff at the southern end, where a track ascends to the right (south-east). The track returns to the river and immediately climbs another bluff. When water levels are normal, this extra climbing can be avoided by simply following the Waiohine and fording it at appropriate places.

Within 1½ hours of the hut, the track swings inland and crosses Makaka Creek, identified by its sharp descent and the distinctive S-curve of the Waiohine at this point. Cross the stream several metres upstream from the confluence, then pass through a dry creek bed and climb a short distance up a steep embankment.

On top of the embankment, the track swings right and climbs again to reach a signposted junction with the Cone Saddle Track (to the south-west) and the track to Walls Whare Camp Site (which continues south along the river terraces).

The Cone Saddle Track (the right fork) begins with a steep climb of 300 metres to a roundish knob, and then sidles down to Clem Creek; the track reappears on the other side of the creek and is marked by a large cairn. It then makes a gentle ascent to the saddle and a signposted junction of four tracks.

Head for the Tauherenikau River and follow the track down a steep 240-metre descent over the next half hour. The track arrives at Cone Hut, a historic slab hut that is still used occasionally by those who like to reminisce about tramping in days gone by. For those with a tent, there are excellent camp sites just a short way downriver.

The last segment of the day is a three-km walk across grassy flats towards Tutuwai Hut. Most of the time, the track remains just below the bush-line, but it's easy to make your own way across the flat for a much more scenic walk. Eventually, a sign points to a hut that sits on a terrace above the river, an hour's walk or less from Cone Hut. Tutuwai Hut has mattresses, gas cookers and a nice view of the river flats.

Stage 3: Tutuwai Hut to Kaitoke

Walking Time: five to six hours
Accommodation: Smith Creek Shelter (20 bunks)

Twenty minutes after leaving Tutuwai Hut, you arrive at the swing bridge across the Tauherenikau River. If the river is flooded, an all-weather track on the true right side will keep you away from the water by ascending the bluffs which surround most side streams.

There are some steep climbs around Gorge, Blue Rock and Boulder streams during the six km to Smith Creek, but the views of the valley are worth the effort. The alternative is to follow the river all the way to Smith Creek Shelter; in normal conditions, this would involve following the flats most of the way, with only an occasional ford to avoid the steep bluffs.

As the track nears Marchant Stream, it swings inland. The stream is easily identified by the cable strung across it to assist trampers during flooded conditions. When water levels are normal, you can cross it without getting your boots wet. Smith Creek Shelter, 10 to 15 minutes from the stream, is in sad shape because of its proximity to the road; there are no mattresses, no tables and no water.

The track from the shelter is a popular day walk. It's a wide path most of the way, and soon passes a track to the former Dobsons Hut site (the hut was removed in 1994). It crosses Smith Creek in an hour and then begins a steep climb to the saddle, reached after the track sidles the ridge for the last few hundred metres. From the saddle, there are impressive views of the sheep stations and farms in Hutt River Valley.

From here, it's a half-hour descent to the car park, and there are plenty of views along the way. You'll also pass the signposted Southern Crossing Track to the Marchant Ridge and Alpha Hut.

You pick up a metalled road at the car park, and in 10 minutes arrive at the three-sided Kaitoke Shelter. It takes another 20 minutes of walking to arrive at State Highway 2 and the Kaitoke Youth Hostel.

OTHER TRACKS
Southern Crossing

This is the classic crossing of the Tararua Range, usually made from near Otaki to Kaitoke, climbing Mt Hector (1529 metres) along the way. This extremely challenging trip should not be undertaken by trampers without extensive alpine experience. The route is usually walked in two to three days, following Fields Track to Mt Hector, crossing Dress Circle and descending by way of Marchant Ridge. There are three huts along the track: Field, Kime and Alpha. The Parawai Lodge at Otaki Forks is at the western start of the track.

Haurangi Forest Park

The Haurangi Forest Park straddles the Aorangi Range in the south-eastern corner of the North Island. This little-known area is predominantly beech forest, with steep-sided valleys and no open tops.

A good two to three-day walk from the DOC Te Kopi field centre (☎ (06) 307 8230) to Cape Palliser crosses four low saddles. Along the route, there is a choice of four huts – Washpool, Pararaki, Kawakawa and Mangatoetoe – all six-bunk, Category Three huts. The tracks are well maintained and marked, but this is definitely a walk for those who like to get away from it all.

South Island

Marlborough Region

So often the poor cousin of the popular Nelson region to the west, the Marlborough Sounds area is now being discovered by overseas travellers. New Zealanders have been enjoying the Sounds for well over a century, but often neglected the area's tremendous tramping potential. This is now being redressed, and trampers are starting to comb the ridges and forests that border the beautiful waterways.

Marlborough Sounds

The convoluted, labyrinthine waters of the Marlborough Sounds have many bays, islands, coves and waterways, which were formed by the sea invading deep valleys after the ice ages. Parts of the area are now included in the 52,000-hectare Marlborough Sounds Maritime Park (actually many small reserves separated by private land).

The region has increased in popularity as a tramping destination in recent years because of the number of good tracks that have been developed. Two of the tracks covered here, the Queen Charlotte Walkway and the Nydia Track, give trampers an opportunity to see two different parts of the picturesque Sounds. The third walk, the Pelorus Track, links the Pelorus Scenic Reserve with Nelson via a series of tracks through the Mt Richmond Forest Park.

HISTORY
The Sounds are very much part of the legend of Kupe. After fighting with the octopus in the waters of Raukawa (now Cook Strait), the exhausted Kupe sent his pigeon, Rupe, to find forest plants for food. At the same time, his shag, Te Kawau-a-Toru, was sent to learn the sea currents. The shag was drowned in the whirlpools near Rangitoto Island (now D'Urville Island) and the mainland. Kupe,

saddened by the loss of Te Kawau-a-Toru, returned to Hawaiki, his homeland.

The argillite quarries of D'Urville Island are just some of the many archaeological sites in the Sounds which yield information about the long Maori occupation of the area. It appears that the pa and the sites surrounding them were not permanently occupied, and that the Maoris were highly mobile, moving with the seasons to harness different resources.

The first European to visit the Marlborough district was Abel Tasman, who spent five days sheltering on the eastern coast of D'Urville Island in 1642. It was to be more than a century before the next Pakeha, James Cook, turned up, in January 1770. Cook stayed 23 days and made four more visits to the stretch of water he named Queen Charlotte Sound during the next seven years. Cook found the native plant *Lepidium oleraceum* (scurvy grass) a good source of vitamin C for his crew. In 1827, the French navigator of *L'Astrolabe*, Jules Dumont d'Urville, discovered the narrow strait now known as French Pass, and his officers named the island to the north in his honour.

In the same year, a whaling station was set up at Te Awaiti, in Tory Channel, which led to the first permanent European settlement in the district. In June 1840, Governor Hobson's envoy, Major Bunbury, arrived on the HMS *Herald* to hunt for Maori signatures to the Treaty of Waitangi. On 17 June, at Horahora Kakahu Island, Bunbury proclaimed British sovereignty over the South Island.

In spite of this, the Marlborough area was not the site of an organised settlement; it was more of an overflow from the Nelson colony. When Wairau settlers realised that revenue from land sales in their area was being used to develop the Nelson district, they petitioned for independence. The appeal was successful and the colonial government called the new region Marlborough –

approving one of the two settlements, Waitohi (now Picton), as the capital. At the same time, the other settlement, known as 'The Beaver', was renamed Blenheim. After a period of intense rivalry between the two towns, the capital was transferred peacefully to Blenheim in 1865.

As early as the 1870s, the Sounds were becoming a popular recreational area. A great number of guesthouses were established, including the Portage. Many of the first areas developed for tourism lie along or close to the Queen Charlotte Walkway.

CLIMATE

The Marlborough Sounds have a temperate climate. High rainfall is experienced in a number of places, as the lush rainforest attests. Close to Cook Strait, the prevailing westerly winds mean that the outer parts of the Sounds can be subject to severe storms.

In the central Sounds, the weather is mitigated by the surrounding hills. Summer days are particularly pleasant, with the water often still and the only evidence of moisture in the air being the clouds that hug the ridges. The two water stops on the high section of the walkway between Te Punga and the Portage will be well used on many days in summer; it can get extremely dry along parts of the track.

NATURAL HISTORY

The Marlborough Sounds have a variety of natural habitats – grassy areas of farmland, gorse-covered regenerating forest and, most importantly, undisturbed natural forest. The Queen Charlotte Walkway and the Nydia Track offer good chances to experience this great diversity and are representative of much of the Sounds.

Of particular interest is the remnant podocarp coastal forest, such as that seen on the Nydia Track. Ngawhakawhiti Bay is a good example of a broadleaf, almost subtropical, coastal forest, with pukatea, tawa, matai, rimu, miro, beech and nikau palm, and a blanket of riotous kiekie. The Queen Charlotte Walkway is distinctly divided into three recognisable forest types: coastal forest at Ship Cove, regenerating forest from Kenepuru to Torea saddles, and mature beech forest between Mistletoe Bay and Anakiwa.

Birdlife in the Sounds is prolific. The birds of the forest include the bellbird, tomtits, silvereyes and tui. In summer, you will hear long-tailed and shining cuckoos and, at night, the morepork and weka. Waders are prominent in tidal estuaries. In the outer islands, you may be lucky enough to spot the king shag, which is common in Pelorus and Queen Charlotte sounds, but quite rare elsewhere. Occasionally, you will see Australasian gannets, masters of the air, plunging into the water to take fish. Accompanying them may be terns and shearwaters.

QUEEN CHARLOTTE WALKWAY

The Marlborough Sounds have long been recognised as one of the jewels of New Zealand. Those put off by the hordes doing the Abel Tasman Track may wish to try this alternative. It's a 67-km track which connects historic Ship Cove with Anakiwa (Cave of Kiwa), passing through privately owned land and DOC reserves. The coastal forest is lush, and from the ridges you can look into either Queen Charlotte or Kenepuru sounds.

The walk can be done in segments (see the Access section) or as a single three to four-day journey. There are many camp sites for those with tents, as well as a number of hostels and hotels. Remember that you are here only through the cooperation of local landowners, so respect their property and carry out what you carry in.

Information

The most convenient place to get information is from the DOC Picton field centre (☎ 573 7582) on the Picton foreshore, or across the road at the station (☎ 573 8838). The Blenheim information centre (☎ 578 9904), in the Forum Building, Queen St, also has information on the track. The book, *Marlborough Sounds Maritime Park* ($15.95), is an excellent introduction to the area. The small DOC pamphlet *Queen Charlotte*

Walking Track has a brief account of the stages, and is useful for planning.

Maps

A good map of the whole Sounds area is the 1:100,000 Holidaymaker No 336-07 *(Marlborough Sounds)*. For complete coverage of the Sounds with the 1:50,000 Topomaps 260 series, you would need four quads: P26 *(French Pass)*, Q26 *(Cape Jackson)*, P27 *(Picton)* and Q27 *(Cook Strait)* – all up, $50 worth.

Huts

There are no DOC huts along the Queen Charlotte Walkway, but there are well-spaced camp sites. A lot of trampers elect to stay in private accommodation along the walk (see Places to Stay in this section).

Access

The best way to complete the walkway is to catch a boat (water-taxi) from Picton to the start of the track at Ship Cove, and return by bus from Linkwater (the turn-off into Anakiwa).

To/From Picton Picton has several water-taxis that can take you anywhere in the Sounds, including hotels and walking tracks accessible only by water. Check first, though, with the tour boat operators. Most tour boats will gladly take you along on the tour, dropping you off and picking you up wherever and whenever you wish; they can be cheaper than the taxis.

If you are planning to walk the whole track, Cougar Line (☎ 573 7925), 10 London Quay, Picton, operates a drop-off service at Ship Cove, the preferred starting point for the walk ($34 per person). It leaves at 8.15 am and arrives at the drop-off point at about 9 am. An afternoon service leaves Picton at 2.15 pm (minimum of two people). They will transfer packs for free (eg Ship Cove to Te Punga). Arrow Water Taxi (☎ 573 8229) goes to Ship Cove on demand; the minimum cost is $120 per trip/$30 per person.

The Beachcomber Cruises 'mail run' boat (☎ 573 7925) departs from Picton at 11.15 am on Tuesday and Friday and arrives at Ship Cove at about 1.30 pm ($28 per person). You can also sail to Ship Cove, or any other part of the track, on the 28-foot yacht *Tamarack* (☎ 578 8236); the cost per person is $35. Rich? Float Air (☎ 573 6433) will fly you to any part of the track accessible by water.

To/From Anakiwa At the Anakiwa end, the mail van (☎ 577 8386) can pick you up at approximately 10 to 10.15 am, Monday to Saturday, for the return trip to Picton. The van leaves Picton at 9 am for those wishing to walk the track in the opposite direction; the cost either way is $5.

Buses operated by Skyline Connections (☎ 542 3159 in Nelson, 573 8857 in Picton) run daily between Picton and Nelson, passing the Linkwater turn-off to Anakiwa. They leave Nelson at 8.30 am (via Queen Charlotte Scenic Route); and they leave Picton at 1.35 pm, arriving in Linkwater at about 2.10 pm ($8). They will go on to Anakiwa for an extra $2; which is worth it, because this is a rather boring stretch of road.

A Havelock-based operator, Sounds Detours (☎ 574 2104), will take a group to the start of the track at Anakiwa ($30 minimum/$5 per person); they will also pick up or drop off at Te Mahia ($60 minimum/ $10 per person). Another operator, Corgi Bus Co (☎ 573 7125), will drop off and pick up

---

Queen Charlotte Guided Walk Options

Beachcomber's Sounds Outdoors (☎ 573 6175) conducts four-day guided walks along the walkway for $495 (minimum two persons); it's a good alternative for those wanting to do the walk in a leisurely manner without having to carry equipment. The Cougar Line (☎ 573 7925) offers a one-day adventure walk from Ship Cove to Resolution Bay; for $76 you get return transport to Picton and the opportunity to walk through some of the beautiful forest. ■

from Anakiwa on demand ($25 minimum/ $10 per person).

Places to Stay
There are plenty of places to stay on the Sounds, some accessible only by boat or floatplane (which means they're often in some beautiful settings). Prices are usually fairly reasonable, and practically all places offer free use of dinghies and other facilities.

In the Sounds There are a number of DOC self-registration camp sites in the area, including six on the Queen Charlotte Walkway. The four on Queen Charlotte Sound are Camp Bay (Punga Cove), Mistletoe Bay, Resolution Bay and Umungata Bay – Cowshed Bay (the Portage) is on Kenepuru Sound and the Bay of Many Coves Saddle is above the Bay of Many Coves.

Various places around the Sounds offer cheap trampers' accommodation. They include the *Resolution Bay Camp & Cabins* (☎ 579 9411) in Resolution Bay ($10) and the *Furneaux Lodge* (☎ 579 8259) on the Endeavour Inlet section of the Queen Charlotte Walkway ($12.50).

The well-known *Portage Hotel* (☎ 573 4309) is on Kenepuru Sound; bunks are $15. The *Te Mahia Resort* (☎ 573 4089) charges $15. *Punga Cove Tourist Resort* (☎ 579 8561), on Endeavour Inlet, Queen Charlotte Sound, and the *Endeavour Resort* (☎ 579 8381), in Endeavour Inlet, have backpackers' beds for $15.

Picton The *Blue Anchor Holiday Park* (☎ 573 7212), on Waikawa Rd about 500 metres from the town centre, has camp sites/ cabins at $16/26. *Alexander's Motor Park* (☎ 573 6378) is a km out, on Canterbury St. It has sites/cabins for $7/24.

Wedgwood House (☎ 573 7797), an Associate YHA hostel at 10 Dublin St, charges $14 per night. The friendly *Villa Backpackers* (☎ 573 6598), 34 Auckland St, charges $14.50/16 for beds in dorms/doubles. This place also provides information, and serves as a booking centre for activities around Marlborough Sounds.

The *Bayview Backpackers* (☎ 573 7668), 318 Waikawa Rd, is on Waikawa Bay, four km from Picton; beds in dorms/doubles are $13.50/16.

The Track
The track is well defined and is suitable for people of all ages and average fitness. It is rated medium because of a long, dry section between Kenepuru Saddle and Portage Saddle. Carry water between Kenepuru and Te Mahia saddles; this is available at the Bay of Many Coves Saddle Camp Site.

Stage 1: Ship Cove to Furneaux Lodge
Walking Time: four to five hours (14 km)
Accommodation: Resolution Bay DOC Camp Site; Resolution Bay Cabins; Furneaux Lodge; Endeavour Holiday Resort

The trip from Picton to Ship Cove takes 45 minutes by water-taxi. On the way, you call in at many of the coves you will pass or look down on in the next four days of walking. It is fitting that the drop-off point and the start of the track is Ship Cove (Meretoto). Cook anchored here five times (once in the *Endeavour* and four times in the *Resolution*), and there is a prominent memorial to this fact on the grassed area beyond the jetty. It's not hard to imagine why Cook returned four times to this poignantly beautiful spot.

The track climbs quite steeply, through podocarp/broadleaf forest of kahikatea, rimu and kohekohe with an understorey of ferns and pigeonwood, into beech forest. About 45 minutes up, there is a lookout over Motuara Island and the outer Queen Charlotte Sound. Cook declared sovereignty over the South Island from Motuara, now a sanctuary for the South Island robin.

It is only 10 minutes or so from the lookout to a saddle at the top of the ridge, which has sweeping views down to Resolution Bay. The track drops steeply to the bay, then sidles the hill until it comes to a signposted junction. The track to the Resolution Bay Camp Site (no fires permitted) is down the left fork, which heads back in the direction of the saddle. Continue south-west (the right fork)

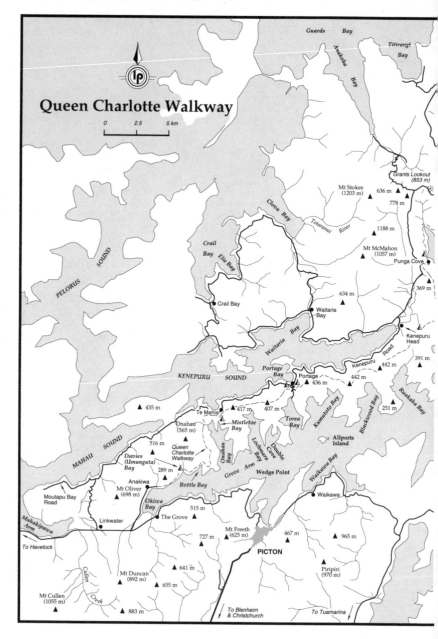

Queen Charlotte Walkway

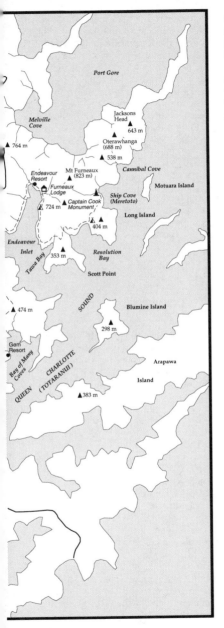

to Resolution Bay, where there is accommodation. The suggested time from Ship Cove is two hours, which gives you plenty of time to enjoy the beauty of the forest.

When the track nears Resolution Bay, you are on private land, so respect the owners' wishes in regard to access and gates. From the distinctive solar panel, a series of New Zealand Walkway markers clearly indicate the path. As you pass through one gate, there is a sign: 'If Spot follows you clip him to the chain' – his owners don't want to catch a water-taxi to Anakiwa to retrieve him.

The track climbs out of Resolution Bay – initially along a new bulldozed path, then along an old bridle path – to a saddle between the bay and Endeavour Inlet. It is about 1½ hours to the saddle and a further 1½ hours downhill along a gentle path to Furneaux Lodge.

There are great views of Endeavour Inlet across to Punga Cove and glimpses of the foreshore as you get closer to Furneaux Lodge. As the track passes through a sprawl of houses, boatsheds and jetties, it is marked by a collection of official and unofficial signs. About 20 minutes beyond the first houses is Furneaux Lodge, ensconced in turn-of-the-century Britishness, with well-manicured lawns, tennis courts and a fountain. Behind the lodge, there is a one-hour return walk to a waterfall, which passes through a magnificent stand of native bush.

Stage 2: Furneaux Lodge to Te Punga Cove
Walking Time: four hours (12 km)
Accommodation: Endeavour Resort; Camp Bay DOC Camp Site; Punga Cove Resort

There is accommodation at the Endeavour Resort, one km beyond Furneaux Lodge, at the northern end of Endeavour Inlet. About 10 minutes past the resort, there is a swing bridge across the stream which empties into the inlet (the track again crosses private land). On the other side of the bridge is a track junction. The path to the north leads to the narrow, dark remains of abandoned antimony mines, a two-hour return walk.

Continue on the south path, a grassy corridor which hugs the western side of the inlet.

Just before the boatshed, which is directly in front of you, strike off to the west, where the track climbs away from the water (a sign indicates 'Big Bay 2 Hrs'). For the next eight km, the track passes through regenerating bush. Farmers have burnt quite high up from the water of the inlet, and only small pockets of original forest remain. Manuka, kanuka and the broadleaf fivefinger line the slopes, and tree ferns are found in the gullies.

Some half an hour from the Big Bay turn-off, you come to a track junction. Take the lower path; the one to the right is a vehicle service track which climbs high above the normal walkway. A little further on, there is a great 'photo opportunity stop', near the point where the track rounds the ridge separating Endeavour Inlet from Big Bay, about an hour from the head of Endeavour Inlet.

Half an hour from the photo stop, you cross a cabled footbridge over a stream entering Big Bay. Over an hour later, you reach the area of Camp Bay and Te Punga Cove. From the grassed DOC camp site, it takes about 10 minutes to reach the Punga Cove Resort.

Stage 3: Te Punga Cove to the Portage

Walking Time: eight to nine hours (20 km)
Accommodation: Bay of Many Coves Saddle DOC Camp Site; Gem Resort (1½ hours down and two hours up); the Portage; Cowshed Bay DOC Camp Site

This is a tough day's walk. It begins at the Camp Bay Camp Site and climbs steeply out of Te Punga Cove to the Kenepuru Saddle, following the road for part of the way (as indicated by markers). It is 20 minutes up to the saddle, where a signpost indicates the way to the Portage and Anakiwa to the south.

The track climbs up steeply here to a prominent knoll, then sidles the ridge on its western side on an old vehicle track. If you don't like lots of 'ups', turn back here, because this is indicative of the rest of the day's journey. About 45 minutes from the

saddle, there is a track junction: the eastern track continues to climb steeply, while the track on the Kenepuru side is blocked. This will eventually be part of the main improved and benched path to the Portage, but until it has been completed and signposted, it's over the top of the knoll (369 metres) for you! The steep slog is rewarded, however, with tremendous views of the Sounds on both sides.

From Kenepuru Saddle, the steep track weaves along the ridge, until you reach the Bay of Many Coves Saddle, three hours later. Some 15 minutes uphill from this saddle is the DOC camp site. This important camp site has a toilet, water, a cooking shelter, and breathtaking views down into the Bay of Many Coves and Queen Charlotte Sound beyond. Replenish water stocks here, because there is only one water point further on.

Climb up from the shelter for 40 minutes to a high point and a signpost indicating 'Gem Resort 1½ Hrs'. From the next prominent rise, you can see the track following the ridge far in front of you and, to the right of your view, the prominent isthmus near the Portage. Be careful with your footing because the track falls steeply in places. More than 1½ hours out from the Bay of Many Coves Shelter, the track goes over the top of yet another prominent knoll (442 metres), then down to a saddle, over another knoll and eventually down to the water point – which is a blue barrel, fed by a piece of plastic hose draining a small creek seepage.

The track is undulating from here to the next high feature (436 metres), which is perched above the Portage. Not far on the south-western side of this feature, the track steepens considerably and then starts to zigzag down to Torea Saddle. It is about 40 minutes down, and where the track emerges, there is a war memorial. The road which crosses this saddle is the same route used by the Maoris to haul their waka (canoes) from one sound to another, thus saving a considerable sea journey. From the saddle, head north and downhill to the Portage (15 minutes) and Cowshed Bay Camp Site (20 minutes).

Stage 4: The Portage to Anakiwa

Walking Time: seven to eight hours (20 km)
Accommodation: Mistletoe Bay DOC Camp Site; Te Mahia Bay Resort; Umungata (Davies) Bay DOC Camp Site

Climb back up to Torea Saddle; the track heads west on the opposite side of the road from the memorial. This part of the walkway also follows the ridge, and involves the ascent of two features over 400 metres. It takes over 45 minutes to get from Torea Saddle to the top of the first knoll (407 metres), from where the track follows the ridge proper.

You look down into the deep dip between the two features; when descending from the first, keep well to the right of the repeater station. There are a number of markers leading to a track which climbs up around the northern flank of the second major knoll (417 metres).

As the track rounds the knoll on its western side, it comes to a junction. The left fork heads east up to the lookout above Mahau, Kenepuru and Queen Charlotte sounds (about half an hour return). This is the best viewpoint of the trip – it's rewarding looking back at the ridge you have traversed all the way from Te Punga Cove.

Drop down to Te Mahia Saddle, to where the track meets the road. Turn south and head towards Mistletoe Bay. Not far down the road, the track to Anakiwa is indicated; it heads west into the bush. If you wish to go to Mistletoe Bay, continue down the road until you come to a signpost indicating the camp site. To the north along the road is Te Mahia, where there is a motel and a camp site.

The track from Te Mahia Saddle to Anakiwa follows old bridle paths above Onahau Bay, passing through regenerating forest, skirting grazing land, then entering mature, black-trunked beech forest before it drops to Bottle Bay.

The vistas along this section are wonderful. You can see down Queen Charlotte Sound all the way to the Grove Arm. Soon, the track is not far above the water, which sparkles through the understorey of ferns, pittosporums, fivefinger, broadleafed rangiora and tawa. Some 2½ hours from Mistletoe Bay, you reach the spacious camping area at Davies (Umungata) Bay. Walk to the water's edge, where you will be rewarded with glimpses of many species of waders.

The last hour of this long 67-km journey is one of the best parts. The track passes through Iwitaaroa Reserve and its splendid stands of beech. There is a car park at the Anakiwa end and a public jetty 800 metres along the road. There is no shop here, however, so it will be some time until that cold can of drink.

NYDIA TRACK

This 22-km, two-day track in the Marlborough Sounds is part of the New Zealand Walkway system. The track was completed in 1979, and most of it follows old bridle paths through pastures, virgin forest and scrubland. The walk is rated easy but it does climb over two low saddles. The only hut on this track is a private, small backpackers' place, but there is excellent camping along isolated Nydia Bay. The walk is reputed to have fewer sandflies than the Abel Tasman Coast Track.

History

Nydia Bay was originally the site of a Maori pa, and its Maori name, Opouri, meant 'place of sadness'. Apparently a hapu (subtribe) was preparing to migrate to the Sounds. The leader of this hapu sacrificed a young boy as an offering to Tangaroa, God of the Sea, in the hope of a safe journey. The father of the boy discovered what had happened and called upon the rest of the tribe to seek *utu* (revenge). In Te Hoiere (Pelorus Sound), they found the relatives who had killed the boy, and killed them.

The attractive little town of Havelock is situated at the confluence of the Pelorus and Kaiuma rivers, 43 km from Blenheim and 73 km from Nelson. Founded around 1860, it was named after Sir Henry Havelock of Indian Mutiny fame. It's the only place where a main road touches the Pelorus Sound.

Information

The DOC field centre (☎ 574 2019) is on Mahakipawa Rd, Havelock. Glenmore Cruises (☎ 574 2532) acts as the tourist information centre. Peter Pannell, at the YHA hostel, has lots of information about the area.

Maps

The best map of the whole Sounds area is the 1:100,000 Holidaymaker No 336-07 *(Marlborough Sounds)*. In the 1:50,000 Topomaps 260 series, you would need the quad P27 *(Picton)*.

Huts

There are no DOC huts along the Nydia Track. There is private accommodation at Nydia Bay, and two DOC camp sites.

Access

You can attempt the track in either direction. The southern end of the track is at the end of Kaiuma Bay Rd, 32 km north of Havelock, and the northern end is at Duncan Bay, 21

km north-east of Rai Valley. Both points can be reached by road, but you can also arrange to be dropped off and picked up by the boat operators in Havelock.

It is best to get dropped off at Shag Point by water-taxi ($10 per person), because it is only a five-minute trip past the mudflats. At the other end, Sounds Detours (☎ 574 2104) can pick you up; the minimum cost is $60, so it pays to go with a few people. Use the phone at Murray Timm's Backpacker Accommodation (see stage one of the walk) to contact either the water-taxi or the shuttle service.

Places to Stay

The *Havelock Motor Camp* (☎ 574 2339), Inglis St, has camp sites from $14 for two. The *Chartridge Tourist Park* (☎ 574 2129), six km south of Havelock at Kaiuma Bridge on State Highway 6, has camp sites/budget rooms for $8/10 per person. The friendly *Havelock YHA Hostel* (☎ 574 2104) is on the corner of Lawrence St and Main Rd (No 46); beds cost $14 in dorms/twins.

The Track

Most walkers get dropped off at Shag Point (near Kaiuma Bay), cross Kaiuma Saddle into Nydia Bay and spend the night there, before tackling the Nydia Saddle the next day. The two easy days should allow you to appreciate the beauty of the Marlborough Sounds and the tracts of forest you will pass through on the way. The Nydia Track is a perfect complement to the Queen Charlotte Walkway – by the time you complete both walks, you will have enjoyed a fair slice of the Sounds.

Stage 1: Kaiuma to Nydia Bay

Walking Time: four to five hours
Accommodation: DOC camp site; Murray Timm's Backpackers (six bunks); Dorie Lodge Homestead

This walk starts with a water-taxi trip to Shag Point, a rocky promontory which juts into Kaiuma Bay in Pelorus Sound. From Shag Point, it is about four km to the start of the

walk proper, at Kaiuma Farm. If you're observant, you may see native orchids along the road and Californian quail darting into the bushes.

The track start is clear. Head through farmland and woolshed yards before crossing unbridged Kaiuma Creek. Follow the track around the base of the 490-metre feature and cross the creek once more, before passing through a deer paddock – make sure you close the gate.

The track passes hillsides of bracken fern, which thrives in the full sunlight but soon peters out closer to the saddle. After crossing another intermittent creek, you are soon in beech forest, and the path climbs steadily to the Kaiuma Saddle. This is not a high saddle, only 387 metres, but it will have taken you about 2½ hours to reach it from the start point at Shag Point. Near the saddle, there is a display about logging in the Nydia Bay region. Fortunately, some podocarp coastal forest is still found along the lower banks of the Nydia Stream.

The track is well defined and benched, with no prominent creek crossings until the bottom. Shortly after leaving the saddle, the track emerges from the beech forest. You get fine views of the water and its forested rim from a number of vantage points. Near Nydia Bay, the track cuts across farmland; follow the walkway signs.

Just before you reach the edge of Nydia Bay, turn left onto the track proper and cross an interesting, one-wire swing bridge. If the tide is out, you can proceed up to the water's edge and cross the stream at its mouth. The walk from the saddle to the bay should take about 1½ hours. Take time to look at the regenerating forest here – manuka, kanuka, ferns and broadleaf abound.

Near the stream crossing is the private Dorie Lodge (☎ (025) 41 2616), which has backpackers' accommodation. Ten minutes along from the stream crossing is Murray Timm's Backpacker Accommodation (☎ 579 8454). This is a six-bed place with toilets, showers and cooking facilities. It charges $10 per person, and there is space for tents as well. From Murray's, it's a further

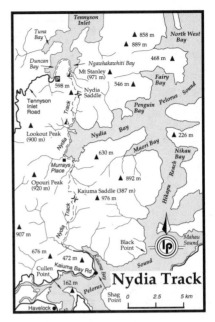

hour's walk to the DOC's Nydia Bay Camp Site. Pass some houses on the left, cross a bridged stream and walk around the edge of the lake on a good track to the camp site; tent sites are $2. There is a small creek nearby and great views of Nydia Bay.

Stage 2: Nydia Bay to Duncan Bay
Walking Time: four to 4½ hours
Accommodation: Ngawhakawhiti Bay DOC Camp Site

The track leaves the northern side of the camp site and soon enters the bush. There are signposts and the track is benched all the way to the Nydia Saddle. From the saddle, at 347 metres, there are good views down to Tennyson Inlet. The walk from the Nydia Bay Camp Site to the saddle should take about 1½ hours.

The rest of the track down to Ngawhakawhiti Bay is also through thick bush and is adequately benched and signposted.

Again, the bush is worth more than just an upward glance. The forest is predominantly beech, kamahi and tree ferns, with the odd kahikatea and rimu. The Ngawhakawhiti Camp Site is on the true right bank of the stream which flows into the bay, so watch for the signpost if you wish to go there. There is a sign which describes birdlife found along the walk. The broadleaf coastal forest here is beautiful, with miro, nikau palm, beech, matai and rimu.

Most trampers will probably stop for a rest or a browse in the forest, then continue anti-clockwise, around the ridge which juts into Duncan Bay, to the track end. The track along this section is flat and easy going. It will take an hour from the saddle to the camp site and another hour from there to Duncan Bay car park – the best place to get picked up by prearranged transport.

Mt Richmond Forest Park

Often overlooked by trampers rushing off to Abel Tasman, Mt Richmond Forest Park is right on the doorsteps of Havelock, Picton, Blenheim and Nelson. The Richmond Range forms the backbone of the 177,109-hectare park, which covers most of the steep, bush-clad mountains between Nelson and Blenheim and reaches north to the Tasman Sea near Whangamoa Head.

There are over 250 km of cut and marked tracks in the park, with about 30 huts scattered along them. The tracks range from challenging alpine routes to easy, overnight walks suitable for families. The park's climate is similar to that of nearby Kahurangi National Park (see the Nelson Region chapter).

HISTORY

Maoris had a number of argillite quarries in the Mt Richmond area, where they mined the hard mudstone for weapons and tools. About 40 quarries have been located in the area and artefacts from the region have turned up in many other parts of New Zealand.

The first European visitors were attracted

by minerals – initially copper and chromium. There was a mining company on Dun Mountain as early as 1856, and Hacket chromite was being removed from open shallow-cuts by the 1860s. There are still parts of an old, benched, bullock track – the Old Chrome Rd – near Hacket, on the western side of the park. Chromite prices slumped at the time of building, so it was never really used.

The tiny township of Pinedale, in the Wakamarina Valley eight km west of Havelock, got the nickname Canvastown back in the 1860s – gold was discovered in the river in 1860, and by 1864 thousands of canvas tents had sprung up as miners flocked to the prosperous goldfield, which was one of the richest in the country. The boom lasted only until 1865 but life was tough for the diggers on this unruly field – although a number were successful.

When most of the accessible alluvial gold had been removed, quartz reefs were developed. Companies operated in the Wakamarina Valley from 1874 until the 1920s. Elsewhere in the area, there were other mines, stamper batteries and even two dredges. In 1986, a tourist panned a five-gram nugget from the river.

NATURAL HISTORY

The whole park is covered by forest, with the exception of small patches of alpine tussock around the summits of taller peaks. The bush includes all five species of beech, as well as the podocarp species of rimu, miro, totara, matai and kahikatea. Uncommon birds found in the park include the rare whio (blue duck), the yellow-crowned parakeet, kaka and, occasionally, kiwis.

PELORUS RIVER TRACK

One of the more popular walks in the Richmond Forest Park, especially with anglers, is the Pelorus River Track, a three-day walk of 40 km that begins in the Pelorus River Scenic Reserve and ends at the Hacket picnic area, some 27 km from Nelson.

It is, however, difficult to get from the Hacket picnic area to Nelson unless you have arranged your own transport. For this reason, an alternative route to Nelson, the more popular Dun Mountain Track, has also been included. This track leaves the Pelorus Track shortly after Middy Hut, goes via Rocks Hut and Dun Mountain, and conveniently lands trampers at The Brook, not far from Nelson.

Information

Near Blenheim, there is a DOC field centre (☎ 572 9100), in Gee St, Renwick. The DOC regional office (☎ 546 9335) is in the Munro Building, 186 Bridge St, Nelson, and their visitor counter (☎ 548 2304) is in the Nelson visitor information centre. There is also a DOC district office (☎ 573 7582) in Picton, on the Picton foreshore, Auckland St. At a pinch, you might be able to get information from the DOC representative (☎ 571 6019) in the Rai Valley, at Pelorus Bridge.

Maps

Two quads of the 1:50,000 Topomaps 260 series, O27 *(Nelson)* and O28 *(Wairau)*, are needed to cover the park, or you can purchase the 1:100,000 Parkmaps No 274-06, *Mt Richmond Forest Park*.

Huts

Rocks Hut is the only Category Two hut ($8); Captain Creek, Middy, Roebuck, Browning and Hacket are all $4 huts.

Access

The east end of the track is 13 km up the Pelorus River Valley from the Pelorus Bridge Scenic Reserve, along the Pelorus River and Maungatapu Rds. The reserve, which has a camping ground, a caravan park, a small store and renowned tearooms, is eight km south of Rai Valley, on State Highway 6 (the Nelson-Blenheim Highway).

The western end of the Pelorus Track is at the Hacket picnic area, at the confluence of Hacket Creek and Roding River, in the Aniseed Valley. This picnic area is 27 km from Nelson and is reached by driving 1½ km south of Hope on State Highway 6 and turning east onto the Aniseed Valley Rd. If you take the alternative route to The Brook,

which is by far the most popular option, you arrive a few km from the city centre, so transport will not be a problem.

There are six Skyline Connections (☎ 528 8850) buses daily between Nelson and Picton, which pass through Pelorus Bridge. These depart from Nelson at 8.30 am (via Queen Charlotte Scenic Route), 10.30 am and 4.30 pm (via Blenheim). In the other direction, they leave Picton at 11.10 am and at 1.35 and 7.15 pm. InterCity (☎ 577 2890, 548 1539) also has three services daily in each direction (westwards 11.20 am and 1 and 1.40 pm, eastwards at 10.20 am and 1.10 and 1.45 pm). Pelorus Bridge is halfway between Nelson and Picton, about 1¼ hours from both townships.

A Havelock-based operator, Sounds Detours (☎ 574 2104), will take a group to the start of the track for a minimum of $60/20 per person. Hitching or walking the 13 km to the start are the only options for those without a vehicle. You can walk from the bridge to the first hut in a day without too much difficulty, because it is only a 2½ to three-hour walk from the start of the track.

You can get to the Roding River Rd on an InterCity bus from Nelson, leaving at 7.30 am Monday to Friday and passing the turn-off about 30 to 40 minutes later. From there, it is 11 km up the metalled road to the Hacket picnic area at the western end of the track. If you have a vehicle, you can easily turn the trip into a loop by hiking the side tracks to the new 20-bunk Rocks Hut.

If you want to complete a loop with minimal backtracking, start at the western end of the track and hike into Roebuck Hut, a six-hour walk. On the second day, walk six hours to Rocks Hut. On the third day, tramp to Totara Saddle and return to Hacket picnic area.

Places to Stay

Near the Park The *Trout Hotel* in the Wakamarina Valley (☎ 574 2120) has single/double rooms at $25/40. The *Pinedale Motor Camp* (☎ 574 2349) has camp sites for $6 per person and cabins from $25 for two. Wakamarina Valley is a local DOC camp

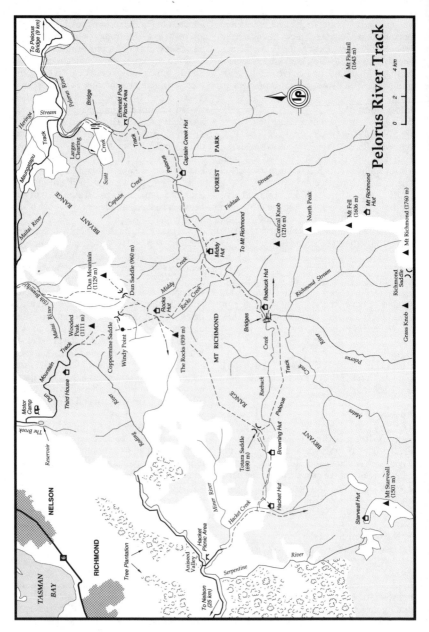

Pelorus River Track

site, and within the Pelorus Bridge Scenic Reserve there are camp sites which cost $6.

Nelson For budget accommodation in Nelson, see Places to Stay for the Abel Tasman Coast Track (in the Nelson Region chapter). The *Brook Valley Motor Camp* (☎ 548 0399), in the upper Brook Valley, has camp sites/cabins at $7/10 per person. *Alan's Place* (☎ 548 4854), 42 Westbrook Terrace, is also close to the end of the Dun Mountain Track; it costs $14 per night. For Havelock accommodation, see Places to Stay for the Nydia Track (in this chapter).

The Track

This trip, a one-way, three-day walk from Pelorus Valley over the Bryant Range into Aniseed Valley, is rated medium. For those without their own transport, there is a modified east-west alternative which gets trampers into Nelson. The Dun Mountain route leaves the Pelorus Track after Middy Hut and heads north-west via Rocks Hut and Dun Mountain to The Brook. It is a far more popular trail than others in the area, but it still has surprisingly few trampers.

The Pelorus and Aniseed valleys receive some of the highest rainfall in the park. When there are extremely heavy falls of rain, streams might become impassable, though if you wait for a day (or sometimes for just a few hours), the water levels will drop enough for you to ford safely. Flooding should not be a problem on the Pelorus River, because the track runs high above it. Where the track does cross the river, there are cable swing bridges.

Stage 1: Road's End to Middy Hut

Walking Time: 4½ to five hours
Accommodation: Captain Creek Hut (six bunks); Middy Hut (six bunks)

Start the walk at the signpost in the car park at the end of Maungatapu Rd. The track begins in private property and follows the edge of the Pelorus River on the true left (west) side. It's two km to the boundary of

the forest park, and along the way you cross a swing bridge over Scott Creek.

Once inside the park, follow the valley through native forest and drop gently in 15 minutes to a terrace above a sandy river beach and a deep pool. This is the Emerald Pool picnic area, a popular day walk, because the track up to this point is well benched and graded. The pool is an excellent swimming hole and marks the start of the good trout waters up the Pelorus.

The track leaves the river and climbs 100 metres from the terrace through a thick forest of rimu, tawa (quite rare in this forest), matai and beech. It arrives at the crest of the main ridge, then levels out until it reaches the edge of a bluff. The track follows the bluff for an hour and then begins descending towards the river, gradually at first but ending with a series of switchbacks.

Before reaching the Pelorus River, the track swings to the west and crosses a bush-clad terrace to reach the short side track to Captain Creek Hut – located in a clearing just above the river, a three-hour walk from the car park.

From here, the main track continues to follow the river and soon crosses Captain Creek. In another five minutes, the track crosses a swing bridge to the true right side (south) of the Pelorus, where there are accessible pools down below for anglers to fish. Once on the true right bank, the track begins to climb steeply, then follows the narrow valley through open forest and sparse scrub before crossing a swing bridge over Fishtail Stream, upstream of its confluence with the Pelorus.

The track continues to stray from the river as it crosses an undulating terrace where the Pelorus has formed a loop in the valley. You walk along this forested terrace the rest of the way to Middy Hut, an hour's walk from Fishtail Stream or two hours beyond Captain Creek Hut, a distance of six km. Shortly before Middy Hut, you come to a track junction. The path to the south heads to Mt Richmond and the hut and saddle of the same name; Middy Hut is straight ahead (west), opposite the junction of the Middy Creek and

Pelorus River. Middy Hut has screened windows, because the area is a haven for mosquitoes.

Stage 2: Middy Hut to Browning Hut
Walking Time: seven hours
Accommodation: Roebuck Hut (six bunks); Browning Hut (six bunks)

A swing bridge crosses the Pelorus to its true left side 150 metres upriver from Middy Hut. From here, you climb sharply to the junction with a track that continues up the spur to Rocks Hut (three hours; this direct route to Nelson is described later). The Pelorus Track heads south-west (the left fork), working its way to a saddle above Rocks Creek, and then drops steeply to the creek some distance upstream from the Pelorus River.

After crossing the creek, the walk becomes more difficult because, for the next four km, the track goes through thick forest and you frequently need to step over protruding tree roots. The forest is lush here, a mixture of beech and rimu along with tree ferns, pepper trees and an understorey of ferns.

Eventually, the track descends to Roebuck Creek and a pair of swing bridges. The first one crosses the creek; the second extends over the Pelorus River, 200 metres upriver. Roebuck Hut is situated on an open terrace directly across from the junction of the creek and the Pelorus, which at normal water levels can be forded here.

From Middy Hut to Roebuck Hut is a three-hour walk. To continue on, return to the swing bridge over the Pelorus River where, on the true left side, the track immediately climbs the ridge that separates Roebuck and Mates creeks. It's a steep half-hour climb for the first 150 metres and then the track begins to ascend at a more gradual rate to Totara Saddle (690 metres). Before reaching the saddle, the track works its way across the slopes of the Roebuck Catchment, and has good views of Mt Fell and Mt Richmond.

At the saddle, there is a junction with a track heading northwards to Rocks Hut (20

bunks; four hour walk). The main track heads west (the left fork), dropping 180 metres in a km. It traverses an open slip and goes through a beech forest on the way to Browning Hut. This hut is in a large, open area on the edge of the bush, and can sleep six (mattresses are placed on a communal shelf).

Stage 3: Browning Hut to Hacket Picnic Area
Walking Time: two hours
Accommodation: Hacket Hut (six bunks)

The track immediately crosses to the true right (north) side of a tributary of Browning Stream. For the next hour, it's an easy 2½-km walk through forest and across several eroded stream beds. During high water, follow a steep, alternative track around these streams and slips. Just before crossing the Browning for the last time, you pass a side track that leads south (the left fork) over a low saddle to Hacket Hut. The main track crosses the stream five minutes later, near the confluence with Hacket Creek, which is forded immediately as well.

The other side of the Hacket is private farmland, but you don't need permission to walk through it. An easy, benched track follows the creek on its true left (west) side for an hour, almost to the Hacket picnic area. One km before the area, the track crosses a swing bridge over Hacket Creek, and then joins a 4WD track to a wooden footbridge over the Roding River.

ALTERNATIVE ROUTE VIA DUN MOUNTAIN
A more direct walk to Nelson, which suits those without their own transport, is the Dun Mountain Track, via Rocks Hut, to The Brook. This popular, medium route takes three days, with a night spent at Middy Hut and another at Rocks Hut. Rocks Hut is on the edge of the Mt Richmond Forest Park and the latter part of this walk passes through the Hira Forest.

Stage 1: Middy Hut to Rocks Hut
Walking Time: three hours
Accommodation: Rocks Hut (20 bunks)

Shortly after leaving Middy Hut, the track crosses a swing bridge and climbs for 15 minutes to a track junction. The Pelorus Track heads off to the south, while the signposted alternative route, the Rocks Hut Track, heads west (the right fork). The well-marked track continues to climb steadily up a leading ridge through thick beech forest, so there are limited views. The height gain from the junction is about 600 metres.

Near the top of the track, high rock pinnacles are visible, and a creek is crossed about 10 minutes below the hut. This is the first water since Middy Hut, so make sure you carry some, especially in summer. The track emerges into subalpine scrub, and you soon reach the hut.

The well-appointed hut offers views out to Mt Richmond and Mt Fell and the top end of the Pelorus Valley. At the time of writing, Rocks Hut had gas, but because there is talk of its removal, you are advised to take your own cooking equipment. The gas is switched on from behind the hut; don't forget to switch it off when you leave. There is a rainwater supply, but if you choose to take water from the nearby creek, get it from above the toilet system.

South-west of Rocks Hut is the ridge track to Totara Saddle. If you go part of the way down this track, you will reach the Rocks – a worthwhile side trip if you are staying at the hut.

Stage 2: Rocks Hut to The Brook
Walking Time: five hours

Four tracks leave from the vicinity of Rocks Hut. One leads initially south then west to the Roding River; one heads south down the ridge to the Rocks then to Totara Saddle; another heads in a north-westerly direction, crosses the upper reaches of the Roding River and climbs to Windy Point; and the last goes north-east to Dun Mountain. Take the last, most easterly, of the four tracks – the one to Dun Mountain.

The well-marked track through alpine and beech forest follows the ridge towards Dun Mountain, which is almost bare of vegetation because of its high mineral content. As you emerge from the bush into the stunted scrub underneath the mountain, there is a track junction: Dun Saddle (960 metres) is to the north-east, the track to the north-west heads down to Coppermine Saddle.

If the weather permits, take the right fork to climb Dun Mountain (1129 metres), two km away. It is about one km to Dun Saddle. A track heads due north from the saddle to follow the southern branch of the Maitai River to Nelson (about three hours).

From the top of Dun Mountain, return the way you came, until you reach the Coppermine Saddle junction one km past Dun Saddle. Turn north-west (the right fork) and head down through bush to Coppermine Saddle. This is the start of the old Dun Mountain Railway, the first railway in New Zealand, which was constructed to enable horse-drawn carts to haul chrome ore from the mountain to Nelson. It is not particularly distinct here, but as you round the west flank of Wooded Peak (1111 metres), the railway becomes more defined.

The walk from here to Third House Shelter is easy; it's about 3½ hours from Rocks Hut. There is a rainwater supply at Third House, but it may not be that reliable.

The railway track is benched and easy all the way from Third House to the reservoir and motor camp at the end of the track. It is a walk of more than four km from here to Nelson.

OTHER TRACKS
Wakamarina Track

This easy, two-day, 18-km walk in Mt Richmond Forest Park begins at the end of the Wakamarina Rd, 19 km from Canvastown, and crosses the Richmond Range to a car park off Kiwi Rd, in Onamalutu Valley. Most people undertake it as an easy weekend trip, with a two-hour walk to Devil's Creek Hut (six bunks) on the first day and a five-hour walk to the Onamalutu Valley on the second day.

Mt Richmond Alpine Route

This three to four-day circuit along the exposed alpine ridges and peaks of Mt Richmond Forest Park is rated difficult. The trip generally involves leaving Mt Starveall (accessible from Hacket Creek) and crossing Slaty Peak, Pelorus Tops, Ada Flat and Old Man to reach Mt Rintoul. A relatively new track, marked from Bishops Cap to the Lee River, allows trampers to complete the loop of the Alpine Route. It is essential to carry adequate water on this trip, because it can get extremely hot on the exposed tops.

Nelson Region

The Nelson region has a number of New Zealand's famous tramps, including the Abel Tasman Coast Track. This chapter covers the Coast Track, the Abel Tasman Inland Track, the Heaphy Track (one of the Great Walks), the Wangapeka Track, the Leslie-Karamea Track, the Travers-Sabine Circuit and the D'Urville Valley Track.

The Abel Tasman and Nelson Lakes regions are already national parks, and the North-West Nelson Forest Park will soon be given national park status and a new name – Kahurangi.

Abel Tasman National Park

In the early 1980s, the Abel Tasman Coast Track, an easy walk around bays and along sandy beaches, was hardly known outside the Nelson region. Today, overseas hikers arrive at the Nelson visitor centre almost daily, point to a page in their guidebook and speak the only two words they may know of the local language: 'Abel Tasman'!

The change that has taken place since the 1980s is remarkable. This is now the most widely used recreational track in the country, easily surpassing such favourites as the Routeburn and Milford. Those tracks draw over 10,000 trampers a year. In a year, the Abel Tasman Coast Track attracts more than 20,000 walkers who stay at least one night in the park.

If you feel inexperienced as a tramper but desperately want to try one tramp, the Coast Track is perfect. It is not a typical, rugged New Zealand track, and it is easier and better serviced than any other track in the country. It is a well-cut, well-graded and well-marked path that is almost impossible to lose. It can be hiked in tennis shoes, there are no alpine

sections to cross and there are always people just up the track in case a problem arises.

HISTORY

Maoris have lived along the shores of the present Abel Tasman National Park for at least 500 years. They had abundant sources of food from both the sea and the forest, and seasonally cultivated kumara (sweet potato).

In 1642, Abel Tasman anchored his ships near Wainui, and that night four Maori canoes appeared, though no contact was made. The next day, eight Maori canoes put out, eventually ramming a small boat that was ferrying between Tasman's two ships. Four of Tasman's crew were killed in the incident and the Dutch quickly departed. Cook stopped briefly in 1770, but recorded little about the coastal area and nothing of its inhabitants.

It wasn't until Dumont d'Urville sailed into the area between Marahau and Torrent Bay in 1827 that Europeans met the Maoris on peaceful terms. The French navigator made friends with the villagers, and he studied flora & fauna and charted the bays and inlets of the northern coast.

European settlement of the area began in the early 1850s. The new settlers ranged from farmers and fishermen to shipwrights and loggers, but by far the most enterprising was William Gibbs. The farm and mansion he built at Totaranui and the innovations he implemented there were ahead of their time. During the economic depression of the 1930s, however, the farm's pastures reverted to ferns.

The Abel Tasman National Park was formed in 1942 to mark the 300th anniversary of Tasman's ill-fated visit. It was very much the vision of one woman, Perrine Moncrieff. She campaigned to get 15,000 hectares of Crown land put aside for a national park and also suggested that it be named after Tasman. In 1948, the Gibbs estate passed to the Crown and was incorporated into the park.

In 1993, Tonga Island Marine Reserve was created alongside the national park. The marine reserve protects all of the marine life within its boundaries, as well as seals, penguins and seabirds.

CLIMATE

Clearly one of the main attractions of the park is not so much its bush, or even its beaches, but its exceptionally mild and sunny climate. Protection by mountain ranges from southerly and westerly winds, gives Abel Tasman some of the best weather in New Zealand. Extreme temperatures are rare, and in Totaranui the average daytime reading during January is 25° C. The coastal region averages 1800 mm of rain annually, but only over a span of 125 days, resulting in long, dry spells from summer through into autumn.

NATURAL HISTORY

The 22,533-hectare Abel Tasman National Park is the smallest of New Zealand's national parks and rises to a maximum altitude of only 1156 metres. Although it's small in size, the park contains a wealth of natural features. Along with its bays, lagoons and sparkling beaches, the park also contains marble gorges and a spectacular system of caves in its not-so-well-known rugged interior.

Along the coast, where it is moist and warm, the park is characterised by lush rainforest, with vines, perching plants, tree ferns and an abundance of the country's national plant, the silver fern. On the drier ridges and throughout much of the park's interior, the bush is beech forest, and all five New Zealand tree species are found here.

ABEL TASMAN COAST TRACK

There is a widespread belief among trampers that the Coast Track ends at Totaranui, but the track is actually a 51-km walk between Marahau and a car park near Wainui Bay. Those who continue north of Totaranui will discover the most dramatic viewing point (Separation Point), the least crowded hut

(Whariwharangi Homestead) and some of the best beaches (Anapai and Mutton Cove) in the park. The entire trek takes only three to five days, although you almost always meet a deeply tanned tramper who has been on the track for two weeks, sleeping on the beaches and living off mussels.

This track is unlike any other in the country. It has been best described as a relaxed walk, due to the easy nature of the track, the excellent weather and the beaches, lagoons and bays that make up most of the scenery. There is some climbing involved, but the Coast Track is rated easy and can be attempted by most trampers, even those with little or no experience in the bush.

The preferred footwear is tennis shoes, not hiking boots, and occasionally you even see somebody heading down the track in sandals or flip-flops, though park rangers strongly discourage it. You still need a backpack (shoulder bags just won't do), some rain gear and a warm jersey or sweater, because the nights can get chilly, even in summer. But also pack sunglasses, a swimsuit, and a hat of some kind to keep the midday sun off your eyes and face. Make absolutely sure you have a bottle of insect repellent and a sunscreen.

Another piece of equipment you should take on this track is a tent, because accommodation is relatively scarce in the busy season. There are five huts, each an easy day's walk apart, but from November to February they fill rapidly. You must arrive at the next hut before noon to get a bunk; otherwise plan on sleeping on the floor or a bench. A tent, however, guarantees you shelter and allows you to sneak away from the crowds and spend a relatively peaceful evening at a small bay or beach. Camping fees are $6.

If you plan to stay in a tent, keep in mind that in recent years possums have become a problem, often stealing food, so keep all food and equipment in your tent. Wasps have also become a problem, and are a nuisance from February onwards.

Information

The DOC regional office (☎ 546 9335) is in

Top Left: Marahau, Abel Tasman Coastal Track (JW)
Top Right: Falls River Bridge, Abel Tasman National Park (JW)
Centre: Coastal Track signpost, Abel Tasman National Park (JW)
Bottom: Seals at play, Abel Tasman National Park (JW)

Left: Dune formations, Ninety Mile Beach, Northland (JW)
Top Right: Camp site, Abel Tasman National Park (NZTB)
Centre Right: Musterer's Hut, Mt Somers (JW)
Bottom Right: Te Pukatea Bay, Abel Tasman National Park (NZTB)

the Munro Building, at 186 Bridge St, Nelson. The office is open on weekdays from 8 am to 4.30 pm. The DOC visitor counter (☎ 548 2304) in the Nelson visitor information centre, at the corner of Trafalgar and Halifax Sts, is open from 8.30 am to 5 pm on weekdays.

Headquarters for Abel Tasman National Park (☎ 525 8026) is in Takaka, at 1 Commercial St. The Motueka DOC field centre (☎ 528 9117) is at the corner of King Edward and High Sts; it is open from 9 am to 5 pm on weekdays.

Maps

The 1:50,000 Parkmaps No 237-07 *(Abel Tasman National Park)* is more than adequate for this trip, or you can purchase quads N26 *(Takaka)* and N25 *(Tarakohe)* of the 1:50,000 Topomaps 260 series.

Huts

Huts and camp sites along the Coast Track (a Great Walk) are $6 a night, even if you end up sleeping on the floor. There may be a hut warden to collect the fees but the DOC requests that you pay for a hut or camp pass before you enter the track. Developed camp sites are mentioned in the track description.

The huts on the track are Anchorage, Awaroa, Bark Bay, Torrent Bay and Whariwharangi. The huts on the Inland Track – Wainui, Awapoto, Castle Rock and Moa Park – all cost $4.

Access

Bus There's quite a variety of transport heading west to Motueka and Golden Bay from Nelson. Mt Cook Landline's Golden Bay Connection (☎ 528 7280), has buses to Motueka and Takaka. The depot is next to the information centre, at 238 High St, Motueka. Other companies, such as Skyline Connections and Abel Tasman Enterprises, provide transport from Nelson, Motueka and Takaka to the Abel Tasman Track. Skyline Connections (☎ 528 8850) operates buses between Nelson, Motueka, Kaiteriteri, Marahau and Totaranui from October until mid-April. For the rest of the year, there are only services to

and from Takaka and Totaranui. Fares are: Nelson to Totaranui $25, Nelson to Marahau $10, round trip $30, Totaranui to Marahau $18, round trip from Motueka $22.

Motueka Taxis (☎ 528 7900) has an inexpensive ($6) service to Marahau on its weekday mail run from Motueka. It leaves the Motueka post office at 2.30 pm and departs from Marahau at 3 pm.

Abel Tasman National Park Enterprises has buses linking Motueka with Nelson and Kaiteriteri, connecting in Kaiteriteri with a launch that goes up and down the coast following the Abel Tasman Coast Track – but with this company you *must* book ahead.

It is unfortunate that there's no transport available from the Wainui car park. For those without a vehicle, the only alternative at this point is to hike across the tidal flats of Wainui Bay at low tide, or wander down the road to Cowshed Corner and hitch a ride towards Clifton and Takaka with traffic or buses leaving Totaranui. Many trampers turn around at the Whariwharangi Homestead Hut and return to Totaranui.

Boat You can now take a boat directly from Nelson to Abel Tasman National Park. Catalina Cruises (☎ 546 9885) goes directly from Nelson to the start of the track, leaving at 8 am. It costs $20 from Nelson to Tinline; the return fare from Nelson to Totaranui is $40.

The *Spirit of Golden Bay* (☎ 525 9135) departs daily from Tarakohe at 9 am, picks up at the Awaroa Lodge at 9.40 am, arrives in Nelson at 12.30 pm, and leaves Nelson at 2.15 pm to drop trampers off along the track. Costs from Tarakohe are $15 to Awaroa, $20 to Tonga Roadstead/Bark Bay, $25 to Torrent Bay/Anchorage, $30 to Coquille Bay/Tinline and $35 to Kaiteriteri.

Abel Tasman Seafaris operates daily out of Marahau (☎ 527 8083). Boats leave Marahau at 9 am and will pick up and drop off trampers anywhere along the track. Fares from Marahau are $15 to Torrent Bay/Anchorage, $18 to Bark Bay, $20 to Tonga, $25 to Awaroa and $28 to Totaranui.

Abel Tasman National Park Enterprises (☎ 528 7801) has 6½-hour launch services departing from Kaiteriteri at 9 am, dropping off trampers in Totaranui at 12.15 pm. It picks up returning trampers, and arrives back at Kaiteriteri at about 3.30 or 4 pm.

With all operators, you can easily combine a walk along part of the Abel Tasman Coast Track with the cruise, being dropped off at one bay and picked up later at another.

Places to Stay

Nelson The *Nelson YHA Hostel* (☎ 548 8817), at 42 Weka St, has rooms for $14 per night. A great place to stay before and after the track is *Baigent Villa* (☎ 548 8468), 114 Rutherford St, which costs $14/15 for a dorm/double; it's popular, so book ahead.

The *Tasman Towers* (☎ 548 7950), at 10 Weka St, is $15 per night. *Boots Backpackers* (☎ 548 9001), on the corner of Trafalgar and Bridge Sts, has dorm beds for $13.50. In the centre of town, at 8 Bridge St, *Bumbles* (☎ 548 2771) has dorm beds for $14. A little bit of an uphill walk away is *Dave's Palace* (☎ 548 4691), at 18 Mount St, where dorm beds are $13. The *Centre of New Zealand Backpackers Hostel* (☎ 546 6667), 193 Milton St, is certainly not central; beds are $14 in dorms. The *Backpackers Beach*

Great Walks Ticket

Hostel (☎ 548 6817), 25 Muritai St, Tahuna Beach, charges $13 a night in all rooms; phone for free pick up.

Motueka At the *White Elephant* (☎ 528 6208), 55 Whakarewa St, beds cost $14 in dorm rooms. At 16 Thorp St, *The Gables* (☎ 528 6300) has beds for $15. To reach The Gables from the information centre, cross the road and turn right into Tudor St, then left into Thorp St.

Takaka The *Takaka Summer YHA Hostel* (☎ 525 8463) is in Meihana St. It's open only over the Christmas holiday period and costs $12 a night. The *Shady Rest Hostel* is at 141 Commercial St, 400 metres from the town centre on the Collingwood side; dorm beds cost $14.

In the Park The *Totaranui Beach Camp* (☎ 525 8026) at Totaranui is administered by the DOC; camp sites cost $6.50 per person. At Awaroa Bay, the *Awaroa Lodge & Cafe* (☎ (025) 43 3135) charges $15 per person in share/twin accommodation. You have three ways of getting to Awaroa Lodge: travel by water-taxi, walk part of the Abel Tasman Coast Track from Totaranui, or drive to Awaroa car park then walk. The *Marahau Beach Camp* (☎ 527 8176) at Marahau has tent sites for $9 and cabins for $25. There is also *The Barn* hostel and camping ground (☎ 527 8043), on Harvey Rd, Marahau, at the entrance to Abel Tasman, where beds are $14 and camp sites $8. The *Park Cafe* is nearby – gorge on cakes, muffins and milkshakes before heading out on the track.

The Track

The Coast Track from Marahau to Wainui car park, a journey of approximately 50 km, can be walked in either direction and is rated easy. The following description begins at the southern end, because this is the most popular direction in which to travel.

The track can be hiked at any time of the year. The peak summer season runs from early November to February, with January and February the busiest months. During this

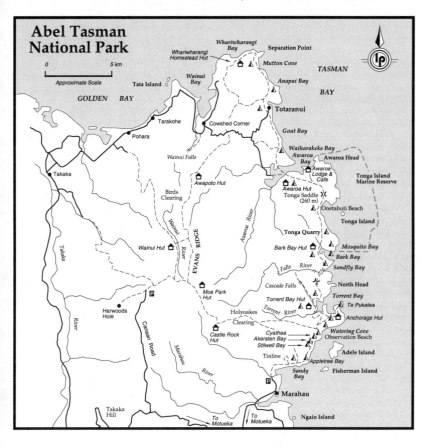

period, Bark Bay looks more like a beach at a seaside resort than one in a national park; there could easily be a couple of hundred trampers with packs, as well as boaties with beer, families with picnics and retired couples who have just arrived for the afternoon. The best time for the Coast Track is probably from the end of February to May, when the crowds thin out but the weather is usually still pleasantly warm.

When walking the track, take notice of the tides. The tidal differences in Abel Tasman are among the greatest in the country, often between three and four metres. At many of the bays (Torrent, Tonga and Bark Bay), waiting for low tide and then crossing is far easier than following the all-tidal track. At Awaroa Bay, you have no choice but to plan on crossing during the two hours before or after low tide. There are current tidal charts in all huts, or you can purchase a book of tide tables for $1 at a Nelson bookshop. Usually, only high tide is listed, but by adding six hours you can determine low tide.

Stage 1: Marahau to Torrent Bay
Walking Time: four hours to Anchorage Beach; 4½ hours to Torrent Bay via tidal flats

Accommodation: Anchorage Hut (26 bunks); Torrent Bay Hut (eight bunks)

The track begins at a turn-off one km outside Marahau. It crosses the Marahau estuary on an all-tidal causeway, climbs gently to a clearing above Tinline Bay and then passes Tinline camp site, 2½ km from the start. Just beyond it, a sign marks one end of the Inland Track. The Coast Track continues around dry ridges, hugging the coast and opening up to scenic views of Adele and Fisherman islands and Coquille and Appletree bays. Signposts indicate side tracks leading down to the beaches and refreshing swims in the surf. There are also scenic camp sites at Appletree.

After passing Yellow Point and its spur track, the track turns inland and climbs along ridges lined with silver fern. At the top, the trees thin out and the track branches. The track to the east (the right fork) descends quickly to Anchorage Beach, half an hour away, and then down the beach to Anchorage Hut and a large camping ground, a very popular spot in summer. The toilets here have been upgraded and are now of the septic-tank variety. Those with a tent can escape the crush of humanity usually found around the hut by following the short side track at the eastern end of the beach to a camp site on Te Pukatea Bay, or backtracking to a developed camp site at Watering Cove.

The fork to the west leads to the Torrent Bay Hut, which is much smaller than Anchorage Hut – note that there are rumours that Torrent Bay Hut may be removed soon. This track descends towards the bay and then splits again, with one track heading for the arm of the bay that separates Anchorage Beach from the Torrent Bay tidal flats. If the tide is right (or the water low enough), you can follow the short track down to the flats and across to the hut in half an hour or so. The other route, the all-tidal track, heads west and circles the bay through bush, arriving at the hut in 1½ hours. There are more camp sites north of Torrent Bay.

An interesting side trip from the all-tidal track is Cleopatra's Pool, a 15-minute walk one-way from the main track. The metre-deep pool, fed by the Torrent River, is surrounded by smooth rocks that lend themselves quite well to sunbathing. The cold, fresh water is invigorating after a day in the sun and sea.

Stage 2: Torrent Bay to Bark Bay
Walking Time: three hours
Accommodation: Bark Bay Hut (28 bunks)

Those staying at Anchorage Hut can head west on the beach and take the short track over a headland to arrive at the Torrent Bay tidal flats, which are easily crossed at low tide. From Torrent Bay, you can cross the lagoon in front of the hut and south of the summer cottages, then turn left up the beach in front of the private residences. Keep going for half a km before the track heads inland.

For those who want to see the various falls and pools of Tregidga Creek and Falls River, stay on the all-tidal track from Torrent Bay Hut and head north-west at the signposted junction. A good, benched track follows Tregidga Creek to modest Cascade Falls after a one-hour walk. You can stay on this track and end up at the Falls River, 15 minutes downstream from its main falls. It's a boulder-hopping scramble, with help from an occasional marker, to reach the impressive cascade.

Once the main track moves inland beyond the summer homes, it climbs 90 metres and sidles around Kilby Stream, before reaching a low saddle where a side track takes you to the first of two lookout points that are passed. The Coast Track descends to a swing bridge over Falls River, where it's possible to climb down to the river and scramble upstream for 20 minutes to view yet more waterfalls. From the swing bridge, you climb to a spur track to the second lookout; this track can be followed for views of Bark Bay to the north and the coastline to the south. From the junction, it's a 20-minute descent to the bay.

Bark Bay is now a major access point for the track, with a launch arriving at 11 am and then cruising back at 2 pm, picking up trampers and day visitors at both times. The hut,

Nelson Region – Abel Tasman National Park 165

the newest on the track, is situated on the edge of the lagoon, a short walk from the beach. The best camping is on the sandy spit overlooking the bay, but there are only a few sites here. More sites have been developed in the bush near the hut. If you don't mind the people, this bay is beautiful.

Stage 3: Bark Bay to Awaroa Bay
Walking Time: three hours
Accommodation: Awaroa Hut (26 bunks); Awaroa Lodge & Cafe (variety of accommodation)

The track follows the spit to its northern end and crosses the tidal lagoon – an easy ford most of the time (except near high tide). The all-tidal track near the hut avoids this but takes an extra 20 minutes to half an hour to hike. Entering the bush, the track begins an immediate ascent, and in a km reaches the junction of the former Stoney Hill Track (which heads north-west to Awaroa Hut). This track, through the interior of the park (four hours), is no longer maintained. It's a challenging route, and it should only be tackled by experienced trampers.

The Coast Track departs from the junction and winds over several inland ridges before dropping sharply to Tonga Quarry, 3½ km from Bark Bay. There is a metal plaque describing the quarry operations that took place here, and several large and squarish stones nearby. What remains of the wharf can be seen in the sand.

The most interesting feature of the bay can only be reached at low tide, give or take 1½ hours on either side. Follow the rocky shore at the southern end of the beach, and after a 10-minute scramble, you come to the sea arches of Arch Point, a set of impressive stone sculptures formed by the repeated pounding of the waves.

The track continues by climbing the headland that separates Tonga Quarry and Onetahuti Beach. After a one-km walk, you come to a clearing overlooking the graceful curve of the long beach. This is another classic Abel Tasman beach, and there are

developed camp sites at the southern end for those who packed a tent. Near the sites, a sign points the way to the delightful, cold, clear freshwater pools, that lie beneath a small waterfall – ideal after a hot day.

The beach is more than a km long. Follow it to the northern end where, on the other side of the lagoon, a track marked by an orange disc departs into the bush. Before heading up the track, you can view some rare Maori carvings not usually seen in this part of the country. They are located in a pair of caves just beyond a small stream at the northern end of Onetahuti Beach. The spiral, abstract carvings are in the left cave – the one not half-filled with water.

The Coast Track leaves the beach by gently climbing above the swamp formed by Richardson Stream, and provides a nice overview of Tonga Roadstead. Eventually, the track comes to Tonga Saddle (260 metres) and you get a quick glimpse of the beaches in the distance. If you're heading for the Awaroa Hut, take the north-west path (the left fork). The signposted path to the Awaroa Lodge is directly in front of you, and descends steeply, almost due north, to the beach.

The path to the Awaroa Hut descends along the contour and crosses a bridge over Venture Creek without crossing private land. The large Awaroa Hut, on Awaroa Inlet, stands on a small beach and has limited space around it for tents. Hopefully, it will be developed further in the future. The Awaroa Lodge & Cafe, to the east of the hut, is worth a jaunt; it sells beer, wine and food (see Places to Stay in this section).

Stage 4: Awaroa Bay to Totaranui
Walking Time: 1½ to two hours
Accommodation: motor camp

Awaroa Inlet can only be crossed in the two hours before or after low tide. Check the tide chart in the hut or at the lodge, then plan your day. Cross the bay directly in front of the hut, and follow the large orange discs which lead to Pound Creek. The track follows the creek until it passes a signposted junction to the

Totaranui-Awaroa Rd, then quickly arrives at Waiharakeke Bay, another beautiful beach. This is a great spot for those with a tent, because it is only 30 to 40 minutes north of Awaroa. The new camp site is 50 metres south from the point where Waiharakeke Stream emerges onto the beach.

The track climbs away from the beach across a rocky ridge and then descends into Goat Bay. It's a 20-minute walk over Skinner Point from here to the Totaranui visitor centre. There's a scenic lookout near the top, complete with a pair of benches, which provides an excellent view of Totaranui.

The visitor centre sells maps, books and brochures on the national park and has a few historical displays. There is also a public phone outside. Scheduled bus services come to this part of the track, but there is no hut and no cabins at the motor camp. The next and final hut is at Whariwharangi Homestead, a 2½-hour walk from Totaranui.

Stage 5: Totaranui to Wainui Car Park
Walking Time: 4½ hours
Accommodation: Whariwharangi Homestead (26 bunks)

Follow the tree-lined avenue in front of the DOC field station and turn north at the intersection, passing the Education Centre. At the end of the road, the Anapai Bay Track begins and quickly reaches a junction with the Headlands Track just before Kaikau Stream. Both tracks head for Anapai Bay, but the left-hand fork is a more direct route. It climbs a low saddle and then descends along a forested stream to Anapai's scenic beach, which is split in two by unusual rock outcrops. There is a camp site here.

The Coast Track continues up the sandy beach, then heads inland. In two km, it reaches Mutton Cove, where there are developed camp sites. Just beyond, before you reach the second beach, the old farm road to the Whariwharangi Homestead starts and heads inland. Halfway to the farmhouse, the vehicle track crosses a low saddle, where there's a junction to Separation Point (half an

hour). The new side track heads east (the right fork), directly to the granite headland that separates Tasman Bay from Golden Bay. The views are worth the walk to Separation Point – the North Island is often visible, along with Farewell Spit, to the north-west. The point is also a favourite haunt of migrating fur seals, but they are usually seen only in autumn and winter.

From the saddle, the farm road continues through regenerating scrubland. Two km from Mutton Cove, it reaches Whariwharangi Bay, another beautiful curved beach. The hut, a restored two-storey farmhouse that was last permanently occupied in 1926, is at the western end of the bay, half a km inland.

At this point, trampers have three choices. You can make the final leg of the journey to the Wainui car park; it's a four-km, 1½-hour walk along the farm road, which involves crossing Wainui Inlet within two hours of low tide. Another option is to take a track that leaves the farm road about halfway between the homestead and the car park, returning to Totaranui by way of Gibbs Hill – a waterless route. Alternatively, you can turn around at the homestead and backtrack to Totaranui (three hours), where there is public transport out of the park.

OTHER TRACKS
Abel Tasman Inland Track
A network of tracks cuts across the interior of the national park, offering a tramp that is a direct contrast to the Coast Track. Inland, the walking is harder and the tracks are more deserted. This track is not maintained and is no longer marked on the Parkmap because it is for seasoned trampers only. There are, however, five huts along the way.

Many begin this tramping track near Marahau, hiking to Castle Rock or Moa Park on the first day. You can reach Awapoto Hut on the second day, and from there it's a four-hour hike to Totaranui, the Wainui car park or the Whariwharangi Homestead. The track, rated medium to difficult, can be combined with a portion of the Coast Track for a five to six-day loop.

Kahurangi National Park

Kahurangi National Park is situated due west of Abel Tasman National Park. It's New Zealand's most recent national park (declared only in 1994). It was once North-West Nelson Forest Park, the largest of the forest parks, at 376,572 hectares; it is now the second largest national park, after Fiordland and ahead of Mt Aspiring. It includes the Tasman Mountains, a chain of steep and rugged ranges whose high point is Mt Snowden (1856 metres).

The best-known walk in Kahurangi is the Heaphy Track. The four-day trek stretches 76 km from Aorere Valley, near Collingwood, to the West Coast, north of Karamea. It is one of the most popular tracks in the country, walked by over 4000 trampers a year.

The Heaphy, however, is just one of the forest park's many walks; it contains more than 650 km of tracks. Two other tracks, which are less used but which many trampers feel are just as interesting, are included in this section.

The Wangapeka Track is a challenging walk, spanning 65 km from the West Coast south of Karamea, to its eastern end on Rolling River. The five-day walk is often linked with the Heaphy by trampers who want to loop back towards Nelson.

Perhaps the most remote walk in the park is the Leslie-Karamea Track, which traverses its namesake rivers for 48 km from the Tablelands to the middle of the Wangapeka Track.

HISTORY

The legendary moa thrived in the north-west region of the South Island, and this important food source led to the establishment of a significant Maori population. Maori occupation along the Heaphy (Whakapoai) River has been dated at least as early as the 16th century, when they had already established a route up the river and over the Gouland Downs to Aorere. They were in search of pounamu (greenstone) from the West Coast (Poutini), for weapons, tools and ornaments.

In 1846, Charles Heaphy, a draftsman for the New Zealand Company, and Thomas Brunner became the first Europeans to hike up the West Coast to the Heaphy River. James MacKay and John Clark completed the inland portion of the Heaphy Track in 1860 while searching for gold between Buller and Collingwood. A year later, gold was discovered at Karamea, inspiring prospectors to struggle over the track in search of it. The Wangapeka Valley was also opened up when gold was discovered in the Rolling, Wangapeka and Sherry rivers in the late 1850s. Dr Ferdinand von Hochstetter was believed to be the first to travel the entire Wangapeka Track when, in 1860, he carried out a geological exploration of the valley.

Miners also had a hand in developing the Karamea River Track, progressing from gold diggings at Mt Arthur Tablelands to the river. By 1878, a benched track had been formed and diggers were active in the Leslie, Crow and Roaring Lion rivers.

The Heaphy was improved when J B Saxon surveyed and graded the track in 1888 for the Collingwood County Council. The sought-after gold deposits were never found, however, and the use of the Heaphy and Wangapeka tracks declined considerably in the early 1900s.

However, the unique flora of the Heaphy area began attracting visiting scientists, who reported, among other things, the track's quickly deteriorating condition, and managed to push for the setting aside of Gouland Downs as a scenic reserve in 1915.

The Heaphy and Wangapeka tracks were improved dramatically after the North-West Nelson Forest Park was established in 1970 and the New Zealand Forest Service began to bench the routes and construct huts. The Heaphy did not become really popular, however, until plans for a road from Collingwood to Karamea were announced in the early 1970s. Conservationists, deeply concerned about the damage the road would do to the environment, especially to the nikau palms, began an intensive campaign to stop the road and to increase the popularity of the track.

In 1994, North-West Nelson Forest Park was upgraded to national park status. Its new name is Kahurangi, a 'treasured possession'.

CLIMATE

All the rivers of the park are fed (and occasionally flooded) by the westerly winds that blow off the Tasman Sea bringing up to 5000 mm of rain to the mountainous areas. The yearly average rainfall for most of the track is 2540 mm, although a rain gauge on the Wangapeka Saddle recorded more than 500 mm of rain in January alone in 1964. Frost is possible in the higher, more exposed regions, particularly the Gouland Downs, at all times except late or mid-summer.

NATURAL HISTORY

The park stretches from the palm-lined beaches of the Tasman Sea to an interior of alpine herb fields, rocky peaks, and rolling flats of red tussock.

About 85% of the park is bush; beech forest covers most of the hills, while rimu and other podocarps are found on the lower slopes in the western fringes of the park. These fringes have a thick, dark green understorey of broadleaf, ferns and toro, which create a jungle-like forest. Five major river systems drain the park: Aorere and Takaka into Golden Bay, Motueka into Tasman Bay, and Karamea and Heaphy into the Tasman Sea.

HEAPHY TRACK

The popular Heaphy Track, an historic crossing from Golden Bay to the West Coast, offers one of the widest ranges of scenery of any walk in New Zealand. Along the 76-km track, you pass through native forest, across red-tussock downs, and along secluded river valleys to a beach lined by nikau palms. There are seven huts and 10 camp sites along the way. It's a considerably easier trek than any other extended tramp in Kahurangi National Park, having been upgraded to Great Walk status in recent years. The four to six-day trip is rated easy to medium.

Information

Information on the track or the forest park can be obtained at the DOC field centre (☎ 525 8026), 1 Commercial St, Takaka, or at the DOC field centre (☎ 782 6852), Waverley St, Karamea.

Maps

The best map for the track is the 1:63,360 Parkmaps No 245 *(Heaphy)*. This can be supplemented by the 1:50,000 Topomaps quads L26 *(Heaphy)* and L27 *(Karamea)*.

Huts

Hut and camping fees are $8 and $6 respectively on this Great Walk; passes should be obtained before you enter the track. The huts are Aorere Shelter, Brown, Gouland Downs, Heaphy, Katipo Creek Shelter, Kohaihai Shelter, Lewis, Mackay, Perry Saddle and Saxon.

Access

Collingwood End The Heaphy is now well serviced by transport at both ends of the track. There are a number of operators who will get you directly to the northern end of the track, near Bainham, in one day from Nelson, Motueka, Takaka or Collingwood.

Collingwood can be reached from Nelson, and towns in between, on Golden Bay Connection (☎ 524 8188). Buses depart from Nelson to Collingwood and the Heaphy Track at 8.45 am on weekdays (late October to late May), arriving at the track at 1.15 pm; a one-way fare costs $30.

An on-demand transport service is operated by NWN Trampers Service (☎ 528 6332); it will drop off or pick up for $35 per person. Tourist Transport or Transport for Trampers (☎ 545 1055) operates from Nelson to the Heaphy Track; the cost is $35 per person. During the walking season, it has a scheduled service from Brown Hut to Collingwood at 1.30 pm, arriving in Nelson at 5.30 pm.

The budget option ($8), is a trip with the mail run (☎ 524 8188), which takes you approximately 10 km down the Bainham Rd

– you walk the other 10 km to the start of the track.

There is a phone at Brown Hut – local calls are free – so trampers finishing here can ring Collingwood Bus Services for the 35-km ride back to Collingwood (the cost is $60 if there is only one person, dropping to $12 if there are five). Collingwood Safari Tours (☎ 524 8257) also provides this on-demand service, for the same price.

Karamea End There's a day shelter on the Kohaihai River, 15 km north of Karamea, at the West Coast end of the track. There is a phone here, so trampers can ring up Karamea Taxi Service (☎ 782 6757), which charges a flat rate of $25 per trip (four to five people) back to Karamea. If you are staying at the camping ground on the southern side of Karamea, the price is $30 for up to four persons. The Karamea Coaster is a courtesy bus service for people staying at the Last Resort (☎ 782 6617).

Cunningham Coaches (☎ 789 7177) departs from Karamea for Westport (100 km south of Karamea) on weekdays at 8 am; the one-way fare is $18. This service departs from Westport at 3.45 pm on weekdays for Karamea.

InterCity (☎ 789 7819) has a Westport to Nelson service which departs from Westport at 4 pm and arrives in Nelson at 7.50 pm. Going the other way, this service arrives in Westport at 11.15 am and arrives in Greymouth at 1.30 pm. White Star (☎ 789 8579) also provides transport from Westport to Nelson or Christchurch, with a bus departing at 10.05 am Sunday to Friday (there is a changeover in Springs Junction); the cost is about $30 to Nelson or Christchurch, $15 to Greymouth.

Trampers with their own vehicles often use a short flight to return to the other end of the track. Heaphy Track Aero Taxis (☎ 525 9428), Takaka, provides flights between Karamea and the Bainham airstrip (located five km from Brown Hut). In Karamea, bookings for the 25-minute flight can be made at the Karamea Tavern (☎ 782 6800). Other operators are Helicopters New

Zealand Ltd (☎ (0800) 50 2002) and Nelson Aero Club (☎ 547 9643).

Places to Stay
Collingwood The Collingwood Motor Camp (☎ 524 8149), William St, has sites ($12 for two) and cabins ($24 for two). The Pakawau Beach Motor Camp (☎ 524 8327) is 13 km north of Collingwood. Camp sites cost $6.75 per person. The Inn-let (☎ 524 8040), on the way to Pakawau, about five km from Collingwood, costs $15 and up; phone in advance.

Karamea The Last Resort (☎ 782 6617) has singles/doubles for $20/15 per person and tent sites for $6. Kohaihai, 15 km north of Karamea, is the site of a DOC camp site; it is not part of the Heaphy Track.

Westport The Howard Park Holiday Camp (☎ 789 7043) is on Domett St, only a km from the post office; camping costs $7/14 a night for one/two people. It also has chalets ($25 for two). Tripinns (☎ 789 7367), 72 Queen St, charges $13.50 per person.

The Track
The following description is for walking the Heaphy Track from east to west, which means that most of the climbing is done on the first day and the scenic beach walk is saved for the last day. For those trekking west to east, allow more time for ascending the spur from Lewis Hut to Mackay Hut and less time for the walk from Perry Saddle to Brown Hut. The walk is rated easy to medium. There are 10 huts and shelters along the way, and five of the huts (Perry Saddle, Saxon, Mackay, Lewis and Heaphy) have gas rings. Camping is permitted at 10 designated camp sites: Aorere and Katipo shelters, Scotts Beach and adjacent to all seven huts. Water, fireplaces and toilets are provided.

Stage 1: Brown Hut to Perry Saddle
Walking Time: five to six hours
Accommodation: Brown Hut (20 bunks); Aorere Shelter; Perry Saddle Hut (40 bunks)

Great Walks Ticket

Brown Hut, a km from the car park at Walsh Creek, is at the eastern end of the Heaphy Track. The hut was built to enable trampers to get an early start on the first leg of the journey – the steep climb to Perry Saddle. The hut has 20 bunks, but during summer there are often quite a few people sleeping on the floor. It has pit toilets and a fireplace.

From the hut, the track follows the Brown River for 180 metres before crossing it on a footbridge. On the other side, the long climb to Gouland Downs begins ascending a steep grass slope on a wide track before moving into bush. Beech forest with scattered podocarps and rata surround the track as it begins a gradual climb along monotonous switchbacks.

At one point, the track passes the junction with the Shakespeare Flat Track, a route that descends south (the left fork) to the Aorere River. Just beyond the junction is a poorly defined short cut that climbs the ridge by a more direct route, a tough climb that saves about half an hour. The main track swings uphill in a wide loop and about three hours from Brown Hut, after a seven-km climb, reaches Aorere Shelter. After another two km of climbing, the track takes a sharp turn and

begins a gentle ascent past Flanagan's Corner, the high point of the trip (915 metres).

From here, it's another 40 minutes (two km) before the track breaks out of the bush into the open tussock and patches of beech found on Perry Saddle. The nearby hut has gas rings, 40 bunks and, at 880 metres, views of the Anatoki Ridge across Aorere Valley. Close to the hut is the deep Gorge Creek – cold, but popular for bathing.

Stage 2: Perry Saddle to Saxon Hut
Walking Time: 3½ to four hours
Accommodation: Gouland Downs Hut (13 bunks); Saxon Hut (20 bunks)

A well-formed track quickly reaches Perry Saddle, and descends through low scrub on the true left (south) bank of Perry Creek. Within three km, the track opens into the bowl of the Gouland Downs, a wide expanse of rolling tussock broken by patches of stunted silver beech or pygmy pine. At the edge of the downs, you cross Sheep Creek and continue over red tussock (*Chionochloa rubra*) until you reach a footbridge over Cave Brook, a stream within sight of Gouland Downs Hut.

Although the small hut is old (built in 1932), it has a nice atmosphere and there are some interesting caves to explore behind it. The fireplace is probably the only original part of the hut which is left. Most trampers push on, however, because the hut is only a two-hour walk from Perry Saddle.

The track leaves the terrace of bush in which the hut is located and emerges again onto the red-tussock downs. Under normal conditions, it is easy to ford Shiner Brook and then Big River. You can use the swing bridges over these in bad weather. Within a km, you cross a footbridge over Weka Creek, and follow the fringe of scrub and bush along the northern part of the downs.

Just before crossing the Saxon River, the track arrives at Saxon Hut (the newest hut on the Heaphy), which is a five-km walk from Gouland Downs Hut. The hut has gas rings and 20 bunks. It was named after John

Saxon, who surveyed the route through here in 1886.

Stage 3: Saxon Hut to Mackay Hut
Walking Time: four hours
Accommodation: Mackay Hut (40 bunks)

The track begins with three km of level trekking, crosses Saxon River and Blue Duck Creek, and swings north. There is a flood track on the true right of the Saxon River; it's well signposted, and will take you over the flood plain to a swing bridge across the Saxon. Eventually, you enter the bush and begin one final climb, regaining all the height lost in the descent to Gouland Downs. From here, you may get your first glimpse of the Tasman Sea and the mouth of the Heaphy River.

From this high point, you move steadily downhill through numerous grass clearings, crossing several small bridges and boardwalks over boggy patches as you skirt the southern edge of Mackay Downs. Seven km after entering the downs, the track reaches Mackay Hut, situated on the fringe of dense bush. From the hut, the views of the Tasman Sea and Gunner Downs are excellent, and the sunsets on a clear evening are extraordinary. Listen for the calls of kiwis at night. The mouth of the Heaphy is about 15 km to the west and 750 metres below.

Stage 4: Mackay Hut to Heaphy Hut
Walking Time: six to seven hours
Accommodation: Lewis Hut (20 bunks); Heaphy Hut (20 bunks)

The track leaves the hut and descends into bush as it works steadily downhill toward the West Coast. Gradually, the valley closes in, and only an occasional glimpse of the Heaphy River is possible through the dense bush. There is a pleasant change in flora when the first nikau palms appear 100 metres above the junction of the Lewis and Heaphy rivers.

The long (12-km) descent finishes at Lewis Hut, which is situated at the confluence of the two rivers, only 15 metres above sea level. The hut, a three to four-hour walk

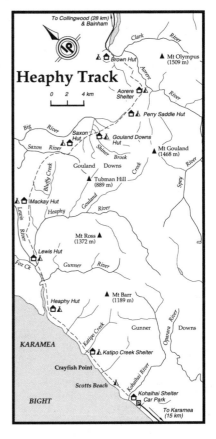

Heaphy Track

from Mackay Hut, has gas rings and 20 bunks. This part of the track used to be notorious for its boggy nature but is now being improved with culverts and track reconstruction.

The track heads north-west from the hut, up the Lewis River to cross the river at a swing bridge. Turn south and follow the true right bank to another long swing bridge over the Heaphy River. Follow the true left (south) bank, where the track remains until it reaches the Tasman Sea. Limestone bluffs keep the track close to the river, and in three km it arrives at a swing bridge over the

Gunner River. The track crosses a large river flat just after the bridge over Murray Creek and cuts through one last stand of bush.

From the bush and hills, the track unexpectedly opens up to Heaphy Hut and the lagoon beyond, an eight-km walk from Lewis Hut. The river mouth is at the junction of two greenstone trails, one over Gouland Downs and the other down the coast. Archaeologists have uncovered evidence of occupation in the area going back at least 500 years.

Not far from the new hut is the old six-bunk Heaphy Hut, which is now staff quarters. The former Heaphy Shelter has been relocated to the camp site. All are only a short hike from the beach on the Tasman Sea.

After struggling over much of the track, many trampers are inclined to spend a full day at Heaphy Hut. There is good swimming in the lagoon, but the Tasman Sea should be avoided because of vicious undertows. To the north, it's possible to cross the Heaphy River at low tide and scramble through a hole in Heaphy Bluff to see if any remains of a wrecked Japanese squid boat are still around. There is also a blazed route over the bluff, which leads northwards up the coast for about an hour. You can occasionally see fur seals from here. To the south, the overgrown McNabb Track begins from the hut and climbs the Bellbird Ridge to Gunner Downs, a full-day side trip.

Stage 5: Heaphy Hut to Kohaihai River
Walking Time: five hours

Unquestionably one of the most beautiful walks in the South Island, the final segment of the Heaphy works its way south along the West Coast, always near the pounding Tasman Sea. The track skirts the bush for most of the way, but in many places well-worn paths show where trampers have decided to forego the track and hike along the edge of the beach.

The track departs from the huts and camp site, passes a small pond, and reaches the sand and surf of the Tasman Sea at Heaphy Beach. It continues south along the coast,

crossing a footbridge over Wekakura Creek, then a bridge over Katipo Creek (generally regarded as the halfway point in the 15-km journey from the mouth of the Heaphy River to the start of the road). Just on the other side of the stream is Katipo Creek Shelter. Not far beyond Katipo Creek is Crayfish Point. The sea here is very dangerous, so use the high-tide track unless you arrive within two hours of low tide.

Still further south, the track crosses a third bridge, over Swan Burn, and arrives at Scotts Camp. Scotts Camp is a grassy clearing near a good beach, about two km from the end of the track. From the clearing, the track makes a gentle climb over a saddle and descends to the Kohaihai River, where a long suspension bridge brings you to a shelter, a public phone and the start of the road.

WANGAPEKA TRACK
The Wangapeka Track is a 60-km journey along the southern border of Kahurangi National Park. There are no beaches or pounding surf on this tramp, but to many backpackers, its rugged scenery and isolation make it a more pleasant hike than the Heaphy. The track could be walked in four days, though due to its rough terrain most trampers spread it over five or six days.

Information
For sources of track information, see Information for the Heaphy Track, earlier in this chapter.

Maps
The best map to use is the 1:75,000 Trackmaps No 335-05 *(Wangapeka Track)*, formerly NZMS 318. Otherwise, you have to purchase three quads of the 1:50,000 Topomaps 260 series: M28 *(Wangapeka)*, L28 *(Mokihinui)* and L27 *(Karamea)*.

Huts
Back-country hut tickets are required to use the huts on this track. The fee is one $4 ticket for each hut – except for the Category Two Taipo and Little Wanganui huts, which are

both equipped with gas and cost $8. There are very few places suitable for camping.

Access
Reaching the remote beginning and end of the Wangapeka requires complicated transport arrangements. The track can be hiked in either direction, but is described here from east to west, because this means easier climbs over the saddles. The eastern end is Rolling Junction Hut, reached by following a narrow metalled road for nine km from the Wangapeka River Rd, after fording the Dart River. You reach this area via the settlements of Tapawera, Tadmor and Matariki.

Wadsworth Motors (☎ 522 4248) runs a 10-seater vehicle from Tapawera to Rolling Junction Hut on demand ($50, regardless of the number of people). They also run daily from Tapawera to Nelson ($6 per person).

You can catch an NWN Trampers Service vehicle (☎ 528 6332) from Motueka to Rolling Junction Hut for $30. From Nelson, there is Tourist Transport or Transport for Trampers, who will pick up or drop off at Rolling Junction Hut for $25.

The western end of the track is a shelter at the end of Little Wanganui River Rd, 25 km south of Karamea. It's three km down the road to a public phone and a total of eight km to State Highway 67, where it's possible to flag down a bus. Cunningham Coaches (☎ 789 7177) transport out of Westport passes the Little Wanganui River Rd junction on weekdays; check the times with Cunningham.

Trampers who are moving directly from the Heaphy to the Wangapeka, using the two tracks to form a semicircular route back towards Nelson, can arrange for a ride between Kohaihai Stream and Little Wanganui River Rd junction through Karamea Motors (☎ 782 6757). The cost from Karamea to Little Wanganui is a flat rate of $33 for up to four persons; if there are five or more, there is a minibus ($7 per person).

The Karamea Coaster (☎ 782 6617) is a courtesy bus service for people staying at the Last Resort in Karamea.

Flights are available from Motueka to Karamea; for details ☎ 528 8772.

Places to Stay
See the Places to Stay sections of the Abel Tasman Coast and Wangapeka tracks.

The Track
The Wangapeka Track is rated medium to difficult, and is described here from east to west. For those who choose to walk it in the opposite direction, more time is needed from Little Wanganui Hut to Little Wanganui Saddle, and less time for the downhill segment from Stag Flat to the Taipo Bridge.

Stage 1: Rolling River to Kings Creek Hut
Walking Time: 3½ hours
Accommodation: Kings Creek Hut (30 bunks); Old Kings Slab Hut (four bunks)

A swing bridge crosses the Wangapeka River near the Rolling Junction Hut, and the track begins on the southern bank. The river is almost always in sight as the well-defined track winds through river flats of grass and scrub. After three hours, you pass Kiwi Shelter, an old bivouac, and cross a swing bridge to the northern bank of the river, passing a signposted junction. The side track crosses Kiwi Stream and heads north (right fork) to the six-bunk Kiwi Saddle Hut (3½ hours).

The main track heads south-west (left fork) and after half an hour reaches Kings Creek Hut via a short side track above the Wangapeka Forks. The gas-equipped hut is a 3½-hour walk from Rolling River. Another 10 minutes up the river is Old Kings Slab Hut, more an historic site than a place to spend the night. The hut was built in 1935 by Cecil King, who prospected in the area until the 1970s.

Stage 2: Kings Creek Hut to Helicopter Flat Hut
Walking Time: six to seven hours
Accommodation: Stone Hut (six bunks); Helicopter Flat Hut (six bunks)

Just beyond Old Kings Slab Hut, the track passes the junction of the North and South

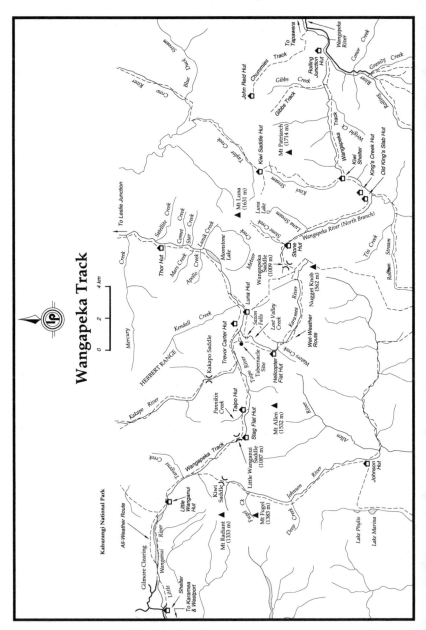

branches of the Wangapeka River. It continues along the true left (east) side of the North Branch and gently climbs towards Stone Hut, passing a deep gorge along the way. It's a 2½-hour (8½-km) walk to the six-bunk hut. Half an hour before reaching it, the track fords Luna Stream and then immediately crosses a footbridge to the true right side of the North Branch. The hut is located on a grassy flat opposite the Stone Creek Junction; it has an open fireplace.

The track leaves Stone Hut in bush but soon comes to an open slip, the result of the 1929 Murchison earthquake. You follow the Wangapeka River to its source, then ascend sharply to the Wangapeka Saddle along a well-marked route until it reaches the pass (1009 metres). At the bush-clad top, there is a signposted junction, with one track heading north-west along a steep, rough route to Luna Hut and another heading east to a clearing on Nugget Knob. The main track goes south-west (straight), towards Helicopter Flat Hut.

Following the main track, you descend gently from the saddle, ford Chime Creek and then begin a more rapid descent along the infant Karamea River into the valley. You cross several side streams before working steadily along the true left (south) bank of the Karamea. The river is crossed twice not far from Helicopter Flat Hut; the fords are easy if the weather is good. If not, there is an alternative all-weather route (marked with poles) that continues along the true left bank. The flood route takes an extra 20 minutes to walk. The routes rejoin on the southern bank, and continue on to Helicopter Flat Hut, just past Waters Creek. If the creek is flooded, there is a walkwire 30 metres upstream.

Helicopter Flat Hut has only six bunks, and there is little camping in the area. Trampers should not pitch tents on the helicopter pad.

Stage 3: Helicopter Flat Hut to Taipo Hut
Walking Time: 3½ to four hours
Accommodation: Taipo Hut (10 bunks)

This is a short three to four-hour walk to one of the newest huts on the track. Trampers can continue past Taipo Hut for another 1½ hours to reach Stag Flat Hut, but this is a smaller and older hut with poor camp sites around it.

From Helicopter Hut, the track follows the Karamea, then sidles up through bush away from the river. The track gradually climbs to Brough's Tabernacle Lookout while the Karamea carves its way through a deep and rugged gorge far below. The Tabernacle is the site of an old A-frame shelter, now long gone, that was built in 1898 by Jonathan Brough when he was surveying the original track. The views from here are excellent – you can see most of the Karamea Valley below.

The track leaves the lookout and after 100 metres passes a side track that descends sharply east (right fork) to Luna Hut. The main track (left fork) heads north then west, and descends steeply for half an hour to a swing bridge over the Taipo River. On the true left (north) side of the river, there is a junction with a track heading east (right fork) to Trevor Carter Hut. It's possible during fair weather to hike a round trip on this track and the track to Luna Hut from the Tabernacle which adds over two hours to the day's walk (allowing time to view Saxon Falls).

The main track is well marked as it heads west and follows the northern bank of the Taipo. You climb gently for several km, and two hours from the bridge, you reach Taipo Hut. This is a pleasant 10-bunk hut with gas stoves, and there are good camp sites below the nearby helicopter pad.

Stage 4: Taipo Hut to Little Wanganui Hut
Walking Time: 5½ to six hours
Accommodation: Stag Flat Hut (four bunks); Little Wanganui Hut (16 bunks)

Soon after leaving the hut, you cross a bridge over Pannikin Creek and then begin a steady climb towards Stag Flats, a tussock area of many creeks, much bog and mud. The climb steepens just before you reach the flats. The track cuts across the flats for 200 metres to reach Stag Flat Hut. After leaving the hut, you enter the bush and begin another steep climb towards Little Wanganui Saddle, an open clearing of snow grass. The climb is a knee-bender but the views from the top are the best of the trip. The saddle is the highest point of the track (1087 metres) and overlooks the Little Wanganui River to the West Coast and the Taipo River to the east.

The track descends past Saddle Lakes and drops steeply to the valley floor, re-entering bush and finally crossing a bridge over Little Wanganui River to its true right (north) side. The track fords Tangent and McHarrie creeks and then climbs steeply around the Little Wanganui Gorge, returning to the river just above the bridge to Little Wanganui Hut.

If the water level is normal, you can skip the track around the gorge and follow the river, fording it when necessary. Little Wanganui Hut, also gas-equipped, is located in a clearing on the true left (south) side of the river.

Stage 5: Little Wanganui Hut to Road's End
Walking Time: 2½ to three hours

Most trampers consider the final seven km of the journey a pleasant stroll, because the hardest walking of the trip is over. Return across the bridge, and follow the track on the true right (north) side of the river. In about 20 minutes, you come to the junction with the all-weather track.

The river route is well marked, and crisscrosses the Little Wanganui four times as it follows the river flats to the road's end. If the water level is normal, you won't have difficulty crossing the fords, which are clearly signposted. Two km before the end of the track, you pass through Gilmore Clearing.

If the river is in flood, follow the all-weather track along the true right (north) side of the river all the way to the end. This track eventually joins an old logging road which, after a km, merges with Little Wanganui River Rd. The all-weather route is a longer walk, because there is considerably more climbing involved. There have been slips near Gilmore Clearing, which add more time

to this part of the trip; take care when negotiating these. Seek advice from the DOC field centres at Motueka (☎ 528 9117) or Karamea (☎ 782 6852).

LESLIE-KARAMEA TRACK
The best tramp into the heart of Kahurangi National Park is the Leslie-Karamea Track. Two river routes combine to form a 48-km trek, but the actual journey is closer to 86 km, because hikers need to walk to and from each end of the track. With this in mind, plan on five to seven days for the trip, which will include tramping half of the Wangapeka Track.

The highlights of the track are its interesting huts and camp sites, a little gold-mining history along the way and the best trout fishing in the park. Just about every river in the national park has fish, and the Karamea River is renowned for its stocks of brown trout, especially where the Leslie empties into it at Karamea Bend. If departing east along the Wangapeka Track, the Wangapeka River is also worth exploring with a rod in hand.

Information
The DOC information offices are the same as those for the Heaphy Track. Get a copy of the pamphlet *Leslie-Karamea* from either the Motueka or Takaka field centres.

Maps
There is no Trackmaps recreational map for the track. Most of the route is covered by the 1:50,000 Topomaps 260 quad M27 *(Mt Arthur)*. See also the maps for the Wangapeka Track in this section. The *Mt Arthur Tablelands Walks* and *Cobb Valley* brochures are useful for the northern access.

Huts
The charge for Salisbury, Little Wanganui and Taipo huts is $8; all the others are Category Three ($4). Rock shelters are free. Mt Arthur, Salisbury, Venus, Taipo, Little Wanganui and King Creek huts have gas; all others have a fireplace or a potbelly stove.

Access
There are two ways to reach the northern end

of the track. The start of the Leslie River Track is technically near the high point of Tableland (1230 metres), on Starvation Ridge, though many people consider Salisbury Lodge to be the beginning. You can reach Tableland by way of Cobb Valley, which lies 110 km north-west of Nelson and 28 km from the Upper Takaka turn-off. Follow the service road along the valley to Mytton Hut, near the end of Cobb Reservoir, and then take the track to Balloon Hut. Tableland is an 11½-km (four-hour) hike.

The most popular approach is from the Graham Valley, on the west bank of the Motueka River. From State Highway 61, cross the river on bridges at Woodstock, Ngatimoti or Pangatotara to the West Bank Rd and then follow AA signs to the valley. It's an hour's drive from Nelson to the Graham Valley. For the last four km up the valley, the road rises some 820 metres to a car park and lookout. You then tramp Flora Track over the saddle of the same name and follow signposts toward Salisbury Lodge (30 bunks). The 14-km tramp via Flora Hut and Flora Stream takes about four hours.

To get to the two start points of the Leslie-Karamea – the Cobb and Graham valleys – you can use either NWN Trampers Service (☎ 528 6332) from Motueka or Tourist Transport or Transport for Trampers (☎ 545 1055) from Nelson. NWN charges $20 to the Graham Valley and $30 to the Cobb Valley; Tourist Transport charges $23 to the Graham and $30 to the Cobb.

The southern end of the Leslie-Karamea Track ends at the Wangapeka Track, and trampers can depart either eastwards to Rolling River Junction or westwards to the Little Wanganui River car park. Although the Little Wanganui River car park is 12 km closer, most trampers need two additional days to cover the final segment of the journey whichever way they head down the Wangapeka Track. Transport can be arranged at either end of the Wangapeka Track (see the preceding Wangapeka Track section), but it's rough going to reach the car parks at the northern end of the Leslie-Karamea if you don't have a vehicle.

Places to Stay
See the Places to Stay sections of the Abel Tasman Coast and Wangapeka tracks.

The Track
The following track, rated medium, begins from Salisbury Lodge, a Category Two hut in the Tablelands. The two alternative access routes to Tablelands are described earlier. The track is described from north to south.

Stage 1: Salisbury Lodge to Karamea Bend
Walking Time: five hours
Accommodation: Splugens Rock Shelter (10 bunks); Leslie Clearing Hut (six bunks); Karamea Bend Hut (12 bunks)

Just beyond Salisbury Lodge is a signpost that points the way to the Leslie River. The track begins as a series of snow poles and a well-worn path through the snow grass to a junction on Tableland Plateau (1280 metres). The track to the north-west (the right fork) heads off to Balloon Hut (half an hour) and the Cobb Valley, while the main track descends south-west into the bush. The drop is steep, with the benched track descending 360 metres in four km.

Within an hour, after passing two good lookout points, you arrive at Splugens Rock. The canvas-fronted shelter is on a platform blasted out of rock and makes for an unusual but very scenic place to spend the night.

The benched track, really an old pack track, continues to descend, emerges on the true left side of Peel Stream, and three km from Splugens Rock arrives at the confluence of the stream and the Leslie River. A swing bridge crosses the Leslie here to its true left bank. You can hike up the Leslie for half an hour from the bridge to reach Arthur Creek, once one of the best gold-bearing streams of the Tablelands. There are still dozens of flume pipes along the creek which were hauled in by packhorse.

Downstream from the bridge, the track moves through beech forest and along flats and terraces. In five km, it reaches Leslie Flats, the site of a six-bunk hut. Leslie Clearing Hut

Leslie-Karamea Track

0   3   6 km

is the latest in a succession of shelters built on the flats since the 1890s. It is an easy four km from the hut to Karamea Bend, where the Leslie and Karamea rivers meet and the Karamea River swings towards the West Coast. The Karamea Bend Hut was built in 1975, and the river here is a noted trout-fishing spot.

Stage 2: Karamea Bend Hut to Venus Hut

Walking Time: 4½ to five hours
Accommodation: Crow Hut (six bunks); Venus Hut (12 bunks)

The track heads upriver (south-west) along the Karamea River, working its way through forest and over terraces and across flats. The track fords several creeks, first Slippery Creek then Little Backwash and Big Backwash, before arriving at Crow River, where there's a swing bridge. It's a 10-km (about a three-hour) walk through mostly beech forest to Crow Hut, just across the bridge.

When the water levels are normal or low, a pleasant alternative (if you don't mind wet boots) is to hike up the river bed. Fords are numerous and range from knee to waist-deep, but the scenery is much more interesting.

The track follows the Karamea for the first half-hour from Crow Hut, passing pools that will tempt any angler. It then swings away from the river and climbs a terrace for the next km, before emerging from the forest to a view of the Karamea swing bridge, located just upriver from Saturn Creek. Once across the bridge, the track remains on the true left side of the river for the rest of the trip.

You remain mostly on the bush terraces as you continue towards the Karamea headwaters, crossing bridges over Jupiter and Venus creeks. It's about three km from the Karamea Bridge to Venus Hut, which is on the southern side of Venus Creek.

Stage 3: Venus Hut to Trevor Carter Hut

Walking Time: 5½ to six hours
Accommodation: Thor Hut (six bunks); Luna Hut (four bunks); Trevor Carter Hut (six bunks)

From Venus Hut, you continue to work your way through bush-clad terraces, and two km (half an hour) from Venus Hut arrive at the footbridge over Mercury Creek. The next major side stream is Atlas Creek, 2½ km further up the Karamea River. From here, the track hugs bluffs above the river until it crosses Thor Creek and arrives at Thor Hut, situated on a small promontory overlooking the Karamea River.

Beyond the hut, you begin climbing undulating bush slopes (where it's easy to get tangled up in the tree roots which crisscross the track) and fording more creeks. Mars Creek is about half an hour from Thor Hut, and Apollo Creek 10 minutes beyond that. The debris and loose rocks that surround the track are the result of the 1929 Murchison earthquake, also responsible for the rubble that spilled down Apollo Creek and the dam that formed Moonstone Lake. The lake extends three km beyond Apollo Creek, and the track skirts the lake by climbing onto the bush-clad slopes above it.

Beyond the head of Moonstone Lake, the track returns to the Karamea River at Orbit Creek, where the valley opens up and the trek becomes an easy walk along river beaches.

In normal conditions, the Karamea is easily forded here, and by crossing it just beyond Orbit Creek, you can pick up a track on the true right (east) bank that cuts across scrub and tussock flats to Luna Hut (half an hour).

An all-weather track continues up the true left (west) side of the Karamea River, crosses bush flats and three km from Orbit Creek fords Kendall Creek. Kendall Creek, draining the Herbert Range, is dangerous; trampers should take care, and on no account cross it in flood conditions – the DOC is looking at the best bridging options for this area. The best ford of the braided stream is near its mouth. The track continues from Kendall, rounds the scrub end of a spur opposite Luna Hut and then enters rubble flats, arriving at Trevor Carter Hut in half an hour (see the Wangapeka Track map).

Stage 4: Trevor Carter Hut to Wangapeka Track

Walking Time: 45 minutes to 1½ hours

There are several ways to reach Wangapeka Track. The most recently built track departs from Trevor Carter Hut and follows the true left (north) side of the Karamea River and its tributary, the Taipo, before reaching the Wangapeka Track at the Taipo Bridge. The 2½-km walk takes about 45 minutes, and from here it takes about another two hours to reach either Taipo Hut to the west or Helicopter Flat Hut to the south-east. From Luna Hut, you can also follow a track on the true right (south) side of the Karamea and cross the river below Saxon Falls. There is a short spur track to the impressive falls, but the main track climbs steeply for 15 to 20 minutes before it reaches the Wangapeka Track at Brough's Tabernacle Lookout. Helicopter Flat Hut is less than an hour away to the south.

A track also departs up the rubble banks of Lost Valley Creek, emerging in 2½ km at a bush-clad saddle with a large tarn. From here, it's a quick drop back west to the Karamea River near Helicopter Flat Hut.

Once on the Wangapeka Track, most trampers need an additional two days to reach either the western or eastern start of the track (see the preceding section on the Wangapeka Track).

OTHER TRACKS
Tableland Walk
This is a two to three-day trip in Kahurangi National Park, from Flora Track car park (in the Graham Valley) to Mytton Hut (at the end of the service road along the Cobb Reservoir – see the Access section of the Leslie-Karamea Track). The 25-km trek could include nights spent at Flora Hut, Salisbury Lodge, Balloon Hut or a number of unusual shelters passed along the way. The trip is rated easy to medium and offers some good views.

Nelson Lakes National Park

Some say that the Southern Alps end in Nelson Lakes National Park. The great mountain range of New Zealand rises out of Fiordland and forms a crest along the South Island until it diminishes in height and importance here, merging with the ranges to the north in Kahurangi National Park and Mt Richmond Forest Park.

The reason most visitors come to Nelson Lakes National Park, located 103 km south-west of Blenheim, is to see lakes Rotoiti and Rotoroa. But once beyond the shores of the lakes, trampers soon discover that this is a land of long valleys and numerous passes, with alpine routes that are not nearly as demanding as those found elsewhere in the Southern Alps.

If you long to climb a mountain and stroll along a ridge, Nelson Lakes is a good place to begin adventuring above the bush-line. It is a mountainous region, with many peaks well above 2000 metres, but the tracks are well benched, and the routes marked with cairns or snow poles.

There are a number of round trips possible in the park, most requiring four to six days of walking and the climbing of one or two passes. The most popular, and the best round trip for trampers with limited experience on alpine routes, is the Travers-Sabine Circuit. The five to six-day walk begins and ends at St Arnaud and includes tramping over Travers Saddle and the Mt Robert skifield. These are not easy climbs, but they are well marked and in good summer weather are within the capabilities of most fit trampers. More remote and more challenging is the D'Urville Valley Track, described here as a round trip out of Rotoroa utilising Sabine Valley and Moss Pass. Without a water-taxi drop off, this is usually a seven-day journey for most trampers, which can end either at Rotoroa or St Arnaud.

The Nelson Lakes National Park is connected to the St James Walkway by two challenging alpine routes. Experienced trampers can hike in a single day from Bobs Hut, on the West Branch of the Matakitaki River, over a very challenging route to Ada Pass Hut. Or it's possible to hike from Blue Lake Hut, on the West Branch of the Sabine River, over Waiau Pass into Waiau River Valley. This trip requires two to three days, joining the walkway near the privately owned Ada Homestead.

HISTORY
The Maoris believed that a giant named Rakaihaitu created the lakes after arriving at Nelson in his canoe *Uruao*. Exploring the land to the south on foot, he picked up a digging stick in upper Buller Valley and gouged out lakes Rotoiti and Rotoroa before continuing down the Southern Alps and creating other lakes. Though they rarely settled here, Maoris did pass through this region, because it was crossed by important routes between the Tasman Sea and Canterbury.

John Cotterell and a Maori guide pushed their way through more than 300 km of trackless terrain to the Tophouse and the Clarence River in 1842. The following January, they retraced their journey and continued on to become the first Europeans to see Lake Rotoiti.

Three years later, another Maori guide, named Kehu, lead William Fox, Charles

Heaphy and Thomas Brunner on one of the best-recorded explorations in the South Island. With Heaphy keeping the diary and Fox using a paintbrush to record the scenery, the group struggled down to Rotoiti under the weight of 34-kg packs. From the lake, Kehu took the party up the Howard River, where they 'discovered' Lake Rotoroa. By September 1846, Fox had sent a pair of surveyors to cut a track towards Rotoiti, and by 1848, a Scot named George McRae had driven 400 sheep from his Rotoiti run to Nelson.

More exploration of the area followed, with Christopher Mailing and William Thomas Locke Travers becoming the first Europeans to explore the Lewis Pass area. Later, Travers returned to take up his own pastoral station in the upper Waiau.

The gold discoveries on the Buller River and in the West Coast region gave the push needed to build a dray road from Nelson to the West Coast goldfields. The road touched the fringes of what is now the national park. It was continually upgraded until it became the present highway, State Highway 6, in the 1920s. Nelson Lakes was gazetted in 1956 as a national park of 57,500 hectares. In 1982, it was increased to its present size, 99,270 hectares, with the addition of over 40,000 hectares, including the Spenser Mountains.

CLIMATE
Nelson Lakes possesses a surprisingly moderate climate for an alpine region. Ranges to the west, south and east protect the park, preventing many storms from arriving and reducing the intensity of others. Rain is brought by the prevailing westerlies that blow in from the Tasman Sea, so the western side of the park is the wettest. In the popular tramping area of Travers Valley, in the eastern half of the park, the average rainfall is only around 2000 mm a year, and at the park headquarters at Rotoiti it drops to 1600 mm.

You must be ready to cope with the sudden weather changes for which alpine areas are noted. A warm, clear day on a mountain pass can become a whiteout, with heavy rain or even a blizzard, in no time at all. Above the bush-line, snow may fall throughout the year, and all trampers should carry warm, preferably woollen, clothing and windproof and waterproof gear. Despite these precautions, the overall climate of the park is pleasantly moderate, characterised in summer by long spells of settled or even clear weather.

NATURAL HISTORY
The landscape of Nelson Lakes was created by the Alpine Fault and carved by glaciers. The fault, where the edges of two great plates in the earth's crust meet, is the major geological feature of the South Island and splits the park almost in half. Movement along the fault created the mountainous terrain millions of years ago, but it was the glaciers of the last ice age that gouged out the land to give the mountains their present shape.

Long valleys were carved by the glaciers which, when they reached the area of St Arnaud, were finally stopped by the hard rock of Black Hill. They forked at this point, pushing up a rocky moraine in the middle. When the glaciers finally retreated, some 8000 years ago, deep holes at the head of Travers and Gowan valleys were left, and these filled with the water of the melting ice to become Lake Rotoiti and Lake Rotoroa. The moraine that surrounds Black Hill became the peninsula that today separates West Bay from Kerr Bay in Lake Rotoiti.

The forests of Nelson Lakes are predominantly beech, with all five New Zealand species found here. In the lower valleys, where the conditions are warmer and more fertile, you'll find red and silver beech interspersed with such species as kamahi, toe toe, kowhai and southern rata (which has a mass of bright flowers when in bloom). Mountain and silver beech become dominant at altitudes above 1050 metres, or where there are poor soils in the lowlands.

The dominant species of bird is the kea, though in character rather than in numbers. Dark olive-green, with scarlet feathers under its wings, this inquisitive alpine parrot is often encountered above the bush-line. It's not uncommon to take a rest stop in the mountains and soon have four or five perched on large boulders around you.

Another park animal that many visitors would like to encounter is the trout. Brown trout is the predominant species caught, and can be found in both the lakes as well as in the main rivers (Travers, D'Urville, Sabine, Matakitaki and Buller). Both spinners and flies are used to entice the fish.

TRAVERS-SABINE CIRCUIT

Unquestionably the most accessible and popular tramping area of Nelson Lakes, Travers Valley provides easy tramping along good tracks with excellent alpine scenery, plenty of huts and a bridge just about every time you need one to cross a stream. Though Nelson Lakes receives only a fraction of the visitors and trampers that Abel Tasman or many of the well-known tracks in Fiordland do, Travers Valley is the one area in the park where the huts will be filled on public holidays and long weekends.

When it's combined with the route in the Sabine Valley next to it, via the Travers Saddle, the trip is ideal for those new to the alpine areas of New Zealand. The passes above the bush-line are well marked but are still part of a 'route', and you wander through meadows, up steep scree slopes and along a winding ridge. The views on a clear day – and there are usually many such days in February – are of spectacular alpine scenery.

Information

The St Arnaud field centre and visitor centre (☎ 521 1806; fax 521 1896) is a five-minute walk from the store in St Arnaud. The centre is open daily from 8 am to 5 pm.

The Lake Rotoroa field base (☎ 523 9369), located at the northern end of Lake Rotoroa, is open from 8 am to 5 pm in summer. Get a copy of the publication *Lake Rotoroa Nature Walks* – here, in one tiny, excellent volume, is all you need to know about the surrounding forests.

Maps

The 1:100,000 Parkmaps No 273-05, *Nelson Lakes National Park*, is adequate. The 1:50,000 Topomaps 260 quads N29 *(St Arnaud)*, M29 *(Murchison)* and M30 *(Matakitaki)* cover the entire trip.

Huts

There are nine huts along the track; all cost $4 a night, except Angelus Hut ($8).

Access

Several local companies have buses to Nelson Lakes National Park. The Nelson Lakes Shuttles (☎ 521 1887), owned and operated by the Yellow House, has a Monday, Wednesday and Friday service between St Arnaud and Picton ($16); it leaves St Arnaud at 9 am, returning at 3.25 pm. It also operates a Tuesday, Thursday and Saturday service between St Arnaud and Westport ($28), leaving St Arnaud at 9 am and returning at 2 pm. Wadsworth Motors (☎ 522 4248) has thrice-weekly buses from Nelson to Lake Rotoiti and Tadmor, plus buses to Tapawera on weekdays.

Nelson Lakes Transport (☎ 548 6858, 521 1802) runs a scheduled return bus between Nelson and St Arnaud daily (except Sunday), connecting with other buses between Picton and Greymouth.

There is also Sounds to Coast Shuttle Service – Blenheim Taxis (☎ 578 0225), whose twice-weekly Picton-Greymouth-Picton run (Monday and Friday) stops in St Arnaud; it leaves Picton at 7 am, arrives in St Arnaud at 8.35 am, leaves Greymouth at 1.15 pm, arrives in St Arnaud at 4.55 pm and finally arrives in Picton at 6.30 pm. The fare is $15 from Picton to St Arnaud and $30 from St Arnaud to Greymouth.

If you wish to get to Lake Rotoroa, you will usually have to hitch from Gowan Bridge. Nelson Lakes Transport will pick up from here, but this is expensive unless you're in a group. The majority of visitors get here in their own cars.

Water-taxis operate on both lakes Rotoiti and Rotoroa (☎ 521 1894 in Lake Rotoiti, 523 9199 in Lake Rotoroa for bookings). Transport on Rotoiti from the head of the lake costs $10 per person (minimum $40) to Kerr Bay and $12 per person (minimum $48) to West Bay. Kerr Bay to West Bay costs $8 per person (minimum $36). From Rotoroa township to the head of Rotoroa lake costs around $20 per person (minimum of $50).

Keep in mind that by ending the trip at Sabine Hut, you'll miss spending a night at Angelus Hut, easily the most scenic in this area.

Places to Stay

Lake Rotoiti The *Yellow House Guesthouse* (☎ 521 1887) in St Arnaud costs $13 per night. *Alpine Lodge* (☎ 521 1869) charges $80/85 for singles/doubles but also has some backpackers' accommodation. There are also two serviced DOC camp sites (Kerr Bay and West Bay) at the Rotoiti end of the walk – contact the St Arnaud field centre.

Lake Rotoroa There are not many accommodation options here. The basic self-registration DOC camp sites by the lake cost $2 per person. At the *Retreat Camping Ground*, towards Gowan Bridge, camp sites are $6 per night.

The Track

The following trip is a six-day walk, rated medium, but it can be shortened by using water-taxis on the lakes (see the Access section), or if the weather is bad by taking the exit from Sabine Hut to Speargrass Hut. It begins with the Lakehead Track along the eastern side of Lake Rotoiti. You can also follow the Lakeside Track along the west side, but this is a longer walk to the southern end.

Stage 1: Kerr Bay to John Tait Hut

Walking Time: five to seven hours
Accommodation: Lakehead Hut (18 bunks); Coldwater Hut (six bunks); John Tait Hut (30 bunks)

The Lakehead Track is clearly signposted, and begins just beyond the toilets at Kerr Bay DOC camping ground. For the first km, to the junction of the Loop Track, it's a wide and level path. Beyond the junction, it resembles a track but remains an easy walk through the forest on the edge of Lake Rotoiti. After four km, the track passes a gravel clearing, where there are good views of the northern half of the lake, including the peninsula between the bays, and in another 2½ km it passes a second clearing. This time the southern half of the lake can be seen.

Lakehead Hut is nine km (about 2½ to three hours) from Kerr Bay camping ground and is situated on a grassy bank overlooking the mouth of the Travers River. There is good trout fishing in the river here, especially in the lake near the mouth. If the hut is full, Coldwater Hut, smaller and not as pleasant, is about 1½ km and a ford of Travers River away, on the other side of the lake.

At Lakehead Hut, signposts direct you across Travers River and through a grassy flat, to the walking track on the true left (west) side of the river. The alternative during high water is to follow the true right (east) side of the river for five km, to a footbridge across the Travers. The true left side is more scenic, however, because it swings close to the river in many places.

Once on the track along the true left side of the river, you soon pass a signposted junction for Cascade Track, which leads to Angelus Hut (4½ hours). The track then meanders between stands of beech and grassy flats until it reaches the footbridge across the Travers, then continues to follow the river closely in the forest, emerging in 3¼ km onto another flat, where Mt Travers dominates the view. Just beyond the end of the flat you arrive at a footbridge over Hopeless Creek, and on the other side is the signposted junction indicating the track to Hopeless Hut (2½ hours).

The sign also says John Tait Hut is two hours away, but most trampers cover the remaining five km in less time. The track now begins to climb gradually. The hut is located in a small, grassy clearing, with good views of the peaks at the head of the valley.

Stage 2: John Tait Hut to Upper Travers Hut

Walking Time: two to three hours
Accommodation: Upper Travers Hut (16 bunks)

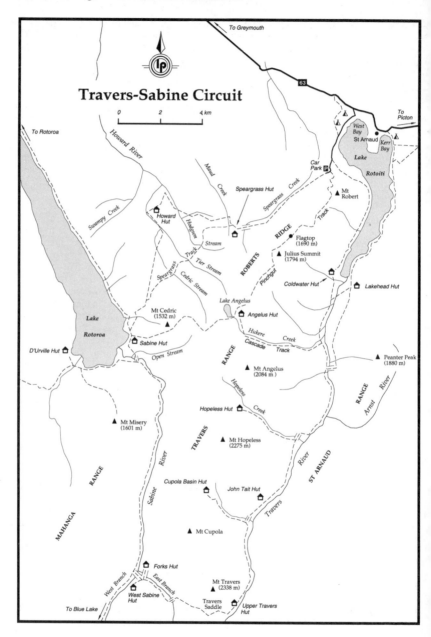

Travers-Sabine Circuit

The track continues to climb the valley. Within a km of the hut it passes the junction with the track to the Cupola Basin Hut (two hours). The climb steepens at this point, and within another km the track passes the side track to Travers Falls. It's well worth dropping the pack and descending to this beautiful cascade of water, a three-minute walk away. The 20-metre falls drop into a sparkling, clear pool.

From the falls, the track climbs gently, soon crossing a bridge over Summit Creek. You cross a second bridge in 1½ km, and at this point you begin a much steeper climb to the bush-line. At the edge of the bush, a little over two km from the second bridge, trampers are greeted with good views of the peaks of both the Travers and St Arnaud ranges.

The Upper Travers Hut is in a grassy clearing before the last stand of mountain beech towards the saddle. It's a beautiful spot, surrounded by gravel and scree slopes which can be easily climbed for better views.

Stage 3: Upper Travers Hut to West Sabine Hut

Walking Time: five to six hours
Accommodation: Sabine Forks Hut (eight bunks); West Sabine Hut (eight bunks)

The route over Travers Pass is well marked with rock cairns and snow poles. The ascent begins when you emerge from the final stand of trees into an area of tussock-covered slopes and scattered, large boulders. From here, you are technically following a route, but due to its popularity, a track exists most of the way. The route climbs gently towards the saddle for a km, until you reach a 'Travers Saddle' sign pointing up a steep gravel slope. The stiff zigzagging climb lasts several hundred metres; it's best to take your time, stopping often to admire the fine views.

Once at the top of the slope, a 450-metre ascent from the hut, the climb to the true saddle is easy; the sharp-edged Mt Travers (2338 metres) looms overhead to the north. The saddle, marked by a huge rock cairn, is a nice spot, but for an awe-inspiring view you should scramble to one of the nearby ridges.

From the saddle, you begin descending rapidly, passing first through tussock slopes then over a rock slide before returning to grass. At one point, about 1½ km from the saddle, there is a superb view of the Mahanga Range, just before you descend into the tree line and return to the track.

You remain in the stunted mountain beech only momentarily, because the track quickly swings onto a scree-covered gully and embarks on a very rapid descent – some 600 metres over a span of three km. This is probably the hardest section of the day, and care has to be taken on the steep sections of loose rock. Halfway down, at the tree line, the track reappears – follow it as it levels out next to the gorge of the East Branch of the Sabine River.

Shortly afterwards, you cross a small bridge over the gorge; it's impossible to see the water, but it can certainly be heard roaring between the narrow rock walls. The best view is from the river bank upstream. Once on the other side, the track follows the steep valley for the next four km and in many places is a maze of tree roots.

The final leg of this long day is a very steep drop down the East Branch to a swing bridge crossing the river. Forks Hut is on the other side of the river. The main track swings south to West Sabine Hut, which is a five-minute walk past the swing bridge over the Sabine River. The West Sabine Hut is in a much sunnier and prettier location than Forks Hut, which may be removed in the near future.

Stage 4: West Sabine Hut to Lake Rotoroa

Walking Time: five to six hours
Accommodation: Sabine Hut (16 bunks)

Return to the swing bridge over the Sabine River and cross to the true left side (west) of the river, following the level route for the first two km. This is a very pleasant stretch because the track remains close to the water, and it's an easy start for those who still ache from the climb over Travers Saddle. The track remains in the wooded fringe along the river for seven km before breaking out onto a grassy flat.

The track crosses the flat for the next two km and climbs steeply at its northern end, only to descend onto another flat. At the northern end of this flat is a climb to a small knob that overlooks Deep Gorge. This is the steepest ascent of a relatively easy day. Once the track descends to the other side, it follows the river to the junction with the track to D'Urville Hut. If you're heading for Sabine Hut, cross the bridge over the deep gorge. The gorge is impressive from either end, and from the middle of the bridge you can look down into the pale green water, and occasionally spot large trout. It's easy to scramble down to the water level – trampers have even been known to float through the gorge for a refreshing dip on a hot day.

From the bridge, the track climbs up and out of the narrow valley, then spills out onto a grassy flat. You are now less than a km from the hut along a wooded, level path. Sabine Hut has 16 bunks, but it's rather a crowded place when full. There are lots of sandflies here, but there are also excellent sunsets over Lake Rotoroa that can be enjoyed from the hut's jetty.

Stage 5: Lake Rotoroa to Angelus Hut
Walking Time: six to eight hours
Accommodation: Angelus Hut (36 bunks)

Fill your water bottles before embarking on the alpine trek to Lake Angelus – there is no water along the way. Also keep in mind that this route is very exposed, with little shelter once you climb above the bush-line.

The track to the alpine hut is signposted 'Mt Cedric' and begins right behind Sabine Hut. The first portion is extremely steep – you gain well over 900 metres in four km – but it has a partial view of Lake Rotoroa on the way up. This section ends once you break out of the bush-line, where you are greeted with an immense view of the entire lake, Sabine Valley and the surrounding mountains. The track now becomes a route, and you follow the poles to a high point which has views of the round-domed Mt Cedric

(1532 metres) to the north, 2½ km from the bush-line.

The snow poles continue along a ridge to the north-east, where you reach the high point of the day (1650 metres) and then skirt the flank of Peak 6150. For most of this ridge walk, you circle a basin below, marked by a small tarn which feeds Cedric Stream. Once the route goes around the peak, it returns to the crest of a ridge, and Hinapouri Tarn soon comes into view below.

In a short distance, the poles direct you off the ridge and you begin to descend towards Lake Angelus. This section involves hopping over huge rocks – good footing is important. At one point you'll spot Lake Angelus, and even the top of the hut, while still a good 20 minutes away. Lake Angelus, actually two lakes, lies in a beautiful basin surrounded by ridges and peaks. This is a good spot to spend a spare day if you have one. The roomy Category Two hut was built in 1970 (the old one is now the loo), and there are plenty of ridges to scramble along for a scenic day hike.

Stage 6: Lake Angelus to St Arnaud
Walking Time: five to seven hours

There are two ways to return to the park headquarters. If the weather is clear, the route along the ridge past Mt Robert skifield is a spectacular walk. But keep in mind the whole length of the ridge is exposed to south-east winds, with few places for shelter on the lee side. In bad weather with low visibility, it is easy to become disorientated and wander off the route. During poor weather, follow Cascade Track, which drops quickly into the safety of the valley. Plan on five to six hours to reach the park headquarters when combining this track with the Lakehead Track.

The ridge route begins as a series of metal poles heading east from the hut and climbing a scree slope to a saddle on the rim of Angelus Basin. The route drops down a scree slope on the other side into a saddle and then climbs up the western side of the main ridge, over a knob of 1814 metres. Follow the ridge in a north-easterly direction, scrambling over or sidling the steep rock outcrops that are encountered. The route comes to a basin below the Julius Summit (1794 metres), passes under the peak on the western side, and returns to the main ridge by first climbing a small saddle immediately north of it.

The well-marked route continues along the ridge past the Third Basin and ascends Flagtop (1690 metres), from which you can view the skifield and shelters. You drop 160 metres over 1½ km along a well-worn track before reaching one of the oldest skifields in New Zealand, Mt Robert, where there are a number of ski lodges. From here you continue along the poled route that follows the ridge to Mt Robert (1411 metres), then pick up Pinchgut Track. The trail drops steeply to the skifield car park and shelter, which is still a seven-km walk from the park headquarters.

D'URVILLE VALLEY TRACK

Most people find the tramp through D'Urville Valley an easy stroll; it's the alpine pass that makes this five-day trek a much more challenging one than the Travers-Sabine Circuit. It's better to walk the loop in an anticlockwise direction and drop into D'Urville Valley from Moss Pass because in the opposite direction, there's a steep ascent of 1500 metres.

Information
Information can be obtained and intentions registered at the Lake Rotoroa field base (☎ 523 9369), located at the northern end of Lake Rotoroa. The St Arnaud field centre and visitor centre (☎ 521 1806; fax 521 1896) is a five-minute walk from the store in St Arnaud.

Maps
The 1:100,000 Parkmaps No 273-05, *Nelson Lakes National Park*, is adequate. The 1:50,000 Topomaps 260 quads N29 *(St Arnaud)*, M29 *(Murchison)* and M30 *(Matakitaki)* cover the entire trip.

Huts
All of the huts along this route are Category Three ($4).

Access
The trip described here starts from Rotoroa, goes along the eastern shore of Lake Rotoroa into Sabine Valley and heads over Moss Pass to the D'Urville River. It ends at D'Urville Hut, near the south-western shore of Rotoroa, and from here there are several ways to exit. You can backtrack along Lake Rotoroa (an eight to nine-hour walk); follow the new Speargrass Track, a nine-hour walk to St Arnaud; tramp to Lake Angelus over the Mt Robert skifield to the park headquarters (see Stage 6 of Travers-Sabine Circuit section); or take the Tiraumea Track to the village of Tutaki.

To complete the circuit in five days, or even to reduce it to a four-day trip, you can arrange to be dropped off at Sabine Hut and picked up from D'Urville Hut by Lake Rotoroa Water Taxi (see Access for Travers-Sabine Circuit). There is no bus service into or out of Rotoroa. The closest spot you can reach by public transport is the Gowan Bridge, 11 km to the north on State Highway 6, on one of a number of shuttle buses. If you hire a water-taxi, the operator will arrange to pick you up there. For other transport and accommodation details, see the Access and Places to Stay sections for the Travers-Sabine Circuit.

The Track
This 65-km, five-day trip, rated medium to difficult (because of Moss Pass), is described from Sabine Valley to D'Urville Valley, which is the easiest way to cross Moss Pass.

Stage 1: Rotoroa to West Sabine Hut
Walking Time: two days (11 to 13 hours)
Accommodation: Sabine Hut (16 bunks); Sabine Forks Hut (eight bunks); West Sabine Hut (eight bunks)

The Rotoroa Track begins at the northern end of the lake, at the picnic area and camping ground, and follows the eastern bank for 18 km to Sabine Hut. The track, which stays in the forest, makes for a tedious day crossing many small ridges and gullies; it's a six to seven-hour tramp to the hut.

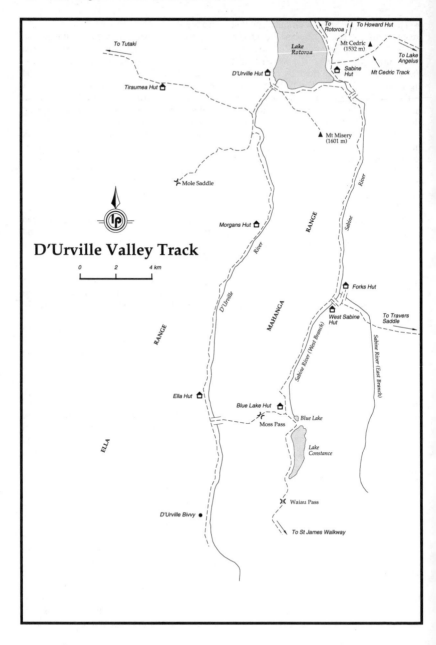

To Tutaki

To Rotoroa

To Howard Hut

Mt Cedric
(1532 m)

To Lake
Angelus

Lake
Rotoroa

D'Urville Hut

Sabine
Hut

Mt Cedric Track

Tiraumea Hut

Mt Misery
(1601 m)

Mole Saddle

Sabine River

RANGE

Morgans Hut

D'Urville River

D'Urville Valley Track

0   2   4 km

Forks Hut

MAHANGA

West Sabine
Hut

To Travers
Saddle

Sabine River (West Branch)

Sabine River (East Branch)

RANGE

Ella Hut

Blue Lake Hut

Blue Lake

Moss Pass

ELLA

Lake
Constance

D'Urville Bivvy

Waiau Pass

To St James Walkway

Those coming from St Arnaud can also reach the hut by hiking the new Speargrass Track. The Speargrass Track begins at the car park for the Mt Robert skifield, descends to Speargrass Creek and then follows the true right bank until it crosses a footbridge just before Speargrass Hut. It's 2½ hours to the hut (six bunks) and another five to six hours to Sabine Hut (four bunks) via the new Speargrass Track. There is a well-benched track that heads up Sabine Valley (see the description for Stage 4 of the Travers-Sabine Circuit, but this way you walk it in the reverse direction). After crossing a deep ravine, most of the day is spent traversing grassy meadows and beech forest to the confluence of the East Branch and West Branch of the Sabine River, where there are two huts (Forks and West Sabine) located across swing bridges. If you don't hire a water-taxi, plan on two days to reach the river forks from either Rotoroa or St Arnaud.

Stage 2: West Sabine Hut to Blue Lake
Walking Time: three to four hours
Accommodation: Blue Lake Hut (16 bunks)

Cross the swing bridge to return to the true left (west) side of the West Branch of the Sabine River, and continue south along the track. From the river fork, the track climbs over beech roots and traverses scree slopes, gaining 400 metres over the next six km. It traverses forest and clearings, many of them made by avalanches, until it enters a basin encircled by mountains. At this point, the track veers left and climbs the forested hillside for a km, until it reaches Blue Lake Hut, just at the tree line.

The hut is set back from the lake, and camping is discouraged near the shores because of its impact on the delicate terrain. Although it's only a three to four-hour walk to Blue Lake, this is a popular place to spend a day resting up before tackling Moss Pass.

The lake itself is enchanting, with its vivid colours of turquoise and emerald green. There is an even better view if you take the track that climbs the remaining km through one last stand of stunted beech – from here,

there is an excellent view of Lake Constance and a good overview of Blue Lake. This is one of the most scenic spots in the park.

Stage 3: Blue Lake to Ella Hut
Walking Time: five to seven hours
Accommodation: Ella Hut (16 bunks)

The route over Mahanga Range is well marked, but good visibility is necessary for a safe crossing of the pass. Snow poles mark the route, beginning behind Blue Lake Hut, and heading in a south-westerly direction through tussock and beech forest to a small creek. The route quickly climbs along the creek to a shingle scree, then makes a steep ascent in a north-westerly direction to an obvious shoulder that extends to the north.

From the shoulder, you can spot Moss Pass, a gap to the northern (right) side. Follow the snow poles as they traverse the scree slopes to the base of the steep gully. It's a hard climb up to the pass, at about 1800 metres, but once on top you're greeted with a view of Mt Ella across Upper D'Urville Valley. The pass often has snow well into summer.

On the D'Urville side, follow the snow poles carefully if visibility is poor – this section has many bluffs and waterfalls that need to be avoided. The long, steep descent first swings to the south then curves back in a westerly direction, passing two small tarns and finally reaching the bush-line.

Here, a well-marked track heads through the beech forest, descending steeply until it levels out at a swing bridge across the D'Urville River. Cross to the true left (west) side of the river and follow the track north (the right fork) as it stays close to the river. Ella Hut is reached within a km.

Stage 4: Ella Hut To D'Urville Hut
Walking Time: eight hours
Accommodation: Morgans Hut (14 bunks); D'Urville Hut (10 bunks)

After a challenging day over Moss Pass, it's easy going down D'Urville Valley, and most trampers have no problem reaching Lake Rotoroa in a day. The track remains on the true left (west) side of the river the entire way and close to the water for the first five km. Two hours from the hut, however, it departs from the river and passes through forest to an outcrop of rock above a gorge. Here, if you inch carefully to the edge, there is a great view of the river below – a swirl of white water thundering through huge boulders.

The track descends from the high point and returns to being a gentle valley walk. In another six km, you pass Morgans Hut, a four-hour walk from Ella Hut. The trout fishing improves from this point on, until you reach the mouth of the D'Urville River at Lake Rotoroa, a favourite with anglers.

The tramp downriver crosses beech-clad terraces and river flats for the next six km, until it passes a signposted junction with Bull Creek Track (to Mole Saddle, outside the park).

At this point, you are only two or three km from D'Urville Hut. In a km, you will pass a second junction with the Tiraumea Track (heading west over the saddle of the same name). In about 1½ km, the valley track ends at a junction. The northern fork is the short spur to D'Urville Hut, while the eastern fork leads around the end of Lake Rotoroa and then inland a short way before returning to the lake at Sabine Hut. It's a two to three-hour walk between the two huts.

Canterbury

Canterbury has been divided into two regions for this guide. Three tramps are covered in this chapter, but Arthur's Pass – because of its wealth of walking possibilities – has a chapter of its own.

Canterbury includes the private Banks Peninsula Track, near Akaroa; the Mt Somers Subalpine Walkway, in the Mt Somers Recreation & Conservation Area near Methven and Geraldine; and the very popular St James Walkway, which traverses the Lewis Park National Reserve, Lake Sumner Forest Park and private land. Canterbury also includes Mt Cook National Park, but because that park's main attraction for trampers, the Copland Pass, ends in Westland National Park, it has been included in the West Coast & Southern Alps chapter.

Banks Peninsula

The hilly Banks Peninsula, formed by two giant volcanic eruptions, contrasts with the flat area around the city of Christchurch. The peninsula's many tiny inlets are interesting spots to explore, especially the areas of high cliff and small bays sandwiched between the harbours of Le Bons, Pigeon and Little Akaroa, which radiate from the centre of the peninsula.

Once heavily forested, the land has been cleared for timber and farming, making this one of the few walks where trampers pass through paddocks full of grazing sheep. Fortunately, there are still patches of beech forest, and this walk passes through some of them.

HISTORY

Maoris have occupied the peninsula for centuries. First came the moa hunters, followed by the Waitaha, and then the Ngati Mamoe from the North Island. In the 17th century, the Ngai Tahu landed at Parakakariki, near Otanerito Bay, and overcame the Ngati

Mamoe. The Ngai Tahu population was depleted by intertribal fighting, the attacks of Te Rauparaha in the 1830s and, later, diseases introduced by Europeans.

Captain Cook sighted the peninsula in 1770, although he mistook it for an island. He named it after naturalist Sir Joseph Banks. Close European contact began in the 1820s when traders arrived searching for dressed flax, which was used to make sails and rope. In 1836, the British established a whaling station at Peraki.

Two years later, the French captain Jean Langlois chose the attractive site of Akaroa as a likely spot for French settlement. In 1840, a group of 63 French and six German colonists set out for New Zealand in the *Comte de Paris* from Rochefort, France. In 1849, the French land claim was sold to the New Zealand Company and the following year the French were joined by a large group of British settlers. However, the small group of French colonists clearly stamped their mark on this place.

The land was cleared for timber milling and dairy farming, industries which were eventually superseded by sheep farming, which is now the dominant industry on the peninsula.

CLIMATE

The westerly winds drop their moisture on the Southern Alps, dry as they cross the Canterbury Plains, and weaken by the time they reach the Banks Peninsula.

Summer is a good time to walk here, but make sure that you take precautions, because it is hot on higher ground. Mist hangs around the higher summits, especially in the mornings, but usually burns off on warm days. Winter can be bitterly cold on the exposed headlands, and squalls and storms can buffet the coastline. Cold southerly gales can also bring snow to higher levels.

Akaroa averages about 1000 mm of rain each year, most of it falling between April and July. The warmest months are December to March, with average temperatures around 21°C maximum and 11°C minimum.

NATURAL HISTORY

Banks Peninsula is composed of the remnants of huge, twin volcanoes, now attached to the mainland of the South Island by gravel pushed down from the eroding Southern Alps. It is believed to have been an island until recently (geologically speaking) and was surrounded by a 15-km band of swamps and reeds only 150 years ago.

The Lyttelton volcano was already extinct when the Akaroa volcano began to erupt some nine million years ago. Both volcanoes were once much higher: Akaroa is estimated to have peaked at around 1370 metres; Lyttelton was slightly smaller. Since then, the volcanoes have been eroded. During ice ages, when the sea level was considerably lower, valleys were gouged on the slopes of the volcanoes. When the sea rose, the valleys drowned and the peninsula took on its present form, with rugged sea cliffs and skylines studded with basalt plugs.

Much evidence of this fiery, volcanic past can be seen today: Redcliffe Point is composed of tuff (airborne material from the volcano), Akaroa Harbour is a sunken (once radial drainage) river from the former volcano, and the basalt plugs on the ridges and summits are volcanic in origin.

The sides of the dormant volcanoes were once cloaked in forest, but much of it was cleared for agriculture. Weeds and introduced grasses took over the flanks, and only pockets of beech forest remain.

Despite the lack of forests, three exciting wildlife species should draw inquisitive trampers to this peninsula – yellow-eyed penguins, fur seals and Hector's dolphins. In four days of walking, you could possibly see all three. From late winter to early summer, you might also see the white-flippered penguin.

Other native birds abound. Birds of the bush include the bellbird, kereru (wood pigeon), fantail, tomtit, rifleman and paradise duck. Shore and seabirds are prolific,

and include the spotted shag, little shag, gulls, terns, oystercatchers, sooty shearwaters and petrels. The not-so-common fairy prion nests on Island Nook, between Flea and Stony bays.

BANKS PENINSULA TRACK

This track is New Zealand's first private walk venture. A $90 to $100 package tour includes transport from Akaroa to the first hut, four nights' hut accommodation, landowners' fees, track registration and a booklet which describes the history and features of the track. Numbers are limited, so an absence of crowds is guaranteed.

There is also a two-day option (four-person limit), which includes a quaint one-night stopover at Stony Bay; the two-day walk costs $55.

Information

Booking is essential, so ☎ 304 7612 or write to Banks Peninsula Walk, PO Box 50, Akaroa. Get hold of a copy of *Banks Peninsula Track: a guide to the route, natural features and human history* – it's free if you've paid to walk the track.

Maps

One of the disappointing features of this walk is the white paint which has been liberally splashed along the track; the organisers say people still get lost. There are sketch maps in the booklet provided and, used in conjunction with the white paint, they should keep you on track. The 1:50,000 Topomaps 260 quads N37 *(Peraki)* and N36 *(Akaroa)* cover the area of the walk.

Huts

The cost of overnight accommodation in the huts is included in the track booking fee. The night stops are in Trampers' Hut (Onuku Farm); Flea Bay Cottage; The Lodge and Outhouse (Stony Bay); and Otanerito Cabins. Two-day walkers stop for a night at the Outhouse in Stony Bay.

Access

There are regular buses to Akaroa, which is

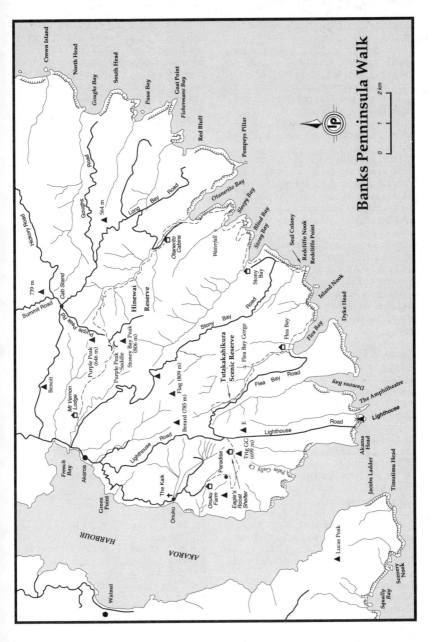

Banks Penninsula Walk

Crown Island

North Head

Goughs Bay

South Head

Paua Bay

Goat Point

Fishermans Bay

Red Bluff

Pompeys Pillar

Long Bay Road

Goughs Road

Hickory Road

564 m

Otanerito Bay

Sleepy Bay

Otanerito Cabins

Waterfall

Hinewai Reserve

Blind Bay

Stony Bay

Seal Colony

Redcliffe Nook

Redcliffe Point

Island Nook

739 m

Cab Stand

Summit Road

Stony Bay Road

Stony Bay

Dyke Head

Benoit

Purple Peak Road

Purple Peak (646 m)

Purple Peak Saddle

Stoney Bay Peak (806 m)

Flag (809 m)

Tutakahikura Scenic Reserve

Flea Bay Gorge

Flea Bay

Flea Bay

Stony Bay

Mt Vernon Lodge

Berard (785 m)

Flea Bay Road

Danons Bay

The Amphitheatre

Lighthouse Road

Lighthouse Road

Lighthouse

French Bay

Akaroa

Green Point

The Kaik

Lighthouse Road

Paradise

Trig GG (699 m)

Palm Gully

Akaroa Head

ARAKOA HARBOUR

Onuku

Onuku Farm

Eagle's Roost Shelter

Jacobs Ladder

Timutimu Head

Waimui

Lucas Peak

Scenery Nook

Squally Bay

only 82 km from Christchurch. Akaroa Tours
(☎ 304 7609 in Akaroa, 379 9629 in
Christchurch) operates a daily Akaroa
Shuttle minibus, departing from the post
office in Akaroa at 8.30 am and 2.20 pm and
from the information centre in Christchurch
at 10.30 am and 4.00 pm from the end of
November to April. The cost is $14 one-way
(students and hostel members $12) and $24
return. Phone to find out about their winter
services.

There is a daily InterCity service (☎ 377
0951) to Akaroa from Christchurch; it leaves
Christchurch at 8.30 am and arrives in
Akaroa at 11 am, then leaves Akaroa at 3.35
pm to arrive in Christchurch at 5.20 pm. The
InterCity depot in Akaroa is on Aubrey St,
close to the centre.

A smaller operator, the French Connection
(☎ 304 7643), leaves for Christchurch at
3.40 pm from the main wharf and information centre ($15).

Trampers without their own transport are
picked up daily from Akaroa post office at 6
pm by the rainbow-coloured Onuku Farm
truck.

Places to Stay

When you undertake the Banks Peninsula
Track, accommodation is provided from the
night before you begin walking until the
night before the last day of walking. More
than likely, you will spend a night in Akaroa.

The *Akaroa Holiday Park* (☎ 304 7471)
on Morgans Rd has tent sites/on-site cara-
vans for $16/32 for two. At the northern end
of the track, the *Mt Vernon Lodge & Stables*
(☎ 304 7180) on Rue Balguerie is a combination hostel and guest lodge; it costs $50 for
four in a four-bed unit.

The *Onuku Farm Hostel* (☎ 304 7612) at
the southern end (the start) of the track, six
km south of Akaroa, charges $7/10 for camp
sites/summer huts. *Chez la Mer* (☎ 304
7024), Rue Lavaud, has dorm beds for $14.

The Track

Advertised as 'Four nights, four days, four
beaches, four bays', this 30-km track allows
you to make a two to four-day walk across

private farmland, and around the dramatic
coastline of Banks Peninsula. Both the two
and four-day options are rated medium in
difficulty, because there are two steep climbs
from sea level up to 600 metres. Other than
that, the small distances travelled each day
make for a leisurely walk suited to families,
walkers wishing to take in the marvellous
scenery, or those wishing to explore further
during the day.

Stage 1: Onuku Farm to Flea Bay

Walking Time: four to six hours
Accommodation: Trampers' Hut (16 bunks);
The Cottage, Flea Bay (12 beds)

After a compulsory night spent in the
Trampers' Hut at Onuku Farm, take the track
back up to the hostel. Near the hostel gate,
there's a sign indicating the Banks Peninsula
Track. The marked track rises steeply
through sheep paddocks, swings east, sidles
around a rocky promontory on a ridge and
traverses a patch of bush to the site of Paradise Farm. Stockyards and exotic trees are all
that remain of the farm. From the track, there
are great views of the harbour and Onuku
Farm.

The track swings west, and about 45
minutes from Onuku, you come to a prominent track junction on a ridge. To the west is
a marked track to a lookout and an alternative
route back to Onuku. The main track is indicated by a sign 'BP Track', which points
uphill and to the east. Keep following this
track until you come to some park benches
overlooking Akaroa Head. There is a side
trip from here to a rock-studded knoll on the
ridge.

The main track switches back from the
benches, crosses an electric fence and aims
for the highest point in the area, Trig GG
(699 metres). This was once a Maori obser-
vation pa, known as Otehore. Observe how
the wind has shaped the vegetation here. If
you're lucky, you may also see Mt Cook,
some 230 km distant. From Onuku to this
point is a solid two-hour climb.

From Trig GG, it is a mere canter down
the path to the Eagle's Roost shelter hut, to

the north-east. The clearly marked track leads from here to a road junction. Lighthouse Rd heads north to Akaroa and south to the lighthouse near Akaroa Head. Ignore this road and follow signs to Flea Bay Rd; follow this downhill for just over a km. Keep an eye out for the turn-off (a sharp left fork) to the track, which passes through the DOC Tutakakahikura Scenic Reserve. This patch of remnant red beech *(Nothofagus fusca)* has survived the once extensive logging on this part of the peninsula. Climb the stile where it is signposted and follow the track down a serene gully, eventually joining the main stream which drains into Flea Bay.

There are a number of cascades and waterfalls shrouded in mamuku (tree fern) in this stretch, all signposted. About an hour after entering the gully, the track emerges into an open area and drops steeply. Park your packs here and do some exploring. There is a waterfall which you can walk behind and a sidetrack into Flea Bay Gorge. From near this point, look across to the south and see nikau palms at their southern natural limit.

From the Flea Bay Gorge junction, follow the stream on its true left (east) bank for about 1½ km. The track crosses the stream a couple of times before arriving at Flea Bay Cottage, the first of the buildings you reach. This is fully equipped and provides accommodation for four-day trampers. Those doing the two-day walk can stop here for lunch.

Stage 2: Flea Bay to Stony Bay

Walking Time: 2½ to four hours
Accommodation: Stony Bay Lodge (12 beds); The Outhouse (four beds)

Head to the beach from the cottage, follow the road east to the gate, then walk onto the beach and follow it until you see a stile. Use the stile to cross the fence and then climb upwards as the track gains altitude to circumvent high cliffs on the eastern side of Flea Bay. If you're lucky, you may see Hector's dolphins (the world's rarest and smallest) in the waters below. The track heads south to

the tip of the headland, rounds it, and heads north-east to the gully above Island Nook.

The remarkable transitions of this walk now become apparent. One moment there are sheep paddocks, the next ancient forest, and then cliffs that seem to be at the edge of the world – indeed, the next landfall across the Pacific is South America.

In the next two days, the track comes close to the precipitous cliffs on several occasions. Don't go too close to the edge, because the cliffs are unstable, even undermined in places. They are particularly dangerous on windy days.

From Island Nook, the track sidles the cliffs to Redcliffe Point, where iron oxides have stained the compacted volcanic ash. From this point, the track heads north-west and crosses a stream, before dropping into Seal Cave, about two hours from Flea Bay. There are usually a number of fur seals here, sunning on the rocks or curled up asleep in the cave behind.

It is quite a steep climb out of Seal Cave to the intersecting ridge between the cave and Stony Bay. From the top of the ridge, there are great views across to Pompeys Pillar, on the northern side of Otanerito Bay. Just over a km from the cave, the track joins the Stony Bay Rd; follow the right fork for a km.

Keep an eye out for the track turn-off on the right of the road, which allows you to avoid the last section of road down to Stony Bay. This track heads through coastal scrub, and after a steep descent, you walk along the beach to Stony Bay.

Stony Bay is a beautiful, idyllic spot with unusual amenities. There are two outdoor wood-heated baths, a swing, an unusual shower, fresh produce, creek-cooled beer, yellow-eyed penguins on the beach and good hosts. Just a night here makes this walk worthwhile. Two-day trampers have a quaint cottage, the Outhouse, for their evening stopover.

Stage 3: Stony Bay to Otanerito Cabins

Walking Time: two to three hours
Accommodation: Otanerito Cabins (12 beds)

This is a short day's tramping – just five km – but it does involve rounding three prominent headlands on an undulating track. Immediately after leaving Stony Bay, you begin to climb a zigzag track to avoid the yellow-eyed penguin burrows below. The track then sidles south-east to the tip of the headland, rounds it, and then heads down in a north-easterly direction to the stream that empties into Blind Bay.

It repeats this pattern to drop into Sleepy Bay. When you get close to the point, however, keep an eye out for the markers which indicate where you should cut over the ridge. Soon, you join a vehicle track which crosses a stream on its way downhill to Sleepy Bay. There is a waterfall about two minutes upstream which is worth a visit.

From the stream, the track heads uphill to a point, where you can look to the southern side of Sleepy Bay and see a huge sea arch. The track then rounds the third headland of the day and drops, in about two km, to the head of Otanerito Bay. The track is signposted in a number of places to steer you through private land, including an abandoned poultry farm.

Head north from the beach, cross a footbridge to the true left (east) side of a stream, follow this for a km, and cross back to the true right (west) side when you reach a track junction. The cabins are across the bridge in the Hinewai Reserve, about 100 metres away, but there are plans to move them nearer to the beach.

Stage 4: Otanerito Cabins to Akaroa
Walking Time: three to five hours

From the cabins, cross the bridge to the eastern side of the junction. The track heads north-west into Hinewai Reserve. After crossing the road bridge, cut over to the true right (west) side of the stream. You now follow the stream on this side to its source near Purple Peak (almost 4 km).

For nearly the whole climb to the saddle (600 metres), you are in the 980-hectare Hinewai Reserve, managed privately for the protection and restoration of native vegetation and wildlife. There are more than 30 waterfalls in the valleys of the reserve, and a number can be visited from the track. As the track gains altitude, the vegetation changes; near its highest point there's a red beech forest, while lower down there are some ancient kahikatea *(Podocarpus dacrydioides)*.

The track from the cabins is well signposted, which is just as well because there are a number of alternative routes, especially as you get higher up the valley into the forest. You leave the reserve at a stile and cross into private land. Follow the vehicle track in a south-westerly direction to the saddle (590 metres), south of Purple Peak. Stony Bay Peak is almost due south, Akaroa Harbour is to the west and Otanerito Bay to the south-east. This is a solid two-hour walk from the cabins.

The track snakes downhill from the saddle and, after a sharp drop, joins a vehicle track, which eventually links up with the Stony Bay Rd. The official end of the walk is Mt Vernon Lodge, where a number of trampers elect to stay. Others continue to the Akaroa post office to get a lift back to their vehicles at Onuku.

Mt Somers Recreation & Conservation Area

Mt Somers is one of the large Canterbury foothills that abut the Southern Alps. Mt Hutt and Mt Peel are the other two large foothills in this region, which incorporates the headwaters of the rivers which drain into the Pacific south of Christchurch.

The forests of the Canterbury foothills are all surviving remnants of greater forests which once covered these mountains. *Nothofagus* (beech) was the dominant type on Mt Somers; whereas Mt Peel has broadleaf podocarp forest.

The Mt Somers Subalpine Walkway is only one of a number of tramping options in the mid-Canterbury region. There are several good walks in and around Mt Peel; ask at the Peel DOC office or in Geraldine about other alternatives. See the Information section which follows.

HISTORY
People came here to hunt moa over 500 years ago, and they burnt the forest and ground cover as they searched for their prey. The path followed by State Highway 72 near Alford Forest is believed to have been used by these seasonal hunting parties. There is evidence of early visitors to the park in primitive drawings in rock shelters on Mt Somers.

There are plenty of signs of modern occupation and exploitation. Coal was discovered in 1856, and by 1864 a number of collieries in the area were producing coal. Two of these – Blackburn and McClimonts – are near the start of the subalpine walkway. The latter was closed in 1915 by fire, although Blackburn, which was served by a jig and tramway, did not begin operation until 1928.

CLIMATE
Mt Somers is in a partial rain shadow, created by the higher western range of the Southern Alps. But surprisingly, it is very dry on the western side of the mountain, and wet in the east, where it is most heavily vegetated. The southern slopes are exposed to snow blown in by south-westerly winds.

NATURAL HISTORY
While much of the mid-Canterbury area is composed of greywacke, Mt Somers is of more recent volcanic origin. The harder nature of the rhyolite rock has resulted in low soil fertility and poor drainage. In particular, the steep southern and northern faces of Mt Somers indicate major faulting.

A highlight of the subalpine walkway is the several altitudinal plant sequences which walkers pass through. Bog species proliferate because of the infertile soil and poor drainage. These are easily seen in Slaughterhouse Gully. Get a copy of the excellent pamphlet *Plants in Peel Forest* (DOC, 1990), which is equally applicable to the forests on Mt Somers as well. It will make your walk much more interesting, because the pamphlet's drawings help you to identify plants you are passing.

Lower down, in both Woolshed Creek and the lower reaches of Bowyers Stream, there are well-preserved examples of the extensive beech forests that covered mid-Canterbury before burning, milling and pastoralism.

Mountain beech and black beech are found in Sharplin Falls Reserve, where there is a subcanopy of broadleaf and southern rata *(Metrosideros umbellata)* on the rocky outcrops. The ancient forest in Woolshed Creek is black beech. The beech attracts wasps seeking honey dew and, at certain times of year, these insects can be a pest to walkers.

MT SOMERS SUBALPINE WALKWAY
The 29-km Mt Somers Subalpine Walkway traverses the northern face of Mt Somers, linking the Sharplin Falls with Woolshed Creek, in the mid-Canterbury foothills. It is a good two-day walk, with the choice of a relatively easy first day and a longer second day, or vice versa. The walk has been split into three stages, based on the two huts where overnight stops are possible. There is nothing to stop you turning the trip into a thoroughly enjoyable three-day walk.

Whichever option you choose, the trip will take 11 to 12 hours if you incorporate the Canyon Route – a must for avid trampers. If the canyon is included, you have a walk of real contrasts: a rugged mountain stream, open areas of subalpine vegetation and thick bush. These features are made all the more special when you consider that the walk begins and ends in farmland on the Canterbury Plains.

Information
There are a number of places where you can get information and maps for this region. In Christchurch, there is the Canterbury Conservancy (☎ 379 9758), Forestry House, 133 Victoria St. Closer to the conservation and recreation area are Raukapuka field centre (☎ 693 9994), North Terrace, Geraldine, and the Peel Forest DOC office (☎ 696 3826),

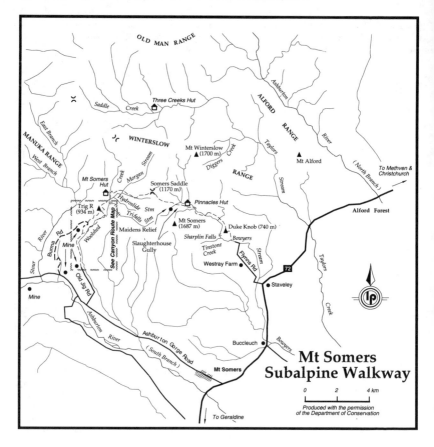

Mesopotamia Rd. You can pay hut fees at these places.

Maps

The best map for this walk is the 1:50,000 Topomaps 260 quad M36 *(Methven)*. The map provided here is for reference only.

Huts

There are two huts on the walk (The Pinnacles and Mt Somers), each costing $4 per adult. Mt Somers huts is a former musterer's hut.

Access

The Sharplin Falls Reserve, the eastern end of the subalpine walkway, is 110 km southwest of Christchurch, 19 km from Methven and three km north-west of Staveley. There is an InterCity bus service during summer and winter to Methven (☎ 302 8044); the cost to/from Christchurch Airport is $40 return. Both InterCity and Mt Cook Landline buses pass through Geraldine (some 45 km south of Mt Somers township). The InterCity depot is at A&W Books (☎ 693 9155), Peel St, while Mt Cook Landline (☎ 693 8144) has a depot in Waihi Terrace. InterCity's

Queenstown-Christchurch service passes through Mt Somers at 5.25 pm (northbound) and 9.40 am (southbound).

It is assumed that most trampers will have their own vehicles, because it's 19 km from Methven to the start of the walk at Woolshed Creek. The best way to arrange transport is to have your car shuttled by a local. Drive to Staveley, north-east of Mt Somers township, and turn up Flynns Rd in the direction of Sharplin Falls. Keep a lookout for Westray Farm (☎ 303 0809), the third building on the western (left) side of the road. The owners, Bruce and Marilyn Gray, will drive your car around to the Woolshed Creek car park to drop you off, then return the car to their secure storage until you return from the walk; they charge $20 per car. Their farm is two km from the Sharplin Falls car park, making this a most satisfactory arrangement. It is half an hour from Staveley to Woolshed Creek.

If you are driving your car to the beginning of the walk, take the Ashburton Gorge Rd from Mt Somers for nine km and take the right-hand turn onto the gravel Old Jig Rd. From the road, you can see an historic lime kiln, the Old Stone House, and the scar on the hill to the south-west is the Cavendish lime works. Drive four km down Old Jig Rd and turn left just before the hay barn. You pass through some gates, which you should leave as you found them. Coalminers' Flat picnic area and the start of the walk are after the last gate. Take it easy through the small creeks on this road because they could damage your car.

Places to Stay
Methven *Methven Caravan Park* (☎ 302 8005), on Barkers Rd, has $10 tent sites (for two people). *Mt Hutt Accommodation – The Bedpost* (☎ 302 8508), near the corner of Mt Hutt Rd and Lampard St, has beds for $14 ($16 to $18 in winter). On the corner of Alford and Allen Sts is *Pinedale Lodge* (☎ 302 8621); rooms are $12 ($16 in winter). The *Redwood Backpackers Lodge* (☎ 302 8287) is near the corner of South Belt Rd and Jackson St; rooms cost $8 ($16 in winter).

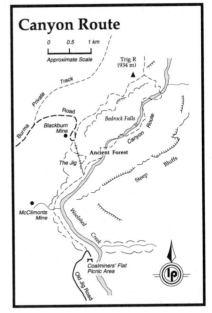

Canyon Route

Geraldine The *Geraldine Motor Camp* (☎ 693 8860), Hislop Rd, has tent sites/cabins for $7/14. At the *Farmyard Holiday Park* (☎ 693 9355), seven km from Geraldine, cabins are $22 for two. *The Olde Presbytery* (☎ 693 8308), 13 Jollie St, costs $13.

The Track
The Mt Somers Walkway is rated medium if you elect to do the Canyon Route. It makes little difference which direction you walk in because there is a climb at each end (Sharplin Falls to Pinnacle Hut and Coalminers' Flat to Trig R). Be warned that this subalpine route is subject to sudden changes in weather.

Stage 1: Woolshed Creek via Canyon Route to Mt Somers Hut
Walking Time: 3½ to four hours
Accommodation: Mt Somers Hut (18 bunks)

From the Coalminers' Flat picnic area, follow the track up the true right (west) side of Woolshed Creek.

You pass the entrance and exit to the Rocky Top loop and an old mine adit. After half an hour, you come to the area known as The Jig, where there's a handmade jig line that leads up to the Blackburn Mine.

The jig was built to transport coal from the mine to wagons on the Mt Somers branch railway below. As each full hopper hurtled down to the bottom of the jig, the momentum pulled an empty one to the top. Even today, there are scattered remnants of hoppers. Those wishing to avoid the Canyon Route, can follow the jig up to the track to Trig R.

To get to the canyon, continue into the ancient forest on the true right of the stream. This small patch of silver beech forest (*Nothofagus menziesii*) is believed to be the only one to survive a fire which swept through the Ashburton Gorge in pre-European times. Turn east (the right fork) at the junction of Sidewinder and Canyon tracks (2½ hours), and cross the creek.

You soon enter the stream; follow it for a short distance until signs direct you back up onto the true right bank, to Pete's Porch. You soon cross to the eastern side of the creek, the first of several crossings in this stretch because the route basically goes through the stream. There are, however, adequate markers in the trees, though you must keep an eye out for them. There is some boulder-hopping, especially near Bedrock Falls, until you come to a junction about 1¼ hours out of Coalminers' Flat. You can choose between the Bluff and River tracks, depending on the condition of the river.

The river option follows the river bed along the true left bank until a bluff bars the way. Look across for markers and a cairn on the true right; cross and follow the track until another crossing is indicated. At one stage, on the true left bank, you come to an impassable boulder. Cross to the true right and follow the track through the bush.

About two hours or more from the start, you reach a point in the river where two big boulders block the stream. The track, on the true right (west) side of the stream, climbs steeply out of the canyon to Trig R (934 metres). It's a good half-hour crawl up the steep track to the bush-line and tussock. The magnificent vista from the trig includes the Manuka Range, the once-glaciated U-shaped valley of the Stour River and, across to the east, Mt Somers.

Take the signposted track to the north, which leads to another great vantage point (with views of Mt Somers Hut on the true right bank of Woolshed Creek). The track swings down and north-west, to the confluence of upper Woolshed Creek and Morgan Stream. Take the track to the bubbling 'Spa Pool' Waterfall, via the stepladder. Allow an hour from Trig R to Mt Somers Hut, including stops and diversions.

Mt Somers Station owns the original musterers' hut, but it is administered by the DOC. There are a number of interesting walks in the region of the hut, including the 1½-hour Trifalls Stream loop and the rock formations in Morgan Stream.

Stage 2: Mt Somers Hut to Pinnacles Hut
Walking Time: four hours
Accommodation: Pinnacles Hut (18 bunks)

From Mt Somers Hut, head east across the creek to a series of markers which lead sharply uphill to a disued vehicle track. Join this track and follow it down to Morgan Stream. It heads east and uphill from here until it reaches the Somers Saddle (1170 metres), the highest point on the walk. The climb is steady, in parts steep, for over 2½ km. If the weather is clear, you are rewarded at the saddle with vistas of the Winterslow, Old Man and Taylor ranges – however, this subalpine stretch is often covered in cloud.

Follow the vehicle track from the saddle, until you come to a barrier. Look for the signpost which indicates where the track continues to the south-east. Follow the snow-pole marker stakes which loop under the northern face of Mt Somers. There are also occasional red paint blazes on rocks. About an hour from the saddle, you come to the 'Maidens Relief', where a waterfall spills over a rhyolite cliff into a clear water pool. Be careful descending this section in wet weather.

From the creek at the base of this cliff, climb a short distance to the saddle before Slaughterhouse Gully. It's a very steep and slippery descent from the top (Heli-Pad 3) down to an unbenched track to Pinnacles Hut. There are many examples of alpine vegetation in the gully, including bog pine *(Dacrydium bidwillii)* and toatoa *(Phyllocladus alpinus)*.

Pinnacles Hut is near the junction of Slaughterhouse Gully and the walkway, about four hours from Sharplin Falls or two hours from Mt Somers Saddle. It has a good potbelly stove, 'space-age' toilet, water supply and mattresses, and at night you can see the glow from the lights of the towns on the Canterbury Plains. In summer, there is a warden on duty to collect fees.

Stage 3: Pinnacles Hut to Sharplin Falls
Walking Time: three to 3½ hours

From the hut, the track descends briefly to the creek before climbing up to One Tree Ridge. It then drops quickly through beech forest on the true right of Bowyers Stream, winding around bluffs.

The track can get extremely muddy in places, so exercise caution as you descend. In one place, the track actually passes under a waterfall. Nearer the river, you pass Heli-Pad 6, then cross a small side stream before emerging onto the bank of Bowyers Stream. Follow this down on the true right (south) side, keeping a look out for markers. At times, you are in the bed of the stream.

At a prominent and well-marked crossing, about 1½ hours from Pinnacles Hut, head to the true left (north) bank and follow this for the rest of the valley.

A final track sign indicates the route to the steep half-hour climb out of Bowyers Stream, up to Duke Knob (740 metres). The short detour through regrowth forest to Duke Knob (a rhyolite outcrop) is a must, because it offers panoramic views over the beech forest below and the plains to the east and south.

There are two ways to descend from Duke Knob. You can take the steep, muddy Zigzag Track or the longer Ridge Track – both end up near the swing bridge across Bowyers Stream. At the bottom of the Zigzag Track, you come to a junction; the southern fork leads to the Sharplin Falls. Allow about half an hour for the descent from Duke Knob to the car park. If you've stored your car at Westray Farm, it's about two km along Flynns Rd.

Lewis Pass National Reserve

The St James Walkway begins in the Lewis Pass National Reserve, which borders Nelson Lakes to the south. It's a five-day, 66-km trek – the longest walkway in the country. The track is well benched and marked, and has an excellent series of huts. Although it winds through pastoral land and beech forests, it is considered a subalpine tramp because the trip involves climbs over Ada Pass (998 metres) and Anne Saddle (1136 metres). However, it is not as challenging as most round-trip tramps in Nelson Lakes, and is well within the abilities of moderately fit trampers.

Although the St James Walkway was built by the New Zealand Walkway Commission and is administered by the DOC, it runs through a variety of public and private land, including Lewis Pass National Reserve, St James Station, Lake Sumner Forest Park and Glenhope Station. The heart of the track – from the upper Boyle River along the Anne River to the Ada River – runs through St James Station, one of the largest in New Zealand. Trampers must not deviate from the track or interfere with livestock along this section. Stiles have been erected over fences, so all gates should be left untouched.

If you plan to tramp from Nelson Lakes National Park to the walkway through Waiau

Valley (via the Waiau Pass from Blue Lake), then you should contact the Hanmer Springs DOC field centre (☎ 315 7128) to find out about obtaining permission to cross this land.

HISTORY

The Lewis Pass National Reserve and the other reserves and private land along the St James Walkway share the history of the Nelson Lakes area.

Although the region was only sparsely settled, Maoris did pass through it, particularly along the portion of the St James Walkway that was part of a popular route from the Tasman Sea to Canterbury. The Ngati Tumatakokiri tribe, the most powerful to use the route, was constantly warring with a rival tribe, the Ngai Tahu. The rivalry ended in a particularly grisly manner when a Ngai Tahu party was trapped in a gorge along the Maruia River by the Ngati Tumatakokiri and massacred. The site of the carnage is now known as Cannibal Gorge, and is passed on the walkway.

In the 1970s, the area was chosen as the site of the first long-distance walkway in the South Island. The St James Walkway, named after the historic sheep station through which it runs, was opened in November 1981. Flora and fauna are similar to Arthur's Pass.

CLIMATE

Extreme weather can be encountered in this subalpine area, with heavy rain or even snow occurring at almost any time of the year. Pack warm clothing (gloves, hat) as well as the usual rain gear.

ST JAMES WALKWAY

The St James Walkway is a well-benched and marked track, with five huts spaced a reasonable day's walk apart. The track should not be underestimated – 66 km is a long journey. The trek from Nelson Lakes over Waiau Pass to the walk is for experienced trampers only.

Information

Information about the track can be obtained at Hanmer Springs, and from the DOC regional offices in Nelson and Christchurch. The DOC Hurunui visitor information centre (☎ 315 7128) is the closest to the St James Walkway. It is open on weekdays from 10 am to 6 pm in summer (until 4.30 pm in winter) and from 10 am to 4.30 pm every weekend. Register your intentions and pay your hut fees at this centre.

Maps

Two quads, M31 *(Lewis)* and M32 *(Boyle)*, of the 1:50,000 Topomaps 260 series cover the walk. You can also use the 1:80,000 Parkmaps No 274-16 *(Lake Sumner Forest Park)* and the 1:100,000 Parkmaps No 273-05 *(Nelson Lakes National Park)*; you will need both of them.

Huts

Hut fees for the Category Two huts – Boyle Flat, Anne, Christopher, Ada Pass and Cannibal Gorge – are $8 per night; the other huts are Magdalene ($4) and Rokeby (free).

Access

Both ends of the walkway are located off State Highway 7, which crosses Lewis Pass from North Canterbury to the West Coast. Transport to and from the track is easy, because the bus drivers along the highway are used to dropping off, and being flagged down, by trampers.

The northern end of the track, and the preferred starting point, is Lewis Pass, on State Highway 7. The southern point of the track, and the usual finishing point, is seven km north of Hope Bridge, which crosses Boyle River almost halfway between the turn-offs to Hanmer Springs and Maruia Springs. It's a 15-minute drive between the southern and northern ends of the track.

As a rough guide, a White Star (☎ 768 0596, 352 1556) bus passes the Boyle Shelter heading to Christchurch at about 1.15 pm daily; a bus heads to Nelson (with connections to Westport and Greymouth), in the opposite direction, at about the same time. The Mount Cook Landline bus (☎ (0800) 80 0737) from Christchurch to

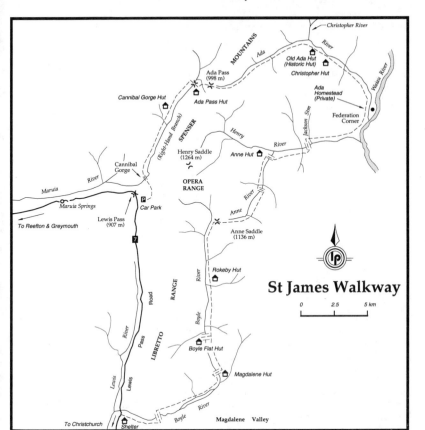

Nelson passes at about noon; in the Nelson to Christchurch direction it passes at about 2.15 pm. There is also the East-West Shuttle (☎ 364 8721); phone for the timetable.

Trampers with their own vehicles tend to use buses to return to the car park from which they departed. There is a car park at either end, but it is best to leave vehicles in secure storage at the Boyle Outdoor Education Centre ($10 per night), because vandalism and theft have been problems at Lewis Pass.

Places to Stay

In Hanmer Springs, the *Mountain View*

Holiday Park (☎ 315 7113), on the southern edge of town, has camp sites for $7.50. The *AA (Central) Tourist Park* (☎ 315 7112) is on Jacks Pass Rd, and has camp sites/cabins for $15/37 for two. The *Pines Motor Camp* (☎ 315 7152) is also on Jacks Pass Rd; camp sites/bunk beds cost $6/12.50 per person.

The Track

The walkway can be tramped in either direction, but is described here from Lewis Pass to the Boyle River. Lewis Pass is the most popular starting point because there is less climbing when the track, rated medium, is walked from this end. For most trampers, it's a five-day walk.

Stage 1: Lewis Pass to Ada Pass Hut
Walking Time: 4½ to five hours
Accommodation: Cannibal Gorge Hut (20 bunks); Ada Pass Hut (20 bunks)

Follow the Tarn Nature Walk from the car park and picnic area located just south of Lewis Pass. It immediately passes the Rolleston Pack Track and then comes to the junction with the walkway. The St James Track heads north-east (the right fork) and is actually a continuation of the old pack track. You begin a sharp descent into beech forest, and in half an hour the track drops 170 metres to a swing bridge over Cannibal Gorge, with the Right-Hand Branch of the Maruia River below.

From the bridge, the track continues along the true right (west) bank of the gorge and, in half an hour, passes Phil's Knob, an excellent lookout point. A staircase assists you around the knob, and you continue along the gorge, climbing in and out of numerous gullies. This is not the easiest tramping, but the walkway is well marked and much work has been done with chainsaws to cut log steps over fallen trees. When you come to a bridged stream, about three hours from the car park or six km from the Cannibal Gorge swing bridge, Cannibal Gorge Hut is not far away.

Beyond the hut, the track follows the Maruia River on a gentle gradient, through beech forest and open alpine fields. It then begins a short, steep climb up a bush-clad terrace and then around a slip. Just minutes from Ada Pass Hut, you enter Ada Pass Flats, where there are views back down the valley, and of Gloriana Peak to the north. Just before reaching the hut, the track crosses a swing bridge over the Maruia River once again. Ada Pass Hut, like most of those along the walkway, is a roomy facility, with 20 bunks. Allow 1½ hours from Cannibal Gorge Hut to Ada Pass Hut.

Stage 2: Ada Pass Hut to Christopher Hut
Walking Time: four to five hours
Accommodation: Old Ada Hut (two bunks); Christopher Hut (20 bunks)

The track departs from the eastern end of the hut and gently ascends Ada Pass (998 metres), fording the Right-Hand Branch of the Maruia River (now a stream) along the way. The bush-clad pass is recognisable by the large sign marking the border between Lewis Pass National Reserve and St James Station. The walkway now descends into Ada Valley along the true right (south) side of the Ada River, passing through a small alpine clearing and then a much larger tussock grassland with a few patches of bush on it.

It's a km across, and orange discs are used to point out where the track resumes in the beech forest. The birdlife is good in this area, and you might spot cattle or a few wild horses along the edges. Looming overhead are the peaks of Faerie Queen, a beautiful sight on a clear day. Two hours from Ada Pass, the track emerges from beech forest to reach the wide expanse of the station. The flats (and the track) swing south-east at the confluence of the Christopher and Ada rivers.

Old Ada Hut, also known as Historic Hut, is near the confluence. Built in 1956 for deer hunters, the two-bunk hut is now more a monument to the old New Zealand Forest Service than a place to stay. One km (15 minutes) down the track is the roomy Christopher Hut (20 bunks), which has a good view of the Waiau Valley.

Stage 3: Christopher Hut to Anne Hut
Walking Time: five hours
Accommodation: Anne Hut (20 bunks)

The third day of the journey is spent almost entirely on grazing land. During the summer, this can be a hot walk because there is little shade. The track is often a 4WD track or a route marked by cairns and posts with orange discs.

After leaving Christopher Hut, you cut across grassy flats along the true right bank of the Ada River. Follow the open flats until they converge with the river at Federation Corner, about 1½ km above Ada Homestead, a St James outstation. The homestead, on the opposite side of the river, is private property; trampers should keep out.

The track stays west of the river and is well benched as it hugs the hillsides and passes the wide flats of Waiau Valley to enter the valley of Henry River. The track keeps to the lower slopes of Mt Federation, through matagouri thickets, and eventually sidles up a terrace to reach a junction with a 4WD track. The walkway heads west (the right fork) on the 4WD track and within half an hour fords Jackson Stream. Leave the vehicle track here and cross a swing bridge over the Henry River to its true right (south) bank. In another km, the track rejoins the 4WD track as it gently climbs to Irishman Flat and then descends to a swing bridge over the Anne River.

Anne Hut and an old shelter are just on the other side of the bridge. If the weather is good and water levels normal, you can save some time and climbing by following the vehicle track all the way to the hut, bypassing the track and bridge near Jackson Stream.

Stage 4: Anne Hut to Boyle Flat Hut
Walking Time: six to seven hours
Accommodation: Rokeby Hut (two bunks); Boyle Flat Hut (20 bunks)

The track winds up the Anne River for two km, then climbs a bush-clad spur to a swing bridge that takes you to the true right (east) side. It continues up the valley towards Anne Saddle, not a difficult climb, about 4½ km from the swing bridge. Halfway up to the saddle, or 45 minutes after crossing Anne River, the track fords Kia Stream; just before the creek, you get a final view of the Anne Valley.

Anne Saddle (1136 metres) is still bush, but a short climb up the ridge north of it brings you to a clearing with good views of the mountains at the head of Boyle Valley.

The half-hour descent from the saddle is steep, dropping 210 metres over two km. Follow the Boyle River for the next 3½ km, remaining on its true left (east) side all the way to Rokeby Hut. At several points, the track climbs high above the river to avoid flood conditions. If the water level is normal, it is far easier and quicker to ford the river and continue along its banks.

Rokeby Hut is an old shelter (two bunks) and not a desirable place to stay. The track remains on the true left (east) side of the Boyle as it continues south. Boyle Flat Hut, just 3½ km further on (one to 1½ hours), stands on the true right (west) side of the river and is reached by a swing bridge.

Stage 5: Boyle Flat Hut to Boyle Car Park
Walking Time: four to five hours
Accommodation: Magdalene Hut (12 bunks)

Return and cross the swing bridge, then head south along the track, now a series of red and white markers, through the tussock grass of Boyle Flat. The edge of the bush is the border between St James Station and Lake Sumner Forest Park. The track shortly descends into the Boyle River Gorge, where it stays 150 metres above the river on a wide, well-benched path, which traverses the gorge and then drops to the river's edge.

An hour from the hut, the track arrives at a swing bridge over the Boyle River. If you ignore the bridge and continue along the true left (east) side of the river, the track leads to Magdalene Hut, one km away. Cross the bridge instead, and follow the track on the true right (west) side down into Magdalene Valley. Once the track enters the valley, it's seven km through river flats and patches of bush along the northern side of the Boyle to a swing bridge. The track crosses the bridge and soon joins St Andrews Station Rd, on the opposite bank.

About 1½ km along the road, you reach the three-sided Boyle Shelter and the car park. Head south down the road a short way to reach Windy Point (at the end of the Lewis Pass to Arthur's Pass – via Harper Pass –

Track) and the Amuri Area School Outdoor Education Centre. A lot of trampers leave their cars here.

OTHER WALKS
Southern Bays Walkway
The second of New Zealand's private walkways, this track is also located on Banks Peninsula. It winds, climbs and dips from Birdlings Flat (near Lake Forsyth) past Oashore, Te Oka Bay, Hell's Gate and Devil's Gap, and ends at Little River. It takes four days and four nights, and because some days involve seven hours of walking, it is more than a jaunt.

Along the way, you will see precipitous cliffs, bays replete with Maori and early whaling history, and the rim of an ancient volcanic crater. The walkway is open from October to May; contact Southern Bays Walkway (☎ 329 0007), Little River, for details.

Arthur's Pass National Park

Visitors come from all over the world to see the mountains at Arthur's Pass. Climbers, hunters and skiers are all attracted to this alpine area, but most of all Arthur's Pass is a tramper's park.

The 99,270-hectare national park is located 154 km north-west of Christchurch. It straddles both sides of the Southern Alps, two-thirds of it lying on the Canterbury side of the Main Divide and the rest in Westland. This rugged mountainous area, cut by deep valleys, ranges in altitude from 245 metres at the Taramakau River to 2402 metres at the highest peak.

There are many tracks for day walks, especially around the park headquarters, but the longer trips are generally routes rather than tracks, and involve following the valleys and then climbing the saddles that link them. Cut tracks are usually provided only when necessary, so much of the time you will be boulder-hopping along river beds. Where tracks do exist, they are rarely signposted and usually only marked with rock cairns; most streams are unbridged. Here and there you'll find unofficial paths, formed by repeated usage around a bluff or up a side creek, but they soon fade.

Park staff consider trampers' tracks to be those routes in the heart of the park which connect valleys and passes to form a loop off State Highway 73. These are not benched walkways like the Heaphy, Routeburn or Abel Tasman Coast tracks, so a good map and an accurate compass are essential.

Arthur's Pass village can be used as the departure point for the three trips described here. It's even worth scheduling some extra days at this one-road town hemmed in by towering mountains because there are plenty of day walks to spectacular vistas.

HISTORY

The Maoris often passed through the Waimakariri basin. Signs of their earlier occupation are evident in the Hawdon Valley, where the forest was burnt by hunting parties. They found shelter in the limestone landscape and overhangs of Castle Hill, where they left charcoal drawings on the walls. The highly prized pounamu (greenstone) lured them across Arthur's Pass, but only occasionally because the easier route over Harper Pass was preferred.

In September 1857, Edward Dobson travelled up the Hurunui River as far as Harper Pass, and possibly into the Taramakau Valley, before turning back. But it was 20-year-old Leonard Harper who, in the same year, became the first European to cross the swampy saddle and descend the Taramakau River to reach the West Coast. Harper was escorted by Maori guides.

Edward Dobson didn't get a pass named after him, but his son, Arthur, did. In March 1864, 23-year-old Arthur Dobson and his 18-year-old brother Edward journeyed up the Bealey Valley and camped above the tree line. The next day, they crossed the pass and descended a short distance into Otira Gorge. Another of Arthur's brothers, George, was later commissioned to find the best route from Canterbury to the West Coast gold fields, and it was George who first referred to the pass as 'Arthur's Pass'.

At the same time that George Dobson was selecting the 'best' route, two parcels of gold had been sent from Hokitika to Canterbury. A gold rush followed and in one week in March 1865, 1000 people poured over Harper Pass (the 'easiest' route) on their way to the West Coast; some 4000 made the trip between February and April. The gold rush and the poor condition of the Harper Pass track intensified the efforts of Christchurch citizens to build a dray road to the West Coast. Work began on the Arthur's Pass road, and by 1866 the first coach drove all the way from one side of the South Island to the other.

The Otira Rail Tunnel was completed in 1923. Trains quickly ended the era of horse-drawn coaches, and today the run from

Greymouth to Christchurch through Arthur's Pass National Park is the most spectacular train ride in the country. The train brought tourists, and it wasn't long before there was a growing push to make the area the South Island's first national park. In 1929, only six years after the Otira Tunnel was opened, Arthur's Pass became New Zealand's third national park, after Tongariro and Mt Egmont.

CLIMATE

The mountains of Arthur's Pass not only attract bad weather, they create it. Like all alpine areas in New Zealand, the mountains of Arthur's Pass make the park colder, windier and wetter than the nearby lowlands. The wettest areas are on the western side of the Main Divide: Otira township averages 5000 mm of rain a year, while Bealey Spur, on the eastern side of the mountains, averages about 1500 mm. Rain falls on Arthur's Pass village 150 to 175 days of the year, with the most unsettled weather occurring in spring and autumn.

The best weather is experienced in February and March, but bring rain gear and warm clothing whenever you visit the park. The high altitudes mean that temperatures fluctuate widely – the average maximum for Otira in January, for example, is 28°C, while the average minimum for the same month is just 10°C.

NATURAL HISTORY

The Main Divide marks a sharp contrast in the park's flora. The Westland slopes, with their higher rainfall and milder temperatures, are covered with lush forests of tall podocarp and, higher up, kamahi, rata and totara. On the eastern side, however, trampers encounter mountain beech forests with less understorey, and drier conditions on the forest floor. The thick bush on the western side of the park also contains more birdlife; commonly seen are the tui, bellbird, South Island tomtit, rifleman and grey warbler.

The bird to watch out for, literally, is the kea. This naturally inquisitive alpine parrot is easily recognised by its olive-green plumage and piercing 'kea-aa' cry. It searches

Kea

huts for food or just for amusement. Its most notorious traits are stealing shiny objects, including knives and car keys, dissecting boots and backpacks and airing sleeping bags with its strong, curved bill. It's an entertaining bird, however, sighted often above the tree line and occasionally in the village itself.

GOAT PASS TRACK

The Goat Pass Track – also referred to as the Mingha-Deception Track (the two rivers the route follows) – is a popular two-day walk and one of the least complicated routes to follow in the park. It's rated medium, and is an excellent introduction to tramping around Arthur's Pass. The Mingha-Deception is also the running leg of the now-famous triathlon which crosses the South Island from the Tasman Sea to the Pacific Ocean by a gruelling combination of cycling, kayaking and running.

Information

The Waimakariri (Arthur's Pass) field and visitor centre (☎ 318 9211) is on State Highway 73; it is open daily from 8 am to 5 pm (shorter hours in winter).

Top Left: Trampers admiring the view, Flea Bay, Banks Peninsula Walk (JW)
Top Right: Rocky Beach Walk, Flea Bay, Banks Peninsula Walk (JW)
Bottom: Waterfall, Banks Peninsula Walk (JW)

West Matukituki Valley, Mt Aspiring National Park (JD)

Maps

Use 1:80,000 Parkmaps No 273-01 *(Arthur's Pass National Park)* or 1:50,000 Topomaps 260 quads K33 *(Otira)* and K34 *(Wilberforce)*.

Huts

Both the Goat Pass and Upper Deception huts are $4; the Mingha Bivouac is free.

Equipment

Arthur's Pass is one place where you don't want to be carrying any excess gear. Free storage is available at the visitor centre and at the youth hostel. Remember that the headquarters close at 5 pm; if you plan to arrive later, store your excess gear at the YHA.

There's a store in town with a good but expensive selection of supplies. It's open daily from 8 am to 6 pm.

Access

You can get to Arthur's Pass by road or rail; the latter option is expensive but a possibility if you enjoy travelling by train.

There is good transport to and from each end of the track along State Highway 73. The Chalet Restaurant, just north of the youth hostel, serves as the bus depot. Buses can be used by trampers heading down State Highway 73 to the start of a track. They can also be flagged down when you emerge from the track.

InterCity (☎ 377 0951) has resumed its summer Christchurch-Greymouth service; it departs from Christchurch at 8.30 am, reaches Arthur's Pass at 11.10 am and Greymouth at 12.45 pm, returns to Arthur's Pass at 3.40 pm and is back in Christchurch by 6 pm.

Coast to Coast (☎ (0800) 80 0847) has a daily bus service which leaves Christchurch at 8.30 am, reaches Arthur's Pass at 10.30 am, returns to Arthur's Pass from Greymouth at 3 pm and arrives in Christchurch at 5.40 pm. This service drops off trampers at Greyneys Shelter and picks up at Aickens. Greyneys is a 10-minute drive south of Arthur's Pass; Aickens is a 10-minute drive south-east of Jacksons. The costs from Christchurch are $25 to Greyneys Shelter, $25 to Arthur's Pass and $35 to Greymouth or Hokitika. There is a concession fare of $60 for a return west-east trip completed within four days – enough time for this trip.

Alpine Coach & Courier (☎ 736 9834) offers a similar schedule to Coast to Coast.

The Arthur's Pass Passenger Service (☎ 318 9233) offers minibus transport to the ski areas and walking tracks. If you're tramping, you can arrange to be picked up at the other end when you finish. The cost of this will vary, depending on the tramp.

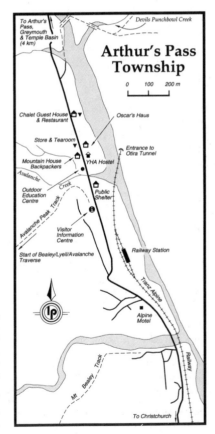

Places to Stay

The *Sir Arthur Dudley Dobson Memorial YHA Hostel* (☎ 318 9230) in Arthur's Pass township has bunks for $18. The nearby *Mountain House* (☎ 318 9258) has bunks for $15. You can camp at the *Public Shelter* for $3 per night, but the facilities are basic (cold water and a flush toilet). Camping is not permitted at Greyneys Shelter, but you would be rich if you had a dollar for every tramper who has slept there. The *Otira Hotel* (☎ 738 2802), 14½ km west of Arthur's Pass, has beds from $12.

The Track

The Goat Pass Track is a 25-km walk, rated medium. Most people accomplish it in two days, spending the night at the popular Goat Pass Hut. The hut is above the bush-line, and an extra day can be spent scrambling on the surrounding ridges. The track can be walked in either direction, but this description is from the Mingha to the Deception River, allowing trampers to undertake the shorter day first.

The southern end of the track is the confluence of the Bealey and Mingha rivers, near Greyneys Shelter, on State Highway 73, five km south of Arthur's Pass. The northern end is the confluence of the Otira and Deception rivers, six km along the road to the West Coast from Otira. Both the Mingha and Deception rivers can be difficult or impossible to ford when high, and should not be attempted at such times.

Stage 1: Greyneys Shelter to Goat Pass

Walking Time: four to five hours
Accommodation: Mingha Bivvy (two bunks); Goat Pass Hut (20 bunks)

If you're travelling by bus, the driver will drop you off at Greyneys Shelter. It's a 10-minute walk north along the road to the junction of the Bealey and Mingha rivers, easily spotted from State Highway 73 as a huge, gravel plain.

Ford the Bealey, then round the point into the Mingha Valley and head up the valley along the true right (west) side of the river.

In about a km, you have to ford the Mingha to the true left (east) side, where the easy walking continues for another three km. In about 1½ hours, a huge rock cairn appears on the true right (west) side of the river, and there's a small, red marker on a tree nearby. Ford the river again and follow the track, which very soon comes out of the trees and crosses a wide rock slide.

On the other side of the rock slide is another large rock cairn and a 'Mingha Track' sign. At first, the track runs level with the river, but then it makes a steep ascent to the top of Dudley Knob. It's a good climb, and once on top you'll be able to see both sides of the river valley. The track descends the knob a short way and then begins a gentle climb towards Goat Pass. This stretch used to be very boggy but has been extensively boardwalked. A little more than two km from the knob, the track passes Mingha Bivouac, a two-bunk hut.

For the next 1½ km you follow the river, fording it a number of times before a large rock cairn and a red sign appear on the true left bank. This marks the final climb. The track passes the impressive bowl of Mt Temple, then follows the gorge to Goat Pass, though you rarely see it. This tussock slope is quite wet and boggy in places, with long sections of boardwalk. The climb is easy though, and from the pass you can look down on its northern side and spot the hut below.

Goat Pass Hut is a great place to spend a night or two. It's a roomy hut, and it has a radio link with the Waimakariri field centre that can be used to receive the latest weather report. There is no fireplace in the hut at present because of the firewood situation.

An excellent climb for a layover day is to ascend the spur to the east and follow the ridge to Lake Mavis. The 500-metre climb to the lake, perhaps the most accessible lake at this level in the park, should take no more than two hours.

Stage 2: Goat Pass to State Highway 73

Walking Time: five to seven hours
Accommodation: Upper Deception Hut (six bunks)

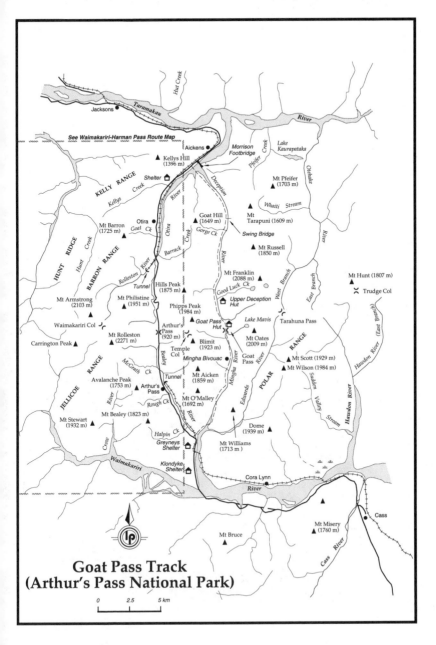

Goat Pass Track
(Arthur's Pass National Park)

0   2.5   5 km

The day begins at the stream behind the hut, where a couple of snow poles have been placed. Follow the small stream, stepping from boulder to boulder, and you soon emerge at Deception River. Here, a huge rock cairn and a large pole alert trampers walking towards the pass to leave the river and avoid the gorge ahead.

Those heading down the valley continue boulder-hopping along the river on the true left (west) side most of the time, though a series of cairns indicate when you should cross to the other bank. There are also short sections of unmarked track that can be used if found. In about two km, you pass the Upper Deception Hut on the true right (east) bank just before Good Luck Creek; look for it carefully because it's easy to miss.

In less than two km, you break out into a wide section of the valley. The walking becomes considerably easier, and again most of the track encountered will be on the true left (west) side of the Deception. In two hours, you enter a gorge, pass the junction of Gorge Creek at the northern end and then in two km enter another small gorge. Both gorges are easy to walk through, with only one or two fords of the river.

At the end of the second gorge, 10 km from Goat Pass, you arrive at a swing bridge (see the note later in this section). Continue under it, and soon Deception Valley swings to the north-west and begins to widen. It's about 5½ km from the bridge to State Highway 73, with the final two km on a track on the true left side of the river through grazing land (watch out for the cows). The Morrison footbridge across the Otira is just north of the confluence, on the true right bank of the Deception River.

Under normal conditions, the Otira River is easily forded, and the road is just on the other side. However, if recent rain has flooded the rivers, you should under no circumstances ford the Deception River to try and reach the Morrison footbridge. If you have any doubt, stay put until the river goes down, or try the Mingha. Backtracking may be tough but it's a small price to pay for your safety.

The route to the Morrison footbridge from the swing bridge across the Deception, down

the true right (east) bank of the river, is arduous and should only be attempted by strong, experienced trampers.

WAIMAKARIRI-HARMAN PASS ROUTE

This excellent five to six-day tramp, which crosses two alpine passes and covers a variety of terrain, is rated difficult because much of the track involves trackless river valleys where long stretches of slogging over boulders will quickly tire ankles and calves, and crossing the two passes involves steep routes that are only lightly marked with rock cairns. Part of this track crosses the neighbouring Taipo Forest.

It is a walk for experienced trampers, but a rewarding one. Highlights include excellent views from Harman Pass and Kelly Saddle, superb trout fishing in the Taipo River and an evening soak in the hot springs at Julia Hut. If short on time or experience, you can shorten this tramp by hiking up the Waimakariri River and spending two nights at the roomy Carrington Hut before backtracking to State Highway 73. The spare day can be used to climb Harman Pass, the easier and more scenic of the two alpine crossings.

Information

The Waimakariri field and visitor centre (☎ 318 9211) is on State Highway 73; it is open daily from 8 am to 5 pm (shorter hours in winter).

Maps

Use the 1:80,000 Parkmaps No 273-01 *(Arthur's Pass National Park)* or 1:50,000 Topomaps 260 quads K33 *(Otira)* and L33 *(Dampier)*.

Huts

The Anti-Crow, Carrington, Julia, Mid-Taipo and Carroll huts are all Category Three ($4), while Greenlaw and Seven Mile huts are free.

Access

The trip begins at Klondyke Shelter, the next day-use facility south of Greyneys Shelter on State Highway 73, just north of where the road crosses the Waimakariri River. It terminates to the north at Kelly Shelter, also on State Highway 73, three km north of Otira township. Neither shelter is set up for overnight use, but both can be reached by bus services coming in and out of Arthur's Pass village (see Access for the Goat Pass Track section).

Places to Stay

This walk has a similar entry and exit point to the Goat Pass Track (except they are on the opposite side of State Highway 73), so see Places to Stay in that section.

The Track

This five to six-day trip, rated difficult, is described from the Waimakariri River north to Taipo River and then over Kelly Saddle, the easiest direction to cross the alpine pass.

Most trampers hike into Carrington Hut the first day and climb Harman Pass the next, spending the second night at the Julia Hut. It is difficult, however, to know where to spend the third night. The natural destination is Seven Mile Hut, but in 1994 this was in bad shape. To continue to Carroll Hut makes for a 12-hour walk, which is beyond the capabilities of most trampers. Even if you stop at Mid-Taipo Hut – the one before Seven Mile Creek – you still face a nine-hour walk to Carroll Hut.

A small stove is almost a necessity on this trip because Carroll Hut does not have gas rings or a stove of any kind, while starting a cooking fire in Seven Mile Hut is nearly impossible.

Stage 1: Klondyke Shelter (State Highway 73) to Carrington Hut

Walking Time: five hours
Accommodation: Anti-Crow Hut (six bunks); Greenlaw Hut; Carrington Hut (36 bunks)

There are two separate ways up the Waimakariri River to Carrington Hut. In normal conditions and using a degree of caution, the river can be forded in most places. The shortest and easiest route is along

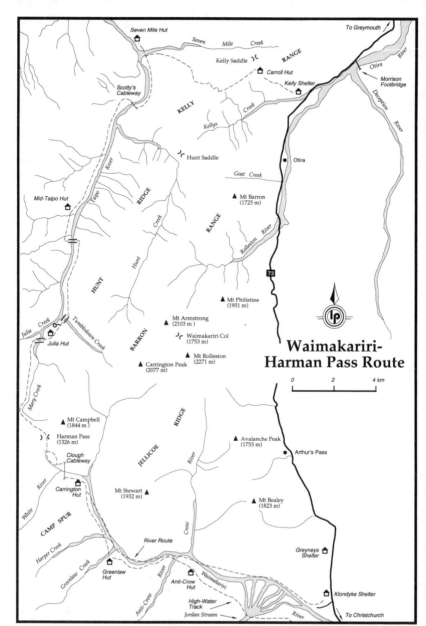

Waimakariri-
Harman Pass Route

the river bed, where trampers cross the Waimakariri and its side streams numerous times.

If the river is flooded, however, you can use the high-water track that runs along the southern bank, near the bridge on State Highway 73. It's about 2½ hours to Anti-Crow Hut from the bridge. After a boggy section to the Anti-Crow, the track hugs the river bed to Greenlaw Creek; the Greenlaw Hut is 10 minutes up the true right (east) side of this stream and about two hours from the Anti-Crow Hut. The track continues up river flats, crosses Harper Creek and re-enters bush until it reaches Carrington Hut (1½ hours from Greenlaw Hut).

You still have to exercise caution on this route because many of the side streams are not bridged and can be dangerous in flood. This track can also be muddy at times and there is often little to see except the trees around you. The average tramper can follow the river to Carrington Hut in around five hours but would need six to seven hours to hike the high-water track.

For the preferred river route, begin at the 4WD track opposite the Klondyke Shelter on State Highway 73 and follow the track west to the small car park at the end. The route continues along the open grassy flats of the Waimakariri River catchment area – you will save time here if you avoid the meanderings of the braided river by hiking it from 'corner to corner'. Most trampers stick to the true left (north) bank until they reach the confluence with the Crow River, about 4¾ km from the highway. Fording the Waimakariri can be avoided along this stretch, except where Turkey Flat forces the river to swing into the forested banks to the north of it.

As you near Crow River, the easiest route is often to cross the Waimakariri to the true right (south) bank, then cut across the flats between the knobs and the mouth of the Anti-Crow River. If you plan to stay at Anti-Crow Hut, ford the Waimakariri early and keep an eye on the tree line for the shelter. Once past Anti-Crow River, ford the Waimakariri again to the true left (north) bank and follow this side to the distinct forested

'corner'. The river swings sharply round this corner, so it is best to ford back to the true right (south) side before reaching it.

From the true right bank, it is easy to reach Greenlaw Creek, recognised by a large two-metre log sticking out of a pile of rocks. You can look up the creek to see a portion of the DOC Greenlaw Hut among the trees. Beyond Greenlaw Creek, a series of poles swing north across the flats for a km to Harper Creek. Stay on the true right side of the river after crossing the creek; the bushy knob that marks the confluence with the White River should quickly become visible.

It's roughly 3¼ km from Greenlaw Creek to the knob, at which point a well-beaten track heads west for five minutes to Carrington Hut. The hut is massive, with four separate sleeping areas and two common rooms. This facility can sleep 36 people comfortably without anybody having to endure the floor. It also contains a radio, which can be used in the morning to receive the latest weather report from the field centre in Arthur's Pass.

The hut is named after Gerald Carrington, who in 1925 proposed to his friends around a campfire that they form a club and promote this valley for tramping. The Canterbury Mountaineering Club was formed, but before the original hut was built here, Carrington drowned at the Waimakariri Gorge.

Stage 2: Carrington Hut to Julia Hut
Walking Time: five to seven hours
Accommodation: Julia Hut (six bunks)

A track departs west from the large hut, up the true right of White River. Just over a km through the forest, you reach Clough Cableway. Under normal conditions, you can ford the river at this point.

If you're forced to use it, the cableway is an interesting device (for those who have never used one before), and definitely easier if there are people cranking the car from both banks – then all the passenger has to do is keep away from the spinning handle inside the car and enjoy the great view of White River Gorge below. Once on the true left (north) side of the gorge, a short track runs from the cableway to the Taipoiti River.

For most of the climb to Harman Pass, you follow the river, hopping from one boulder to the next. There are a few rock cairns (but never when you need one) and even a few segments of beaten path, but during most of the climb you have to pick and choose your own route. It's probably easier to follow the true left (west) bank of the river for the first 1¼ km, until a rock bluff forces you to the other side.

More bluffs force you back to the true left side, and eventually you climb towards what appears to be a granite bowl with steep walls and a waterfall. There is only one route up from here – on the true right (east) side of the river, where several large cairns mark the way up an easy rock and tussock slope.

Once on the slope, a distinct track appears, and crosses two gullies before making the final ascent to Harman Pass. From the pass, you can see Whitehorn Pass to the west and, more importantly, the three branches of Mary Creek to the north. On the bluff opposite the pass, an obvious route allows trampers to skirt a gorge.

Take time to study the route from the pass down to the branch of Mary Creek. Cross the stream and then ascend the bluff before the gorge. There are rock cairns to assist you, but make sure you climb the bluff high enough to avoid the gorge totally. You then drop back down to the creek. Descend through the tussock grass and rocks (not as easy it appears) until you reach Mary Creek near the junction of its third branch. Ford the creek to its true left (west) side and begin boulder-hopping down the stream. The quickest route is to ford the creek from corner to corner and stay along the banks.

An hour or so from the pass, you reach the bush-line. Continue along the stream banks until you pass a rock slide on the true left (west) side and see a huge rock cairn (the biggest since crossing the pass); this is the start of the Julia Track, which is marked by white metal tags. The three-km track twice climbs steadily up the side of the valley and then descends again. The first time you get

an excellent view of Mary Creek. Eventually, the track descends to a swing bridge, just a few minutes from Julia Hut. Be aware that at one point the track comes to a rock slide five metres above the river and resumes on the other side 30 metres up the scree.

Julia Hut, a very pleasant six-bunk facility with views of peaks all around it, was rebuilt in 1987. The feature of this hut is the nearby hot springs, reached in 10 to 15 minutes by passing the old Julia Hut and continuing down the valley. Once you pass a tarn, look for a side track marked with white metal tags. The track drops steeply to cross the Taipo River. Don't cross the river; instead, hike downstream 150 metres or so and look for the greyish pools on the true right (east) bank.

During a dry spell, the water might be too hot to enter. If there has been too much rain, the pools could be impossible to locate in the swollen river. But if conditions are right, you can deepen the pools by scooping out the gravel with the bucket from the hut. Lay back and soak in the warm water, with the Taipo rushing by an arm's length away. After climbing Harman Pass, nothing could be more pleasant.

Stage 3: Julia Hut to Seven Mile Hut

Walking Time: 5½ to six hours
Accommodation: Mid-Taipo Hut (six bunks), Seven Mile Hut (six bunks)

A track leaves the new hut, climbs a terrace and passes the old Julia Hut before heading down the valley along the true right (east) side of the Taipo River. In a km, it crosses a walkwire over Tumbledown Creek and continues as an easy walk, although it tends to get boggy in places. It reaches a swing bridge five km from Julia Hut and crosses to the true left (west) side of the Taipo. From the middle of the bridge, it's possible to see a portion of the Mid-Taipo Hut, still a 15 to 20-minute trek away through grass and scrub flats. The six-bunk hut is a 2½ to three-hour walk from Julia Hut but is in much better shape than the one at Seven Mile Creek.

From the hut, a track continues through open flats for 20 minutes, then climbs steeply around a gorge. After descending to the river bed, the track becomes a route more or less through open flats for the next four km as it works it way towards the noticeable knob located just before Scotty's Cableway. This is a good stretch for anglers to seek pools in the river that might hold trout.

Eventually, you reach the northern end of the flats, with the knob looming overhead, and find a white metal marker pointing to a track leading up into the bush. If the weather is clear and the river easy to ford, trampers should seriously consider continuing through the gorge instead of using the cableway to cross it. The track to Scotty's Cableway involves an extremely steep climb, part of which is along an old stream bed, and an equally steep descent.

Either way, you emerge from the gorge on the true right (east) side of the Taipo and continue down the river, where the terrain quickly changes into grassy flats and terraces that make for easy walking. It's about 3¼ km from the cableway across the flats and past One Mile Creek to Seven Mile Creek.

Cross the creek (do not head upstream) and look for the hut, which is in the open flats but near the bush-line. The hut is old and rapidly deteriorating but still keeps out the weather. It's in a crucial location, however, and hopefully will soon be replaced.

Stage 4: Seven Mile Hut to Kelly Shelter

Walking Time: five to six hours to Carroll Hut; six to eight hours to Kelly Shelter
Accommodation: Carroll Hut (eight bunks)

You begin the day by recrossing Seven Mile Creek to its true left (south) side and hiking upstream to the distinctive white pole, high on a bank. Go just beyond the pole (a 15-minute walk from the hut) and look for white metal tags which signal the start of a track.

Once on the track, you climb steeply and soon pass through an eerie, old mining trace. You then ascend sharply to the bush-line, climbing 800 metres in four km. It's about a 2½ to three-hour hike from the hut to the small knob, marked by a large cairn just

beyond the last stand of mountain beech. There are good views in almost every direction, even of Seven Mile Hut, where the day began.

From the knob, a well-defined track climbs the ridge through scrub and flax but quickly becomes obscured. There are a few white metal markers and segments of worn track here and there, but basically you make your own route up to the top of the ridge, where a large cairn and a pole with a yellow disc are located. This is a very important marker for trampers walking in the opposite direction because it puts you in line with the start of the track at the bush-line.

Once on top, a couple of cairns point the way along the most northern ridge, the lower of the two viewed running east. There are very few markers up here – try to stay to the north, keeping Seven Mile Creek in view below. Hike east up the ridge and over small knolls until you emerge at a series of small tarns. The route continues north-east from the small ponds, over a tussock basin and up the main ridge of Kelly Range. When you reach the crest of the range, you will be able to view at least a portion of Otira Valley.

From the tarns, it's a km to the main ridge if you follow a direct route, then another 1½ km to Carroll Hut. You will actually see the hut soon after reaching the main ridge, but stay on the crest of Kelly Range because the south-eastern side is very steep and has rugged bluffs. The ridge will lead to slopes that you can easily descend to the hut.

Carroll Hut, rebuilt in 1981, has eight bunks but no gas rings or heat of any kind. It's a very pleasant spot, and has excellent views of the surrounding mountains, so it's a great place to spend an extra day. The hut is named after Patrick Carroll, who died in the mid-1930s following a mountaineering accident. A chilling newspaper account of the mishap is framed on the wall.

Beyond Carroll Hut, it is only 1½ hours to Kelly Shelter, maybe two hours if it's raining. The first km is above the bush-line, through tussock, while the rest is in the forest. The drop to Kellys Creek is quite steep. You emerge at State Highway 73.

ACROSS HARPER PASS

This is a five to six-day walk along an important historic route which connects Arthur's Pass and Lewis Pass. The track runs from Arthur's Pass National Park in the west to Lake Sumner Forest Park in the east, crossing the Main Divide over Harper Pass, a low saddle of only 963 metres. The segment in the national park is a valley route along the Taramakau River, but in the forest the track is well cut and marked. This, combined with the low alpine pass, makes crossing the Harper Pass an easier trip than many others in the area, including the Waimakariri-Harman Pass route.

Trampers have to be cautious with the Taramakau, however. It is a large and unruly river, located in a high rainfall area, making it prone to sudden flooding. The best direction to walk the track is debatable because of the unpredictable nature of the river. The easiest way is from east to west because less climbing is required when crossing from the valley of the Hurunui River to the Taramakau River. But the trip will be described here from west to east because the track is easier to reach from Arthur's Pass, and by follow-ing the Taramakau first, you won't get blocked if a sudden rainfall makes the river impassable.

Unlike the Taramakau below Locke Stream Hut, there is a well-defined track along the Hurunui and Hope rivers and bridges at all major crossings. Once you cross Harper Pass into the forest park, the track can be walked during most foul weather.

History

Maoris may not have lived in this rugged region, but they often traversed it on their way to the West Coast in search of pounamu (greenstone). Their favoured route included much of the walk described here. Family groups headed up the Hurunui, scaled the bluffs into Maori Gully using a fibre ladder, then continued up the Hurunui's southern branch to the lakes (Sumner, Katrine and Taylor), where they would restock food supplies. After negotiating the pass, which they called Ngoti Taramakau, they would follow the Taramakau to the area around Lake Kaurapataka, where there was a plentiful supply of food.

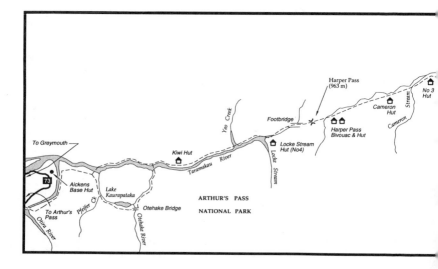

The Maoris were the first to guide Europeans through this area. In 1857, the two guides Wereta Tainui and Terapuhi took Leonard Harper across the pass that now bears his name. Three years after the first bridle paths were surveyed, in 1862, this route served as the main gateway for diggers in the 1865 gold rush to the West Coast. All along the route were stores and grog shops. When the rush ended, the track fell into disrepair until its modern use as a tramping trail.

Information

You can obtain information, register intentions and pay hut fees at the Waimakariri (Arthur's Pass) field centre. There is a DOC field centre in Hanmer Springs (☎ 315 7264), and the DOC also runs the Hurunui visitor information centre (☎ 315 7128). The visitor information centre is open on weekdays from 10 am to 6 pm in summer, 10 am to 4.40 pm in winter, and from 10 am to 4.30 pm every weekend.

Maps

Use the 1:80,000 Parkmaps No 273-01 *(Arthur's Pass National Park)* and the 1:80,000 Parkmaps No 274-16 *(Lake*

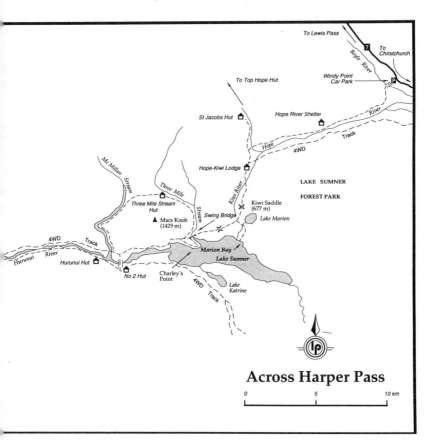

Across Harper Pass

0   5   10 km

Sumner Forest Park). Good track notes are available from the Waimakariri field centre in Arthur's Pass.

Huts

The Hurunui Hut and Hope-Kiwi Lodge are Category Two ($8) huts; the others (Locke Stream (No 4), No 2, No 3, St Jacobs, Harper Pass, Hope River and Kiwi Hut) are all Category Three ($4) huts.

Access

At the western end of the track is the DOC Aickens base hut, 1½ km north of Aickens railway station on State Highway 73. It can be reached from Greymouth or Christchurch by bus with InterCity (☎ 377 0951), Alpine Coach & Courier (☎ 736 9834) or Coast to Coast (☎ (0800) 80 0847). Alternatively, take the Tranz-Alpine train (☎ (0800) 80 2802), which drops you at Aickens (see Access in the Goat Pass Track section for details). At Arthur's Pass, an InterCity bus departs at 11.10 am and the Coast to Coast Shuttle at 11 am for Greymouth. They pass the DOC Aickens base hut about half an hour along their route.

The eastern end of the track is Windy Point, on State Highway 7, seven km north of the Hope Bridge, across the Boyle River, almost halfway between the turn-off to Hanmer Springs and Maruia Springs. Current bus schedules are usually posted in Hope-Kiwi Lodge, the last hut for most trampers, but as a rough guide, a White Star bus passes Windy Point at about 1.15 pm daily for Christchurch, and also at 1.15 pm for Nelson (with connections to Westport and Greymouth). The Mount Cook Landline bus (☎ (0800) 80 0737) from Christchurch to Nelson passes at about noon; in the Nelson to Christchurch direction it passes at about 2.15 pm. There is also the East-West Shuttle (☎ 364 8721 for timetable information).

The walk from Hope-Kiwi Lodge takes most trampers five hours, so an early start is necessary if you hope to catch one of the buses. It is best to be at the highway, ready to flag down the bus, 30 minutes before it is due to arrive.

Places to Stay

The west to east crossing from Arthur's Pass to Lewis Pass often involves staying overnight at one end of the track. See Places to Stay for the Goat Pass Track (in this chapter) for possibilities at the western end and Places to Stay for the St James Walkway (in the Canterbury chapter) for options at the eastern end.

The Track

This tramp, rated medium, begins at the national park base hut north of Aickens. If the Otira River is flooded, think twice about setting off. A walk confined to the true left (south) side of the Taramakau, using the Morrison swing bridge over the Otira near Deception River and the Otehake Bridge and the side track south of Lake Kaurapataka, would take 10 to 12 hours to reach Locke Stream Hut.

Stage 1: State Highway 73 to Locke Stream Hut

Walking Time: six hours
Accommodation: Kiwi Hut (eight bunks); Locke Stream Hut (18 bunks)

From behind the DOC Aickens base hut, follow the paddock fence to the Otira River. Ford the river and head for the obvious gap in the bush-line on the other side. There is a shelter shed here. A track leads through scrubby bush to grassy flats, which provide an easy walk to Pfeifer Creek.

Near the creek is a junction with a track that leads south (the right fork) to Lake Kaurapataka, a beautiful body of water in the former Otehake Wilderness Area (it has since reverted to national park, no longer deemed a wilderness because of the presence of huts and tracks). This is also a flood track because it connects with a route along the Otehake River, which joins the Taramakau. The high-water alternative would take two to three hours to walk.

The main route continues from Pfeifer Creek, fording the Taramakau to the true right (north) bank, where the travel is easier. It's about six km from Pfeifer Creek to Kiwi

Hut and, 1½ km before reaching it, you pass the confluence with the Otehake River. Stay on the true right (north) side of the Taramakau River and keep a sharp eye out for an old track that departs for a grassy clearing. Trampers have been known to miss the hut because it sits well back from the river, but the track to it is now well marked.

In places, you might find remnants of an old vehicle track, but beyond Kiwi Hut the route is mostly clogged with boulders along the true right (north) side of the river. It's nine km from Kiwi Hut to Locke Stream. The river bed begins to narrow halfway up near Townsend Creek, and steep northern banks force you to ford to the true left (south) side.

Continue along the gravel beds until you reach Locke Stream. A track on the other side leads through the bush for 10 minutes to Locke Stream Hut (No 4), an 18-bunk facility with a radio link to the Waimakariri field centre in Arthur's Pass. You can use the radio to pick up the latest weather report every morning at around 9 am.

Stage 2: Locke Stream to No 3 Hut

Walking Time: seven hours
Accommodation: Harper Pass Bivouac & Hut (two/six bunks); Cameron Hut (four bunks); No 3 Hut (18 bunks)

Above Locke Stream, the valley continues to narrow and the Taramakau appears more like a mountain stream. Signs of recent flooding, slips and fallen logs mar the banks of the stream. Harper Pass Track begins at the hut, and winds in and out of the forest as it climbs towards the alpine crossing. Keep a sharp eye out for trail markers that will indicate when the track moves back into the bush. This section is challenging and slow, but within 1½ hours you should reach the footbridge located three km above Locke Stream.

After crossing the stream, you swing to the true right (north) side and follow the Taramakau (though it's rarely visible through the bush) to the headwater gorges. Here, the track begins a steep 280-metre ascent

through forest to Harper Pass, which is reached three hours from the hut.

You do not enter the tussock grasslands on the pass, but drop quickly on the eastern side to the headwaters of the Hurunui River. Within 15 minutes of the stream, the two-person Harper Pass Bivouac and another six-bunk hut are reached – both pleasant places to spend an evening.

The track departs from the creek bed into lush subalpine scrub, and follows terraces along the true right (south) side of the stream. It's a steady 6½-km descent from the Harper Pass Bivouac to the first substantial flat; Cameron Hut is halfway down, on the edge of the forest. From the small hut, it's a short walk to No 3 Hut. The track crosses the flat to an emergency walkwire over Cameron Stream and then stays on the fringes of the forest for the next 1½ km, until it opens onto a flat opposite Waterfall Creek.

No 3 Hut, which looks like a deserted schoolhouse, stands in the middle of the grassy clearing. The old, two-roomed building has a large, wooden porch and an open fireplace.

Stage 3: No 3 Hut to No 2 Hut

Walking Time: four to five hours
Accommodation: Hurunui Hut (20 bunks); No 2 Hut (18 bunks)

A 4WD track departs from the hut and crosses the flats, reaching a signposted junction in one km. The main walking track veers to the south (the right fork) and stays on the true right (south) side of the Hurunui River for the entire day. The track undulates as it bypasses steep embankments cut into the hillsides. If you want flat, easy travel, veer to the north (the left fork) at the junction and follow the 4WD vehicle track all the way along the true left (north) side. If you plan to stay at the Hurunui Hut, it's best to stick to the walking track.

From the junction, the walking track is marked by a series of poles as it crosses the flats and enters the forest. The track sides up and down along the forested hillsides for two km, crosses another flat, and then makes a long descent to the signposted hot springs, a two-hour walk from the hut. The sulphurous, thermal water emerges from rock 30 metres above the Hurunui and forms a cascade of hot water to the river bed below. It's possible to soak in a small pool.

The track departs from the hut and returns to the forest for a km, before emerging onto a flat. The route cuts across the flat, returns to the bush and 1½ hours from the hot springs arrives at the site of the Hurunui Hut. The 20-bunk DOC hut was built in 1987 as alternative accommodation for trampers who dislike sharing with people who drive 4WD vehicles to No 2 Hut.

The walking track continues and in half an hour arrives at the swing bridge across the Hurunui River, a km below the confluence with McMillan Stream. A vehicle track leads from here to No 2 Hut, 15 minutes downriver. The hut features 18 bunks in two rooms, and has an excellent view across the lower flats to Lake Sumner and Mt Longfellow. This hut is a popular destination with 4WD users.

Stage 4: No 2 Hut to Hope-Kiwi Lodge via Kiwi Saddle

Walking Time: four to five hours
Accommodation: Hope-Kiwi Lodge (24 bunks); St Jacobs Hut (eight bunks)

Resist the temptation to cut across the flats and to ford the Hurunui River directly in front of No 2 Hut to avoid backtracking to the swing bridge – this route includes boggy areas and clumps of matagouri that can make the walk tedious and, in the end, more time-consuming. Return to the swing bridge and follow the vehicle track on the other side to where it swings sharply to the west. A route marked with poles heads east (the right fork) from here and crosses the valley along the edge of the forest. To avoid some cliffs, the track dips into the bush once before reaching the head of the lake.

On the northern side of Lake Sumner, the track enters forest again for an easy climb to Three Mile Stream, crossed by a swing bridge. There's a junction here, with one track heading north towards Three Mile Stream Hut and another south to Charley's Point, on the lake. The main track departs east across the stream and begins the steepest climb of the day, gaining 150 metres before levelling off and finally reaching bush-clad Kiwi Saddle (677 metres).

It's a quick descent through bush to the open tussock country along Kiwi River. The track follows the edge of the beech forest along the true left (west) side of the river, and it's an hour's walk through the cattle flats to the Hope-Kiwi Lodge, situated near the western edge of the forest. This hut is large – five rooms, two stoves and 24 bunks. There is more modest accommodation 1½ hours up the true right (west) bank of the Hope River at St Jacobs Hut (eight bunks).

Stage 5: Hope-Kiwi Lodge to State Highway 7

Walking Time: five hours
Accommodation: Hope River Shelter (no bunks)

Begin this day early if you intend to connect with one of the buses (see Access in this section) on State Highway 7. A vehicle track departs from the hut and follows the true right (south) side of the Hope River, reaching the highway at the Hope Bridge. The walking track heads north through beech forest and grassy flats and in 45 minutes reaches a swing bridge over the river. A side track continues north towards St Jacobs Hut (a 45-minute walk), but the main track crosses the swing bridge to the true left (north) side of the river.

The track immediately enters a large open flat, and it's an easy walk for the next hour as you follow poles for four km until a bend in the river forces the track to climb into the forest. The track sidles between bush and more flats and in two km arrives at the Hope River Shelter, a three-sided hut with a stove and benches. The shelter marks the halfway point to State Highway 7 – seven km of the journey remain.

The track remains in beech forest for the next two hours, until it breaks out onto a series of grassy terraces, and crosses farmland for two km to a swing bridge over the Boyle River gorge. On the other side, the track leads past service huts to a picnic area and a small shelter. A metalled road covers the remaining half-km from the picnic area to State Highway 7.

OTHER TRACKS
Casey Saddle-Binser Saddle
This is an easy to medium two-day tramp in the drier, south-eastern corner of Arthur's Pass National Park. The loop begins and ends near Andrews Shelter, reached from State Highway 73 by turning onto Mt White Station Rd and following it for five km, to where it crosses Andrews River.

There is a track most of the way, and no difficult fords of large rivers. The well-cut track crosses two easy saddles, winds through open beech forest and follows the grassy terraces along the Poulter River. You can spend the night at Casey Hut, a modern 16-bunk facility, or at one of the good camp sites along the route. Keep in mind that this track can often be walked when wet weather makes other tramping tracks treacherous.

Three-Pass Trip
This is a challenging four to five-day alpine route, for experienced trampers, through Harman, Whitehorn and Browning passes. On the first day, you hike from Arthur's Pass National Park up the Waimakariri River to Carrington Hut, cross Harman and Whitehorn passes to Park Morpeth Hut on the Wilberforce River on the second day and climb over Browning Pass to Harman Creek Hut on the third. The east-west route ends at the Lake Kaniere-Kokatahi Rd, where most trampers continue the walk into Kokatahi. There are many steep climbs on this trip but the alpine scenery is spectacular.

Craigieburn Forest Park

CASS-LAGOON SADDLES TRACK
One of the easier alpine routes in the Arthur's

Pass region is a well-developed track over two saddles that actually lies just south of the national park. The Cass-Lagoon Saddles Track, a 30-km walk in Craigieburn Forest Park (44,000 hectares), has become a particularly popular weekend trip for Christchurch trampers. Although part of the tramp is technically a 'route', the entire trek is well marked and the alpine saddles are easy to climb. Park authorities have, however, stressed that people do get lost on the Cass-Lagoon Saddles Track. This trip is rated medium and is usually walked in two days, with a night at Hamilton Hut, one of the nicest huts in the South Island.

The track can be reached from Arthur's Pass Village (see the Goat Pass Track section for information on getting to the village). Because the forest park is so close to the Arthur's Pass National Park, its history, climate and natural history are very similar.

Information
The Craigieburn Forest Park is administered by the Waimakariri (Arthur's Pass) field centre (☎ 318 9211). The visitor centre is open daily, and contains displays on the park's features as well as information on recreational opportunities. You can pay hut fees here.

Maps
Maps that cover the track include the 1:80,000 Parkmaps No 274-17 (Craigieburn Forest Park) and the 1:50,000 Topomaps 260 quad K34 (Wilberforce).

Huts
Hamilton Hut is Category Two ($8) and Bealey and Cass huts are both Category Three ($4) huts. All other huts in the forest are free.

Access
There is good transport to and from each end of the track along State Highway 73. The Tranz-Alpine train stops at Cass railway station, where there is also a car park. From here, it's half a km down a road to the signposted track off State Highway 73. At

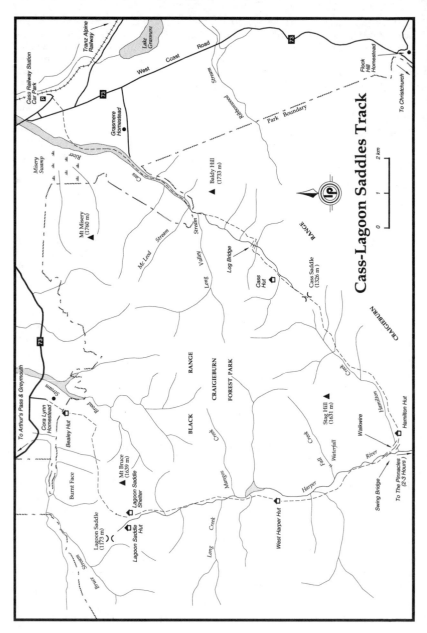

Cass-Lagoon Saddles Track

the other end of the track, near Bealey Hut, a number of buses run in both directions along State Highway 73 and can be flagged down. See the Access section for the Goat Pass Track for bus information.

Places to Stay

For accommodation possibilities in the region, see Places to Stay for the Goat Pass Track.

The Track

It is best to walk this track in early to late summer because of the heavy snowfalls in winter and the danger of avalanches on Cass Saddle.

The track can be walked in either direction, but will be described here from the Cass end to Bealey Hut. You almost have to run along the track from Hamilton Hut to meet any of the morning buses to Greymouth passing on State Highway 73, so a good alternative is to end the second day at scenic Lagoon Saddle, two hours from State Highway 73, or spend the night at Bealey Hut and catch the bus the next morning. If you're heading to Christchurch, there are afternoon buses.

Stage 1: State Highway 73 to Hamilton Hut

Walking Time: five to seven hours
Accommodation: Cass Hut (four bunks); Hamilton Hut (20 bunks)

From the signposted car park near the Cass railway station, follow the road back to the marked start of the track on State Highway 73 (about half a km south of the bridge over the Cass River) and cross the stile into farmland. The route is well marked with poles, and it crosses the paddock to a large display sign that contains a box with an intentions book. The Cass River is just beyond, and you head upstream along the gravel flats, fording from one side to the other when necessary.

If the river is flooded, there is an all-weather route – it's signposted on the Grasmere Homestead access track, near the display sign. Two km up the Cass River, you will see flood route signs on the true right (south) side. These are wrong because the river has recently changed course; check the current status with staff at the Waimakariri (Arthur's Pass) field centre. In normal conditions, the Cass is easily forded and its gravel beds make for a much more pleasant walk than the flood route.

After travelling up the river bed for four km (about 1½ hours) from State Highway 73, a 'Craigieburn Forest Park' sign appears on the true right (south) side; next to it is a well-defined track. You make an immediate climb, steep in some parts, and in three km you cross the Cass River on a bridge made of a huge log. The track then climbs another 90 metres in the next km to reach Cass Hut. As far as bivvies go – most being little more than a mattress in a tin box – this one is not bad. It's near the bush-line, with a small table, a stove and some space inside.

Within minutes of leaving the hut, you begin climbing towards Cass Saddle (1326 metres). Once you break out of the trees, there are panoramic views. During the winter, this area is avalanche-prone, and in the summer it's easy to see why – there are steep scree slopes on both sides of the alpine route. Poles lead through open tussock for the remaining 1½ km from the hut to Cass Saddle; the pass is marked by an exceptionally large pole. You can look down into the Hamilton Creek valley and, on a clear day, even see the light-brown roof of Hamilton Hut.

From the saddle, the route veers left for 100 metres and then begins a quick descent into the bush and down a narrow ridge. The track drops more than 300 metres before it levels out in the upper portion of Hamilton Creek valley, where it crosses several streams.

One km from the hut, the track emerges from the bush onto the grassy terraces along Hamilton Creek. The hut is on a ledge above the creek, and has a commanding view of the valley. Inside, it's an impressive structure, with 20 bunks, a wood stove, and even a drying rack that can be lowered and raised.

Stage 2: Hamilton Hut to State Highway 73

Walking Time: six to seven hours
Accommodation: West Harper Hut (five bunks); Lagoon Saddle Shelter (one bunk); Lagoon Saddle Hut (three bunks); Bealey Hut (six bunks)

The track heads west from the hut and almost immediately arrives at a walkwire across Hamilton Creek (unnecessary in normal conditions and best left for emergency use). You continue up the Harper River on the true left (east) side and soon come to a swing bridge.

The track resumes on the true right (west) side and follows the valley through forest and open flats for the 4½ km to West Harper Hut, an older-style hut, built in the 1950s. West Harper Hut is 15 to 20 minutes beyond Tarn Creek and is strictly a hunter's bivvy, with dirt floor, canvas bunks, a fireplace, and even an impressive set of antlers mounted on the wall.

Keep in mind that the track is well marked with red and white metal tags. Hunter's trails abound in the area, especially up side streams like Tarn Creek, and it's easy to mistakenly depart on one and not notice the main track resume on the other bank.

From the hut, the track soon arrives at a short gorge, which it bypasses with a steep climb. In fine weather, it is easier to follow the river, fording it once or twice, to avoid the climb. The track returns to the Harper and becomes more of a route along the river bed, with rock cairns marking the way. In about three km, you ford the river to a cairn on the true left (east) bank and pass a posted flood route before arriving at the confluence of the Harper River and Long Creek.

At this point, Long Creek usually looks like the major channel, so a sign has been erected in the middle of the confluence which points the way to 'Lagoon Saddle'. You continue to follow the river bed for another half-km, until a track on the true left (east) side leads into the bush and climbs to the saddle. The climb is steady but not steep, and in 1½ to two hours from Long Creek you come to a sign pointing the way to the saddle or to the short spur track to Lagoon Saddle Shelter. The shelter is a clean A-frame with two mattresses, a wood stove and an inside toilet. Nearby, across the river, is Lagoon Saddle Hut, which sleeps three.

The main track leaves the junction and climbs steeply through beech forest for 120 metres until it reaches the bush-line. Above the trees, there is an excellent view of the saddle and the tarn in the middle, which is actually bypassed by the track. The climb continues but is much easier, and the views of the snowcapped peaks of Arthur's Pass National Park to the north get better and better. It's about three km across the alpine region, with snow poles marking the route around Mt Bruce, until you return to the forest edge at Burnt Face.

There are plans to reroute the Lagoon Saddle to State Highway 73 section of the track to avoid an ecologically sensitive section on the flanks of Mt Bruce; check with the DOC at the Waimakariri field centre in Arthur's Pass.

The final leg is a steep, boggy, slippery 2½-km descent to Bealey Hut. The hut is in surprisingly good shape, considering its proximity to the road, and has a stove, a table and six canvas bunks. It's a five-minute walk to the car park and, from there, a 4WD road leads 1½ km through Cora Lynn Homestead to State Highway 73.

West Coast & Southern Alps

You can go for a tramp almost anywhere in Westland. From the end of the Heaphy Track down to the Te Wahipounamu world heritage region, the 'Coast' is almost all wilderness. A main road hugs the coast, and small tracts of farmland act as a buffer against the relentless regrowth of the beautiful forests. Only a couple of walks are described in this chapter, but look eastwards at the powerful bulk of the Southern Alps and realise that tramping is a way of life here. Just step off the road...

Paparoa National Park

Most tourists travelling down the isolated West Coast between Westport and Greymouth are enthralled by the rugged seascape, but the region usually receives little attention from trampers passing through.

The common notion is that the only reason to stop is to take a quick walk through the Pancake Rocks Reserve. That opinion is slowly changing, however, thanks to the development of one of New Zealand's newest national parks. Paparoa National Park was officially opened in 1987 as part of the country's national parks centennial celebration. It includes the rugged granite peaks of the Paparoa Range and the lowlands and river valleys west of it – ironically, it does not include the spectacular seascape seen along State Highway 6.

The park boasts beautiful scenery – within an easy walk inland lie river valleys made tropical by groves of nikau palms, and there are also spectacular limestone formations, narrow gorges, and interesting caves to explore. All these features remain hidden from most travellers, but can be seen by trampers who take the park's most noted tramp, the Inland Pack Track.

The 25-km walk extends from Punakaiki to the spot where State Highway 6 crosses the mouth of Fox River. There are no huts along this track, only the Ballroom, one of the largest (if not the largest) rock bivvies in New Zealand. There are no alpine passes to negotiate or excruciating climbs above the tree line, but the tramp is no easy stroll. There is mud to contend with and a couple of rivers to hike.

Dilemma Creek flows through a gorge so steep and narrow that trampers just walk down the middle of it. Occasionally, you can follow a gravel bank, but much of the trek involves sloshing from one pool to the next. When water levels are normal, the stream rarely rises above your knees, and if it's a hot, sunny day, this can be the most pleasant segment of the trip.

HISTORY

The area around Punakaiki is significant in Maori history as the first place settled on the Poutini (West Coast). Middens have been recorded at Barrytown, suggesting that Maoris must have made many seasonal excursions to the nearby bays and rivers to gather food. The name suggests that there was an abundance of food – 'a spring of food in plenty' – and Maori travellers on coastal journeys must have replenished their food stocks here. The coastline, as rugged as it appears, was a trade route for Maoris carrying Arahura greenstone north.

The first European explorers to walk through the area were probably Charles Heaphy and Thomas Brunner, who were led by the Maori guide Kehu on a five-month journey down the West Coast in 1846. These men passed 23 Maoris heading north, but the first settlement encountered was Kararoa, 20 km south of Punakaiki.

Heaphy was impressed by the Paparoa region and he devoted a dozen pages of his diary to it. But he also wrote about the 'incessant rain', delays caused by swollen rivers and of climbing rotting rata and flax ladders up the steep cliffs of Perpendicular Point at the urging of his Maori guide. Later that year,

Brunner and Kehu made a return trip to the area. It was an epic journey, one that lasted 18 months, in which they completely circumnavigated the Paparoa Range, traced the Buller River from source to mouth and travelled as far south as Paringa.

Gold was discovered on the West Coast as early as 1864, but the hunt for the precious metal really only gained momentum two years later, when famed prospector William Fox and a companion chartered the SS *Woodpecker* and landed it on the lee side of Seal Island in May 1866. The area, just south of where the Fox River empties into the Tasman Sea, became known as Woodpecker Bay, and miners by the thousands stampeded to this stretch of the coast. They scattered around Charleston to the north and then formed the town of Brighton near the Fox River. Historians estimate that by 1867, Charleston had a population of 12,000 and Brighton, where there is almost nothing today, was a booming town of 6000.

Reaching the areas along the 'beach highway' was extremely challenging for miners. Despite the Nelson Provincial Government replacing the Maori flax ladders up Perpendicular Point with chains that had saplings forced through the links, miners still looked inland for a safer route. In 1866, work began on the Inland Pack Track, which headed south from Brighton, thereby avoiding the hazardous Perpendicular Point. It was cut through the western lowlands of the Paparoa Range and, in 1868, was used to extend the Christchurch to Greymouth telegraph line north to Westport. The line, which also passed through Brighton and Charleston, was one of the most expensive ever installed in New Zealand, costing 'about 104 pounds, 10 shillings and eight pence per mile', due to the wet weather and the thick, jungle-like bush.

After the miners left, tourism was the main activity in the region. A coastal track being cut by the early 1900s was to eventually become State Highway 6. When passenger cars first travelled the Westport-Greymouth Rd, in the 1920s, few rivers had bridges, so tourists often had to ford a stream to a vehicle waiting on the other side.

Nearby Pancake Rocks has long been a popular tourist sight, but the Paparoa Range and lowlands were thrust into the consciousness of the nation only in the 1970s, when there was interest in logging the area. This sparked a heated conservation campaign that led to the establishment, in 1987, of the 30,560-hectare national park.

CLIMATE

Trampers must be prepared for the rainy weather for which the West Coast is renowned – gentle streams can quickly turn into raging rivers. The park's lowlands are a lush, almost subtropical forest because of the warm ocean current that sweeps past the coast and the moist westerlies that blow in off the Tasman Sea. The effect is a wet but surprisingly mild climate.

Average annual rainfall in the western lowlands is between 2000 and 3000 mm, much of it falling in late winter and spring. Midsummer to autumn, on the other hand, can be exceptionally sunny with long spells of settled weather. Both Westport and Punakaiki average almost 2000 hours of sunshine annually.

NATURAL HISTORY

The Paparoa Range is composed mainly of granite and gneiss peaks that have been carved by glaciers and weathered by rain, snow and wind into a craggy chain of pinnacles and spires. This is a low but extremely rugged set of mountains, between 1200 and 1500 metres high. Routes over the alpine areas of the Paparoas are only for experienced trampers willing to endure the impenetrable bush, the consistently cloudy weather at the top and the rough terrain of a true wilderness area.

The western lowlands area, which lies between the ocean and the mountains, is totally different in character. This is a karst landscape – a limestone region where the soft rock has been eroded by rivers and underground drainage. What remain are the deep canyons and gorges whose limestone walls may rise 200 metres above the river. There are blind valleys, sink holes, cliffs, streams that disappear underground, overhangs and, perhaps most intriguing to trampers, numerous caves.

The nikau palms which line the beaches and cliffs along the coast and give State Highway 6 its tropical character extend inland. The palms combine with a profusion of black mamuku tree ferns, smaller ferns and supplejack vines to form a jungle-like canopy. Still further inland, the lowland forest becomes a mixture of podocarps, beech and broadleaf trees, with rimu and red beech often the most dominant species.

The size of the forest and the fact that it's been left relatively unmolested by humans has led to the park's profusion of birdlife. Commonly spotted along the tracks are bellbirds, tomtits, fantails, grey warblers, kereru, riflemen and tuis. One of the favourites encountered is the western weka, a brown flightless bird often spotted in the Fossil Creek area. There are also good numbers of great spotted kiwis, but you'll hear them at night more often than you'll see them. On the coast, there is a colony of the rare Westland black petrel.

The other resident of the park that attracts attention is the trout. Anglers planning to walk the Inland Pack Track should take a rod and reel because they will be passing enticing trout pools along the way. The first three km of the Pororari River from State Highway 6 can be an especially productive stretch.

INLAND PACK TRACK

Even if you don't carry a tent, the Inland Pack Track can be walked by using the Ballroom, a giant limestone bivvy, for overnight shelter. This involves a long day from Punakaiki to the bivvy, located north of the junction of the Fox River and Dilemma Creek, then a short two to three-hour tramp the next day out to State Highway 6. It is better to carry a tent, however, as a precaution against rapidly rising streams, which can delay trips or prevent you from crossing Walsh Creek and reaching the Ballroom. A tent also allows the tramp to be divided more evenly into two days or walked at a more leisurely pace over three days.

Information

The Paparoa National Park visitor centre (☎ 731 1895) is next to the highway, opposite the entrance to the Pancake Rocks. It's open every day from 8.30 am to 4 pm, and in summer stays open until about 8 pm. Many of the inland walks are subject to river flooding, so check at the visitor centre before setting out.

Maps

The best coverage of the track is the 1:50,000 Parkmaps No 273-12 *(Paparoa)*. Another good map is the 1:50,000 Topomaps 260 quad K30 *(Punakaiki)*.

Huts

You don't have to pay hut fees on this walk, because there are no huts. There is no rental charge at the Ballroom for those wearing top hat and tails or ball gowns, so dance the night away.

Access

Punakaiki serves as the departure point for this trip, and many trampers spend a night here at the beginning or end of their walk.

White Star (☎ 768 0596, 789 8579) operates a bus service on the western side. The Greymouth to Westport bus departs at 8.05 am, passing Punakaiki at 8.45 am ($9); it connects with other services to Nelson and Christchurch at Springs Junction. The Westport to Greymouth service departs at 2.30 pm and passes Barrytown at 3.40 pm ($9).

InterCity (☎ 768 4199) has daily services north from Greymouth to Westport and Nelson; the northbound bus leaves Greymouth at 1.50 pm and arrives in Punakaiki at 2.30 pm. The southbound bus departs from Westport at 11.20 am and arrives in Punakaiki at 12.20 pm. Kea West Coast Tours (☎ 731 1802, 768 5101) has an 18-seater bus which goes from Greymouth to Punakaiki ($22 return).

Both these buses cross the bridge over Fox River at the northern end of the Inland Pack Track. Trampers can use these services to get

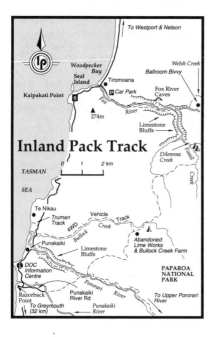

Inland Pack Track

to and from the ends of the track or to move up the coast. Check with the companies for advice on the best times to be waiting on State Highway 6.

Places to Stay

The *Punakaiki Camping Ground* (☎ 731 1894) has tent sites ($7 per person) and cabins ($26 for two). It's operated by the DOC (☎ 731 1895). *Te Nikau Retreat* (☎ 731 1111) is three km north of Punakaiki, on the sea side of the road, 200 metres past the entry to the Truman Track. Follow the no-exit drive for 450 metres until you reach the self-catering lodges ($10/25 per person/couple).

The Track

The Inland Pack Track is rated medium. Trampers should not wander off the track because this is karst limestone country and there are a number of hidden sink holes and underground streams in the area, some quite near the track.

The track can be walked in either direction, and many trampers arriving in the afternoon start at the Fox River end, from which it's a shorter walk to the Ballroom. However, the track will be described here from Punakaiki, the direction you should follow if you don't have a tent. By staying overnight at the motor camp, you can get the latest report on the weather conditions and water levels from the DOC visitor centre before departing the next morning.

If the forecast is poor, wait another day or move down the coast. To be trapped out on the track by rising rivers with no tent makes for a very long night. On the other hand, if the forecast is good, you can take the longer walk with no problems and be safely at the Ballroom by nightfall.

Stage 1: Punakaiki to the Ballroom
Walking Time: seven to eight hours

You can begin the track either at a farm road near the Punakaiki River, 1¼ km south of the Pancake Rocks (Punakaiki) visitor centre, or at the Pororari River Bridge on State Highway 6, just north of the motor camp.

Punakaiki River is part of the original track, but many feel the route along Pororari is more scenic. For the purists, proceed up Punakaiki River Rd (east) to the ford, 1½ km from State Highway 6. Cross the river, leave the logging road at the signpost and head north-east. The track passes through some logged swamp to the base of the hill that separates the Punakaiki from the Pororari. A well-benched track climbs up to a low saddle and then drops gently 80 metres to the Pororari River basin. It levels off as it approaches the signposted branch track down the Pororari, about an hour from the saddle. The ford is about 300 metres further upstream.

The scenic Pororari River alternative follows the river closely along the true left (south) bank from the bridge on State Highway 6, through a spectacular landscape of towering limestone cliffs graced by nikau palms and tree ferns. Within 15 minutes, it passes Punjabi Beach. Keep an eye on the deep green pools of the river because you can often spot trout or freshwater eels early in the morning.

In 3½ km, the track comes to a junction with the loop back to Punakaiki River and State Highway 6 (which would take two hours to walk). Then, in another 300 metres, you reach a signposted ford of the Pororari River. In normal conditions, it's an easy crossing to the junction on the other side. The Pororari River Track continues along the true right (north) side of the river to a fine viewing point over the Pororari Gorge (two hours one-way). The Inland Pack Track heads north (the left fork) and for the next four km works its way through a silver beech forest. The track can become muddy in places, with little to look at except the surrounding bush and an occasional signposted sink hole, but it is easy to follow.

In 1½ hours, you enter a clearing and then join a 4WD track. To the east are good views of the rugged Paparoa Range; to the north, pairs of white posts direct you through private property. The route passes the shacks of an abandoned lime works, some farm sheds and the signposted vehicle track along Bullock Creek to State Highway 6 before arriving at the creek itself. This is a nice spot, and the first decent place to set up camp for those who got off to a late start.

After fording Bullock Creek, the track resumes as a rough vehicle route for almost a km and then enters bush again. The track stays in the beech forest but sidles an open area and passes some immense patches of flax. After two km, the track begins ascending to a low saddle. There's a lot of mud here, but the climb is easy and the descent on the other side is rapid.

The track remains fairly level until it emerges at Fossil Creek, which is 2½ hours from Bullock Creek and marked by a large rock cairn and a small sign. There is no track at this point – you simply follow the creek downstream towards its confluence with Dilemma Creek. You may want to change into tennis shoes to follow the river, though

if your boots are already caked in mud, this is a good way to clean them. The one-km walk under a thick canopy of trees takes you through pools which are easy to wade through in normal conditions.

It takes about half an hour to reach the junction with Dilemma Creek, marked by another rock cairn and a small sign. There are grass flats around this area – good places for camping. There are even larger flats several hundred metres further up the Dilemma.

The next stretch is a walk downstream through Dilemma Creek, which is the most spectacular segment of the trip. You follow the creek bed beneath massive limestone walls, with no room for a track of any kind. You make numerous fords to avoid deep pools or to follow short gravel bars. The Fox River can probably be reached in well under an hour, but most trampers, so overwhelmed by the stunning scenery, take 1½ to two hours to cover this short stretch.

A signpost located on the true left side of Dilemma Creek, just before the confluence with the Fox River, indicates where the track resumes. The confluence is an easy spot to recognise because a sharp rock bluff separates the two canyons.

Occasionally, someone will scale this bluff during high water to continue up the Fox River to the Ballroom. The easier way is to drop down the river and then ford it. Once on the true right side of the Fox, follow it back up past the confluence (left branch facing upstream) to reach the Ballroom. The bivvy is about a km up the river, not far upstream from where Welsh Creek enters the Fox River, and is easy to spot. It takes about 20 minutes and three or four fords to reach it.

The rock overhang is appropriately named because it's about 100 metres long and has a cavern and a towering arched ceiling in the middle. The roof is a hanging garden of sorts, with grass, vines, rows of ferns and even small trees growing out of it. Its popularity has led to benches and a large fire pit being built, but there is little firewood in the immediate area. There is, however, good swimming nearby in the Fox River.

Stage 2: The Ballroom to State Highway 6
Walking Time: two to 2½ hours

Return to the small track sign on Dilemma Creek just before its confluence with the Fox River. A rough and very bushy track begins here and follows the true left (south) side of the Fox. It's rough at first, but turns into a pleasant walk along the gorge high above the river. It follows the valley for three km before dropping down to the Fox River and fording it to the true right (north) bank.

On the other side is a junction; the track heading east goes to Fox River Caves. The 35-minute climb to the caves is a gentle one, with the exception of the final 100 metres. The entrances to the three impressive caves are inside a huge rock overhang. The best cave to enter is the upper left-hand one (when you face the caves), which is accessible by stone steps. A few metres inside, you'll encounter stalagmites and stalactites.

An alternative route is a side track that runs straight up a moss-covered stream from the Fox River to the caves. This track is difficult to find when travelling downriver but it can save you from backtracking up the Fox from the point where the main track fords the river. For the adventurous, the shortest route down to the ford from the caves lies in the Fox; you follow it in the same way you followed Dilemma Creek. This should be done only in good weather – even then some fords will be almost waist deep.

After returning to the main track at the ford of the Fox River, stay on the true right (north) side and follow the track west along the river, crossing numerous gravel bars and using the little footprints designed to keep wandering trampers on course. This section takes about 40 minutes. You emerge at a car park where the Inland Pack Track is signposted. State Highway 6 is another 200 metres down the metalled road.

CROESUS TRACK

The history of the Paparoas is inextricably interwoven with the search for gold, and these mountains are crisscrossed with the tracks made by miners. You have to admire

the tenacity they showed in crossing the rugged barrier of the Paparoas between the Grey Valley and the Tasman Sea near Barrytown, 29 km north of Greymouth. The leisurely two-day Croesus Track is a pleasing blend of history and scenery, making a great introduction to the windswept tops of the Paparoas.

The views from the high points of the walk, Croesus Knob and Mt Ryall, are superb, with the bald tussock tops stretching north and south. To the east are the ranges across the Grey River valley beyond Blackball, while to the west is the rugged seascape which ends in the south near the Twelve Apostles, Point Elizabeth Track and the Big Rock. The Croesus Track is littered with gold-mining sites for almost its entire length on the eastern side of the range.

The track is not in the Paparoa National Park, but the forest through which it passes is administered by the DOC. There's an ecological reserve in the catchments of the Roaring Meg and Blackball creeks, which has been established to preserve altitudinal changes in the vegetation.

Information
There is a DOC field base (☎ 768 0427) in Greymouth, on the corner of Johnson and Swainson Sts. The Paparoa National Park visitor centre (☎ 731 1895) is at Punakaiki.

Maps
The best coverage of the track is the 1:50,000 Topomaps 260 quad K31 *(Ahaura)*.

Huts
There are three huts along the track. The Cec Clarke Hut is Category Two ($8); the other two, in poor condition, are Category Four (free).

Access
The track on the Blackball or Grey Valley side starts from the Smoke-Ho Creek car park. The road to Smoke-Ho (rough in spots) is well signposted as it leaves the main road between Blackball and Roa. On the western side of the Paparoas, at Barrytown, the track

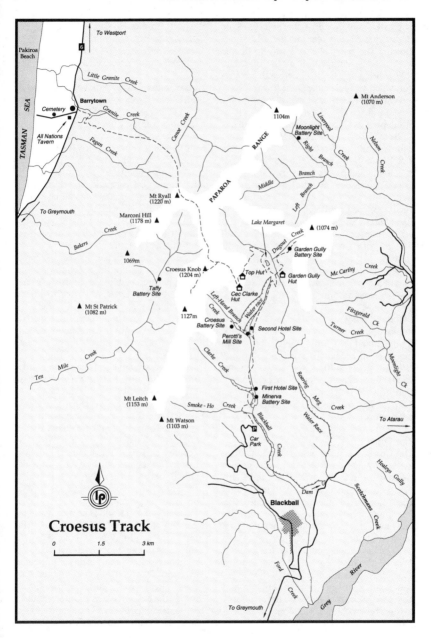

Croesus Track

0   1.5   3 km

is clearly signposted at the side of State Highway 6, directly opposite the All Nations Tavern. The most practical way to do the walk is to be dropped off on the Blackball side, picking up a bus to Greymouth or Westport when you reach the Barrytown side.

White Star operates a bus service on the western side. The Greymouth to Westport bus departs at 8.05 am, passing Barrytown at 8.30 am ($9); it connects at Springs Junction with services to Nelson and Christchurch. The Westport to Greymouth service departs at 2.30 pm and passes Barrytown at 3.55 pm ($9). There is also an InterCity service (see Access for the Inland Pack Track). For a small fee, you could probably get a lift from Blackball to Smoke-Ho with a local.

One unusual way to get to the Blackball side is with Coastwide Helicopters Heli-Hike (☎ 731 1823). This company flies you across the Paparoas from Barrytown to the start of the Croesus Track, near Blackball, for $50 per person (minimum of four).

Places to Stay

In addition to the places in Punakaiki listed for the Inland Pack Track, there is a fascinating place in Blackball called the *Blackball Hilton* (☎ 732 4705), which has dorms, double or twin rooms for $13 per person. At Barrytown, 16 km south of Punakaiki, the *All Nations Tavern* (☎ 731 1812) charges $12 per person.

The Track

The Croesus Track crossing can be done as a seven to eight-hour one-day walk, or over two days with a stop in the Cec Clarke Hut. The walk from Smoke-Ho car park (on the Blackball side) to the top of the range takes 3½ hours, across the tops to the bush-line 1½ hours and from the tops down to Barrytown 2½ hours.

Even the two-day option is rated medium, because the track crosses the exposed tops around Croesus Knob and Ryall (it is only a route) and involves a good deal of climbing and a steep descent from the tops to Barrytown. The brochure *Croesus and Moonlight Walks: Paparoa Forest* is handy.

Stage 1: Smoke-Ho Car Park to Cec Clarke Hut

Walking Time: three to four hours
Accommodation: Cec Clarke Hut (20 bunks)

At the Smoke-Ho car park you can climb up the hill near the exposed coal seam for good views of the area. From Smoke-Ho, head in a north-westerly direction along a well-benched track and descend for a km to cross Smoke-Ho Creek. Soon after crossing Clarke Creek, you come to a track junction near the first hotel site, about half an hour after leaving the car park. The track to Cec Clarke continues north. You can back track slightly on the signposted south (the right fork) track to the Minerva Battery site. The stamper battery was used to crush quartz in gold-mining operations.

Continue north for half an hour to another junction, just before the second hotel site. The signposted path to the north-west leads across Blackball Creek to Perotti's Mill site (five minutes) and the Croesus Battery site (25 minutes). Return to the main track. Not far to the north is the second hotel site and, if weather permits, you will get great views of the tops.

From the second hotel site to the Garden Gully Hut junction, follow the true left (east) bank of Blackball Creek for an hour. At a fork, you can continue west up to Cec Clarke Hut and the tops, or continue north on a signposted track to see the two-bunk Garden Gully Hut, located in the headwaters of Roaring Meg Creek (five minutes). About 10 minutes further on from the hut is the Garden Gully Battery site, the only one still standing in the area, and the mine entrance (half an hour from the junction).

Return to the fork and head west, climbing steadily uphill towards the Cec Clarke Hut. You will get glimpses of Lake Margaret below as you pass through an area that is still regenerating from the bushfires of several years ago. During the hour climb, the track heads roughly west, then south, emerging through the bush-line at Top Hut (two bunks) before rounding a spur to head north to Cec Clarke Hut. This Category Two hut ($8) has mattresses, a stove, water supply and a wonderful location – well worth a night's stopover. Both Garden Gully and Top huts are Category Four.

Stage 2: Cec Clarke Hut to State Highway 6
Walking Time: four to 4½ hours

From Cec Clarke Hut, the rough path heads north-west through the tussock to the main ridge of the Paparoa Range; it is poled all the way to the bush-line on the western side. It is hard to resist the climb to the rocky Croesus Knob (1204 metres), which gives the track its name. The path to the knob strikes off south-west from the main track along a distinctive ridge. Return to the main path and follow the poles to the north-west until you come close to the summit of Mt Ryall (1220 metres). From Cec Clarke to this point, near the bush-line, takes about two hours, including a side trip to Croesus Knob.

The well-marked track then plunges into the bush, which in this area is predominantly subalpine species and beech, and drops steeply towards the West Coast. Further down towards State Highway 6, the gradient eases as you join an old miners' benched track. After about 2½ hours, you emerge onto State Highway 6 near the conveniently situated All Nations Tavern in Barrytown.

OTHER TRACKS
Kirwans Track
Located in Victoria Forest Park, on the eastern side of the Paparoa Range, this three-day loop includes nights at two huts, tramps across river flats and climbs to open tops of tussock. Ore buckets, giant return wheels, tools and boots remain from the quartz-mining operations that took place here in the late 1890s. The track starts at Capleston, a mining ghost town at the end of Boatmans Rd, off State Highway 69 between Reefton and Inangahua Junction. Ask at the DOC's Reefton field centre (☎ 732 8391).

Mt Cook & Westland National Parks

Even in a country as rugged and mountainous as New Zealand, where towering peaks are commonplace, the Southern Alps are mind-boggling. This great range, revered by climbers throughout the world, stretches along the length of the South Island, forming a backbone of greywacke and granite from Fiordland to the Nelson Lakes.

The heart and soul of the Southern Alps, however, lie in a pair of national parks that straddle the Main Divide. Mt Cook National Park comprises 69,923 hectares of peaks, subalpine scrub, tussock, river bed and permanent snow. The 117,547-hectare Westland National Park rises dramatically from the Tasman Sea at Gillespies Beach and extends to the Main Divide.

The two national parks form a bastion of towering peaks and glaciers capped by Mt Cook (3754 metres), the tallest summit in New Zealand. Surrounding the famous mountain are 18 other peaks that are over 3000 metres. Glaciers, including the 29-km Tasman, cover 40% of Mt Cook. Westland contains 60 named glaciers, two of which, the Franz Josef and the Fox, are renowned features of the West Coast.

It's not surprising that with so much rock and ice, these national parks are not trampers' parks. Though the scenery is phenomenal and the day walks to viewpoints are numerous, this is really climbing territory.

Most valleys west of the divide are extremely rugged, with steep gorges and thick bush, while to the east they inevitably lead to glaciers requiring experience and special equipment to traverse. Crossing the passes between the valleys is a major climbing feat.

The Copland Pass, an historic crossing of the Main Divide, is traditionally done in three to four days from east to west. Although 300 to 500 people make the crossing each year, it is an extremely challenging trek that demands more fitness and technical skill than any other popular walk in New

Zealand. The route involves a 1029-metre scramble up a loose rock ridge, the final 150 metres involving a climb up a 35° snow slope.

The walk down the Copland Valley is a pretty straightforward tramp but, since 1993-94, the Hooker Valley has been in a treacherous condition, with about four areas of wash outs between the terminal lake of the Hooker Glacier and the Hooker Hut (see Guides in this section).

The second walk is an overnight trip to Mueller Hut, at the end of Sealy Range. Although the trek to the hut is a stiff climb, it is not as technical as the Copland, nor does it normally require the use of crampons and ropes. But the trip is, nevertheless, a journey into the alpine world of Mt Cook, and if the weather is clear, the views from the hut are spectacular. For most trampers, this one-way track is the only opportunity to depart from Mt Cook village and spend an evening among the peaks and glaciers.

Even if you don't have the experience to continue on to the famous pass, you can make a very pleasant two to three-day journey from the West Coast up the Copland Valley in Westland. A common trip is to hike into the Welcome Flats Hut, site of some very popular hot pools, and then spend a spare day exploring above the bush-line around the Douglas Rock Hut. On the third day you tramp back out from Welcome Flats to the highway.

HISTORY

Only a small group of Maoris and a handful of European explorers lived or travelled in South Westland before the 1865 gold rushes brought miners to Okarito and Gillespies beaches. Maoris knew of Mt Cook and called it 'Aoraki'. Tasman and Cook remarked on the rugged land as they sailed by, but it's doubtful that they ever saw the towering peaks that now bear their names.

The first European to mention Mt Cook was Charles Heaphy. Travelling with Thomas Brunner along the West Coast in 1846, Heaphy made sketches of the mountain after learning about it from his Maori

guides. In 1857, John Turnbull Thomson was the first non-Maori to actually explore the Mt Cook region. Five years later, Julius von Haast and Arthur Dobson spent four months exploring the rivers, valleys and glaciers of what is now the park.

Haast prepared a colourful account of their findings for the Canterbury Provincial Government. 'Nothing...' he wrote, '...can be compared with the scenery, which certainly has not its equal in the European Alps.'

Climbers soon staged a race to its peak. The first serious attempt was made in 1882 by Reverend William Green. He had seen photographs of Mt Cook and was so inspired that he convinced two Swiss guides to help him attempt the summit. Their first attempts, up an ice ridge from the south and then up a route along Ball Glacier, were unsuccessful.

They then turned their attention to the northern side and, following Haast Ridge, came within several hundred metres of the top before bad weather forced them back down. The three men spent a long night clinging to a narrow rock ledge at 3050 metres, listening to the boom of avalanches around them, and the next morning retreated to their base camp. They never reached the top, but encouraged others to climb the peak.

In 1894, Edward Fitzgerald, a famous English climber, announced his intention to scale Mt Cook. He left Europe with Italian guide Mattias Zurbriggen, but soon after he arrived he found three New Zealanders – Tom Fyfe, George Graham and Jack Clarke – had beaten him to it (at 3 am on Christmas Day 1894). Fitzgerald, infuriated, didn't climb Cook at all. Instead, he made the first ascent of peaks around the mountain – Sefton, Tasman and Haidinger.

The first Hermitage Hotel, built in 1884 near White Horse Hill (a fireplace is all that remains today), sparked interest in discovering an east-west route to the West Coast. In 1892, the Canterbury Provincial Government sent explorer and surveyor Charles Douglas to search for a pass over the Main Divide suitable for mule traffic. From the West Coast, Douglas went up the Copland Valley and explored several passes. He finally decided that the Copland Pass offered the best possibilities.

Fitzgerald and Zurbriggen made the first recorded crossing from east to west, in 1895, when they climbed what is now Fitzgerald Pass. They then spent three arduous days without supplies trying to find a way down the Copland Valley. Construction of the existing track began in 1910, and by 1913 the first Welcome Flats Hut was built. Its hot springs quickly made it a popular spot.

Climbs on Mt Cook continued to dominate the history of this region, giving the Hermitage the unique status and aura of adventure that it still enjoys today. Much easier routes were pioneered after the first ascent, which was not duplicated for 61 years. One by one, the faces of Mt Cook were climbed, including the South Ridge, in 1948, by a team of three headed by Sir Edmund Hillary. The last major approach, the hazardous Caroline Face, was finally ascended in 1970, by New Zealanders Peter Gough and John Glasgow.

CLIMATE

As might be expected, the weather in this region is harsh and extremely volatile. The Southern Alps form a major barrier to prevailing westerly wind and create their own climate. The annual rainfall in Mt Cook village is 4000 mm, and it rains an average of 149 days a year.

The park does experience spells of fine weather, but it is the long periods of foul weather for which it is most noted; visitors often leave disappointed at not having viewed 'the mountain', while many arranged treks over the Copland Pass never get further than the Hermitage Hotel.

Come prepared for strong winds, heavy rain and even snow, then rejoice if the skies clear and Mt Cook comes into view.

NATURAL HISTORY

The Mt Cook and Westland national parks are both part of the Te Wahipounamu world heritage region. They have diverse geography and geology, and an abundnace of flora & fauna. If you want to witness the incredi-

ble forces of nature at work, go to these back-to-back parks and see their massive glaciers and rivers carving through the valleys between the peaks.

On the Westland side, there are primeval rainforests, rata and beech higher up, and a profusion of ferns, shrubs and trees lower down. There are many lakes to explore on the narrow coastal plain and the soaring, ice-covered mountains provide a dramatic backdrop. The two glaciers, Fox and Franz Josef, appear to slice the forest in two as they push towards the sea.

If the weather permits, the scene on the eastern side of the Southern Alps is even more spectacular. Mounts Cook and Sefton dominate the skyline around Mt Cook village, and the Hooker and Tasman glaciers almost reach the settlement.

Distinctive flora of the subalpine and alpine regions include the Mt Cook lily, the New Zealand edelweiss and the mountain daisy. The birdlife is prolific, especially on the Westland side, and includes rare white heron (kotuku) crested glebe, morepork (ruru), kaka, parakeet, tui and the South Island brown and greater-spotted kiwi. Many keas are found around Mt Cook village.

For those wishing to explore the natural history of the region in greater depth, *The Alpine World of Mt Cook,* by Andy Dennis and Craig Potton, is an excellent resource. Visits to the DOC visitor centres in Mt Cook, Fox Glacier and Franz Josef will also enhance your enjoyment of the landscape.

COPLAND PASS

The complete Copland Pass trek, from the Hermitage to State Highway 6 on the West Coast, offers an incredible cross-section of New Zealand terrain, from glaciers and steep snowfields, to rock ridges, thermal pools and the lush rainforest on the western side.

This is usually a once-in-a-lifetime adventure that can only be completed under good conditions. For those who aren't properly prepared, it can turn into a life-threatening nightmare. This alpine area experiences sudden changes in weather, with heavy snow, rain or gales that can pin trampers down for days. If you question your own physical stamina or alpine experience, don't even consider crossing the Copland Pass. A modified one-night trip to the Welcome Flat Hut would be a much more enjoyable tramp.

The DOC offers this advice on the skills required to cross the Copland Pass:

A commonly asked question is 'How much experience is needed to cross the Copland Pass?' Our advice is: previous practical experience with the use of an ice axe is essential, eg methods for holding an ice axe while ascending a snow slope; support, brace and shaft dagger positions and self-arrest techniques. Also essential is previous experience at ascending steep snow slopes using zigzag technique and step kicking. Crampons may not be needed for every crossing, but it is essential that they are carried, and previous experience is necessary in correct fitting of crampons and French cramponing techniques. General experience in alpine route finding where there is no trail is also required.

At least half of your party should be experienced in the techniques outlined above – do not attempt the crossing alone unless you're very experienced. If you are seeking companions for the crossing, organise your group before departing from the village rather than trying to find someone at Hooker Hut. Make certain you know how experienced your companions are.

Information

All trampers attempting the Copland Pass must register their intentions at the visitor centre in Mt Cook (or Fox Glacier if crossing from the west). At the same time, check out current weather and track conditions. Make sure that you notify national park staff when you conclude the trip. There is a book at the western end of the track, at Karangarua, if you are heading south to Queenstown or Wanaka.

Mt Cook The National Park field centre (☎ 435 1819), open daily from 8 am to 5 pm, will advise you on all tramping routes. This is also the place to register your intentions, check the weather (which is recorded every day at 9 am) and pay hut fees.

Franz Josef Glacier The Franz Josef field centre (☎ 752 0796) is open from 8 am to 5 pm daily.

Fox Glacier The Fox Glacier field centre (☎ 751 0807) is open from 8.30 am to 4.30 pm daily. In the summer and during the holiday season, it's open much later.

There's a petrol station in the town – if you're driving south, this is the last fuel stop until you reach Haast, 120 km away.

Guides

If you feel that you don't have the experience required to cross the Copland, hire a guide. The Alpine Guides Mountain Shop (☎ 435 1834), open every day from 8 am to 5.30 pm, will advise on current conditions and costs. Since most parties employing a guide have considerable tramping experience, they usually hire a person for only 1½ days. The guide shepherds trampers up the dangerous part of the Hooker Valley to the Hooker Hut, leads you over the pass to safe ground (400 metres across on the West Coast side), and then returns to Mt Cook village with any equipment that was rented.

The cost of a trip that includes a guide, guide's food, hut fees at Hooker and equipment rental is $420 for one client and $290 per person for a party of two (one guide for two people is the maximum ratio). Experienced climbers can hire an ice axe and crampons for $55; these can be returned to Alpine Guides in Fox Glacier.

Maps

The 1:100,000 Parkmaps No 273-10 (*Mount Cook/Westland National Parks*) is sufficient if you are only hiking the valleys of the

Copland Pass track. For the entire pass crossing you need the 1:50,000 Topomaps quad H36 *(Mount Cook)* which covers the track from the village to Welcome Flats Hut. This quad can be purchased or hired from the visitor centre.

Huts

It costs $14 per night for Hooker Hut (Category One) and $8 a night for Douglas Rock and Welcome Flat huts in Westland (Category Two). You can pay hut fees at the Mt Cook or Fox Glacier visitor centres. There is no charge if you are forced to use the Copland Shelter in an emergency.

Equipment

Every person attempting the pass needs an ice axe (to assist climbing in snow) and crampons (in case the snow is too hard for boots to grip). To hold a fall if somebody slips, there should be one rope in every tramping party, and at least half the party should have the mountaineering experience to put in effective belays capable of holding a fall on snow or rock. Helmets are necessary in the section from Hooker Glacier terminal to Hooker Hut and on to the ridge leading up to the Copland Pass.

You can rent or buy just about any piece of climbing equipment from Alpine Guides, which also sells camping and tramping gear. Food supplies can be obtained from a small store just down the street from Alpine Guides, though it's cheaper to bring your own food.

Access

The Copland Pass walk begins in Mt Cook village and finishes at the end of the Copland Valley, on State Highway 6. Getting to Mt Cook is no problem – Mt Cook Landline (☎ 435 1849) has daily buses to Queenstown, Te Anau and Christchurch. Most of its services connect with the longer routes through Twizel, 70 km (an hour's drive) from Mt Cook. There are year-round daily buses, but in summer there are extra, more direct services, making travel quicker. From November to April, special excursion buses

run between Christchurch and Queenstown, or on day trips out of Christchurch; all stop at Mt Cook for about 3½ hours.

InterCity also has a daily Queenstown-Christchurch route with a 40-minute stop at Mt Cook. The Mt Cook and InterCity buses both stop at the front door of the Mt Cook YHA Hostel.

The Mt Cook field centre offers free storage, but most people who cross the Copland Pass arrive carrying only what they need for the trek to avoid an expensive return to the village.

On the West Coast, there is a northbound InterCity bus which passes the track end at around 3.30 pm daily and reaches Franz Josef at 4.40 pm. A southbound bus reaches the track end at around 9.10 am daily and arrives in Queenstown at 4.50 pm. There are additional summer services from Queenstown to the Copland or Franz Josef. A one-way fare from the track to Franz Josef or Fox Glacier, where there are a number of accommodation options, is about $20.

Along the West Coast, hitching prospects can be very bleak. If you're lucky, you might do Greymouth to Queenstown in three days – if you're not, you could well stand on the same spot for a couple of days.

From Greymouth, there are onward connections to Westport, Nelson, Picton and Christchurch.

Places to Stay

Mt Cook Camping is allowed at the White Horse Hill camping area at the old Hermitage site, the starting point for the Hooker Valley track, 1¾ km from Mt Cook village; it costs $3 per night. The excellent *Mt Cook YHA Hostel* (☎ 435 1820), on the corner of Bowen Drive and Kitchener Drive, gets crowded in the high season (December to April); beds cost $17 per night.

Franz Josef The *Franz Josef Holiday Park* (☎ 752 0766) is a km south of the township; tent sites are $7 per person and dorm beds are $8. The *Franz Josef Glacier YHA Hostel* (☎ 752 0754) at 2-4 Cron St, just off the main road, charges $14 a night for beds. Next door is the *Chateau Franz Josef Backpackers* (☎ 752 0738), where share rooms are $13.50 and tent sites are $6. On State Highway 6 is *Franz Josef Lodge – Backpackers* (☎ 752 0712); beds cost $14.50 in twins/quads.

Fox Glacier The *Fox Glacier Holiday Park* (☎ 751 0821) is 400 metres down the Lake Matheson Rd from the town centre; tent sites cost $7.75/15.50 for one/two people and bunks are $11. The *Ivory Towers* (☎ 751 0838) on Sullivans Rd charges $13.50.

The Track

Crossing the Copland Pass from east to west is strongly recommended because this is the easier and safer route to follow. The following description is a four-day trip, with nights spent at Hooker, Douglas Rock and Welcome Flats huts. To save a day, you can pass Douglas Rock and spend the second night at Welcome Flats. This trip is rated extremely difficult.

Stage 1: Mt Cook Village to Hooker Hut
Walking Time: three to four hours
Accommodation: Hooker Hut (12 bunks)

The first day was once an easy three-hour walk from Mt Cook village to Hooker Hut. This is no longer the case because there have been several wash outs in the streams draining the western side of the Hooker Glacier, and some are subject to periodic rock fall. Alpine Guides even encourage their clients to wear a climbing helmet in this section.

The track begins in front of the Hermitage Hotel on the Kea Point Nature Walk as a well-graded tourist path, before quickly branching off and passing White Horse Hill, half an hour from the hotel. It continues through old moraines towards Hooker River where, if the day is clear, Mt Cook dominates

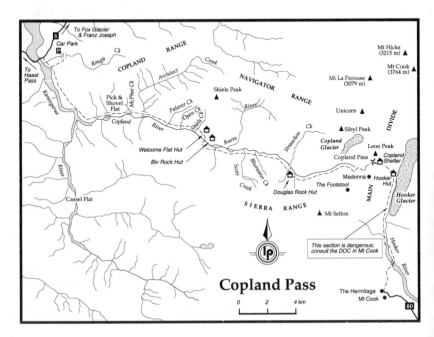

Copland Pass

Tramper admiring the view, Mt Aspiring National Park (JD)

Top Left: Routeburn Track, Otago (VB)
Top Right: Crossing Architect Creek, Copland Track (VB)
Bottom: Hooker Valley from Mueller Hut route, Mt Cook National Park (JD)

the valley. Eventually, the track reaches the Hooker River, crosses a swing bridge to its true left (east) side and then, in half an hour, crosses back over to the true right (west) side.

About 1½ km from the second bridge, the track reaches an alpine meadow; there is a shelter here, on the northern side of Stocking Stream. At this point, the track begins to climb, reaching the terminal lake of the Hooker Glacier – the end of the Hooker Valley Track – in half an hour.

A marked route takes over, following the beach for 150 metres. The route then heads diagonally uphill, crossing the rocky bed of a side stream. From here, rock cairns indicate the way and stretches of track appear as the well-defined route leads across a moraine terrace to a second side stream. This is an avalanche path in winter and spring, and since 1993-94 has been subject to rock fall in the wash outs (see earlier warnings).

The route crosses the gully and works its way up a terrace. Once across the terrace, the route zigzags through another side gully and a section of rocky scree before finally dropping to the grassy basin where the Hooker Hut is located. The hut has 12 bunks, but can be very busy and cramped during summer. It has kerosene cookers and fuel, lanterns, cooking utensils, a radio and a beautiful view of Mt Cook's southern face.

Stage 2: Hooker Hut to Douglas Rock Hut
Walking Time: 10 to 14 hours
Accommodation: Copland Shelter (emergency use only); Douglas Rock Hut (12 bunks)

Leave Hooker Hut early because the 1020-metre climb to the top of the pass takes three to six hours, depending on the fitness of the group. Most parties leave at 5 or 6 am and work steadily towards the Copland Pass, knowing that even clear weather can deteriorate in as little as two hours. Cloud and mist often blow in from the west during the afternoon, obscuring visibility.

The route, marked by rock cairns and poles at the beginning, heads up the valley, then climbs steeply along a deep rocky gully before crossing it. On the other side, a well-formed path descends slightly and then climbs to the main ridge to Copland Pass. Rock cairns indicate the way along the main ridge, through broken rock bands and scree slopes. It is safest to follow the ridge, though you will be exposed to steep drop-offs here. If conditions become icy on the ridge, you'll have to rope up and put on crampons before continuing.

The ridge is easy to follow to a step, 152 metres below the pass, where the Copland Shelter, an orange barrel-shaped emergency shelter, is located. The shelter has capacity for about four people and contains a sleeping platform (no mattresses) and a radio. It has no water. Use the shovel attached to the roof to gain access to the door if it's been snowing.

The hut is reached by most parties in about three hours and is often used as a rest stop for the second breakfast of the day. Beyond the shelter, the route to the pass is on permanent snow. The snow slope lies at an angle of about 35°, so parties should rope up before continuing. Usually, the snow is soft enough to 'kick' steps, but late in the summer it might become icy, so good cramponing techniques are needed to negotiate the pass safely.

The snow slope lies on the right of a rocky ridge that makes a line from the shelter towards the pass. The slope follows the ridge until it nears the top, then veers further right to the actual pass, a small notch in the Main Divide. It takes about an hour to travel from the shelter to Copland Pass (2150 metres). If the weather is clear, the view from 'the roof of New Zealand' is immense. To the south is the Tasman Valley, to the west is the Tasman Sea and all around are the peaks of the Southern Alps, dwarfed by the overpowering size of Mt Cook.

The descent into Copland Valley begins with a tricky 45-metre, steep rocky gully, which is sometimes coated in ice. Again, this is a section where many parties will rope up. The route continues through two rocky scree basins, often filled with snow. Keep towards the bottom of the basins. The second will run into the rocky gully of a stream. A well-defined track begins on the true left of the stream, at about 1300 metres.

This track, marked by rock cairns, wanders through tussock to large rocks and a waterfall. It then follows a series of switchbacks to the head of the Copland Valley, crossing a number of avalanche gullies before reaching the bush-line. Five minutes after entering the bush, you arrive at Douglas Rock Hut, having completed a 1430-metre descent from the pass. Douglas Rock Hut has platform bunks, a potbelly stove with coal, and a radio link to the Westland National Park headquarters, providing trampers with weather reports every morning.

Stage 3: Douglas Rock Hut to Welcome Flat Hut
Walking Time: two to three hours
Accommodation: Welcome Flat Hut (30 bunks)

The easy eight-km walk to Welcome Flat Hut takes most trampers only two to three hours. But after the hard climb over Copland Pass, many find a short hike and a long afternoon in the hot springs the ideal way to spend the next day. The well-defined track leaves Douglas Rock Hut, almost immediately crosses a bridge over Tekano Stream, then works its way through forest around a ridge. It follows a broken Copland River and crosses a number of open slips before descending to Scott Creek. Under normal conditions, the creek is easy to ford.

The track continues on the other side, where it breaks out into the open tussock of Welcome Flat. This pleasant area along the river is surrounded by peaks and snowfields. It's not hard to justify an extended break here, even though you're less than an hour from the hut. The flats are marked with rock cairns that lead back into bush, and in half an hour the track arrives at a swing bridge. The hut is on the true right (north) side of the river.

Welcome Flat Hut, built in 1986, is an excellent facility, offering a potbelly stove with coal, a radio, and enough platform bunks to accommodate about 30 people. In summer, there is usually a warden stationed here.

Nearby are the hot pools first noted by Charles Douglas in 1896. The water emerges from the ground at 60°C and flows through a series of pools towards the Copland River. Most bathers prefer the second pool. A midnight soak on a clear evening is one of the highlights of this trip; weary hikers can lie back in the heated water and count the falling stars streaking across the sky.

Stage 4: Welcome Flat Hut to State Highway 6 Car Park
Walking Time: six hours

The track climbs for one km through a ribbonwood forest, first crossing Foam Creek, to the high point of the day. It then makes a quick descent to the bridge across Shiels Creek. It's another 25-minute descent to Open Creek and the next footbridge, and an even shorter walk to Palaver Creek, where you cross the third bridge of the day. You continue to descend gradually, in two km reaching a swing bridge over Architect Creek, a 300-metre drop from the Welcome Flat Hut.

The track swings towards the river's edge after crossing Architect Creek, forcing trampers to hop from one large boulder to another. From here, the track alternates from the river bed to the bush. Trampers should keep an eye out for the orange markers where the track enters the forest again. It's a km from Architect Creek to the bridge over McPhee Creek, then another two km to a bridge over an unnamed stream, which drains the Copland Range to the north.

The track eventually departs from the Copland River and crosses a forested terrace to a side track that leads to a view of the confluence between the Copland and Karangarua rivers. The track, now well graded, continues in a forest of rimu and totara for two km, until it emerges onto open river flats. Poles mark the route across the flats where, on the other side, the track enters the forest for a short distance before coming to Rough Creek. There is a footbridge half an hour upstream, but normally the creek can be easily forded. (Note that the river valley can flood easily. There is a signposted high-level track through the bush which you can follow when the flats are under water. This track, though muddy in places, is the only alternative in wet conditions.)

The car park is on the other side of Rough Creek (don't forget to sign out in the intentions book), and from here it's 200 metres to State Highway 6. Time your arrival to coincide with transport because the sandflies are voracious – fighting them off for hours may well be the memory you take away from this magnificent tramp.

MUELLER HUT

A round-trip walk to Mueller Hut can be done in a single day, but to fully appreciate the scenic setting of the hut and its unique mountain character, a night should be spent on the alpine ridge. Mueller Hut also makes it possible to venture away from the bustling village and into the mountains unencumbered by mountaineering equipment and without the many complications of the Copland Pass.

Information

For sources of information on this walk, see Information for the Copland Pass. Before heading out in the morning, stop at the national park visitor centre to read the weather forecast for the day. Also, register your intentions here and pay your hut fees. See the Places to Stay and Access sections of the Copland Pass for accommodation and transport information.

Maps

The best map for this trek is the 1:50,000 Topomaps quad H36 *(Mount Cook)*, which can be purchased at the Mt Cook visitor centre for $12.50.

Huts

There is only one hut on this walk – Mueller Hut ($14 per night).

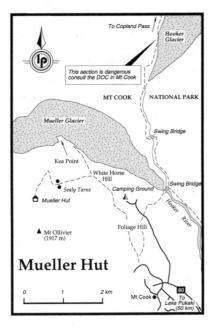

Mueller Hut

Equipment

Many trampers take an ice axe on this walk, though crampons and rope are usually unnecessary during summer. Experienced trampers can easily handle this overnight trek, but keep in mind that this is still an alpine trip and should not be undertaken in poor weather.

See the Copland Pass section for information on renting equipment or purchasing supplies in Mt Cook village.

The Track

This five-hour trip is rated difficult because it involves a steep climb. The return trip, along the same track, takes three hours.

Stage 1: Hermitage to Mueller Hut

Walking Time: five hours in good conditions
Accommodation: Mueller Hut (12 bunks)

The trip begins at the Hermitage Hotel on the Kea Point Nature Walk, a very level and well-maintained path that heads up the open scrub of Hooker Valley towards White Horse Hill. Within half an hour, you pass Foliage Hill; you'll see two lodges and the camping ground shelter near the base of White Horse Hill. The track begins to climb gently, moves into bush and comes to the signposted junction of the Sealy Tarns Track. Kea Point is to the north (right fork), a 15-minute walk away. The side trip is worth it because the viewpoint is on an old lateral moraine above Mueller Glacier, with Mt Sefton overhead.

The route to Mueller Hut continues west (left fork) on the Sealy Tarns Track. It's a two-hour climb to the tarns, a knee-bender at times but not that difficult because the track has been improved recently. As soon as you begin climbing, you are greeted with excellent views of the lower end of the Hooker Valley to the south, including Mt Cook village. Higher still, there are views of the upper portions of the valley, and the Mueller Glacier. The tarns, a series of small pools, make a natural rest stop because they are located on the ridge in a narrow meadow of alpine shrubs, grasses and herbs.

Just south of the tarns, look for a huge rock cairn that marks the route continuing to Mueller Hut. It begins as a well-worn track that involves a lot of scrambling, then eventually fades out altogether on a slope of rocky scree. At this point, more rock cairns mark the way over boulders towards a large orange and black pole – impossible to miss on a clear day. Take your time hopping from one boulder to the next to avoid any mishap.

Once at the pole, the route swings around to head in a more northerly direction, then continues towards the end of the ridge. This section is often covered by snow – an ice axe may come in handy. It's a 20-minute scramble up the snow or scree slope to the end, from which there are excellent views of the upper portion of the Mueller Glacier and the peaks of the Main Divide. Rock cairns continue around the side of the ridge and lead south for about 20 minutes to the hut, on the crest of the ridge. Keep a sharp eye out for the hut because trampers can miss its orange roof.

The original hut was built in 1914-15, closer to Kea Point than to the top of the ridge. It was replaced in 1950 but was almost immediately destroyed by an avalanche. The present hut, at 1800 metres, has gas rings and a radio. Needless to say, the views are excellent, including not only the namesake glacier below but, if you are blessed with clear weather, the peaks of the Main Divide, crowned by Mt Cook. It's possible to scramble up Mt Ollivier (1917 metres) – the first peak Sir Edmund Hillary climbed – which commands an even better panorama of the area.

Otago

Otago is a large province with a range of landscapes in its sweep from the sea, across the old gold fields, to the majestic alpine region of Mt Aspiring. All the walks described in this chapter lie completely or partially in the Mt Aspiring National Park – a raw yet beautiful environment. However, these walks only scratch the surface of tramping possibilities, and the ardent tramper could find many adventures in between.

Mt Aspiring National Park

Mt Aspiring National Park is a fitting end to the Southern Alps. It has wide, rounded valleys with secluded flats, more than 100 glaciers, and mountain ranges with peaks of over 2700 metres, including 3027-metre Mt Aspiring, the tallest mountain in New Zealand outside Mt Cook National Park.

The park is more than 355,518 hectares, stretching from the Haast River in the north to the Humboldt Mountains in the south, where it has a common border with Fiordland National Park. The park is now part of the Te Wahipounamu world heritage region, which includes Mt Cook, Westland and Fiordland national parks.

From a tramper's point of view, the national park has a split personality. Although this is the country's third largest park, most trampers walk only the small portion around Glenorchy. Within this region, there are several popular tracks, including the Routeburn – second only to the Abel Tasman Coast Track as the most heavily used trail in New Zealand. This three-day walk draws over 10,000 trampers a year, most of whom walk the track sometime between November and March.

The Routeburn is a tramp over the Main Divide from the Milford Rd (in Eglinton Valley) to the lower portion of the Dart Valley. It passes through thick rainforest with red, mountain and silver beech forming the canopy and ferns, mosses and fungi covering everything below like wall-to-wall carpeting. But it's the alpine sections that most appeal to trampers. The tranquillity of a tussock meadow sprinkled with giant buttercup and flowering Spaniard, and the dramatic views of entire valleys or mountain ranges are ample rewards for the steep hikes and the frequent encounters with other trampers.

The other tracks in this area are not nearly as busy, but draw large numbers of trampers during the summer. The Greenstone, a two-day walk renowned for its trout fishing, is a relatively level walk that draws between 2000 and 3000 hikers a year; it is often combined with the Routeburn to form a circular walk. Nearby is the Caples Track, a two-day walk which shares Greenstone's starting and finishing points. It crosses open river flats of tussock grass along rivers with clear pools and rippling currents, and it's often possible to spot trout lying in their holes.

North of Glenorchy is the Rees-Dart Track. This is a walk along the valleys of the Dart and Rees rivers, which are joined by the Rees Saddle. The Dart River separates the Forbes Mountains from the Southern Alps on the west, while the Rees River separates them from the Richardson Range on the east. Both rivers drain into the head of Lake Wakatipu. The four to five-day trip is more difficult than the other three Glenorchy tracks but still draws about 1500 trampers a year.

In contrast to the popularity of the Glenorchy region, the other tramping areas of the national park, near the towns of Wanaka and Makarora, are little used. While the Routeburn draws more than 10,000 trampers a year, the equally beautiful Wilkin Valley, near Makarora, is walked by only about 700. Much the same is true of the West and East Matukituki valleys. These areas offer spectacular alpine scenery and more challenging trips, but far fewer encounters with other people. The Wilkin-Young Valleys Circuit is a three-day trip that involves bush tracks, grassed valleys and a climb over the 1490-metre Gillespie Pass.

Near Wanaka, there is the challenging but scenic Cascade Saddle Route – a two to three-day walk along the West Branch of the Matukituki River, over the 1500-metre pass and along Dart Glacier to the mid-point of the Rees-Dart Track. The entire trip, from the West Matukituki Valley to the end of the Rees-Dart Track, is a four to five-day journey whose alpine beauty, many trampers believe, is unmatched even by the Routeburn or Milford tracks.

HISTORY

There are traces of a Maori village at the mouth of the Routeburn, oven sites at the point where the Matukituki meets Lake Wanaka, and a moa-hunting site near Glenorchy. But the real value of this area to the Maoris was as a trade route between South Westland and Central Otago, and as a source of pounamu (greenstone), which was highly valued for tools and weapons.

Maori expeditions in search of greenstone are said to have been conducted as late as 1850 – about the same time the first Europeans began exploring the region. The veil of obscurity over the upper Wakatipu area was first lifted by W G Rees. In September 1860, after establishing his sheep station near Queenstown, he sailed to the head of Lake Wakatipu and discovered the Rees and Dart rivers draining into it.

In 1861, David McKellar and George Gunn, part explorers and part pastoralists, shed some light on the Greenstone Valley when they struggled up the river and climbed one of the peaks near Lake Howden. What they saw was the entire Hollyford Valley, but they mistakenly identified it as the George Sound in Fiordland. The great Otago gold rush began later that year, and by 1862 miners were digging around the lower regions of the Dart and Rees as well as in the Routeburn Valley.

Prospector Patrick Caples made a solo journey up the Greenstone from Lake Wakatipu in 1863, and discovered the Harris Saddle before descending into the Hollyford Valley and Martins Bay. Caples returned through the valley that now bears his name, ending a three-month odyssey in which he became the first European to reach the Tasman Sea from Wakatipu.

It was not until late in the nineteenth century that the first European crossed the Barrier Range from Cattle Flat on the Dart to a tributary of the Arawata River. William O'Leary, an Irish prospector better known as 'Arawata Bill' roamed the mountains and valleys of this area and much of the Hollyford River for 50 years, searching out various metals and enjoying the solitude of the open, desolate places.

Mountaineering and a thriving local tourist trade began developing in the 1890s, and by the early 1900s it was booming, even by today's standards. Hotels sprang up in Glenorchy, along with guiding companies who advertised trips up the Rees Valley by horse and buggy. Sir Thomas Mackenzie, Minister of Tourism, pushed for the construction of the Routeburn trail and hired Harry Birley of Glenorchy to establish a route. In 1912, Birley 'discovered' Lake Mackenzie, and the next year began cutting a track.

The famous track reached Lake Howden by the outbreak of WW I, but the final portion wasn't completed until the road from Te Anau to Milford Sound was built by relief workers during the Depression – until then a tramp on the Routeburn had meant returning on the Greenstone.

The first move to make Mt Aspiring a national park came in 1935, but for all its beauty and popularity with trampers and tourists, the park wasn't officially preserved until 1964. Some valleys, such as the Greenstone, Caples and much of the Rees, still lie outside the park, with little protection from road-building enthusiasts.

CLIMATE

Weather varies dramatically from one end of

Mt Aspiring National Park to the other. A rain gauge just west of the Homer Tunnel (actually Fiordland National Park) measures 7110 mm a year, while Glenorchy, 34 km to the east, receives only 1140 mm annually.

In general, the Routeburn, the Dart River valley and the western half of the Greenstone and Caples tracks receive about 5000 mm of rain a year, and there is the possibility of snow above the 1000-metre level in almost any month. But the lower Rees, Matukituki and Wilkin valleys are considerably drier, receiving an annual average of about 1500 mm. The old homestead at Mt Aspiring Station, where the mean annual rainfall is 2940 mm, once recorded 330 mm in 26 hours!

The weather tends to be more settled from late December to March, and February is often suggested as the best month for walking. But keep in mind that the park is a typical alpine region and you must be prepared for sudden changes in weather and unexpected storms regardless of what month it is.

In spring and early summer, there is considerable chance of avalanches in the valley heads and on the steeper slopes; check with the park authorities in Wanaka, Makarora, Glenorchy and Queenstown. To tramp any track but the Greenstone outside the months of November to May requires much experience and special equipment.

NATURAL HISTORY

The landscapes of the park are predominantly of glacial origin. During the ice ages, massive glaciers carved into the metamorphic and sedimentary rock. Evidence of this glaciation is everywhere. A huge glacier carved the side of the Darran Mountains and over Key Summit, and fingers of it pushed to lakes Wakatipu and Te Anau via the Greenstone and Eglinton valleys.

When the glaciers retreated, they left a sculpted landscape of U-shaped valleys, small hanging valleys and rounded cirques and ridges. The park's mountains still contain over 100 glaciers, ranging from the large Bonar to the smaller ones which hang from the sides of the Matukituki valley.

Much of the park is predominantly silver beech, with red and mountain beech in the southern half. This makes for semi-open forests and easy tramping in most valleys, unlike in the Fiordland forests, where you rarely step off the track because of the thick understorey. West of The Divide, there is rainforest of rimu, matai, miro and kahikatea. Between the valleys are mountain meadows that support one of the greatest ranges of alpine plants in the world. There are a number of bog communities in the area around Key Summit.

In alpine areas, there are beautiful clusters of snow berry *(Pernettya)* and coprosma in subalpine turf. In the Routeburn Valley, look for mountain daisies, snow grass and veronica. Other beautiful plants of this region are *Ranunculus buchanani* and New Zealand edelweiss.

The forests are alive with native birds – riflemen, bellbirds, fantails and pigeons. In alpine areas, you may be lucky enough to see the diminutive rock wren and, along the rivers, blue (whio) and paradise ducks.

ROUTEBURN TRACK

Combine the well-cut track with the great alpine views and the notoriety the Routeburn enjoys in tramping and travel literature and you have the reason why more than 10,000 people walk the track every year, the vast majority between December and February. Overseas visitors who tackle only one track during their stay, usually walk the Routeburn.

During most of the summer, the huts along the track are so full that many trampers are thankful just to get a spot on the floor. There is also a constant flow of foot traffic between huts, and usually a small gathering at Harris Saddle. You put up with the large numbers of people because the mountain scenery is truly exceptional, or you go somewhere else to tramp.

It is rumoured that a booking system may be introduced on this track, with numbers limited to fit the availability of accommodation.

Information

The Queenstown DOC field centre (☎ 442 7933; fax 442 7932) is at 37 Shotover St, opposite the Trust Bank (there's also one in Ballarat St). It's open from 9 am to 4.30 pm Monday to Friday all year round, and also from 10 am to 3 pm on Saturday and Sunday from mid-December to mid-February.

The Information & Track Walking Centre (☎ 442 9708) is also on Shotover St. It arranges bookings for the Routeburn, Greenstone, Caples and Rees-Dart tracks, and also for the Kepler and Milford tracks – see the following Southland chapter. It's open from 8 am to 8 pm in summer (until 7 pm in winter).

In Glenorchy, there is a field and visitor centre (☎ 442 9937) on the corner of Mull and Oban Sts. The centre is open daily during the summer.

Maps

The best map is the 1:75,000 Trackmaps No 335-02 *(Routeburn Track)*. Another option is to use the 1:150,000 Parkmaps No 273-02 *(Mt Aspiring National Park)*.

Huts

Between late October and mid-May, the four huts on the Routeburn Track – Routeburn Flats, Routeburn Falls, Mackenzie and Howden – are well serviced. All the huts have gas rings for cooking, as well as a wood or coal stove. During these months, they are also very crowded.

Bunks cost $14 a night, because this is a Great Walk, and there are hut wardens who check to see that you have a Great Walks hut pass. Unlike the Milford Track, bunks cannot be reserved, and you still have to pay whether you end up with a mattress or a spot on the floor.

Camping is allowed at Routeburn Flats (50 sites, $6), Lake Mackenzie (nine sites, $6) and 20 minutes away from Lake Howden (15 free sites). It's a good idea to camp because the huts are notoriously crowded and will remain so until a permit system is introduced.

Overnight use of the Harris Shelter and track-end huts is not permitted – strange how they always seem to be full with packs, humans and smelly socks.

Equipment

Most equipment can be bought or rented in Queenstown. It's also possible to outfit your trip in Glenorchy, where there is a store with an excellent selection of tramping food – freeze-dried dinners, noodles, cereal and fresh fruit – at prices not much higher than those you'd pay in Queenstown.

Access

The track can be hiked in either direction, and there is now a variety of public transport going to each end. Most trampers pass through Queenstown and begin the track from the Glenorchy side, ending up at The Divide, where they can catch transport to Te Anau (after first viewing Milford Sound) or back to Queenstown. Alternatively, you can loop back to the Glenorchy side of the Humboldt Mountains by walking either the Greenstone or the Caples tracks.

To Queenstown This is the central point for New Zealand's best tramping region. Air New Zealand, Mt Cook Airlines and Ansett New Zealand all fly into Queenstown. Mt Cook Airline (☎ 442 7650) has daily direct flights to Auckland, Christchurch, Dunedin, Te Anau, Milford Sound, Wanaka, Mt Cook, Nelson and Rotorua, with additional connecting flights from Christchurch to Wellington, Auckland and Nelson. Ansett New Zealand (☎ 442 6161) has daily direct flights to Christchurch with connections to Wellington, Auckland and Rotorua. Air New Zealand operates one daily jet service on the Christchurch-Queenstown route.

There are a number of bus options. The InterCity booking office (☎ 442 7420) is on the corner of Shotover and Camp Sts, next to the visitor information centre. Mt Cook Landline buses leave from the depot on Church St (☎ 442 7650). Great Sights Gray Line buses (☎ 442 7028) depart from the Mt Cook Landline depot. Backpacker Express (☎ 442 9940) departs from the Information

& Track Walking Centre on Shotover St, but will pick you up anywhere in Queenstown.

InterCity has several daily routes to and from Queenstown. The route to Christchurch (10 hours) goes via Mt Cook village (4¼ hours). Other routes are to Te Anau (2½ hours) and Milford Sound (five hours), Invercargill (3½ hours) and Dunedin (5¼ hours).

InterCity also has a daily West Coast service to the West Coast glaciers via Wanaka and the Haast Pass, taking two hours to Wanaka, 7½ hours to Fox Glacier and eight hours to Franz Josef Glacier. If you want to continue up the coast from the glaciers, you have to stay overnight at Fox or Franz Josef. It takes a minimum of two days (longer if you want to see more than a bus window) to get up the West Coast to Nelson.

If you want to go up the coast to Nelson by bus, the best alternatives are probably the backpacker buses (West Coast Express, Kiwi Experience or Flying Kiwi), particularly if you have the time and you want to get out and see things.

Mt Cook Landline also has several bus routes from Queenstown, with daily buses to Christchurch, Wanaka, Mt Cook village and Te Anau. From November to April, it has a special daily bus service to Christchurch which includes a 3½-hour stopover at Mt Cook village.

Several companies have buses to Milford via Te Anau, including InterCity and Fiordland Travel. For an interesting variation on travel to Milford Sound from Queenstown, see MV *Wanderer* in the Milford Sound section of the Southland chapter.

Queenstown End The Backpacker Express (☎ 442 9939; fax 442 9940) runs to and from the Routeburn, Greenstone, Caples, and Rees-Dart tracks, all via Glenorchy. Approximate prices for the Backpackers Express are:

- Queenstown to the Routeburn $20
- Queenstown to the Greenstone/Caples $25
- Queenstown to the Rees $22
- Queenstown to Glenorchy $10

- Glenorchy to the Rees $12
- Glenorchy to the Greenstone/Caples $15
- Dart to Glenorchy $12
- Greenstone/Caples to Glenorchy $15

If you are taking a Fun Yak trip as a conclusion to the Rees-Dart Track, transport back to Queenstown is included.

The Divide/Te Anau End There is trampers' transport between The Divide, Te Anau and Milford during the summer, with bus frequency scheduled according to demand – enquire at the Te Anau DOC visitor centre because operators come and go as frequently as the rain.

There are also InterCity, Mt Cook Landline and Fiordland Travel buses from Te Anau via The Divide to Milford and back every day. Check the latest schedule details so that you know what time to expect the bus. Transport to Glade House, on the Milford Track, departs from Te Anau.

It's possible to hitch to the track from Te Anau (you have to leave in the morning) or Milford (leave early morning or mid-afternoon). Hitching out is much easier, leaving early morning to Milford, mid-afternoon to Te Anau; the object is to connect with people driving up to Milford from Te Anau for the day.

Places to Stay

Queenstown This is very much the hub of this region, and if you are tramping you will not be able to avoid at least one night in town. Contact the Queenstown visitor information centre/InterCity Travel (☎ 442 8238), on the corner of Shotover and Camp Sts, for accommodation information. The office is open from 7 am to 7 pm daily. There's a DOC camp site at 12-Mile Creek Reserve, Glenorchy Rd, just five km from Queenstown.

Glenorchy This is a small town, with a limited choice of places to stay. The *Glenorchy Holiday Park* (☎ 442 9939), 2 Oban St, offers camping and transport to various walking tracks. Camp sites are $6 per person, cabins and hostel beds are $12 per person.

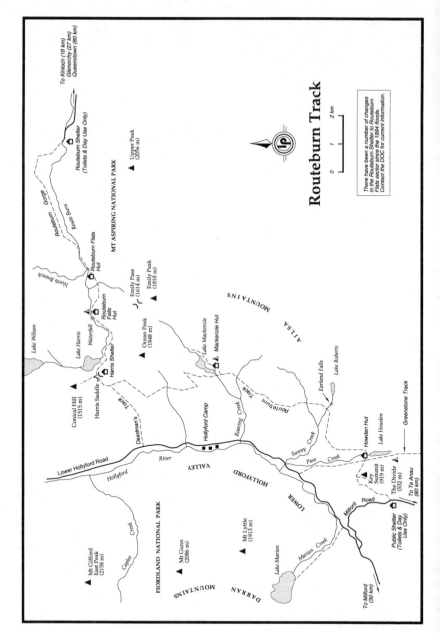

Routeburn Track

The Glenorchy Hotel offers backpackers accommodation in the *Glenorchy Backpackers Retreat* (☎ 442 9902), where a bed costs between $13 and $15 per night. The *Glenorchy Cafe* is the local hang-out for trampers; it serves freshly baked bread, organic salads and vegetables, and home-cooked meals.

The Track
The Routeburn is a classic alpine crossing over the Humboldt Mountains to The Divide on the Milford Rd. Most trampers take three days to walk the 39 km, but leave an extra day in case foul weather holds them up between the Routeburn Falls Hut and Lake Mackenzie or obscures the panoramic alpine views enjoyed along this stretch. The track is rated easy to medium.

The following description starts from the end of the track just north of Kinloch and finishes at The Divide on the Milford Rd. One possibility for those who want to do a round trip on the Routeburn is to hike from Lake Mackenzie back to Routeburn Flats via Emily Pass. This is a difficult, poorly marked route with stretches of unmarked bush and scrub. Interested trampers should consult the DOC staff at Glenorchy or the hut warden at Lake Mackenzie before attempting it.

There is a considerable amount of climbing to do on the Routeburn because you have to cross the Harris Saddle (1277 metres). But the track itself is well benched and graded; in fact it's surprisingly wide in many places, and difficult to lose.

The two most popular places to spend the nights are Routeburn Falls and Lake Mackenzie, two huts located near the bush-line. The route between them is the most spectacular section of the walk, so it's a shame to see some people hustling through just to get a bunk at the next hut. You can completely avoid the huts by camping, but you are pretty much restricted to the camp sites at Routeburn Flats, the nine at Lake Mackenzie and the site 20 minutes from Lake Howden.

The Routeburn Falls Hut, which has only 30 bunks, is a bottleneck and is seemingly always crowded. To ease the problem, the Routeburn Flats Hut was recently upgraded

Great Walks Ticket

to encourage more trampers to spend the night here. The views from the hut are not as dramatic as those from the porch of the Routeburn Falls Hut, but it's only a 1½-hour walk between the two.

In 1994, the track was severely damaged by slips and wash outs. It may mean the track between Routeburn Shelter and Routeburn Flats has been rerouted – check with the DOC at Glenorchy or Queenstown. The track between these points was closed for most of the 1994 season, so it may vary slightly from the following description.

Stage 1: Routeburn Shelter to Routeburn Falls
Walking Time: four hours
Accommodation: Routeburn Flats (20 bunks); Routeburn Falls (30 bunks)

Routeburn Shelter is next to the car park where the buses drop trampers off. From here, the track crosses the Route Burn on a swing bridge to its true left (north) bank and winds a km through forest of red, silver and mountain beech to a footbridge over Sugarloaf Stream. Once across the stream, the track climbs gently for 20 minutes until it reaches another bridge, over Bridal Veil Stream, and then begins to sidle Routeburn Gorge.

The track follows the narrow valley around the gorge and then breaks out onto beech and grass flats before crossing a swing bridge over the Route Burn and emerging onto Routeburn Flats, 6½ km from the shelter. From the flats, you can clearly see Routeburn Falls Hut up the valley, just above the bush-line at 1005 metres. It's an easy half-hour stroll through the flats to a junction where the right-hand fork leads to Routeburn Flats Hut, a 20-bunk facility.

The main track (the left-hand fork) begins a sharp ascent towards Routeburn Falls Hut. The track covers 270 metres over three km (about 1½ hours) before reaching the hut above the bush-line. The verandah of this hut offers spectacular views of the flats and the surrounding Humboldt Mountains. There is no camping around this hut, and the wardens are strict about enforcing the rule. If all the bunks are taken (normally the case), trampers either sleep on the floor, double up on bunks or return to Routeburn Flats, an hour's walk going down.

Stage 2: Routeburn Falls to Lake Mackenzie

Walking Time: four to five hours
Accommodation: Lake Mackenzie Hut (53 bunks)

Right behind the hut are the impressive Routeburn Falls, tumbling down a series of rock ledges. A series of orange snow poles indicates the track, which cuts across an alpine basin to begin a steady climb to the outlet of Lake Harris. The track passes a square rock, ascends sharply, and arrives at Lake Harris. The lake takes away any other thought (even of sore legs), especially on a clear day, when the water reflects everything around it.

The track works its way around the lake along bluffs and moraines. You get a second jolt 1½ hours from the hut, when you sight the grassy meadows of Harris Saddle. From this 1277-metre vantage point, the entire Hollyford Valley comes into view, all the way to Martins Bay if the weather is clear. If you are blessed with such weather, drop the packs and climb the side track to Conical Hill, about an hour's round trip. The 360° view from the 1515-metre peak includes the Darran Mountains, Richardson Range (in Otago) and the Hollyford Valley.

There is an emergency shelter on Harris Saddle, which is a popular place for tea and lunch. From here, the track descends a stone gully, then turns sharply south. The narrow stretch of track which follows clings to the Hollyford Face of the ridge high above the bush-line – the best part of the trip. Make sure you keep to the track because the areas on either side are very fragile.

After half an hour, the track arrives at the junction with Deadman's Track, an extremely steep route to the floor of the Hollyford Valley (five hours). The immense views continue, and two km from the junction with Deadman's Track the track passes an emergency rock bivvy. The rock is huge, but should not be used as a way to avoid hut fees or a crowded hut at Lake Mackenzie.

Two hours from the saddle, the track ascends and rounds a spur to Lake Mackenzie, a jewel set in a small, green mountain valley. The track zigzags down to the lake, dropping sharply for the final 300 metres. It then skirts the bush and arrives at Lake Mackenzie Hut, a two-storey hut with a spiral staircase.

Camping is tightly restricted (to nine sites) around the lake because of the fragile nature of the ground and alpine plants. Trampers should also remember that the lake doesn't have a conventional outlet, so if you wash yourself or your clothes in it, the soap will be seen for weeks or months.

Stage 3: Lake Mackenzie to The Divide

Walking Time: four hours
Accommodation: Lake Howden Hut (28 bunks)

The track begins in front of the hut, passes a private hut and cuts across a tussock meadow. It then climbs for an hour to a bridge over a branch of Roaring Creek. The climb is to make up for the height lost in the descent to Lake Mackenzie, and at one point the track breaks out of the trees to fine views of the Hollyford Valley and the Darran Mountains on the other side.

A further hour from Roaring Creek, the track arrives at the thundering Earland Falls, an ideal spot for an extended break. The spray will fog up camera lenses and quickly cool off any overheated trampers. If it's raining, the falls will be twice as powerful so use the nearby swing bridge to cross the flooded stream.

The track steadily descends and in three km emerges at Lake Howden and a major track junction. The Routeburn Track is straight ahead (west); the Greenstone track is the left fork (south-east); and the right fork (north-west) is a route to Hollyford Rd used by trampers heading directly to the Hollyford Track. You can either stay at the split-level Howden Hut on the shores of the beautiful lake or camp at the far end of the lake by following the Greenstone Track.

The Routeburn Track swings past the flanks of Key Summit and in 15 minutes comes to a junction. The 30-minute side trip (left fork) to the top is worth it on a clear day, if you're not racing down to catch a bus – from the 919-metre summit, you can see the Hollyford, Greenstone and Eglinton valleys.

From the side track, the Routeburn Track descends steadily to the bush, where thick rainforest resumes, before reaching The Divide, the lowest east-west crossing of the Southern Alps. It's three km (about an hour's walk) from Lake Howden to The Divide, where there is a car park, and a shelter for those waiting for the bus.

GREENSTONE TRACK

The Greenstone and Caples valleys are linked by McKellar Saddle. The Greenstone and Caples tracks are described separately in this chapter but can easily be linked together to make a four to five-day trip.

This two to three-day walk is the antithesis of the Routeburn. Some trampers just

coming from the dramatic alpine scenery of the Routeburn or Milford feel let down by the Greenstone, but most find it a pleasant change from the crowds of the more popular track. The Greenstone is an historic trail and at one time was the only way to return to Lake Wakatipu from the Routeburn. It runs from Lake Howden to Elfin Bay along the almost dead-flat valley of the Greenstone River, which is why the tramp is rated easy.

Although more and more people tramp the Greenstone every year, especially now that there is good public transport to the Greenstone car park, the walk is still nowhere near as popular as the Routeburn.

Anglers will enjoy this track because the Greenstone River is renowned for its brown and rainbow trout, which average somewhere between $1\frac{1}{2}$ and three kg. Access to the river's pools and holes is very good because the track remains quite close to the Greenstone from Lake McKellar to near its mouth at Lake Wakatipu.

Information

From Lake Howden to Lake McKellar, the Greenstone lies in the Fiordland National Park, but the majority of the track is in Wakatipu Forest, which forms the southern border of Mt Aspiring National Park.

Intentions can be registered and information obtained from the DOC Queenstown visitor centre (☎ 442 7933), Glenorchy field centre (☎ 442 9937) or Te Anau field centre (☎ 249 7921).

Giardia is present in the area, so boil or sterilise all drinking water. Always use the hut toilet.

Maps

The best map is the 1:75,000 Trackmaps No 335-02 *(Routeburn Track)*.

Huts

There are two Category Two huts on the Greenstone (Mid Greenstone and McKellar); both are $8 per night. The other hut, Sly Burn, is a Category Three ($4). The Category Two huts both have coal fires, and all three huts have mattresses and running water. Hut fees can be paid at the Glenorchy field centre or at the Queenstown field centre. Wardens are present from late October until mid-April, and will check for back-country hut tickets.

Access

Backpacker Express (☎ 442 9939; fax 442 9940) supplies transport between the Greenstone car park and Glenorchy, a 40-km trip along a dirt road. The service is provided on request, but turns out to be a daily run most of the summer. If the road is blocked for any reason (as it was in 1994 after the floods), they operate a water-taxi from Glenorchy to the Greenstone Bay wharf, on the western side of Wakatipu.

The western end of the track is at Lake Howden Hut, on the Routeburn Track, and transport can be picked up from The Divide on the Te Anau to Milford highway (see the Access section of the Routeburn Track).

Places to Stay

For accommodation in Glenorchy and Queenstown, see the Places to Stay section for the Routeburn Track. For Places to Stay in Te Anau and Milford, see the Places to Stay section for the Milford Track (in the Southland chapter).

The Track

The track, rated easy, can be walked in either direction but is described here going from west to east. See the Routeburn Track description for details of the walk from The Divide to Lake Howden Hut.

Trampers planning to loop back on the Greenstone from the Routeburn can easily walk from Mackenzie Hut to Lake McKellar, a 5½ to six-hour day. Two more days would be needed to complete the track, with a six-hour walk to Mid Greenstone Hut on the first day and then a 6½-hour tramp out to the car park. The Greenstone can also be combined with the Caples (see the next walk) to form a four-day loop.

Stage 1: Lake Howden to McKellar Hut

Walking Time: three hours from The Divide; two hours from Lake Howden
Accommodation: McKellar Hut (20 bunks)

Take the southern fork at the signposted junction near Lake Howden Hut and follow the western side of the beautiful lake. In 20 minutes, the track passes the camp sites at the southern end of the lake. It then leaves the lake and gently climbs to the Greenstone Saddle, though few trampers realise when they have reached the low pass. Less than an hour from Lake Howden Hut, the track emerges onto a grassy flat to the signposted junction to the McKellar Saddle and Caples Track.

The Greenstone Track heads south (the right fork) and gently climbs the forested edges along Lake McKellar. Within an hour, it passes Lake McKellar Lodge (a private hut for guided walks), and then shortly arrives at McKellar Hut, situated near the swing bridge that crosses the Greenstone River to its true left (east) side.

Stage 2: Lake McKellar to Mid Greenstone Hut

Walking Time: six to seven hours
Accommodation: Mid Greenstone Hut (12 bunks)

The track immediately crosses the Greenstone River to the true left (east) side and cuts through beech forest for about 15 minutes until it emerges onto Greenstone Flats. The track is well marked as it runs down the flats to Rat's Nest Hut, on the opposite bank of the river, a 1½-hour walk from McKellar Hut. Rat's Nest is a private hut for musterers.

A short way beyond the musterers' hut, the track climbs past a deep chasm where the river can be heard thundering below. The view is spectacular and the chasm makes a nice place for an extended break. An hour from Rat's Nest, the track leaves the river to avoid swamps and bog areas, and eventually arrives at Steele Creek. Just before the swing bridge over the creek is a junction with a track heading north (the left fork) to Steele Saddle and Upper Caples Hut, a very difficult route (10 hours).

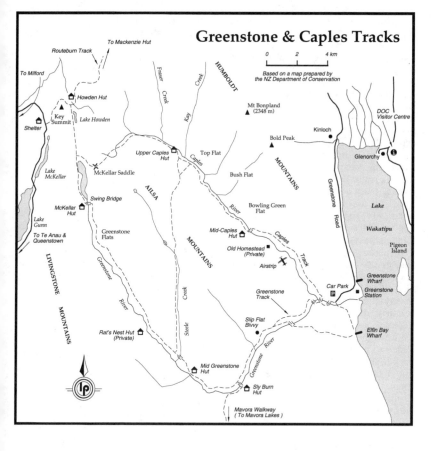

Greenstone & Caples Tracks

Based on a map prepared by
the NZ Department of Conservation

Once on the other side of the swing bridge, the Greenstone Track follows the flats for 20 minutes or so and passes the private Steele Creek Lodge before it reaches the Mid Greenstone Hut, a km below Steele Creek. The 12-bunk hut is located close to the edge of the bush, on a terrace.

Stage 3: Mid Greenstone Hut to Greenstone Car Park

Walking Time: five to six hours
Accommodation: Sly Burn Hut (10 bunks); Slip Flat Bivvy (four bunks)

The track continues skirting the forest edge along the open flats for about an hour beyond Mid Greenstone Hut, until it enters the bush across from the junction with Pass Burn. The hut seen near the confluence on the true right (west) side of the Greenstone River is private. Once in the bush, the track begins to ascend above the Greenstone Gorge, and comes to a junction with a track to Pass Burn bridge. The swing bridge is only a short descent down the side track and is a good vantage point from which to view the narrow rock walls of the gorge. Just across the swing bridge is Sly Burn Hut, the junction point of the Mavora Walkway (a two to three-day walk to Mavora Lakes via Pass Burn).

The main track continues on the true left (north) side of the river, climbs high above the gorge and swings left with the valley before emerging onto the western end of Slip Flat. The track quickly passes Slip Flat Bivvy, on the edge of the forest, and then re-enters the bush close to the river. (There is an emergency bridge upstream if the creek across Slip Flat is in flood.)

In 20 to 30 minutes, the track crosses a stream and comes to a junction. The track to the east (right-hand fork) stays close to the river to cross a swing bridge and head for Rere Lake (one hour). The main track, to the north (left-hand fork), remains on the true left (north) side of the river and climbs through the rest of the gorge.

In about 1½ to two hours, the track reaches a swing bridge over the Greenstone River, and on the other side crosses Caples Flat. After about 20 minutes of traversing the grassy flats, a second swing bridge is reached; the signposted junction to the Caples Track is just beyond it. The track to the west (the left fork) heads up the Caples Valley to the Caples Hut (2½ hours). The track to the east (the right fork) follows the true right bank of the Greenstone River for another 15 minutes before it crosses another footbridge. From here, it's a short distance to the car park.

CAPLES TRACK

The Caples Valley separates the main body of the Ailsa Mountains from the Humboldt Range. Although it's a smaller and, at times, steeper valley than the Greenstone, the Caples is thought by many to be more scenic, with its 'park-like' appearance of small grassy clearings enclosed by beech forest. There is also good trout fishing in the lower portions of the Caples River, from its confluence with the Greenstone to the Mid Caples Hut. About 1600 trampers tackle the Caples every year and the numbers are increasing.

Information

The majority of the Caples Track is in DOC stewardship land, which forms the southern border of Mt Aspiring National Park. Intentions can be registered and information obtained from the DOC Queenstown visitor centre (☎ 442 7933), Glenorchy field centre (☎ 442 9937) or Te Anau field centre (☎ 249 7921).

Giardia is present in the area, so boil or sterilise all drinking water. Always use the hut toilet.

Maps

The best map is the 1:75,000 Trackmaps No 335-02 *(Routeburn Track)*.

Huts

Both the Mid Caples and Upper Caples huts are Category Two and the fee, $8 per night, can be paid at the Glenorchy field centre or at the Queenstown field centre. Both centres have coal fires, mattresses and running water. Wardens are present from late October until mid-April, and they check for hut tickets.

Access

Both ends of the Caples are located on the Greenstone Track, with the eastern end of the track a 20-minute walk from the car park. The western end joins the Greenstone Track at the head of Lake McKellar, about an hour south of the Lake Howden Hut. Transport for the Caples is the same as for the Greenstone, and the two tracks are often combined to form a loop.

Places to Stay

For accommodation in Glenorchy and Queenstown, see the Places to Stay section of the Routeburn Track; for accommodation in Te Anau and Milford, see the Places to Stay section for the Milford Track (in the Southland chapter).

The Track

The Caples Valley is linked to the Greenstone Valley by McKellar Saddle, so this

Top: Mt Cook from Tekapo, Central Otago (NZTB)
Bottom: Routeburn Valley, Otago (VB)

Tramper on Mt Arthur, Kahurangi National Park (DOC)

walk can be tramped separately or combined with the Greenstone Track to make a four to five-day trip.

The Caples, which involves a climb over McKellar Saddle (945 metres) is rated medium. It's described here starting from the Greenstone car park and going to Lake McKellar.

Stage 1: Greenstone Car Park to Upper Caples Hut

Walking Time: five hours
Accommodation: Mid Caples Hut (12 bunks); Upper Caples Hut (20 bunks)

The track departs from the car park and in a couple of minutes crosses a footbridge to the true right bank of the Greenstone. In about 15 minutes, it reaches a signposted junction with the Caples Track, which is the fork to the north across the swing bridge.

The Caples Track continues along the true left (east) side of the Caples River, but stays in the beech forest above the valley to avoid crossing the grazing land of Greenstone Station. At one point, an airstrip and a wood-shed might be spotted on the far bank.

It's a 2½-hour walk along the true left (east) bank before the well-marked track descends past a small gorge and crosses a swing bridge to Mid Caples Hut (12 bunks). The hut is on an open terrace above the river, near the edge of the forest. From the hut, the track remains on the true right (west) side of the river and crosses open grassy flats for the first hour. You then ascend into beech forest to round a small gorge before quickly return-ing to the flats, where there is a fence to protect the forest from station stock.

Eventually, the track turns into bush before it emerges at the southern end of Top Flat. It takes about 25 minutes to cross the flat and cut through more beech forest to Upper Caples Hut. Just before the hut is the signposted junction with the Steele Saddle route to the Greenstone Track, an extremely difficult walk (10 hours). Upper Caples Hut is in a scenic setting, on a grassy flat, with the Ailsa Mountains rising directly behind it.

Stage 2: Upper Caples Hut to Greenstone Track

Walking Time: four to five hours to Green-stone Track

The track leaves the valley floor and begins ascending towards McKellar Saddle, climb-ing 150 metres, past the junction of Fraser Creek and Caples River to a small, boggy meadow. From here, the track continues to climb and sidle past upland basins, marked with snow poles, and two hours from the hut you ford the Caples, now a mountain creek, to its true left side. The track crosses back to the true right side of the Caples and makes its final ascent through open alpine terrain to the saddle, a climb of 450 metres from the hut.

The saddle (945 metres) is free of bush, but can be extremely boggy after heavy rain. After an especially bad summer in 1988, trampers were asked to stay off the Caples Track while Mt Aspiring National Park trail crews laid a planked trail across it. The views are good from McKellar Saddle – on a clear day the peaks and hanging valleys of Fiord-land can be seen to the west.

The track is well signposted where it leaves the saddle, and quickly descends 100 metres before swinging north. The track drops another 200 metres with a series of switchbacks, and it takes about 1½ hours to descend the steep track from the saddle to the point where you break out of the bush near the head of Lake McKellar. Here, the track swings north to bypass swampy lowlands, then crosses a bridge to the signposted Greenstone Track.

To the north (right fork), the track leads to Lake Howden Hut, 45 minutes to an hour away. The other fork (south) can be followed to reach McKellar Hut, an hour's walk away. Those trampers heading all the way from Upper Caples to The Divide on the Te Anau-Milford Highway should plan on a 6½ to seven-hour day.

REES-DART TRACK

The least-used track in the Glenorchy region is the Rees-Dart, a four to five-day route that

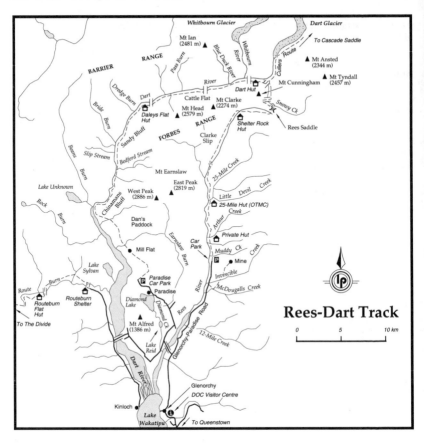

Rees-Dart Track

connects two splendid valleys, winds through a variety of scenery (including grassy flats, lush forests and high bluffs) and even climbs over an alpine pass. Although the 70-km trip is rated medium, it's longer and definitely more challenging than either the Routeburn, Greenstone or the Caples. However, most of the track is well marked and maintained, making the Rees-Dart a journey within the capabilities of average trampers.

Information
The Rees-Dart lies within Mt Aspiring National Park. Intentions can be registered and information obtained from either the Queenstown DOC visitor centre (☎ 442 7933) or the Glenorchy field centre (☎ 442 9937).

Giardia is present in the area, and you should boil or sterilise all drinking water. Always use the hut toilet.

Access to the special protected area on the western side of the Dart River below Bride Burn is by permit only.

Maps
The best map is the 1:150,000 Parkmaps No

273-02 *(Mt Aspiring National Park)*. Otherwise get S113 *(Tutoko)* (1974) and S114 *(Earnslaw)* (1984) of the old NZMS 1 series.

Huts

The three DOC huts on this trip – Shelter Rock, Dart and Daleys Flat – are serviced with solid-fuel fires for heating, mattresses and running water; fees are $8 a night. Camping is permitted, except in the fragile alpine and subalpine areas between Shelter Rock Hut and Dart Hut.

Access

For a long time, the only public transport to and from the track was provided by buses that dropped you off at the Rees River Bridge on their way to the Routeburn Track. Now, Backpacker Express (☎ 442 9939), operating out of Glenorchy and Queenstown, has a pick-up and drop-off service at both ends (see Access for the Routeburn Track in this chapter).

Places to Stay

For accommodation options in both Glenorchy and Queenstown, see Places to Stay for the Routeburn Track.

The Track

Most people hike Rees Valley first and then return down the Dart River – the easiest direction in which to climb the Rees Saddle – and this is the way the tramp is described here. Nights are usually spent at Shelter Rock and at the Dart and Daleys Flat huts, with an extra night at Dart Hut if you plan to undertake the side trip to Dart Glacier (see the next section). The trip is rated medium.

Stage 1: Muddy Creek to Shelter Rock Hut

Walking Time: seven hours
Accommodation: 25-Mile Hut (eight bunks); Shelter Rock Hut (20 bunks)

A 4WD track leads up the Rees Valley to the Otago Tramping & Mountaineering Club's (OTMC) 25-Mile Hut. But the official and traditional start of the track is the Muddy

Creek car park. From here, you ford the creek and head up a bulldozed track, reaching the private Arthur Creek Hut, just beyond Bridges Creek, in two km.

Grassy flats lie beyond Arthur Creek, and it's four km of open travel on the true left (east) side of the Rees River until the track fords 25-Mile Creek. 25-Mile Hut is just before the creek, two to three hours from Muddy Creek.

The route continues along open river flats for another 1½ hours until a track, marked by a park boundary sign, enters the bush. Within a km, the track crosses a swing bridge to the true right (west) side of the Rees River. The track continues on this side of the river, passes through Clarke Slip, over grassy flats, and then begins a climb through beech forest. Within two km, the track passes the site of the old Shelter Rock Hut, now used occasionally by those who carry a tent. From here, it's another km along the true right (west) bank of the Rees, through stands of stunted beech, before· the track crosses a swing bridge back to the true left (east) bank to arrive at the new Shelter Rock Hut.

Stage 2: Shelter Rock Hut to Dart Hut

Walking Time: five to seven hours
Accommodation: Dart Hut (20 bunks)

The climb over the alpine pass of Rees Saddle begins by following the river on the true left (east) side for a short time to pick up a well-marked track which rises through alpine scrub. The track gradually sidles up the valley until it reaches a tussock basin below the saddle, about four km from the hut. Rees Saddle is the obvious low point to the north, and you keep to the stream bed before climbing up the steep slope to the top of the saddle.

The final ascent is marked with poles and a well-beaten path. As you would expect, the saddle (1447 metres) provides good views of the surrounding peaks and valleys, making it the natural place for lunch if the weather is clear.

Follow the orange poles from the saddle to Dart Hut. They quickly descend 90 metres to a terrace and group of tarns above Snowy Creek. The track traverses steep slopes, which can be dangerous when wet or covered with snow.

The route stays on the true left (west) of Snowy Creek before dropping suddenly to a swing bridge and crossing to the true right (east) side. The track climbs above the bridge, passes some good views of the upper Dart Valley and Dart Glacier, and descends across broken slopes of rock and shrub.

Dart Hut is visible on the true left bank of the Dart River during the final descent, which ends at a swing bridge across Snowy Creek (replaced in winter by a four-wire crossing). There are some camp sites just before you cross the bridge to the true left side of the creek, but the hut is only five minutes away. Dart Hut is the only one on the track that has both gas rings and a wood stove. This hut tends to be a bottleneck on the track and occasionally will be full at night.

There are some excellent day trips from here, including walks to view the Dart and Whitbourn glaciers.

Stage 3: Dart Hut to Daleys Flat Hut

Walking Time: six to eight hours
Accommodation: Daleys Flat Hut (20 bunks)

The track climbs away from the hut and along a bluff above the river, offering an occasional view of the rushing water below or the valley in front of you. In two km, you pass the junction to the swing bridge that crosses the river to the track to the Whitbourn Valley and the lower Whitbourn Glacier (three hours). The main track continues along the valley through thick forest. You can often hear the river below, but rarely get to see it.

Within 4½ km of the Whitbourn Bridge, the track climbs sharply, but then drops into a rocky stream clearing near the eastern end of Cattle Flat. The track quickly emerges from forest onto the flat, an almost endless grassy area where the trail appears as a path of trampled grass marked occasionally by a rock cairn. The Dart is seen as you cross the

flat, as is a portion of the Curzon Glacier, high in the mountains across the river. The track follows the middle of the flat and in three km passes a sign to a rock bivvy. The bivvy, a three-minute walk up a side track, is a huge overhanging rock that can easily hold half a dozen people or more. If it's raining, this is an excellent place for lunch because it is almost halfway to the next hut.

The track continues across Cattle Flat for another 1½ km, crosses a fence on a stile and finally returns to the bush. From here, it's a steady drop towards the river, with the track reaching the banks of the Dart in 2½ km. Along the way, you pass another rock bivvy, much smaller than the one at Cattle Flat. Eventually, the track breaks out at Quinns Flat, a beautiful stretch of golden grass surrounded by mountains, and then returns to the bush.

The track crosses a few more streams and, in 30 minutes, arrives at Daleys Flat. Follow the trampled grass across the flat to reach Daleys Flat Hut on the far side.

Stage 4: Daleys Flat Hut to Paradise

Walking Time: six to eight hours

This last leg of the journey is not a difficult hike but, at 26 km, it makes for a long day. If you plan to catch the afternoon transport to Glenorchy, it's best to be out of the hut by 7 am, allowing yourself a full eight hours to reach Paradise. The morning begins in forest, but within 15 minutes the track comes to a small, grassy flat, only to return to the bush on a high bank above the river.

Four km from the hut, the track breaks out onto Dredge Flat and cuts across it. Use the markers to locate where the track re-enters the bush in the middle of the grassy flat. At the lower end of the flat, Sandy Bluff looms overhead and another marker directs you to the track.

As soon as the track enters the forest, it begins climbing the steep bluff, where at one point a ladder and steel cable are needed to get up a rock face. This is very adventurous, but at the top you are rewarded with a fine view of Dredge Flat and the valley beyond.

Not far from here is the pick-up point for Fun Yakkers and weary trampers catching the jet-boat back to Glenorchy (the pick-up point is well signposted).

The track immediately descends to a grassy flat, crosses it and stays close to the river for the next seven km. Eventually, the track enters an open flat, with Chinamans Bluff straight ahead and an impressive waterfall from Lake Unknown visible high in the mountains across the Dart.

The track skirts the bluff, requiring only a fraction of the climbing endured at Sandy Bluff, descends onto Chinamans Flat, and arrives at another sign for a rock bivvy. The bivvy, a rock overhang, is up in the bluff, a short scramble away. It has enough room for about six people.

Once on the flats, you come almost immediately to a 4WD track. It's about 6½ km to the car park, a good two-hour trek (unless you're late for the transport and have to start running down the track). The 4WD track passes through Dan's Paddock, an old grassed scree fan, and begins a gentle descent. From here, trampers can either follow the vehicle track or a walking track to the car park; the walking track is shorter.

CASCADE SADDLE ROUTE

Cascade Saddle is one of the most scenic alpine crossings in New Zealand that can be walked without the aid of mountaineering gear or climbing experience. It is still a very steep, hard climb to the pass, and should not be attempted in adverse weather conditions. Steep snow grass slopes on the Matukituki side become treacherous when wet or covered by fresh snow.

By hiking the route from Matukituki to Dart Valley, you receive the latest weather report, via a radio in Aspiring Hut, on the morning before you attempt the steepest section, a four-hour climb from the hut to the Pylon (1835 metres). The stretch from Aspiring Hut to Dart Hut on the Rees-Dart Track is a long 10 to 11-hour day for those without a tent. With a tent, you can break the hike and spend a glorious night camping in an alpine

meadow near the pass, with Mt Aspiring looming overhead.

History

The Ngati Mamoe and Ngai Tahu tribes established named settlements around the shores of lakes Wanaka and Hawea. One of these was Nehenehe ('forest'), on the northern side of the Matukituki River where it flows into Lake Wanaka – several sites and ovens for cooking cabbage tree roots remain.

The Maoris referred to Mt Aspiring as Tititea ('peak of glistening white'). Aspiring was first seen by a European when government surveyor John Turnbull Thomson explored the region in 1857. He was followed by James Hector, who explored the West Matukituki Valley in 1863, crossing the col in an epic journey and almost reaching the West Coast via the Waipara Valley. Pastoralists and timber millers came next, and the valley was carved up in the 1870s.

Information

The Mt Aspiring National Park (Wanaka) field centre and visitor centre (☎ 443 7660; fax 443 8776) is located on Ardmore St at the eastern edge of town. It's open daily from 8 am to 5 pm from mid-December to mid-January, and on weekdays during the rest of the year. It has informative natural history displays, audiovisual programmes and, of course, loads of information and brochures for trampers. It also has books, maps and the latest weather report. It's a good idea to pick up a copy of the *Matukituki Valley Walks* pamphlet ($1).

Mountain Recreation Wanaka (☎ /fax 443 7330) can provide guides for the difficult Cascade Saddle route to the Rees or Dart valleys.

Maps

The 1:150,000 Parkmaps No 273-02 *(Mt Aspiring National Park)* is fine for the Dart or Rees valleys, but it's reassuring to have the 1:50,000 Topomaps 260 quad E40 *(Earnslaw)*, if it's available, which covers the route over Cascade Saddle to Dart Hut.

Huts

Aspiring Hut was built by the New Zealand Alpine Club. It's maintained by the DOC and a hut warden is stationed there to collect fees ($14 a night). The hut is an interesting place to spend a night because there are usually a number of climbers, with their piles of mountaineering gear, to give it an atmosphere of high adventure. The huts on the Rees-Dart cost $8; a warden is stationed at Dart Hut to collect fees.

Access

To/From Wanaka The InterCity bus depot is on Ardmore St, opposite the Clifford's Resort Hotel. Daily buses from Queenstown stop at Wanaka on the way to the glaciers via Haast Pass, so does a connecting bus from Tarras on InterCity's daily service from Queenstown to Christchurch via Mt Cook. InterCity has a connecting bus from Cromwell on the Queenstown to Dunedin route every day except Sunday.

Mt Cook Landline buses operate from the Wanaka Travel Centre (☎ 443 7414) on Dunmore St in the town centre. Buses run daily to Christchurch, Dunedin and Mt Cook, daily (except Saturday) to Queenstown and on weekdays to Invercargill. Travel times from Wanaka are Queenstown (two hours), glaciers (six hours), Mt Cook (4¼ hours), Christchurch (10 hours) and Dunedin (seven hours).

West Matukituki There is good public transport at the end of both the Matukituki and Dart valleys

Transport services can be arranged from Wanaka to the end of the track in the West Matukituki Valley through Matuki Services (☎ 443 7980, 443 8540) or Mt Aspiring Express (☎ 443 7414, 443 8876), Wanaka United Travel, 99 Ardmore St.

From mid-December to the end of January, Matuki Services departs from the Kaleidoscope Gift Shop, Helwick St, on Monday, Wednesday and Friday at 10 am and from Raspberry Creek at 11 am. A one-way fare to the road end is $15. It will provide a service any time for a set fee if you

have a group; telephone for prices. The Mt Aspiring Express operates from November to April; a one-way fare to Raspberry Flat is $20. See the preceding section for transport out of the Dart or Rees valleys.

Places to Stay

The *Wanaka Motor Park* (☎ 443 7883) is on Brownston St, about one km from the town centre; powered camp sites/bunks are $8/11.50 for one and cabins cost $27 for two. The *Pleasant Lodge Holiday Park* (☎ 443 7360), three km from Wanaka on Glendhu Bay Rd, has cabins at similar prices.

The *Wanaka YHA Hostel* (☎ 443 7405), at 181 Upton St, is $14 per night. There is backpacker accommodation at *Cliffords*, in the old staff quarters at the back of Clifford's Resort Hotel (☎ 443 7826); singles/doubles are $13.50/20. The *Wanaka Bakpaka* (☎ 443 7837) is at 117 Lakeside Rd; a bed costs $13.50/15 in dorms/doubles.

The Track

The easiest way to climb Cascade Saddle, a route rated as difficult, is up the Dart Valley from the west. But the safest way is east to west because you tackle the steepest and potentially the most treacherous segment in the morning, only a few hours after receiving the latest weather report at Aspiring Hut – this is the way it is described here.

It takes three days to reach Dart Hut and a further two days to walk to the end of either the Rees or Dart valleys, making this a five-day adventure. Trampers should schedule an extra day (or more) to ensure good weather to cross Cascade Saddle. If the weather is fine, the spare day can be spent at Dart Hut undertaking side trips, including a climb of Rees Saddle.

Stage 1: Road End to Aspiring Hut

Walking Time: 2½ to three hours
Accommodation: Aspiring Hut (26 bunks)

Either the Aspiring Express or Matuki Services will take trampers to the road end, a car park at Raspberry Creek, 54 km from Wanaka. Cross the bridge to a 4WD track on

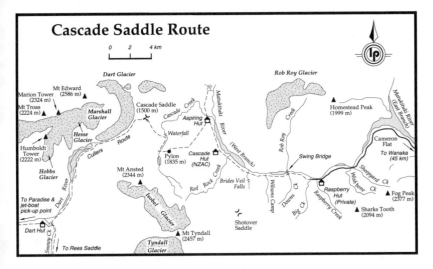

the other side; the track cuts across the open valley of grassy flats on the true right (south) bank of the Matukituki. The scenery up the river includes Shotover Saddle and Mt Tyndall to the left (south), Cascade Saddle straight ahead (west) and occasional sheep or cattle. Within two km, the track passes the swing bridge which provides access across the West Branch of the Matukituki River to the Rob Roy Glacier route (a five-hour round trip), and on a good day, the hanging glacier can clearly be seen above it.

The 4WD track ends at the bridge, and beyond it you can either follow the river bed and grassy flats, fording when necessary and enduring wet feet, or follow a marked track that climbs into the valley. At one point, near Wilsons Camp, the track climbs to the left to bypass a small bluff hidden in a clump of beech trees. Four km from the bridge, the track climbs away from the river a second time, passing Brides Veil Falls. Cascade Hut can be seen from the ridge. At this point, the track swings north-west along the valley floor, passing Cascade Hut, and in another 2½ km (half an hour) reaches Aspiring Hut.

The stone and wood hut is a classic climbers' lodge, built by the New Zealand

Alpine Club. There is a huge floor-to-ceiling window overlooking Mt Aspiring, and even a telescope to enabling you to watch climbers attempting ridges. Also in the common room is a stone fireplace, surrounded by easy chairs, with a mantel that contains books, photos and other mountaineering memorabilia. A warden is stationed here in the summer to collect fees, and to receive weather reports every morning and evening.

Stage 2: Aspiring Hut to Cascade Saddle
Walking Time: four to six hours

The trip to Dart Hut is a long day, so an early start is important, but ironically many trampers wait until 8.30 am or later, until the hut warden receives the morning weather report from park headquarters in Wanaka. The track begins behind the hut and heads south-west into the trees, where it is signposted. It climbs steeply through beech forest and, within an hour, there are views of Mt Aspiring to the north and the rest of the valley to the south.

The track makes a steady ascent, works around a waterfall and, two to three hours from the hut, breaks out above the bush-line.

For most trampers, this is a glorious moment. If the day is clear, there will be stunning views the minute you leave the last few stunted beech trees.

The next section is difficult. The route is marked by orange snow poles (metal standards) and follows a steep snow grass and tussock ridge upwards. Occasionally, you're on all fours working from one pole to the next because the route sidles a few ledges and outcrops and at times becomes very steep. You are never more than 100 metres from the left of the spur. From the bush-line, it's a good two hours before the track swings to the left and then, veering right again, climbs an easy slope to Pylon, the marker at 1835 metres. Take a break – the views are wonderful and you've just climbed 1335 metres over four km.

From the marker, the track skirts the ridge to the south and then descends steadily through rock and scree to Cascade Creek (follow the standards). The route crosses the stream to its true left (west) side and climbs some easy slopes towards the saddle to the north. The route veers left just before the saddle, but you can continue to the low point (at 1500 metres), where you can look from its edge (be careful!) straight down a 1000-metre sheer rock face to a small valley below. It's an incredible feeling standing there looking at so much scenery, with Mt Aspiring to one side and the Dart Glacier to the other.

Just before you climb to the saddle, there are grassy alpine meadows that provide a degree of protection for those who plan to pitch a tent. If the evening is clear, this is a once-in-a-lifetime camping experience – watch the pink *alpenglow* on the peaks around you and then watch the stars emerge overhead.

Stage 3: Cascade Saddle to Dart Hut
Walking Time: four to five hours
Accommodation: Dart Hut (20 bunks)

For those heading to Dart Hut, you have only completed the first half of the walk. As soon as the route veers off the saddle, you get your best view of the Dart Glacier, from its beginnings among the peaks right down to the gravel-covered ice of its snout in the valley. If it's fine weather, this is a good place to lie down, enjoy lunch and study a wonder of nature.

The snow poles continue down the tussock slope to a ledge on the top of a moraine, then descend quickly along the ledge. The glacier is an impressive sight, but you are forced to keep one eye out for the next pole (or, when they run out, for the next rock cairn). The cairns are hard to see at times.

You steadily descend slopes of loose rock as you head for the valley floor, finally coming to it near the end of the glacier, where the ice is black. You continue down the true left (east) side of the river and, eight km from the saddle, pass the hanging ice of Hesse Glacier as the track drops out of the mountains towards the Dart. At this point, the route departs from the rocky moraine hills, and it's an easy tramp for the next two km across grassy benches along the wide river bed.

Eventually, the valley closes in and the route is forced to climb around a few steep banks. It also fords several side streams which roar down from the mountains, before the Dart makes a wide swing to the west – a sign that you are only half an hour from the hut. Stay on the true left side of the river; the final half-km to the hut is along a steep bank above the river. Hike a short distance up Snowy Creek and cross it on a swing bridge to reach the hut.

From Dart Hut, trampers can reach the road either by continuing along the Dart or climbing the Rees Saddle and following the Rees River. The Dart is actually a longer (two-day) walk but is the preferred choice of many who, having seen its beginning at the glacier, want to follow the river all the way to Lake Wakatipu.

WILKIN-YOUNG VALLEYS CIRCUIT
Wilkin Valley offers two features that are hard for most trampers to pass up once they 'discover' the Makarora region: the mountain scenery is outstanding, easily rivalling that of Matukituki Valley near Wanaka or

even the tramps in the Glenorchy area, but the number of trampers is light. Compared to the 10,000 who hike the Routeburn Track every year, probably around 700 trampers use the huts and tracks of the Wilkin Valley, and the same is true of the forested valley of the Young River, another tributary of the Makarora River. The two valleys can be combined in a loop that offers superb scenery but few people, except during the brief holiday periods around Christmas and Easter.

History

Maoris from coastal Otago and Southland visited this region to hunt birds and fish. They knew of Makarora as Kaika Paekai, the 'place of abundant food', and camped around the shores of Lake Wanaka and in the Makarora Valley. Some ventured to the West Coast in search of pounamu (greenstone).

In January 1863, a prospector looking for gold was the first European to cross Haast Pass. A few weeks later, he was followed by explorer-geologist Julius von Haast. A pack track was established up the Makarora Valley and over to the West Coast in the 1880s. Road building began as unemployment relief work in 1929, but it wasn't until 1960 that a proper road over the pass was completed. The difficult Paringa-Haast section was opened in 1965.

Information

The Makarora DOC visitor centre (☎ 443 8365) is one km north of the township, on State Highway 6. It's open on weekdays from 8 am to 5 pm (and on weekends in the summer months). Gather information here and register your intentions. Excess gear can be left for a small charge. On the other side of Haast Pass is the South Westland World Heritage visitor centre (☎ 751 0809), where you can get information on the entire world heritage area.

A stop at the visitor centre is almost mandatory if you intend to tramp the whole Young-Wilkin Circuit. The big rains of 1993-94 caused widespread damage to the track in the Young and Wilkin valleys, but not enough to close it. The park officials can show you the tricky slips and the easiest ways to get over them.

Maps

The 1:150,000 Parkmaps No 273-02 *(Mt Aspiring National Park)* covers the entire route but doesn't supply much detail. The new 1:50,000 Topomaps 260 quad F38 *(Wilkin)* should be available by the time this book is published. The *Tramping Guide to the Makarora Region* (DOC, 1992) lists a number of excellent walks. Don't forget that the Albert Burn Hut was knocked out by the floods.

Huts

It costs $8 a night for all huts in the Wilkin and Young valleys. All the huts have mattresses, and a potbelly or open stove for heating. Pay hut fees at Makarora visitor centre.

Access

Makarora, located 60 km north of Wanaka or 192 km south of Fox Glacier, has a permanent population of around 30. You can't see the cluster of A-frame units from the road, but they are capable of accommodating about 140 people, which can be useful from time to time, when adventure-seekers arrive in town. Apart from these units, there isn't much in the township, a fact from which it derives its charm.

InterCity has buses that run this route, departing from Fox Glacier daily at 8.50 am and 12.50 pm and from Wanaka at 10.10 am and 3 pm. Northbound buses pass through the small town of Makarora at around 12.10 and 4.30 pm. Southbound buses have the same times because drivers swap over here. The afternoon service does not operate in winter.

Makarora Rivertours Ltd (☎ 443 8372) offers jet-boat transport on the Wilkins River, which can be useful if you are short of time or if the river is swollen. If rivers in the area are in flood, many trampers avoid the dangerous ford of the Makarora near its confluence with the Wilkin by catching a

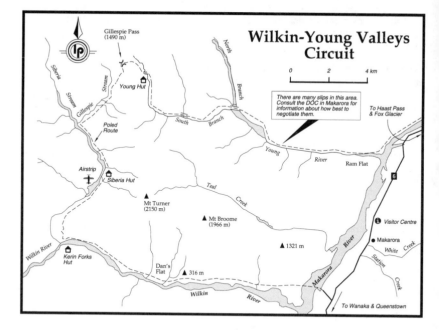

It is wise to ask at the visitor centre about the best spot to ford the Makarora River. To reach the Young Valley, the river is generally forded at Sawmill Creek, four km north of the village on State Highway 6. Study the Makarora carefully, then choose the best ford between its confluence with the Young River

jet-boat from Kerin Forks back to Makarora. The jet-boat will also drop off trampers in the Young Valley. You can arrange this service at the store in Makarora; it's cheaper, naturally, if you travel in a group

Places to Stay

There are DOC camp sites on State Highway 6 at Cameron Flat , 11 km north of Makarora, and at Davis Flat, a further 3 km north. At Makarora, *A-Frame Motels & Cabins* (☎ 443 8372) charges $32 for a cabin for two, and $7 for a tent site.

The Track

This three to four-day trip, rated medium to difficult, is described from the Young Valley, the easiest way to cross Gillespie Pass, to the Wilkin Valley.

Most trampers spend the first night at Young Hut. The second day is spent climbing Gillespie Pass, a 1520-metre saddle, with a night stop at Siberia Hut. On the third day,

you can return to Makarora on a jet-boat down the Wilkin River.

The boat ride eliminates three to four hours of walking, as well as allowing you to spend the night at Siberia Hut and still make the afternoon InterCity bus out of Makarora. Trampers with more than three days, however, should seriously consider spending a day or two hiking the upper portions of the Wilkin Valley, where the best mountain scenery of the park lies.

Stage 1: State Highway 6 to Young Hut
Walking Time: six to eight hours
Accommodation: Young Hut (10 bunks)

and Brady Creek. At this point, the crossing is within the ability of most trampers, when the water level is normal.

Once on the true right (west) side of the Makarora, you round the corner into the Young Valley, where you will find a good track leading up the river's true left (north) bank. The track remains close to the river and makes for an easy stroll up the valley. Within three hours, you enter the flats below the junction of the North and South branches of the Young River. Continue to just above the confluence, where a swing bridge allows you to safely cross the North Branch.

A track on the other side continues on the true left (north) side of the South Branch and immediately climbs and crosses unstable slips – they are well marked with rock cairns, but exercise caution. It then descends to the first flat along the South Branch, where there is a small rock bivvy across the river, a little more than an hour from the forks. The track continues to climb through bush and small clearings until it reaches the alpine zone. The Young Hut lies another km up the valley on the true right (south) side; a bridge five minutes upstream gives safe access to the hut. The hut has a small stove, 10 bunks, and a view of Mt Awful (2202 metres) framed by the valley walls.

Stage 2: Young Hut to Siberia Hut
Walking Time: six to seven hours
Accommodation: Siberia Hut (20 bunks)

Continue up the valley along the true right (south) side of the South Branch for a km. Within half an hour, you reach the start of the track to Gillespie Pass, on your left. A large rock cairn and signs mark the start of the route, up a north-easterly facing slope of scrub and tussock. Make sure you have filled your water bottles because this is the last water until well over the pass.

It's a steep climb of 400 metres up the slope alongside a rock bluff, and then along the crest of a spur, where orange snow poles mark most of the route. Just before reaching the 1490-metre pass, the route swings left up a small gully. It takes three to four hours to

reach the saddle from the hut, and for many trampers the alpine setting is a good spot for an extended break or lunch, with Mt Alba (2355 metres) dominating the skyline.

You leave Gillespie Pass by following the orange snow poles south-east along a ridge for a km, until the route swings to the south-west. At times you are sidling down through snow grass basins, which are very slippery when wet so exercise caution. The track enters the forest on a small predominant spur and leads down to Gillespie Stream, a good spot for a rest. You continue down through forest, sidling above Gillespie Stream on its true left (south) bank, before descending steeply to the Siberia Stream.

The walk through Siberia Stream Flats is an easy one and the mountain scenery surrounding you is spectacular. It takes about an hour to cross the grassy flats to Siberia Hut, on the true left (east) side of Siberia Stream. Plan on three to 3½ hours to reach the hut from the top of the pass. Recently, this part of the track has been marked with poles, to keep trampers to a set path and thus minimise damage to the vegetation.

You can arrange to fly out from Siberia – the airstrip is on the other side of Siberia Stream from the hut, 400 metres downstream.

An excellent side trip from the Siberia Hut is a walk up to Lake Crucible, a true alpine lake nestled under Mt Alba. It takes three to four hours from the hut (and about the same to return). You may be lucky enough to see the tiny rock wren bobbing among the large boulders at the lake outlet.

Stage 3: Siberia Hut to Kerin Forks
Walking Time: two to three hours
Accommodation: Kerin Forks Hut (10 bunks)

Head to the southern end of Siberia Flats to reach a marked track that enters the forest. This is about a half-hour walk. The track remains on the true left (east) bank of Siberia Stream, and gradually descends away from the flats through bush. It sidles around a shoulder, then follows a series of switchbacks over the final 450 metres to the Wilkin

River, a short distance upstream from Kerin Forks.

The Kerin Forks Hut is located on the grassy flats below the confluence of the Siberia Stream and Wilkin River, 400 metres downstream on the true right (south) bank of the Wilkin. The hut cannot be seen from Kerin Forks, and the Wilkin River has to be crossed to reach it. It takes three to four hours to reach the hut, where most trampers will have arranged to be picked up by a jet-boat.

To continue down the river, follow the well-marked track along the true left (north) bank. The walk is easy, and within four hours the track comes to the confluence with the Makarora River. Much caution has to be used when fording this river, and it is best done upstream from its junction with the Wilkin.

OTHER TRACKS
Wilkin-East Matukituki Route
This very challenging route, for experienced alpine trampers only, takes you from Wilkin Valley, over the 1430-metre Rabbit Pass into East Matukituki Valley. A jet-boat ride to Kerin Forks (in Wilkin Valley) and then a lift back to Wanaka (at the end of the walk) can be arranged (see Access for the Wilkin-Young Valleys Circuit). Plan on five to six days.

Pick up the *Wilkin Valley* brochure from the Makarora DOC visitor centre. It explains the route over Waterfall Face, a dangerous segment unless the weather is good. There are no huts in the East Matukituki Valley.

West Matukituki
Those without the time to complete the Cascade Saddle trip can enjoy shorter tramps in the upper portion of the West Matukituki Valley and then return to Wanaka. Get a copy of *Matukituki Valley Tracks* from the Wanaka visitor centre.

Liverpool Bivvy Arrange transport to the road end with Matuki Services (see Access for the Cascade Saddle Route section), then hike into Aspiring Hut for the first night. The next day is a four to five-hour walk up the valley to the eight-bunk Liverpool Bivvy, with its majestic views of Mt Aspiring and surrounding peaks. You can easily return to the road end on the third day to catch the van back to Wanaka. This trip is rated medium. The tussock can be treacherous and slippery when covered in snow.

French Ridge There are spectacular views from this 14-bunk hut perched high on Mt Aspiring's flanks. A medium three-day walk up the West Matukituki would involve a stopping for the night at Aspiring Hut, walking five to six hours (with a 'grunt' of a climb) to French Ridge Hut the next day, and returning to the road on the third day. The upper part of the route is very exposed in bad weather.

If you wish to venture beyond the hut to the Quarterdeck and the Bonar Glacier, you will need to be an experienced climber and have the necessary equipment. If you are not, then enjoy the view you have from the hut, or hire a guide. The view from the top of the Quarterdeck is one of the best sights on earth, with Aspiring, the 'Matterhorn of the South', as a backdrop.

Mountain Recreation (☎ /fax 443 7330) runs a number of treks in the Matukituki Valley. The head of this company is the very experienced Geoff Wayatt, who owns the climbing school based at Shovel Flat.

Shotover Saddle Trampers can retrace part of the great gold rush that took place on the Shotover River and end up in West Matukituki Valley, where there is transport back to Wanaka. You can get to the start of the track from Queenstown by contacting Nomad Safaris (☎ 442 6699) or Outback Tours (☎ 442 7386), and joining a bus tour to Skippers Canyon. The cost is about $40 per person. The road ends at Branches Flat, and from there it's a four to five-hour walk to 16-Mile Hut and three more hours to 100-Mile Hut. The following day involves a climb through Shotover Saddle – you end up near Cascade Hut, in the West Matukituki Valley.

Southland

Southland has many of New Zealand's best outdoor treasures. The biggest gem is Fiordland National Park, the largest slice of the Te Wahipounamu world heritage region. Although all of the walks described here are within Fiordland National Park, or close to it, trampers will find other areas, such as the Takatimu Ranges, the Catlins and the south-western and south-eastern coasts, equally rewarding.

Fiordland National Park

Anchoring New Zealand's national park system in the south is the 1,252,297-hectare Fiordland, the largest park in the country and one of the largest in the world. It stretches from Martins Bay in the north to Preservation Inlet in the south, bordered by the Tasman Sea on one side and by a series of deep lakes on the other. In between are rugged ranges with sharp granite peaks and narrow valleys, 14 of New Zealand's most beautiful fiords, and the country's best collection of waterfalls.

The rugged terrain, thick rainforest-like bush and abundant water have kept progress and people out of much of the park. The fringes of Fiordland are easily visited, and some tracks, such as the Milford, are crowded in summer. But most of the park is impenetrable by all but the hardiest trampers, making this corner of the South Island a true wilderness in every sense.

The most intimate and personally rewarding way of experiencing Fiordland is on foot. There are over 500 km of tracks, and more than 60 huts scattered along them. Unquestionably the most famous track in New Zealand is the Milford Track. Often labelled 'the finest walk in the world', the Milford is almost a pilgrimage to many Kiwis who, if they never do any other walk, must hike this track. Right from the beginning, the Milford

has been a highly regulated and commercial venture, and this has deterred some. But in the end, despite the high costs, mileposts, sightseeing planes buzzing overhead and the abundance of buildings on the manicured track, it's still a wonderfully scenic walk that is within the ability of most people.

There are, however, many other tracks in Fiordland. The Hollyford, stretching from the end of Lower Hollyford Rd to isolated Martins Bay, is steeped in history and has good fishing holes.

At the opposite end of the park is the Dusky Track. This eight to 10-day walk from the West Arm of Lake Manapouri to Supper Cove is one of the truest wilderness walks in the park. And in 1988, the park opened its newest track, the Kepler, a four-day alpine walk designed to take some of the pressure off the Milford and the Routeburn.

HISTORY
In comparison with other regions of the country, little is known of the pre-European history of the Maoris in Fiordland. There is evidence of a permanent settlement at Martins Bay, and possibly summer villages at Te Anau and Preservation Inlet, which were used for seasonal hunting expeditions in the area. The Maori name for the Dusky Sound was Tamatea, the legendary explorer who travelled the full length of the main islands in the canoe *Takatimu*.

The most significant find in the Fiordland region, however, was made in 1967, when the remains of a Maori sitting burial were discovered in a small, dry cave on Mary Island in Lake Hauroko. It was the best-preserved burial ever recovered in New Zealand, and one of the oldest. The body was that of a woman – presumably a high-ranking one – and dated back to the mid-1600s.

In 1770, Captain Cook arrived in the *Endeavour* and worked his way up the west coast, attempting to land at several of the sounds. He was unsuccessful: dusk arrived too soon in one instance, while in another he was doubtful about the direction of the wind. Cook returned three years later, bringing the *Resolution* into Dusky Sound, where the crew recuperated after three months at sea. Recorded in his log in 1773 was probably the first written description of sandflies: 'most mischievous animals...that cause a swelling not possible to refrain from scratching'.

Cook's midshipman, George Vancouver, returned to Fiordland in 1791, taking his ship up Dusky Sound as his former captain had. The following year, a sealing gang of 12 men were left in the sound for a few months; they reaped a harvest of 4500 skins, constructed one of the first buildings in New Zealand and nearly completed a ship with the emergency iron work left behind. They were eventually taken away by the mother ship, but more sealers returned, and by 1795 there were 250 people in Dusky Sound.

Whaling followed sealing for a brief period, and in 1829 the first station of any size in the South Island was built in Preservation Inlet. The two industries wiped out seals and whales but did promote exploration of the coast. The Welsh sealing captain John Grono was the first to sail into the Milford Sound, in 1823, naming it after his home town, Milford Haven.

Fiordland continued to be explored from the sea until pastoralist C J Nairn reached Te Anau in 1852 from the Waiau Valley. Nine years later, two more cattle drivers, David McKellar and George Gunn, climbed to the top of Key Summit and became the first Europeans to view the Hollyford Valley.

Patrick Caples was the first European to descend into the Hollyford Valley from the Harris Saddle, in 1863. A few months later, Captain Alabaster made his way from Martins Bay to Lake Howden. He was followed by a prospector, James Hector, who worked his way up the Hollyford, and eventually back to Queenstown to a hero's welcome from miners. Each man thought he was the first to make the journey, because news travelled much more slowly in those days.

Miners continued to move deeper into Fiordland, in search of the golden stream that would make them rich. In 1868, the Otago provincial government added stimulus to the growth of the area when it decided to start a settlement at Martins Bay. The town was surveyed on the north-eastern corner of Lake McKerrow, named Jamestown, and many of its lots sold. The settlers who finally moved into the area found life hard and lonely. By 1870, there were only eight houses in Jamestown. Nine years later the settlement was completely deserted, and only a handful of people continued to live in Martins Bay.

The only other permanent residents of Fiordland at the time were two hermits who had settled in the sounds during the 1870s. One was William Docherty; after earning his prospecting licence, he settled in Dusky Sound in 1877 and stayed until the late 1890s. The other was Donald Sutherland, a colourful character who sailed 100 km from Thompson Sound into Milford Sound in 1877 and became known as the 'Hermit of Milford'.

In 1880, Sutherland and John Mackay struggled up the Arthur Valley from Milford in search of precious minerals. The fine waterfall they found was named after Mackay – he won a coin toss for the honour. After several more days of labouring through the thick bush, they sighted a magnificent three-leap waterfall, and it was only fair that

Sutherland name this one after himself. The pair then stumbled up to the Mackinnon Pass, viewed the Clinton River and returned to Milford Sound.

Gradually, as word of Sutherland's Falls leaked back to towns and cities, the number of adventurers determined to see the natural wonder increased, as did the pressure for a track or road to the Milford area. In 1888, Quintin Mackinnon and Ernest Mitchell, with the financial support and blessing of the government, set out to cut a route along the Clinton River.

At the same time, C W Adams, chief surveyor of Otago, and a party of 11 were moving up through the Arthur Valley. In October 1888, Mackinnon and Mitchell stopped track-cutting, scrambled over the pass, spent an icy night above the bush-line, and then made their way past the present site of Quintin Hut to meet Adams. A rough trail was finished and a few flimsy huts thrown up, and by 1890 tourists were using the route, with Mackinnon as a guide.

The government continued to seek improvements to the track and huts, and in 1903 the Government Tourist Department took over all facilities on the track, including the ferry that transported trampers to the trail. While the Milford Sound was attracting people, Martins Bay was driving them away. By the turn of the century, the McKenzie brothers were the sole inhabitants of the area, using a rough track in the Hollyford Valley to drive their cattle out to the stockyards. In 1926, the brothers sold out to Davy Gunn, a Scotsman from Invercargill.

Gunn became a legend in his own time. He improved the track in the valley, constructed huts along the way and gradually went from running cattle to guiding tourists. Gunn's greatest achievement, however, was the emergency trip he undertook to get help for victims of an aircraft crash in Big Bay in 1936. Gunn tramped from Big Bay to Lake McKerrow, rowed up the lake and then rode his horse more than 40 km to a construction camp, where he telephoned for a plane. The trip would take an experienced hiker three days; Gunn did it in 21 hours. He continued

his single-handed promotion of the valley until 1955, when he drowned in the Hollyford River after his horse slipped.

The Milford Track changed significantly when, in 1940, it became possible for trampers to walk through Homer Tunnel (until then most hikers had had to turn around at the Sound and backtrack to Lake Te Anau). The tunnel began as a relief project in the 1930s, and was finally opened to motor traffic in 1954. Fiordland National Park was created in 1952, preserving 100 sq km and protecting the route to Milford Sound.

Until 1965, all the track and hut facilities in the park were controlled by the Tourist Hotel Corporation (THC) and trampers had to take part in a guided (and costly) trip to walk the trail. A protest and demonstration in front of the THC Hotel in the Sound brought change and the creation of huts for the so-called 'freedom walkers'. Today, the freedom walkers (now referred to as independent trampers) share the track with the guided parties, but use different huts.

Fiordland National Park was finally rounded out to its present size in 1960, when the Hollyford Valley and Martins Bay were added. In 1988, during New Zealand's centennial celebration of its national park system, the Kepler Track was finished and officially opened. The track was first conceived in 1986 as a way to relieve walking pressure on the Milford and the nearby Routeburn Track.

In 1888, Mackinnon and Mitchell were paid $60 to cut half of the Milford Track; a century later the Kepler was completed, at a cost of more than $1 million.

CLIMATE

Fiordland has come to mean waterfalls, lakes, fiords and rain – buckets of the stuff. The area's weather is described by park staff as 'violent and wet' all year – storms and winds moving west from the Tasman Sea dump up to 8000 mm of rain on the coast and western portions of the park. Early morning mist and thick layers of fog are quite common in the southern region.

The area averages 200 days of rain a year,

yet sitting in a rain shadow behind the mountains is Te Anau, which receives only 1200 mm a year. When travelling to the park, bring good rain gear, and expect the average summer temperatures in the lowlands to be around 18° C.

NATURAL HISTORY

One of the first impressions trampers gain of the park is of the almost overpowering steepness of the mountains. This impression is accentuated by the fact that the mountains are usually separated only by narrow valleys. The rocks and peaks of Fiordland are very hard and have eroded slowly. The mountains in the Mt Aspiring and Arthur's Pass parks are softer and erode more quickly, consequently presenting walkers with a gentler topography of large shingle screes and wide, open river valleys.

The most important contributors to Fiordland's majestic mountain scenery were the glacial periods of the last ice age, which lasted some two million years and ended a mere 14,000 years ago. The glaciers shaped the hard granite peaks, gouged the fiords and lakes, and scooped out rounded valleys. The evidence of the ice flows can be found almost everywhere, from the moraine terraces behind Te Anau and in Eglinton's U-shaped valley to the pointed peaks of the Milford Sound.

One result of the glaciers is Fiordland's trademark lakes. Te Anau, the largest lake in the South Island and second largest in the country, provides an avenue to most of Fiordland's scenic attractions. It's 66 km long, has a shoreline of 500 km and a surface area of 342 sq km. Another major lake is Lake Hauroko, one access point to Supper Cove in Dusky Sound. It's the deepest lake in New Zealand (463 metres).

Other results of Fiordland's glacial beginnings are the waterfalls. The sheerness of the mountain walls and fiords (some sea cliffs rise 1½ km out of the water) has created ideal conditions for waterfalls. There seems to be one at every bend of every track, cascading, tumbling, roaring or simply dribbling down a green mossy bluff.

The most famous waterfall is the Sutherland Falls, on the Milford Track. With its three magnificent leaps and a total drop of 580 metres, it is the third highest in the world. By the end of a visit to the park, trampers become connoisseurs of falling water, viewing the shape, drops and force of falls with an artist's eye. Some may even secretly pray for rain, which can double the size and the number of the waterfalls along the tracks.

The large amounts of moisture mean lush vegetation as well as waterfalls. On the eastern side, forests of red, silver and mountain beech fill the valleys and cling to the steep faces. In the northern and western coastal sections, impressive podocarp forests of matai, rimu, northern rata and totara can be found.

Much of the forest can be seen growing on a surface of hard rock covered by only a thin layer of rich humus and moss, a natural retainer for the large amounts of rain. It is this peaty carpet which allows thick ground flora to thrive under towering canopies, and sets western Fiordland bush apart from that of the rest of the country.

Fiordland stunned the ornithological world in 1948 when Dr Geoffrey Orbell 'rediscovered' the takahe (Porphyrio mantelli hochstetteri), a 45-cm high, flightless bird with scarlet feet and bill, and brilliantly-coloured blue to iridescent green feathers. The takahe had not been seen for 50 years and was thought to be extinct when Dr Orbell sighted seven birds in what is now the Takahe Valley of the Murchison Mountains. An immense management programme was launched to save the species, and in 1986 it was estimated that 181 birds lived in the park.

The birds trampers will probably spot, however, are the usual wood pigeons, fantails, bush robins, tuis, bellbirds and kakas. In the alpine regions, you may see keas and rock wrens; if you wander around at night you might occasionally come across a kiwi.

Backpackers will encounter something else buzzing through the air: the sandfly. The insect is common throughout New Zealand, but Fiordland has the distinction of being renowned for them. There seems to be an exceptionally high proportion of sandflies around Martins Bay, at Supper Cove (at the end of Dusky Track) and at several points along the Milford Track, including the end which has been appropriately named Sandfly Point. In alpine regions or in wind, rain or direct sun, the sandfly's numbers are reduced significantly, but rarely does it disappear completely. There are also mosquitoes in a few places.

One insect that delights trampers is the glow-worm. Their bluish light is most spectacular in the Te Anau Caves, where they line the walls by the thousand. They can easily be spotted on most tramps, glowing at dusk or at night beneath the ferns and in heavy bush sharply cut by a benched track.

Fiordland offers first-class freshwater fishing for brown and rainbow trout, and some excellent coastal fishing opportunities at Martins Bay and Supper Cove. The lakes are renowned for their trout populations, but trampers, not having a boat at their disposal, do much better concentrating on rivers and the mouths of streams that empty into lakes. Almost any stream in the park will hold trout – the better ones near tracks include the Clinton (off the Milford), the Spey (on the Dusky Track), Hollyford River and its Lake Alabaster (on the Hollyford Track) and the Irish Burn (off the Kepler Track). You need a licence, and there are special regulations and seasons for some waters, so check with the park headquarters before you start casting.

MILFORD TRACK

The 53-km Milford Track is best enjoyed if you accept the fact that it is a highly regulated tourist attraction where every step is controlled. You can walk the track in one direction during the summer season, starting from Glade Wharf. You must stay at Clinton Forks the first night, despite it being only two hours from the start of the track, and you complete the trip in the prescribed three nights and four days. This time limit is perhaps the bitterest point with independent

walkers – if the weather goes sour, you still have to push on and cross the alpine section.

Independent walkers and guided parties rarely see each other on the track. With careful segregation and the one-way travel, the Milford appears much less crowded than you might expect with over 10,000 trampers crossing it every year. The only problem on the track is the scenic flights, which have become a nuisance in recent years. The planes have to follow the same valleys as walkers, and on a clear day several planes will be buzzing around the Sutherland Falls.

Keep all this in mind when considering the Milford: if regulations, high cost and lack of wilderness outweigh its outstanding scenic value, skip this track.

Information

The Fiordland National Park Visitors Centre & Museum (☎ 249 7921) is on Te Anau Terrace, beside the lake. It's open daily from 8 am to 6 pm and 7.30 to 9.30 pm in summer, and from 9 am to 4.30 pm in winter. There is a free car park at the visitor centre; check to see if it's secure. Fiordland Travel (☎ 249 7419), which operates the lake cruises and tours, is on the corner of Te Anau Terrace and Milford Rd. The Mt Cook Airline travel office is on Te Anau Terrace.

Maps

The best map for this walk is the 1:75,000 Trackmaps No 335-01 *(Milford Track)*. You do not need to get any of the quads of the 1:50,000 Topomaps 260 series. At a scale of 1:250,000, the Parkmaps No 273-03 *(Fiordland National Park)* is too small; save it for planning other walks.

Permits

The first and most important step for independent walkers is to secure a reservation for a permit (allowing you to commence the track on a particular day and no other). If your party is larger than two or three people and you want to walk during the period from mid-December to January, book way ahead if possible. (The walking season for the

Milford is from early November to mid-April.)

If you are travelling alone or in a pair, and can wait a few days, you have a reasonable chance of getting on the Milford without an advance reservation because cancellations can make places available. Make independent bookings through the Milford Track Bookings office in Te Anau (☎ 249 8514); office hours are 9 am to 4.30 pm.

Costs
For independent walkers, the cost of doing the walk includes a $70 permit fee (no concession for children), which covers three nights in the huts. Add to this the cost of the bus to Te Anau Downs ($11, children $7), the boat from there to the track ($37.50, children $10), the launch from the end of the track to Milford Sound ($19, children $11.50) and the bus back to Te Anau ($35, children $21), and the grand total will probably come to around $170 per person (children $120). If you stay at the hostel in Milford, add another $16 per night – plus food, which can be expensive, particularly at Milford.

Huts
The independent walkers use three 40-bed huts – Clinton Forks, Mintaro and Dump-

ling. Each has a common room with gas rings for cooking, wood or gas-burning stoves for heating, basins, tables and benches, a communal bunk room with mattresses, and a drying room. Cooking utensils are not provided and no food is available for sale. Camping is prohibited along the track.

Equipment
There is a full range of tramping gear for hire in Te Anau. Two rental places are Bev's Hire (☎ 249 7389), 16 Homer St, and Te Anau Sports (☎ 249 8195), PO Box 5, Te Anau.

Access
To/From Te Anau Mt Cook Airline (☎ 249 7516) has daily flights to Queenstown and Mt Cook, with connections to other centres. Waterwings Airways (☎ 249 7405), an agent for Ansett New Zealand, has flights to Queenstown and Milford. Air Fiordland (☎ 249 7505) also has flights to Queenstown, Milford and Mt Cook.

InterCity (☎ 249 7559) has daily bus services between Queenstown and Milford via Te Anau, taking 2½ hours from Te Anau to either Queenstown or Milford. Buses arrive at, and depart from, the InterCity depot on Milford Rd.

Mt Cook Landline (☎ 249 7516) has daily buses between Queenstown and Milford via Te Anau, and a weekday bus from Te Anau to Invercargill. Topline Tours (☎ 249 8059), 80 Quintin Drive, operates a daily service

---

Milford Track Guided Walk Option
Organised parties are taken through by guides, and stay at a different chain of huts to independent trampers. These huts are usually an hour before the 'freedom walkers' huts, so there is little mingling of the two types of walker. The guided groups stay in Glade House, Pompolona Lodge and Quintin Lodge, cushy establishments with hot showers, hot meals and comfortable beds.

The guided walk – five days and four nights (three in huts on the track and one in Milford) – costs around $1355, somewhat less for children 10 to 15 years old (around $845). Children under 10 are not accepted. Milford Track Guided Walk (☎ (0800) 65 9255, 249 7411) take bookings. ■

between Te Anau and Queenstown. It departs from Te Anau at 10 am and Queenstown at 2 pm. Fiordland Travel (☎ 249 7419), on the lakefront, also has buses to Queenstown and Milford.

Te Anau End Several bus companies have buses from Te Anau to Te Anau Downs, to connect with the Fiordland Travel boat to Glade House, at the head of Lake Te Anau, where the Milford Track begins. The buses leave Te Anau at around 1.15 pm, connecting with the launch which leaves Te Anau Downs at 2 pm.

In addition to the bus companies mentioned above, Kiwi Discovery Track Transport (☎ 442 7430) leaves Queenstown daily at 7.30 am and returns from Milford to Queenstown at 3.45 pm. Another small operator which may provide transport is Trips 'n' Tramps (☎ 249 7081).

Smaller operators charge less for the boat trip or combine it with a package such as a fast boat to Glade Wharf, sea kayak from track finish (Sandfly Point) to Milford and a minibus to Te Anau ($99). There are so many variables in the transport equation that Milford Track Bookings has requested that we advise you to contact them.

Milford End The ferry to Milford departs from Sandfly Point (at the end of the track) at 2 and 3 pm. Buses, which usually leave Milford between 3 and 5 pm, take about 2½ hours to Te Anau, with a stop at The Divide, and there are connections from Te Anau to Queenstown. Hitching out is possible but requires patience. Or you can fly out from Milford to either Te Anau or Queenstown. For bus services, see To/From Te Anau (earlier in this section).

Places to Stay
Te Anau This town is an important stopover for many trampers. The *Te Anau Motor Park* (☎ 249 7457) is opposite the lake, just one km from Te Anau on the road to Manapouri; tent sites are $8.50, bunk beds are $11 and standard cabins cost $30. The *Mountain View Cabins & Caravan Park* (☎ 249 7462),

on Mokonui St, has cabins for $40 for two. The *Te Anau YHA Hostel* (☎ 249 7847) is about 1½ km out of town on Milford Rd; it charges $15 per night, and you can leave gear here while you're away tramping ($2). *Te Anau Backpackers* (☎ 249 7713), 48 Lake Front Drive, has dorm beds for $14.

Te Anau to Milford There are basic DOC camp sites along the road to Milford; these are listed in the pamphlet *Conservation Camp Sites*, available from all DOC offices. At Cascade Creek, the *O Tapara Lodge* (☎ 249 7335) charges $60/75 for singles/doubles. *Hollyford Camp*, formerly Gunn's Camp, is in the Hollyford Valley; tent sites are $3.50 per person and rustic cabins cost $14/24/39 for one/two/three people.

Milford Sound Budget accommodation at Milford Sound is very limited, so it's a good idea to book ahead if you want to stay here. The hostel-style *Milford Lodge* (☎ 249 8071) has tent sites for $8 per person, and beds for $16 in two to six-person rooms.

The Track
Most trampers take the launch across Lake Te Anau, a pleasant trip that is a good introduction to the area. The Milford Track is rated easy.

Stage 1: Glade Wharf to Clinton Forks Hut
Walking Time: two hours
Accommodation: Clinton Forks Huts (40 bunks)

The track from the wharf is a wide 4WD trail which was once used by packhorses to carry supplies to the huts. In 15 minutes, it passes Glade House, the official start of the Milford Track. The track crosses the Clinton River on a large swing bridge, and continues along the true right (west) side as a gentle path without a stone or a blade of grass out of place. The lower portion of the Clinton, from here to past Clinton Forks Hut (the first hut for independent walkers), has excellent trout fishing.

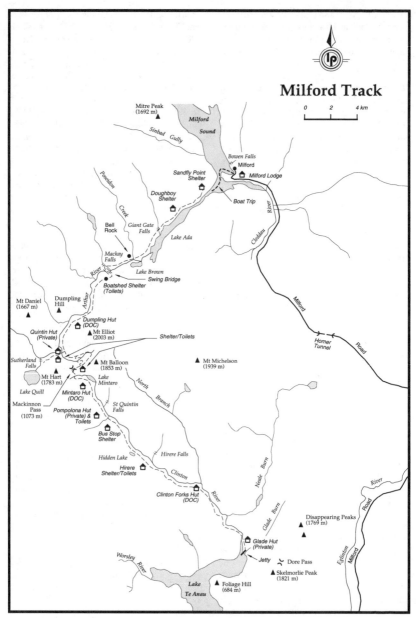

Milford Track

0   2   4 km

Mitre Peak
(1692 m)

*Milford
Sound*

Sinbad Gully

Bowen Falls

Milford

Sandfly Point
Shelter

Milford Lodge

Doughboy
Shelter

Poseidon

Boat Trip

Creek

Cleddau

*Giant Gate
Falls*

Bell
Rock

Lake Ada

Mackay
Falls

River

Lake Brown

Swing Bridge

Boatshed Shelter
(Toilets)

Mt Daniel
(1667 m)

Dumpling
Hill

Milford

Arthur

Dumpling Hut
(DOC)

Quintin Hut
(Private)

Mt Elliot
(2003 m)

Shelter/Toilets

Road

Homer
Tunnel

Sutherland
Falls

Mt Hart
(1783 m)

Mt Balloon
(1853 m)

Mt Michelson
(1939 m)

*Lake
Mintaro*

North Branch

Lake Quill

Mintaro Hut
(DOC)

Mackinnon
Pass
(1073 m)

Pompolona Hut
(Private) &
Toilets

St Quintin
Falls

Bus Stop
Shelter

Hidden Lake

Hirere Falls

Clinton

Hirere
Shelter/Toilets

River

Noale Burn

Clinton Forks Hut
(DOC)

Clade Burn

Disappearing Peaks
(1769 m)

Glade Hut
(Private)

Road

*Worsley
River*

Jetty

Dore Pass

River

Eglinton

Milford

Skelmorlie Peak
(1821 m)

*Lake
Te Anau*

Foliage Hill
(684 m)

At one point, the track offers an impressive view of the peaks next to Dore Pass, but most of the walk along the river is through beech forest. Clinton Forks Hut is reached two hours after leaving the launch at the wharf. All independent walkers must spend the first night here because the hut at Mintaro will be fully utilised by the party that left Glade Wharf the previous day.

Stage 2: Clinton Forks Hut to Mintaro Hut
Walking Time: four to 4½ hours
Accommodation: Mintaro Hut (40 bunks)

Beyond Clinton Forks, the track heads up the West Branch of the Clinton River, and in four km the valley becomes noticeably narrower, with granite walls boxing it in on both sides. The track remains in beech forest until it comes to the Prairies, the first grassy flat. There are good views from here towards Mt Fisher (2131 metres) to the west and Mackinnon Pass to the north. A short side track curves west (left) to Hidden Lake, on the far side of which is a towering waterfall.

The track re-enters bush and begins a rocky climb to the first Bus Stop Shelter, nine km from Clinton Forks, and then to the deluxe Pompolona Hut, the second night layover for guided walkers. The track crosses a swing bridge over Pompolona Creek and continues its winding course over low scrub. The track ascends more steeply as it passes a side track to St Quintin Falls and eventually works its way to Lake Mintaro and Mintaro Hut. The hut is a 3½-km walk beyond Pompolona Hut.

If the weather is clear, you might want to stash your pack and continue to the Mackinnon Pass (1073 metres), to be assured of seeing the impressive views without hindrance from clouds or rain. The pass is a 1½ to two-hour climb from the hut, and offers a spectacular view at sunset on a clear evening.

Stage 3: Mintaro Hut to Dumpling Hut
Walking Time: six hours
Accommodation: Dumpling Hut (40 bunks)

The track leaves the hut, swings west with the valley and resumes its climb to Mackinnon Pass. It crosses the Clinton River a second time and begins to follow a series of switchbacks out of the bush and into the alpine sections of the route. After four km at a knee-bending angle, the track reaches the large memorial cairn that honours the discovery of this scenic spot by Quintin Mackinnon and Ernest Mitchell, in 1888.

The track then levels out and crosses the rest of the alpine pass and there are impressive views all around of the Clinton and Arthur valleys and several nearby peaks. The two most prominent peaks on the pass are Mt Hart (1783 metres) and Mt Balloon (1853 metres). If the weather is fair, trampers like to spend some extra time at the pass; if it isn't, they can't get off it fast enough.

The track passes several tarns, reaches the emergency shelter and swings north for the descent. From the pass to Quintin Hut, the track drops 870 metres over a span of seven km. Soon, the track arrives at Roaring Burn Stream, crosses it and re-enters the bush.

Quintin, another private hut, has an airstrip, several buildings for the guided trampers and a day-use shelter for independent walkers. You should seriously consider leaving your pack and following the spur to Sutherland Falls (a 1½-hour round trip). The falls – three leaps totalling 580 metres – are an awesome sight and, for many, the highlight of the trip. If the weather is bad, wait until the following day and hike an hour back up the track from Dumpling Hut. This allows you to catch the falls at sunrise, when the early morning sun presents the cascading water in a different light.

The track leaves Quintin Hut and descends Gentle Annie Hill, re-entering thick forest, which is often slippery and wet. Within three km (an hour's walk) of Quintin, the track arrives at Dumpling Hut, a welcome sight after a long day over the pass.

Stage 4: Dumpling Hut to Sandfly Point
Walking Time: 5½ to six hours

The last leg of the Milford Track is an 18-km

walk to a shelter on Sandfly Point. The trek takes most people between five and six hours, and if you plan to meet the 2 pm launch to Milford, you should be out of Dumpling Hut no later than 8 am.

The track descends back into bush from the hut, and soon the roar of the Arthur River is heard as the track closely follows the true right (east) bank. Six km (about a two-hour walk) from the hut, the track reaches the private Boatshed Shelter (a morning tea stop for guided walkers) and then crosses the Arthur River on a large swing bridge. Just beyond the swing bridge, the track crosses a bridge over Mackay Creek, then comes to the side track to Mackay Falls and Bell Rock. Both natural wonders are a short walk from the main track and worth the time it takes to see them – especially Bell Rock where the water has eroded a space underneath the rock large enough to stand in.

The track begins to climb a rock shoulder of the valley above Lake Ada, and at one point there is a view of the lake all the way to the valley of Joe's River. From here, the track descends to Giant Gate Falls, passing the falls on a swing bridge before continuing along the lake shore. It takes about an hour to follow the lake past Doughboy Shelter (a private hut for guided walkers) through wide open flats at the end of the valley to the shelter at Sandfly Point.

Though it is important to be on time to meet the boat at 2 or 3 pm, Sandfly Point is not a place to spend an afternoon – it's a haven for the insect after which it was so aptly named.

HOLLYFORD TRACK

The Hollyford is the longest valley in Fiordland National Park, stretching 80 km from the Darran Mountains to Martins Bay, on the Tasman Sea. The upper portions of the valley are accessible by the Lower Hollyford Rd, which extends 18 km from Marian Corner (on the Milford Rd) to the start of the track. The track is generally recognised as extending from the road end to Martins Bay. It also includes a seven-hour segment from Lake Alabaster Hut to Olivine Hut, on the Pyke River.

In recent years, portions of the route have been upgraded, new transport services have emerged and more and more trampers have discovered the lush rainforest, extensive birdlife and unique marine fauna (seals and penguins) at Martins Bay. The track now averages about 1200 walkers a year, both guided parties and independent trampers, but still sees nowhere near the numbers using the Routeburn or Milford.

One reason the Hollyford will always lag behind its two famous counterparts to the south is the length of the trip. The track is basically a one-way tramp, unless a Big Bay-Lake Alabaster loop is taken through the Pyke Forest (a nine to 10-day trip for experienced trampers only). Otherwise it's a four-day walk out to Martins Bay, where you either turn around and retrace your steps to the road end or arrange to be flown out.

Once in Martins Bay, two things are needed: spare time and lots of insect repellent. The isolated bay is a great spot to spend an extra day because it offers superb coastal scenery and saltwater fishing as well as good views of a seal colony and penguins. But be prepared for the sandflies and mosquitoes that quickly introduce themselves to all passing trampers.

Information

See the Information section of the Milford Track. The Hollyford experts are HTC, the Hollyford Tourist & Travel Company (☎ 442 3760), which helps all walkers, not just those using its services.

Maps

The best map for this walk is the 1:75,000 Trackmaps No 335-03 *(Hollyford Track)*. You do not need to get any of the quads of the 1:50,000 Topomaps 260 series. At a scale of 1:250,000, the Parkmaps No 273-03 *(Fiordland National Park)* is too small.

Huts

Trampers have the use of five DOC huts and

one private hut on the track – Hidden Falls, Alabaster, McKerrow Island, Demon Trail, Hokuri and Neil Drysdale's 'Mouse House' and sleepout. The latter, private huts at Martins Bay (accommodation for 10 to 12 people), replace the Martins Bay Hut which was destroyed by fire in December 1990.

These are all Category Three huts ($4), except the private huts ($6). It is essential to book the private huts through Air Fiordland (☎ 249 7505). All DOC huts have mattresses, water and toilet facilities.

Access

Many trampers will avoid backtracking all or a portion of the track by using the transport services of HTC (☎ 442 3760). The company offers a number of possibilities, including flying from an airstrip near Gunns Camp to Martins Bay or from Milford Sound to Martins Bay. They also run a jet-boat along Lake McKerrow and will transport trampers from the head of the lake to Martins Bay in either direction. This saves a day and eliminates walking the Demon Trail, by far the most difficult portion of the track. Arrangements can be made by either calling or writing to the company, or by contacting HTC staff on the track (at their Pyke or Martins Bay lodges).

A number of buses on the Te Anau to Milford run will drop off or pick up trampers at the Marian Corner Shelter. Some buses drive in as far as Gunns Camp. This still puts you about eight km short of the start of the track, and the only way to reach it without a vehicle is to walk or try to hitch a ride.

The Trackwalker (☎ 442 3663) service, run in conjunction with Backpackers Express (see the Access section for Mt Aspiring National Park in the Otago chapter), has a service from Queenstown via Te Anau to the start of the Hollyford. It departs from Queenstown at 9 am and from Te Anau at 11.30 am, reaching Hollyford car park at 1.30 pm; the cost is $50 one-way.

There are a number of operators who will fly you out from Martins Bay, including Air Fiordland (☎ 249 7505).

Places to Stay

For accommodation in Te Anau, Milford Sound and on the road between these places, see Places to Stay for the Milford Track, earlier in this section. Many trampers, especially those coming directly from the Milford or Routeburn tracks, will make their way to Gunns Camp. You can get supplies here – the small store is well stocked with backpackers' food. The next day, it's a two-hour walk to the road end and another three hours to Hidden Falls Hut.

The Track

The following description covers the Hollyford Track from the road end to Martins Bay, a five-day trip that's rated medium. From Martins Bay, trampers either backtrack, arrange to be flown out or continue on the Big Bay-Lake Alabaster loop (see the following Other Tracks section). The track suffered extensive damage in the 1994 floods, so seek advice in Te Anau or from HTC.

Stage 1: Hollyford Rd End to Hidden Falls
Walking Time: two to three hours
Accommodation: Hidden Falls Hut (12 bunks)

A track departs from the shelter at the end of the road. In less than a km it crosses a swing bridge over Eel Creek, then continues sidling bluffs for another km to a second bridge, over Swamp Creek. Sections of raised boardwalk avoid the swampy areas.

At this point, the track closely follows the true right (east) bank of the river, offering an occasional view of the snowcapped Darran Mountains to the west. It's about a three-km walk until the track emerges on the open flat of Hidden Falls Creek and quickly passes Sunshine Hut, an HTC shelter.

Just beyond the private hut, a side track leads to Hidden Falls, which are two minutes upstream from the swing bridge. Hidden Falls Hut is on the northern side of the bridge, five minutes away. It has gas rings as well as a wood stove, and has a good view of Mt Madeline to the west. There is also a

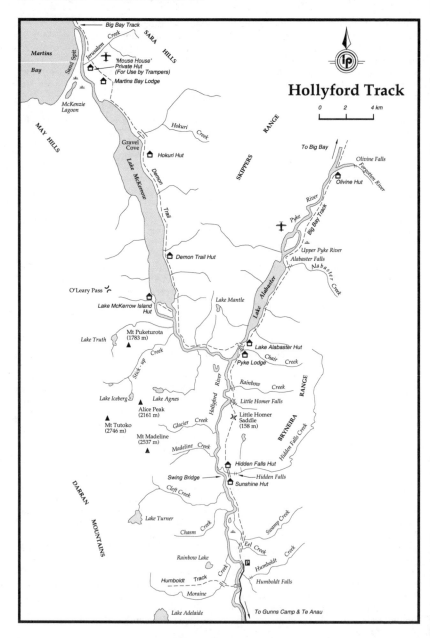

Hollyford Track

0   2   4 km

four-bunk unit adjacent to the hut which can be booked through the DOC in Te Anau.

Stage 2: Hidden Falls to Lake Alabaster

Walking Time: 3½ to four hours
Accommodation: Lake Alabaster Hut (12 bunks)

The track departs behind the hut, and passes through a lowland forest of ribbonwood and podocarp for two km before beginning its climb to Little Homer Saddle, the high point of the trip. It's about a 30 to 45-minute climb through beech forest to reach the saddle (158 metres); through the trees there is a view of Mt Madeline and Mt Tutoko to the west. Tutoko (2746 metres) is Fiordland's highest mountain and one of New Zealand's most inaccessible peaks.

The descent is steeper than the climb, until the track reaches Homer Creek at the spot where nearby Little Homer Falls thunders 60 metres down into the stream. It's another half-hour before the track swings back to the Hollyford and crosses a swing bridge over Rainbow Creek. The track stays with the Hollyford River for two km before it reaches the confluence with the Pyke River and passes Pyke Lodge (another HTC hut).

The track crosses a swing bridge over Chair Creek and then comes to the giant swing bridge over the Pyke River. If you're planning to stop for the night, skip the Pyke bridge and continue up the true left (east) side of the river for another 20 minutes to the hut on the shores of Lake Alabaster. The hut does not have gas rings, but the lake makes it a scenic place to spend the night and it's a favoured spot for trout fishing.

Stage 3: Lake Alabaster to McKerrow Island

Walking Time: four hours
Accommodation: McKerrow Island Hut (12 bunks)

Backtrack for 20 minutes to the swing bridge over the Pyke River and, after crossing it, continue beneath the rocky bluffs along the lower section of the river. Here, the track enters a lush podocarp forest, and all sights and sounds of the two great rivers are lost in the thick canopy of the trees.

The track works its way through the bush for two hours before breaking out into a clearing next to the Hollyford, now twice as powerful as it was above the Pyke River junction.

Before reaching Lake McKerrow, the Hollyford River swings west around McKerrow Island; another channel (usually dry) rounds the island to the east. Near the dry river bed, there is a sign pointing up the main track to Demon Trail Hut. This is also the start of an unmarked route across the eastern channel to a track on McKerrow Island. Follow this track around the northern side of the island to reach McKerrow Island Hut, pleasantly situated near the mouth of the main channel and partially hidden by bush.

If the rain has been heavy, it may be impossible to cross the eastern river bed, in which case trampers can continue on the Demon Trail and, in 1½ hours or so, reach Demon Trail Hut. If you're at McKerrow Island Hut and it rains, there's little you can do but wait until the channel can be safely forded. One of the better fishing spots for trout is usually around the mouth of the main channel – check the log book for the most recent catches.

Stage 4: Demon Trail from McKerrow Island to Hokuri

Walking Time: 6½ to seven hours
Accommodation: Demon Trail Hut (12 bunks); Hokuri Hut (12 bunks)

From the signpost on the main track, it's a 20-minute walk to the start of the Demon Trail, which begins in a clearing that was once the site of a hut. This portion of the track used to be called 'the most exhausting non-alpine track in New Zealand', but has been upgraded in recent years. Still, the trail is rocky, undulating and basically a tedious walk. It's three km (a good hour's walk) to the new Demon Trail Hut, which sits on a terrace overlooking Lake McKerrow, a pleasant spot.

At Slip Creek, considered to be the halfway point, a nearby rock bivvy is large enough to hold six people if emergency shelter is needed. Most trampers, however, try to cover the 12 km from McKerrow Island to Hokuri as fast as possible. For those who push on to Demon Trail Hut, plan on a five-hour walk the next day to Hokuri.

Stage 5: Hokuri to Martins Bay
Walking Time: 4½ to five hours
Accommodation: Martins Bay Private Hut

It's about a 10-minute walk beyond the hut to Hokuri Creek, which can usually be forded near its mouth on Gravel Cove. If not, there is a walkwire 15 minutes upstream. The track continues along the lake shore for 1½ hours and passes the township of James-town, though little remains of the settlement today. In another half-hour you reach the signposted turn-off where the track leaves the lake for good and heads inland.

The track cuts through bush at this point and, in about three km (an hour's walk), it breaks out into the grassy clearing where the Martins Bay airstrip is located. A sign points to Martins Bay Lodge, the last HTC hut, while poles lead across the grassy clearing and around one end of the airstrip. Martins Bay Hut was burnt down in December 1990 and the 'Mouse House', two private huts, and a sleepout with cooking facilities have been made available for trampers. The cost is $6 per person per night, but you must book through Air Fiordland (☎ 249 7505). The hut is on the western side of the track, just before Jerusalem Creek, and it's a good base from which to explore this fascinating area.

After the normally easy ford, the track continues through forest, passing several views of the mouth of the Hollyford River and the sandy spit on the other side. Within three km, the track emerges from the bush, passes some artistic rock formations and then swings north to the site of the former Martins Bay Hut, situated in coastal scrub overlooking Long Reef.

Nearby is a rocky point, with easy access to deep pools offering productive coastal fishing. There is a seal colony just a 15-minute walk down the rocks of Long Reef; it's one of the best in New Zealand. You might also spot penguins shuffling along the shore from one boulder to the next. An old cattle track continues north then east of Long Reef, and this is the track to take to Big Bay and the circular route to Lake Alabaster.

KEPLER TRACK
The Kepler is one of the best-planned tracks in New Zealand: a perfect loop, beginning and ending near the control gates where the Waiau River empties into the southern end of Lake Te Anau. (DOC staff can actually show you the start of the track from a window inside the Te Anau visitor centre.)

It's an alpine crossing, designed to take pressure off the Routeburn and Milford tracks, and includes an all-day trek on the tops above the bush-line, with incredible panoramas of Lake Te Anau, its South Fiord Arm, the Jackson Peaks and, of course, the Kepler Mountains.

The 40-bunk huts are definitely needed. They may even be overflowing as more trampers discover this new, hassle-free walk.

Information
For information about the Kepler Track, see Information for the Milford Track.

Maps
The best map for this track is the 1:50,000 Trackmaps No 335-09 *(Kepler Track)*. You don't need any of the Topomaps 260 quads.

Huts
The Kepler Track is a Great Walk, so between late October and mid-April the three DOC huts on the track are well serviced, with heating, gas for cooking, mattresses, running water, flush toilets, and a warden in residence. Outside the summer season, huts are unserviced and require the purchase of back-country tickets.

The 40-bunk huts are Mt Luxmore, Iris Burn and Moturau, each costing $14 per night. Not far off the track is the Shallow Bay Hut ($4). Alternatively, you can camp at the two camp sites, Brod Bay and near Iris Burn Hut ($6 per person).

Access
This is one of the few walks in New Zealand that can be made into a round trip from a major town. The start of the track is about five km from the Te Anau visitor centre (a good hour's walk). Follow the Manapouri-Te Anau Rd south and take the first right turn which is clearly marked by a yellow AA sign. Continue past the golf course and take another right-hand turn, go past a car park and walk across to the control gates to reach the track.

The Kepler Track Shuttle Bus operates from the Te Anau Motor Park (☎ 249 7457, 249 7106). Its transport package costs $16 and includes 9 and 10.30 am departures on the *Manuska* to Brod Bay or 10 am, 3 and 5 pm departures from the Waiau River swing bridge. Sinbad Cruises has a number of options for transport around the lake, especially to the Brod Bay end of the Kepler Track. Lakeland Boat Hire (☎ 249 8364) provides a water-taxi service; it departs at 8.30 am and then by arrangement.

Places to Stay
For details of accommodation in Te Anau, see Places to Stay for the Milford Track. For accommodation in Manapouri, see Places to Stay for the Dusky Track.

The Track
The Kepler Track begins by ascending to Mt Luxmore Hut on the first day. This means there is almost no climbing on the second day, when trampers are faced with the long alpine crossing.

The track, completed in 1988, is a cut and well-marked trail. But the Kepler is considerably more difficult than the Routeburn and doesn't even compare with the Milford. It's rated difficult because the first day involves a gruelling 850-metre climb, from the shores of Lake Te Anau to Mt Luxmore, above the bush-line. If you have trouble handling the first day, then return – the second day is even longer and more difficult.

The track is designed to be walked in four days, though this can be reduced to three days by eliminating the night in the final hut, on the shores of Lake Manapouri. It's a 5½-hour walk down the Iris Burn Valley to Moturau Hut. In another 1½ hours, you cross the swing bridge over the Waiau River at Rainbow Reach. In 15 minutes you'll be on the Manapouri-Te Anau Road, 11 km south of Te Anau.

Stage 1: Control Gates to Mt Luxmore Hut
Walking Time: six to seven hours
Accommodation: Mt Luxmore Hut (40 bunks)

The track begins by skirting the lake to Dock Bay, staying on the fringe of a beech forest. Within half an hour, the track begins to wind through an impressive growth of tree ferns, with crown ferns carpeting the forest floor, and then reaches the signposted junction to Beer's Farm, a more direct (but tougher) 4½-hour climb to Mt Luxmore. The track continues to skirt the lake's western shore and crosses a swing bridge over Coal Creek.

In another three km, the track crosses another stream and arrives at Brod Bay, a beautiful sandy beach on the lake. There are pit toilets, a table and a barbecue here, and for those who made a late start and have a tent, this is a scenic place to camp.

Great Walks Ticket

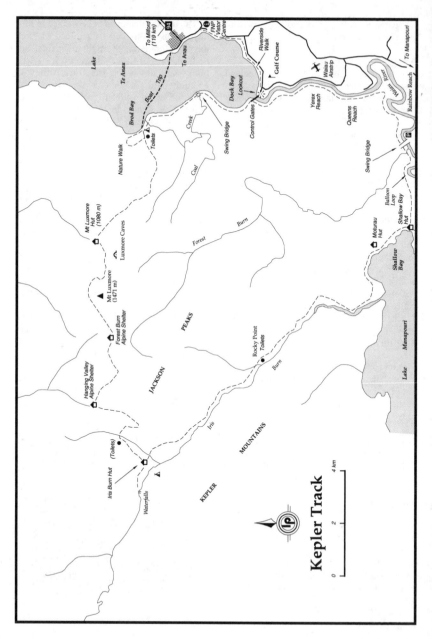

Kepler Track

The track to Mt Luxmore is signposted near the beach, and you now begin the steepest climb of the trip. The track climbs steadily and in three km (two hours) reaches a set of towering limestone bluffs, an ideal lunch spot. At the bluff, the track swings due west, skirts the rock, then swings north and resumes climbing through stunted mountain beech.

Within a km, the track breaks out of the bush-line and you get the first glorious view of the trip, a panorama of Lake Te Anau, Lake Manapouri and the surrounding Takatimu, Snowden and Earl mountains. From here, the track becomes a marked route through the alpine scrub, with planking crossing the wet sections. The track climbs a couple of small rises and, within an hour of breaking out of the bush, skirts a small bluff. On the other side, Mt Luxmore Hut can be seen, with its namesake peak behind it.

This hut, like all huts on the track, was built in 1987, and features two levels, gas rings, great views from the common room and even toilets that flush. From here, Mt Luxmore (1471 metres) can easily be climbed without packs (a two to three-hour round trip). The warden, who collects the fees, receives a weather report every morning, around 8 am.

Stage 2: Mt Luxmore Hut to Iris Burn Hut
Walking Time: seven to nine hours
Accommodation: Iris Burn Hut (40 bunks)

Most trampers will find this a long day. Wait for the weather report in the morning to be sure of good conditions for the alpine crossing, then head out immediately to make full use of the day on the track. Carry a full litre of water because there are only a few streams along the way (and these could be dry during summer).

The track departs from the hut and climbs towards the unnamed peak east of Mt Luxmore but ends up sidling its northern slopes. Mt Luxmore looms overhead. Within three km of the hut, the track swings to the north to skirt the ridge that runs north from the summit. For those interested in climbing the peak, easily distinguished by its large

trig, it's best at this point to scramble to the top of the ridge and drop the packs. From here, it's an easy 15 to 20-minute climb to the top. If the weather is clear, the view is perhaps the finest of the trip – a 360° panorama that includes the Darran Mountains, 70 km to the north.

Backtrack to your packs. From the ridge, you can easily see the track and its snow poles on the west side. The track resumes on the other side of the ridge, skirting a bluff on steep-sided slopes for the next three km, until it reaches a high point on the ridge. Below, you can see the first emergency shelter (1235 metres). The track swings away from the ridge and sidles along the slopes around it to make the final descent to Forest Burn Alpine Shelter, close to the Forest Burn Saddle, reached 2½ to 3½ hours from Mt Luxmore Hut. Beware of strong wind gusts when crossing the saddle.

From the shelter, the track skirts the bluffed end of a ridge, with great views of the South Fiord. In 3½ km, the track rounds the bluffs onto a ridge crest and the walk becomes considerably easier. You follow the ridge, skirt two knobs and then climb another one. Once on this high point, you can see the second emergency hut, Hanging Valley Alpine Shelter.

The shelter sits on a ridge at 1341 metres and is usually reached in three hours from the first shelter (5½ to six hours from Mt Luxmore Hut). The views are great, and if it's still early in the day, spend some extra time here – it takes only two to 2½ hours to reach the Iris Burn Hut and, because most of the walk is through bush, this view is much more inspiring than anything else you'll see along the way.

The track leaves the second shelter and follows a ridge to the south for two km. The ridge crest is sharp, and at times you feel as though you're on a tightrope. Eventually, the track drops off the ridge with a sharp turn to the west and descends into the bush. The descent is a quick one, down an endless series of switchbacks, and the track drops 390 metres before crossing a branch of the Iris Burn.

Once on the other side, the track levels out as it skirts the side of this hanging valley, at one point becoming a boardwalk across the steep face. The views of the Iris Burn below are excellent and there's a seat here, so you can lean back, put your feet on the guard rail and enjoy the scenery.

The final segment of the day covers more switchbacks, with the track dropping 450 metres. Just when it levels out, Iris Burn Hut comes into view, a welcome sight for many.

Stage 3: Iris Burn Hut to Moturau Hut
Walking Time: five to six hours
Accommodation: Moturau Hut (40 bunks)

After the long alpine crossing, this is a very easy, level and enjoyable segment of the track. The walk to Moturau Hut usually takes less than six hours, so many trampers begin with a side trip (20 minutes) to see the impressive waterfalls near Iris Burn Hut.

The main track begins behind the hut with a short climb before levelling out in the beech forest. Within three km, it crosses a branch of the Iris Burn and breaks out into a wide, open area. The cause of the clearing, a huge landslide that occurred in January 1984, is to your right – piles of rocks and fallen trees can be seen everywhere. The track returns to the bush on the other side of the clearing and continues down the valley, at times following the river closely, to the delight of anglers.

The track crosses several small branches of the burn, and remains almost entirely in the bush (one section is through an incredibly moss-laden stand of trees) until it reaches a rocky clearing, where the boulders are bright orange (the result of a healthy growth of red lichen). At this point, 11 km from the hut, the track climbs and follows a bluff above the burn; sometimes it's a boardwalk hanging from a sheer face, and there are excellent views of the river below.

Four km from the red-lichen clearing, the track descends away from the bluff and swings south. In another two km, it passes a view of Lake Manapouri at the mouth of Iris Burn, a popular spot for anglers. The track swings east and, in a km, returns within sight of the lake. In the final leg, the track skirts the shore of Shallow Bay until it arrives at Moturau Hut.

This is a pleasant hut with a view of Lake Manapouri from the kitchen. Much of Shallow Bay has a sandy shoreline. Unfortunately, many trampers skip this hut to save the $14 hut fee, and continue to the Rainbow Reach swing bridge.

Stage 4: Moturau Hut to Control Gates
Walking Time: 4½ to five hours

For the first two km, the track heads south through bush, until it reaches a junction with a short track to Shallow Bay. The main track heads east (the left fork) and within a km comes to a large swamp known as Amoeboid Mire, which is crossed on a long boardwalk. The track skirts the southern side of the grassy swamp, passing a small lake in the middle, before reaching an old river terrace that overlooks Balloon Loop, five km from the hut.

The track bridge crosses Forest Burn, which meanders confusingly before emptying into Balloon Loop. From here, it's half an hour to the swing bridge at Rainbow Reach, 1½ hours from the hut. Along the way, the track skirts bluffs that overlook the wide Waiau River. If you choose to cross the Rainbow Reach swing bridge, it's a 15-minute walk up the metalled road to the Manapouri-Te Anau Rd, where it's easy to hitch a ride in either direction.

Otherwise, the track continues in an easterly direction, and within an hour begins to swing due north to pass Queens Reach. From the reach, the track climbs onto a river terrace, where there are views through the trees of a set of rapids, and then moves into an area of manuka scrub. At Yerex Reach, two hours from the swing bridge, the track passes a few old posts, and a quiet segment of the river known as Beer's Pool. At this point, you're only 30 to 45 minutes from the control gates. In all, it takes about 2½ to 3½ hours to walk the 11 km from Rainbow Reach.

DUSKY TRACK

The Dusky Track starts on two of Fiordland's largest lakes, ends at its longest fiord and traverses three major valleys and two mountain ranges. It offers trampers the widest range of experiences and scenery of any track in the park. It also offers the most remote wilderness setting. But it's remoteness, and the high cost of transportation in and out of the area, means that the Dusky Track, for all its beauty and variety, attracts less than 500 trampers a year.

The Dusky is basically an inverted Y-shaped track that goes to Supper Cove, with its end points on relatively isolated arms of Lake Manapouri and Lake Hauroko. Supper Cove is the scenic eastern end of 44-km long Dusky Sound, the longest fiord in the park.

In recent years, the track has been rerouted and upgraded and the huts improved, but this walk is still a challenging one, even for moderately experienced trampers. It's also a fairly long walk.

Traditionally, many trampers begin the trip by taking a launch across Lake Hauroko, then trekking across Pleasant Ridge to Loch Maree Hut. From here, they head to Supper Cove, backtrack to Loch Maree and then exit at the West Arm of Lake Manapouri, taking another launch to Manapouri. This is the cheapest way to walk the track, and involves the least amount of backtracking. Lake Hauroko can get very rough at times, and it's not unknown for trampers to be stranded while waiting for a scheduled launch. This trip requires eight to nine days.

To reduce the number of days required and to avoid all backtracking, many trampers arrange to be picked up or dropped off by float plane at Supper Cove. Using this option, trampers take a launch trip across Lake Manapouri, hike down the Spey River to Loch Maree Hut, where a spare day is often spent climbing scenic Pleasant Ridge. The trip ends with the walk out to Supper Cove and float-plane transport back to Te Anau. This walk, which requires only four to five days, is the one described here. Additional notes at the end of the section are given for the trek to Lake Hauroko.

Information

See the Information section of the Milford Track for details of The Fiordland National Park Visitors Centre & Museum.

Fiordland Travel (☎ 249 7416) is the main information and tour centre in Manapouri – the office on the waterfront organises most of the trips. Time your visit to the centre so that it doesn't coincide with a boat departure, otherwise they won't have time to help you.

Get the free booklet *Manapouri to Doubtful Sound*. It contains lots of information on how to get to the start of the Dusky Track.

Map

Although the track is well marked, it's best to purchase quads S148 *(Wilmot)* and S157 *(Heath)* of the old NZMS 1 series. There is no Trackmaps production, and the quads of the Topomaps 260 series are not available yet.

Huts

The DOC provides and maintains the following Category Three ($4) huts on this walk: Upper Spey, Kintail, Loch Maree, Lake Roe, Supper Cove, Halfway and Hauroko Burn. The basic West Arm Hut, at the start of the track, has six bunks but no fireplace; it also costs $4.

Equipment

Among items needed for this trip are rain gear (parka and pants) and lots of insect repellent.

Access

InterCity used to have buses to Manapouri, but these seem to have been discontinued. Fiordland Travel has lots of people going from Manapouri to Te Anau to hook up with their Te Anau trips, and vice versa, so they operate a Te Anau-Manapouri bus service for $5 (children $2.50) one-way. Many other tour buses also bring groups in here. The Te Anau Motor Park operates a service to Manapouri ($39 return). Te Anau is still the departure point for most Dusky Track trampers.

The launch across Lake Manapouri is offered through Fiordland Travel (☎ 249

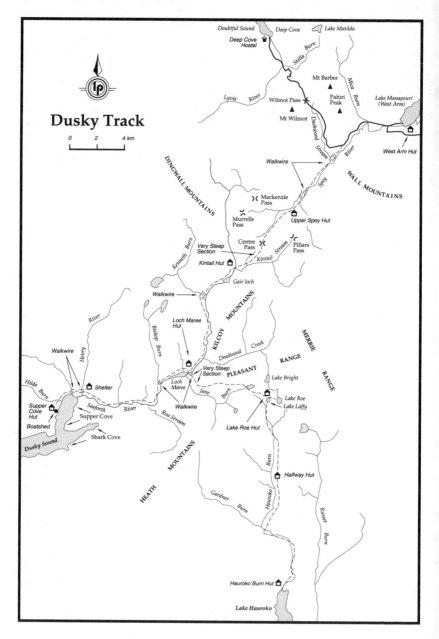

Dusky Track

0   2   4 km

Top: Mitre Peak from Milford Sound (NZTB)
Bottom: Mitre Peak, Fiordland (NZTB)

Tramper on Rakiura Track, Stewart Island (DOC)

7419, 249 6602), on Te Anau Terrace, Te Anau, just down from the visitor centre. The boat leaves twice daily from October to April at 9.30 am. The fare for adults is $25 one-way to the West Arm, or about $40 for the round trip if you decide to backtrack and depart by water. There is also a charge of about $3 for the bus trip from West Arm to the start of the Dusky Track; this arrangement is at the discretion of the driver and is subject to seat availability.

You can arrange the float-plane service through Waterwings Airways (☎ 249 7405) in Te Anau, conveniently located between Fiordland Travel and the national park visitor centre. Check what it costs to be dropped off or picked up in Supper Cove. It's wise to book ahead for the plane because the company is busy in summer offering scenic flights (write to Waterwings Airways at PO Box 22, Te Anau). Fiordland Helicopters (☎ 249 7575) will fly four trampers, plus their gear, to Supper Cove for $680. Others to try are The Helicopter Line (☎ 249 7209) and Southern Lakes Helicopters (☎ 249 7167).

If you're including Lake Hauroko in your trip, you will probably depart from Tuatapere. The town is reached via Invercargill by bus; for details of the current service, contact the Tuatapere DOC field centre (☎ 226 6607), Main Rd.

To get to the Hauroko car park from Tuatapere, try Borland Road Services (☎ 218 3308), Buchanan Motors, Invercargill; Bennetts Passenger Service (☎ 226 6715), 71 Main St, Tuatapere; or A B Mini Tours (☎ 208 7704), Gore.

The Lake Hauroko Tours boat service (☎ 226 6681) provides travel to the end of the lake most Saturdays and Wednesdays. Apart from these days, this is an unscheduled service, so prior arrangements must be made through V & H McKay in Tuatapere.

Places to Stay

Manapouri For accommodation in nearby Te Anau, see Places to Stay for the Milford Track. The *Lakeview Motel* (☎ 249 6624) on the Te Anau Rd has camp sites/cabins for

$15/28 for two. The *Manapouri Glade Motel & Motor Park* (☎ 249 6623) has camp sites/cabins for $15/26.

Deep Cove You can stay at the *Deep Cove Hostel* at Deep Cove on Doubtful Sound for $17 per person. Arrangements to stay and get there must be made through Fiordland Travel. You have to buy sector fares on the Doubtful Cruise to stay here: Manapouri-Deep Cove is $47 (one-way), and if you want the cruise on Doubtful Sound it's $29 extra (book at Fiordland Travel, at the Manapouri wharf).

Tuatapere The *Five Mountains Holiday Park* (☎ 226 6418), 14 Clifden Rd, has twins/doubles for $10/35.

The Track

The following four-day trip, rated difficult, is described from the West Arm of Lake Manapouri to Supper Cove.

Stage 1: West Arm to Upper Spey Hut

Walking Time: five to 5½ hours from the Jetty
Accommodation: Upper Spey Hut (12 bunks)

From the jetty on West Arm, the trip begins on the Wilmot Pass Rd. If you are finishing the track at West Arm and have to wait for transport, West Arm Hut accommodates about six people, but you will need a stove.

The Wilmot Pass Rd crosses a bridge over Mica Burn and comes to a junction with a secondary road on the true right (west) side. Those trampers heading to Upper Spey Hut for the first night continue on Wilmot Pass Rd and in 20 minutes come to the signposted start of the Dusky Track. It is 45 minutes from West Arm to the turn-off to the track.

The track enters a forest of ribbonwood and beech along the true left (west) side of the Spey River. It is well graded at the beginning and in little more than a km comes to two walkwires spanning Dashwood Stream. The track gently climbs the valley, passes through a couple of small clearings and, four hours from the jetty, fords Waterfall Creek. A short distance beyond the creek, the track crosses a second walkwire, to the true right (east) side of the Spey River.

It's a short climb from the walkwire to the edge of a large but swampy clearing. Yellow poles lead you across the clearing to the Upper Spey Hut, at the top end. This hut has a potbelly stove.

Stage 2: Upper Spey Hut to Kintail Hut

Walking Time: five to six hours
Accommodation: Kintail Hut (12 bunks)

The day begins with a steep climb along Warren Burn, the headwaters of the Spey River, before levelling out. The track then leaves the stream and the bush to climb steeply again towards Centre Pass, one of three saddles that lead into the Seaforth Valley. The route up through the alpine scrub and tussock slopes is marked by snow poles. Snow may be encountered on the pass as late as November, but after that it's usually clear until April. Looming over the pass to the north-east is Mt Memphis (1383 metres), and occasionally trampers drop their packs and climb it.

The descent on the west side, to the Seaforth River, is considerably longer and steeper than the climb on the eastern side, but it begins on a slope which has an alpine herb field with mountain buttercups. There are excellent views of Gairloch, Tripod Hill and the Seaforth Valley.

When the track enters the bush, the drop steepens as you descend to the true right (north) side of Kintail Stream. Follow it to a walkwire over the Seaforth just above its confluence with the stream. On the other side, there is a short side track that heads upstream (the right fork) to Kintail Hut, five minutes away. This hut has platforms, so additional people can be squeezed in. Once the potbelly stove is alight, the place heats up quickly. There are also good camp sites along the river's edge, near the confluence with Kintail Stream.

Stage 3: Kintail Hut to Loch Maree

Walking Time: four to five hours
Accommodation: Loch Maree Hut (12 bunks)

Return to the walkwire but remain on the true right (west) side of the river. The walking is easy because the track heads south-west towards Gairloch, the first of two lakes that you pass. At the top end of the loch, the track crosses a boggy area, then skirts the shoreline to its outlet, where you begin to descend a gorge to Kenneth Burn. The tramping is rough, until you arrive at the walkwire across the burn.

The valley flattens out after Kenneth Burn and the travel becomes easier again. Halfway (about three km) to Deadwood Creek, the track crosses a walkwire over an unnamed stream. Several clearings are crossed, and track markers indicate where the track re-enters bush. The track also crosses a number of small gullies that fill with water when the Seaforth is swollen.

Just before the confluence of the Seaforth River and Deadwood Creek, the track climbs over a knob, then continues to sidle the steep valley on the true right (west) side. This is difficult walking, along a stretch that is prone to flooding during heavy rains.

It ends about five minutes before Loch Maree Hut, when you emerge at the six-foot track that was built in 1903 by 60 West Coast miners. The miners' track was originally intended to continue to Lake Manapouri, but was never completed – you can still see picks, crowbars and a hefty anvil along the side of the track just below Loch Maree.

For many, Loch Maree is one of the most scenic spots along the track. The loch is a flooded lake caused by a landslide; fallen tree trunks still decorate the area and stumps can be seen above the water. In the early morning, this can be a most unusual sight. A layer of mist lies over the lake, silhouetting the stumps and transforming the loch into a prehistoric landscape. The Loch Maree Hut is on a little peninsula at the head of the lake. It is equipped with a potbelly stove.

Near the hut, a walkwire across the Seaforth River begins the overland route to Lake Hauroko. A common day trip for those not planning to exit at this lake is a hike up Pleasant Ridge to Lake Roe. The ridge, an alpine area of numerous tarns, offers the best overview of Dusky Sound from anywhere on the track. Lake Roe Hut is actually on Lake Laffy; it's another 20 minutes to Lake Roe itself, a beautiful body of water in a setting of granite outcrops. A round-trip tramp to the lake, without packs, is a seven-hour walk.

Stage 4: Loch Maree to Supper Cove
Walking Time: six hours
Accommodation: Supper Cove Hut (12 bunks)

The route around Loch Maree has been upgraded to an all-weather track, but occasionally the lake still rises enough to make the track impassable for a day or two. After leaving the hut, you climb above the northern shore before descending to a walkwire across Bishop Burn. At this point, the track swings onto the wide miners' track, for an easy stroll down the Seaforth Valley.

The valley is flat, and trampers are aided with a walkwire over Macfarlane Stream and a cable ladder over a cliff. About four hours from Bishop Burn, the track passes several heavily bushed flats, where 10 Canadian moose were released in 1910 (moose were last seen in 1970), and arrives at the old Supper Cove Hut, built in 1903 and reconditioned by park authorities in 1955.

It takes another hour to reach the present hut, the track crosses walkwires over Henry and Hilda burns and then climbs around the hillside into Supper Cove. Some undulating terrain is covered before the track descends to a walkwire across a small stream; the hut is on the other side. At low tide, this segment of climbing can be avoided by simply following the beach. There is a small boatshed next to the hut, with a dinghy for public use. You have to row some distance out into Dusky Sound to catch groper, but if you have a line, it's easy to land a few blue cod in the cove itself or even from shore.

Lake Hauroko to Loch Maree
For most trampers, it is a three-day walk from the lake to Loch Maree Hut. The Hauroko Burn Hut (10 bunks, potbelly stove) is near the jetty on the lake, for those who are dropped off late. Otherwise it's a

six-hour walk to the next facility, Halfway Hut (12 bunks, open fire).

The next day, the track follows a gentle grade until it reaches the forks of Hauroko Burn, where it climbs steeply out of the bush to Lake Roe Hut (12 bunks, potbelly stove). The walking time from Halfway Hut to Lake Roe Hut is five hours.

The final leg is the most scenic. Snow poles mark the route around the outlet of Lake Horizon and then across Pleasant Ridge, where there are good views of Dusky Sound. At the end of the ridge, the track drops steeply to the Seaforth River and Loch Maree Hut. The walk from Lake Roe Hut to Loch Maree takes four to five hours.

OTHER TRACKS
Big Bay-Lake Alabaster Loop
Most of this route is in the Pyke Forest, but access to it is primarily from the Hollyford Track in Fiordland National Park. When the two tracks are combined, they form a wilderness loop that continues from Martins Bay along the coast at Big Bay, inland to Pyke River and then down the shore of Lake Alabaster to return to the Hollyford. The *Pyke-Big Bay Route* pamphlet is available from the park visitor centre in Te Anau.

George Sound
The marked route extends from the Northeast Arm of the Middle Fiord on Lake Te Anau to George Sound. There are three huts along the track and there are rowing boats on Lake Hankinson – it's a three-hour row to the other end, where the track resumes. The second day is a 10-hour trek from Thompson Hut over Henry Saddle to George Sound Hut. The round trip is a four to six-day walk, rated difficult. Get a copy of the *George Sound Track* notes from the DOC visitor centre in Te Anau.

For transport and advice, contact Fiordland Bird & Bush (☎ 249 7078), Lakeland Boat Hire (☎ 249 8364) and Western Safaris (☎ 249 7226). The Helicopter Line (☎ 249 7209), Fiordland Helicopters (☎ 249 7575), Southern Lakes Helicopters (☎ 249 7167) and Waterwings Airways (☎ 249 7405) all offer drop-off or pick-up services from George Sound.

Takatimu Mountains

These mountains, easily accessible from Te Anau and Invercargill, are outside Fiordland National Park. The three $4 huts in the mountains – Becketts, Princhester and Aparima – can be linked by challenging tramps. Ask in Tuatapere or Te Anau for a copy of the *Takatimu Mountains* brochure.

Waitutu Tracks

Two tracks in this area have been developed for tramping: the South Coast Track (a one-way track which runs from the end of Blue Cliffs Beach Rd, along the edge of Te Waewae Bay, south of Tuatapere) and the Hump Track (from Te Waewae Bay to Lake Hauroko).

South Coast Track The track begins after the bridge over Track Burn and extends 44 km to Big River, the boundary between Waitutu Forest and Fiordland National Park. Most trampers tackle only the first half,

which includes an old logging tramway and four impressive viaducts to the mouth of Wairaurahiri River. There are two huts (Port Craig and Wairaurahiri) along this section and one more beyond it, at Waitutu River. A round-trip walk to Wairaurahiri River and back would be a three to four-day trip, rated easy.

Hump Track This track starts at the same place as the South Coast Track, but soon turns north towards the Hump Ridge at Blue-cliffs Beach (on Te Waewae Bay). The track passes above the bush-line and provides spectacular views from the Hump Ridge (1067 metres). It's a good, challenging three-day walk, with overnight stops at the Category Three Hump and Teal huts. The latter is near the shores of Lake Hauroko, a good day's walk from the Hauroko car park.

Pourakino Jet Tours (☎ 234 8512, 224 6130) operates trips upriver from the Wairaurahiri Hut to the Lake Hauroko car park, which opens up interesting tramping permutations.

Stewart Island (Rakiura)

Going to Stewart Island, New Zealand's third largest island, is going to extremes. This is the southernmost part of New Zealand, off the South Island south of Invercargill. It's a most remote area, with only one small village (400 residents), and vast tracts of wilderness that rarely feel the imprint of a hiking boot. Its tracks have the most unpredictable weather, the most birdlife and unquestionably the most mud.

The 165,000-hectare island measures 65 km from north to south and 40 km from east to west. But its real beauty lies in its 755-km coast, with its long beaches, impressive sand dunes, and crystal-clear bays ringed by lush rainforest. The interior is mostly bush and is generally broken by steep gullies and ridges, several emerging above the bush-line. The highest point on Stewart Island, Mt Anglem, is only 976 metres, but the walking here can be almost as rugged as in mountainous areas in the North or South islands.

Time slows down and almost stops in this isolated corner of the country. Visitors find life here simpler, the pace unhurried, and the atmosphere in the village of Halfmoon Bay (formerly Oban) relaxed. The remoteness of Stewart Island is a welcome change from the busy tracks of the South Island. There are very few trampers on the tracks after the Christmas period, and the tracks are undeveloped beyond Port William.

The island has more than 220-km of tracks, maintained by DOC staff at Halfmoon Bay. These include the Rakiura Track, a three-day route that was cut in 1986 and is now classified as a Great Walk; it connects huts at Port William and North Arm and provides the only short loop on the island (all the others require seven to 10 days); it's the most popular Stewart Island tramp.

What's surprising about the trampers who arrive at Halfmoon Bay is that 60% of them are overseas travellers. They are obviously more intrigued by the island's remote southern position than Kiwis are.

Most tramping on Stewart Island is not easy. To hike beyond the fully planked and benched Rakiura Track, trampers should be experienced and well equipped. You encounter mud just a few km from the Port William Hut and have to deal with it for much of the way, rain or shine. It's impossible to avoid on the North-West Circuit and most trampers just slosh right through it, ending each evening with a communal washing of boots, socks and feet. It varies from ankle-deep to knee-deep, and even deeper at some ill-famed spots such as Ruggedy Flat and the track to Mt Anglem.

Gaiters are a good piece of equipment to have, but if you are planning an extensive trip, you just have to accept the fact that socks will be wet, pants will be mud-splattered and boots will never be the same colour again.

HISTORY

Rakiura, the Maori name for Stewart Island, means 'heavenly glow', referring perhaps to the aurora australis which is often seen in this southern sky, or to the spectacular blood-red sunsets. The Maoris have a legend about the creation of Rakiura: a young man named Maui left the Polynesian Islands to go fishing, paddled far out to the sea and, out of sight of his homeland, dropped anchor. In time, his waka (canoe) became the South Island, a great fish he caught became the North Island, and his anchor became Rakiura, holding everything in place.

Excavations in the area provide evidence that, as early as the 13th century, tribes of Polynesian origin migrated to the island to hunt moa. Maori settlements were thin and scattered, however, because the people were unable to grow kumara (sweet potato), the staple food of settlements to the north. They did make annual migrations to the outer islands seeking titi (muttonbird), a favourite food, and to the main island searching for eel, shellfish and certain birds.

The first European to sight the area was Captain Cook, in 1770, but he left confused about whether it was part of the South Island. He finally decided it was part of the mainland, naming it Cape South. By the early 1800s, sealers were staying for months at a time to collect skins for the mother ship. There is evidence that American sealer O F Smith discovered Foveaux Strait in 1804 because it was known briefly as Smith's Strait. The island itself derived its European name from William Stewart, the first officer of the English sealer *Pegasus*. Stewart charted large sections of the coast during a sealing trip in 1809 and drafted the first detailed map of the island.

In 1825, a group of sealers and their Maori wives set up a permanent settlement on Codfish Island. Sealing ended by the late 1820s, to be replaced temporarily by whaling. Stewart Island had been a port of call for whalers since the early 1800s, as a place to recuperate after a season at the whaling bases. Small whaling bases were established on the island itself but they were never really profitable and didn't contribute significantly to the island's progress. Neither did timber. Although the island was almost completely covered in bush, most of it was not millable and little was profitably accessible.

In 1886, gold was discovered at Port William in the wake of the great Otago and West Coast gold rushes. A small-scale rush resulted, and further strikes were made at a few beaches on the northern and western coasts. The influx of miners was large enough then to warrant building a hotel and a post office.

The only enterprise that has endured is fishing. Initially, those fishing were few in number and handicapped by the lack of regular transport to the mainland. But when a steamer service from Bluff began in 1885, the industry expanded, resulting in the construction of cleaning sheds on Ruapuke Island and a refrigerating plant in the North Arm of Port Pegasus.

Today, fishing and, to a much lesser extent, tourism are the occupations of most of the 400 residents of Halfmoon Bay. The main catch is crayfish for the export trade, from June to January, while paua and blue cod are caught for the New Zealand market. A new development to the industry started on Stewart Island in 1982 when the first of three sea-cage salmon farms were built in Big Glory Bay.

CLIMATE

The weather here plays havoc with trampers. The island's overall climate is surprisingly mild, considering the latitude, with pleasant temperatures most of the year – cool in summer, rarely cold in winter. The only place where snow occasionally falls is on the summit of Mt Anglem.

Annual rainfall at Halfmoon Bay is only

Muttonbirding

One industry that survived into the present is muttonbirding. As a direct result of the Deed of Cession, signed in 1864, only Maoris who are descendants of the original owners of Stewart Island are allowed to search and take titi (muttonbirds) from the island – the only Europeans allowed this privilege are the spouses of birders.

The sooty shearwater *(Puffinus griseus)*, known affectionately as the muttonbird, nests in burrows on remote islets in the Stewart Island region, laying a single egg in November and hatching it towards the end of December. The parents stay with their chicks for three months, and then depart on their annual migration in March. It's at this stage that the Maoris search out and capture chicks so laden with fat that they can neither fly nor run very far. By May, the remaining chicks have become proficient flyers and can follow their parents.

Although considered greasy by many Pakehas, muttonbirds are a great delicacy to the Maoris. It is the annual hunt itself, however, that has great significance to Maoris – muttonbirding is one important Maori custom that has successfully withstood the assault of European culture. ∎

1600 mm but it occurs over 250 days of the year. Or, as one member of the DOC staff put it, 'you get a little rain on a lot of days'. In the higher altitudes and along the southern and western coasts, rainfall averages 5000 mm a year, which means a lot of rain on a lot of days. It's important to keep in mind that the daily weather (or, more accurately, the hourly weather) changes frequently – it's not uncommon to experience two or three showers and clear blue skies in between one hut and the next.

NATURAL HISTORY

For putting up with mud, hilly terrain and indecisive weather, the tramper is amply rewarded. The bush and birdlife on the island are unique. Beech, the tree that dominates the rest of New Zealand, is absent from Stewart Island. The predominant lowland bush is podocarp forest, with exceptionally tall rimu, miro, totara and kamahi forming the canopy. Due to mild winters, frequent rainfalls and porous soil, most of the island is a lush forest held together by vines and carpeted in ferns and moss. It is so thick and green that the bush appears to be choking the track.

The birdlife on the island is also unique. The ecological disasters (rats and cats) that

Penguin

have greatly affected the mainland have not had as much impact here, so Stewart Island has one of the largest and most diverse bird populations of any area in New Zealand. Those intent on spotting a kiwi in the wild have a good opportunity while tramping here. There are more kiwis on Stewart Island than there are people, and they are less nocturnal than their cousins to the north. The best areas to spot them are around Mason Bay and on Ocean Beach, on The Neck near Paterson Inlet – see the aside on the DOC's guidelines for kiwi-spotting.

Bush birds such as bellbirds, tuis, wood pigeons (kereru) and fantails are often seen along the tracks, and you may see parakeets and kakas (forest parrots) which are rare on the mainland. The island is also the home of several species of penguin (yellow-eyed, Fiordland crested and blue), and colonies are often spotted near Long Harry Bay. Ulva Island, in Paterson Inlet, is especially rich with birdlife.

The most famous bird, which trampers will not see, is the kakapo, the world's only flightless nocturnal parrot. It is the largest parrot in the world, with the males weighing

---

Kiwi Etiquette

Kiwi-spotting on Stewart Island can be enhanced if you observe the following DOC guidelines, designed to minimise disturbance to the birds. It is especially applicable to visitors to Mason Bay or on kiwi-spotting tours from Halfmoon Bay.

- Absolutely no dogs
- Keep noise to a minimum and keep to the tracks
- Stay five metres from the birds at all times; do not follow them
- When using a torch, screen the light with your hand
- Do not use flashlights when taking photographs ■

up to three kg. Thought to have long been extinct, the bird was rediscovered in the southern half of the island in 1977. The kakapo is now only found on predator-free Little Barrier Island (in the Hauraki Gulf) and on Codfish Island (north-west of Stewart Island).

RAKIURA TRACK

The Rakiura Track was built to provide trampers with a short circular track of moderate difficulty as an alternative to the challenging 10-day route around the northern portion of the island. It immediately became the most popular tramp on Stewart Island, virtually replacing the five-day journey up to Christmas Bay as the standard trip for those trampers who have less than a week to spend on the island. The three-day walk has been planked and benched to eliminate most of the mud for which this island is famous. Nights are spent at the Port William Hut and at the North Arm Hut.

Information

For information on tracks and tramping, contact the DOC (☎ 214 4589), Don St, Invercargill. The Southland Museum visitor information centre (☎ 218 9753), at 82 Dee St, also has information.

On the island, there's a DOC Stewart Island visitor centre (☎ 219 1218; for DOC matters ☎ 219 1130) on Main Rd in Halfmoon Bay. In addition to much useful information on the island, it has good dis-

plays on flora & fauna, and you can store gear here while you're walking ($2.50 for a small locker, $5 for a large one).

Several handy pamphlets on tramps on the island, including *Halfmoon Bay Walks*, *Rakiura Track* and *North-West Circuit Tracks*, cost $1 each.

There is a general store at Halfmoon Bay, open from 9 am to 5.30 pm during the week, 10 am until noon on Saturday and Sunday, and 4 to 5 pm on Saturday (only in the busy period). Make sure you order bread, milk, eggs and newspapers in advance if you want them. The Lettuce Inn sells fruit, vegetables, sweets and film, rents videos, and stocks bulk bins of dried food for trampers.

Maps

The Rakiura Track is covered on quads E48 *(Halfmoon Bay)* and D48 *(Ruggedy)* of the 1:50,000 Topomaps 260 series, and by the 1:150,000 Holidaymaker map No 336-10 *(Stewart Island)*.

Huts

Purchase a date-stamped Great Walks pass from the DOC visitor centre for the huts at Port William and North Arm ($8) and for the camp sites at Port William, Maori Beach and Sawdust Bay ($6). Since the Rakiura Track was upgraded to Great Walk status, the huts on the track have been enhanced.

Access

Air Southern Air (☎ 218 9129) flies from

Collecting Seafood on Stewart Island

Eating seafood that you have caught or gathered is an enjoyable part of any coastal tramp. However, the DOC is attempting to effectively manage seafood collecting on Stewart Island and requests that trampers observe the following guidelines.

Trampers collecting seafood should take only as much as they need. If you are fishing, do not keep any Blue Cod less than 33 cm in length from the tip of the nose to the middle of the tail. If you collect paua, do not remove more than 10 per person and make sure that the shells are at least 125 mm (paua will probably die when removed from rocks, so judge their size before you remove them). Do not scuba dive for paua. Recreational anglers should contact the DOC visitor centre on Stewart Island on arrival for an update on recreational fishing regulations.

Visitors with a penchant for seafood should also check biotoxin levels in Paterson Inlet on arrival. It may be a health hazard to consume mussels when biotoxin levels are high. ■

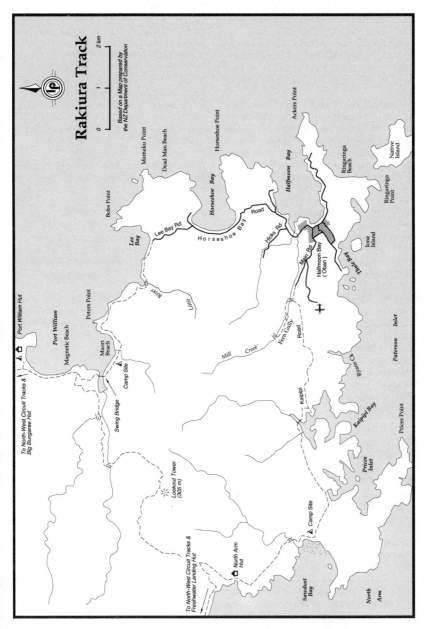

Rakiura Track

Invercargill to Stewart Island for $67.50/118 one-way/return (children half-price). The company also has a student/YHA standby fare ($33.75/67.50 one-way/return); you must present either a YHA or a student card. Be at the airport half an hour before departure.

Southern Air sends a minibus once a day to pick up passengers from the YHA hostel in Invercargill. Other than that, you'll have to make your own way to the Invercargill Airport. The bus from the Stewart Island airstrip to 'town' is included in the airfare.

The free baggage allowance is only 15 kg per person, which is not much if you're carrying camping or tramping gear – if you exceed 20 kg, you'll be charged extra.

Ferry Stewart Island Marine Services (☎ 219 1327, 212 8376) operates the *Foveaux Express* from Bluff to Stewart Island for $37/74 one-way/return (children under 16 half-price). There are departures every day (except Saturday) in summer, and on Tuesday, Friday and Sunday during the winter, often with extra services on public holidays. It's wise to book at least a few days ahead, especially in summer. The crossing takes one hour across the often stormy Foveaux Strait, so take some seasickness pills with you. The ferry operator no longer offers discounts or standby fares which actually makes standby on the plane cheaper. Fly!

Bus Two Invercargill buses connect with the ferry: Campbelltown Passenger (☎ 212 7404) and Foveaux Express Bus Services (☎ 212 8709). They pick up anywhere in Invercargill. Stewart Island Travel (☎ 219 1269) arranges bus tours, taxis and accommodation.

Places to Stay
Invercargill Any trip to Stewart Island includes a stopover in Invercargill. The *Invercargill Caravan Park* (☎ 218 8787) is at the A&P Showgrounds on Victoria Ave, off Dee St and only one km from the centre; tent sites cost $7 and cabins are $22 to $26

for two. The *Coachman's Caravan Park* (☎ 217 6046) at 705 Tay St has tent sites/ cabins for $6/27.50 for two.

The *YHA Hostel* (☎ 215 9344), 122 North Rd, Waikiwi, about three km from the town centre, costs $14 per night. The very comfortable *Southern Comfort* (☎ 218 3838), at 30 Thomson St has dorms/twins for $15/17 per person. The *Coachmans Inn* (☎ 217 6046), 705 Tay St, charges $15 for a bed in a basic cabin.

Rakiura (Stewart Island) There is a free DOC camp site at Apple Bridge, Fern Tree Gully, about half an hour's walk along Main Rd from the wharf, but it's very basic. The *Ferndale Caravan Park* (☎ 219 1176) has tent sites for $5. *Ann's Place* (☎ 219 1065) is $8 per night. The *Shearwater Inn* (☎ 219 1114), Ayr St, charges $28/52 for singles/ doubles, or $20 per person in larger shared rooms; this place has minimal kitchen facilities.

An excellent alternative is to stay in one of the several homes on the island offering hostel-style accommodation; check with the DOC in Halfmoon Bay.

The Track
The following Great Walk, rated medium, is described from Port William to North Arm, the easiest direction to walk the route. For those tramping from North Arm to Port William, you should add two hours to the walking time, for the uphill trek. You need a date-stamped Great Walks pass for this trip, available from the DOC visitor centre.

Stage 1: Halfmoon Bay to Port William
Walking Time: four to five hours
Accommodation: Port William Hut (30 bunks)

Begin at the Halfmoon Bay general store, and walk five km along Horseshoe Bay Rd to Lee Bay, where the track begins. From the track entrance sign, the track cuts through bush, crosses a bridge over Little River, skirts the tidal area on the edge of the forest and then heads inland. Within two km, the track descends onto Maori Beach, where there is a camp site, and follows the smooth sand to reach a swing bridge at the far end, an hour's walk from Little River.

A sawmill began operations here in 1913, and at one time a large wharf and a network of tramways were constructed to extract the rimu. By 1920, there were enough families living here to warrant opening a school. The onset of the Depression led to the closure, in 1931, of Stewart Island's last mill, and now regenerating forest surrounds the old steam haulers and tramways in the area.

From the bridge, the track heads inland to skirt a headland and within a km passes the signposted junction of the Rakiura Track to North Arm Hut. The track to Port William quickly descends the headland and swings close to Magnetic Beach, where the jetty can be seen in the distance. It's possible at low tide to hike along the coast for the last leg to the jetty, instead of following the track.

Port William Hut (30 bunks) is one of the largest huts on the island. In 1876, the government had grand plans for a settlement here, offering 50 families free land to develop the timber resources and offshore fisheries. The settlement was a dismal failure because the utopia which the government had hoped to foster was plagued by isolation and loneliness. All that remains of the settlement today are the large gum trees next to the hut.

Occasionally, a fishing boat will dock at the jetty and the crew will clean their catch of blue cod. You should be able to barter for a few fillets, which makes for an unexpected and delicious dinner.

Stage 2: Port William to North Arm
Walking Time: four to six hours
Accommodation: North Arm Hut (30 bunks)

Backtrack along Magnetic Beach to its southern end, where the track heads inland to cross the headland, almost two km from the Port William Hut. At a signposted junction (45 minutes south of the hut), the Rakiura Track heads west (the right fork), climbs over a hill and descends to a swing bridge over a branch of the unnamed stream which empties onto Maori Beach. The track skirts the valley above the stream's true left (north) side for more than a km, then descends to a second bridge and crosses to the true right (south) side.

The walk becomes tedious, with the track climbing over a number of hills as it heads south, fords another branch of the stream, then swings west. At this point, it makes a 1½-km climb to the high point, at 305 metres. The signposted lookout tower allows you to see Paterson Inlet and the Tin Range to the south.

From here, the track descends sharply, levels out briefly and then descends a second time before ending at the North Arm Hut (30 bunks), reached one to 1½ hours from the lookout.

Stage 3: North Arm to Halfmoon Bay
Walking Time: four hours

This section of the Rakiura Track has recently been constructed and is extensively boardwalked. The track heads south-west for a km, then south-east, and follows the coast above North Arm. At low tide, you can see

Great Walks Ticket

the extensive mudflats of the Freshwater River delta.

The track then comes to a bridge over a creek which drains into Sawdust Bay (a sawmill site between 1914 and 1918). About halfway down the Sawdust Bay beach, there is a camp site, shelter and toilet. From the camp site, the track swings in a more easterly direction, and in one km reaches the head of Prices Inlet. It continues through kamahi and rimu forest, crosses the tidal headwaters of the bay by bridge, and soon reaches sheltered Kaipipi Bay. In the 1860s, the two sawmills at this bay employed more than 100 people.

The track between Kaipipi Bay and Halfmoon Bay is the former Kaipipi Rd, once the best-maintained and most heavily used on the island.

Previously, the old Link Track was used to exit North Arm Hut via Mill Creek and Fern Gully. Since the track has been re-routed, you have to backtrack to see this beautiful profusion of ferns. The gully is north-west of the junction of the end of Kaipipi Rd (Rakiura Track) and the road from Halfmoon Bay; cross the bridge and follow Mill Creek upstream along its true left (north) bank.

From the junction, follow the track south-east as it merges into Main Rd; it's 40 minutes from the junction to Halfmoon Bay. You can follow Main Rd to either the South Sea Hotel or the general store, depending on what you crave most after a tramp.

NORTH-WEST CIRCUIT

This is the classic trip around the northern half of Stewart Island. The trip includes Mason Bay, a 14-km beach where prevailing westerly winds have formed a spectacular set of sand dunes. The beach itself can be an impressive sight, with the surf breaking hundreds of metres out and roaring onto the hard sand. Standing here, you truly feel you're on the edge of the world.

The entire loop is a difficult trip, suitable for experienced trampers only, and requiring 10 to 12 days. Some trampers cut it down to seven days by heading from Benson Peak to Freshwater Landing, skipping Mason Bay altogether. It seems a shame to come so close to this magnificent bay only to bypass it in order to save time.

A much better solution is to incorporate a chartered flight to or from Mason Bay. Southern Air, which flies trampers from Invercargill to Stewart Island, also handles the short (10-minute) flight to Mason Bay. This option allows you to spend seven to eight days hiking to the bay along the best portions of the track and skip some muddy sections along Scott Burn and Freshwater River. The four-seater plane can hold three trampers and their packs. Make arrangements for the flight at the Southern Air desk at the Invercargill Airport, or at Stewart Island Travel (☎ 218 9129) in Halfmoon Bay; they will advise on current charter costs.

There are also a number of charter-boat operators in Halfmoon Bay, and arrangements can be made to be dropped off on the coast, usually no further north than Christmas Village Bay. The Halfmoon Bay DOC visitor centre keeps a list of the current operators.

A highlight of the trip is the offshore fishing. At a number of coastal huts there are rocky points nearby where you can fish for blue cod. The best bait is limpet, the small shellfish that can be gathered easily off the rocks. Cut away the shell and toss your baited hook just off the rocks. Sometimes it's possible to actually see the cod rise to the bait.

See the Information and Access sections of the Rakiura Track for transport, accommodation and tramping details.

Maps

The 1:150,000 Holidaymaker map No 336-10 *(Stewart Island)* covers the entire route, but its scale does not contain enough detail for most trampers. If that's the case, purchase quad D48 *(Ruggedy)* of the 1:50,000 Topomaps 260 series, which covers the entire route except for the well-benched tracks to Port William and North Arm from Halfmoon Bay (E48, *Halfmoon Bay*).

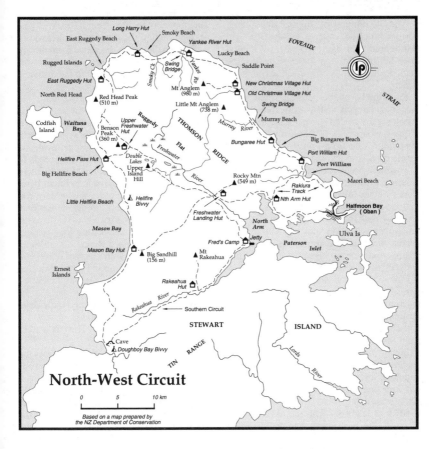

North-West Circuit

0   5   10 km

Based on a map prepared by
the NZ Department of Conservation

Huts

Nearly all huts on Stewart Island, with the exception of the Rakiura Great Walk huts (Port William and North Arm), are $4. There are also some free huts on the island.

The Track

The following trip, rated difficult, is described from Port William to North Arm. See the Rakiura Track section for track descriptions of the segments from Halfmoon Bay to Port William Hut and from North Arm Hut to Halfmoon Bay.

Stage 1: Port William to Christmas Village Hut

Walking Time: seven hours
Accommodation: Big Bungaree Hut (20 bunks); Old Christmas Village Hut (six bunks); New Christmas Village Hut (20 bunks)

From the Port William Hut, return along the side track over the small hump to the main track and head north. You climb a small saddle and cross a footbridge to Sawyers Beach and then head inland, where the famous mud-bashing of Stewart Island begins.

After 40 minutes of slipping and sliding, you are rewarded with a view of the Titi (Muttonbird Islands) to the east. It's a good three-km trek through the bush before the track begins a steady drop to Little Bungaree Beach.

From the beach, you cross a small headland and descend to Big Bungaree Beach, following the golden curve of sand to the hut at the far end. The 20-bunk hut is only a three-hour walk from Port William but is a scenic place to spend the rest of a short day.

The track resumes climbing from the hut, crossing a series of hills and gullies as it works its way inland from Gull Rock Point. In three km, the track descends sharply onto Murray Beach for a two-km stretch of golden sand. This is a good spot to swim, and to collect shells, paua and mussels, but if you attempt to stretch out in the sun, the sandflies will quickly drive you back into your clothes.

Follow the beach, and at the northern end cross the swing bridge over Murray River to reach a side track which leads 100 metres upstream to a well-preserved steam engine half-covered by bush. The engine is left over from mill operations in 1912. A number of tramways were also built, and the main track departs along one of them for a km. The track undulates and crosses numerous streams. In 3½ km, you pass a spur track to the old Christmas Village Hut. The eastern (right-hand) fork leads down to the old hut, then re-enters the bush to ascend to the main track.

The track climbs a hill and then descends to a swing bridge over a stream. On the northern side, near the pebbled beach just north of Christmas Village Bay, is the new Christmas Village Hut. It was built in 1986 and is a vast improvement on the original.

Stage 2: Christmas Village to Yankee River

Walking Time: five to six hours
Accommodation: Yankee River Hut (20 bunks)

Some trampers spend an extra day at Christmas Village Hut to climb Mt Anglem (980 metres), the highest point on Stewart Island.

The junction to the summit track is just beyond the hut; the round trip is a six-hour walk. On a clear day, the views from the top are excellent – you can see most of Stewart Island, and the South Island in the distance. The mud on this side track, however, has been known to be exceptionally bad.

It's a steep climb from the hut to the junction with Mt Anglem Track (the left fork). The main track (right fork) heads north as it works its way through a rimu forest, and remains dry for five km until it descends to a swing bridge and onto Lucky Beach. There is little sand to entice anyone to linger here.

The track begins again at the western end of the beach and climbs through dense ferns and bush. For four km (two hours) you cover undulating terrain, then begin a long descent to the sluggish Yankee River. Just in time, and usually greeted with a sigh of relief, you arrive at a signpost pointing to the hut; five minutes downstream, it comes into view.

Stage 3: Yankee River to Long Harry Bay

Walking Time: five to six hours
Accommodation: Long Harry Hut (six bunks)

Backtrack to the main track. This crosses the Yankee River on a swing bridge, rises steadily for 200 metres over the ridge of Black Rock Point, then descends to Smoky Beach, two hours from the hut. The climb is a knee-bender and the track is often muddy, but the beach and the huge sand dunes are very scenic.

The track continues along the beach for two km to its western end, before heading inland to cross Smoky Creek on a swing bridge. It climbs high above the beach, then begins a tough stretch where it climbs in and out of numerous bush-clad gullies and crosses half a dozen streams. Within three km of Smoky Creek Bridge (a good two-hour trek), the track makes a steady descent to Long Harry Hut, high above the ocean.

The old six-bunk hut is less than inspiring, but the scenic beach along Long Harry Bay is perhaps the best spot on the trip to view a penguin colony. The offshore fishing is also excellent if you scramble onto a nearby rocky point to get away from the kelp beds.

Stage 4: Long Harry Bay to East Ruggedy Hut

Walking Time: three to four hours
Accommodation: East Ruggedy Hut (20 bunks)

The track continues along a terrace behind the hut for a short distance, then climbs along Cave Point Ridge. There are good views along the ridge before the track descends to the broken coast. You follow the coast briefly, then enter the low scrub at a signpost. After a steep 200-metre climb over a ridge, the track descends to a river, with scenic East Ruggedy Beach beyond it.

The track moves inland from the beach, marked by poles through the sand dunes and scrub. A km (about 15 minutes) from the beach it reaches East Ruggedy Hut (20 bunks), which replaced the old two-bunk East Ruggedy Bivvy. You can stay at the roomy hut or head down the side track to West Ruggedy Beach, at the northern end of which is a rock bivvy with room for four people. The rock shelter is a 40-minute walk from East Ruggedy Hut.

Stage 5: East Ruggedy Hut to Hellfire Pass Hut

Walking Time: six to seven hours
Accommodation: Hellfire Pass Hut (20 bunks)

The track works its way to the eastern side of the Ruggedy Range. As it nears the head of Ruggedy Flat, it encounters some extremely deep bogs and mud holes, although boardwalks now span the worst spots. When it reaches the range, the track turns south and offers good views of Red Head Peak to the west. Six km from East Ruggedy Hut, it reaches the junction to Waituna Bay.

The south-western track (right fork) descends to Waituna Bay and continues south to join the track from Benson Peak above Big Hellfire Beach. There is now a 20-bunk hut (Hellfire Pass) along this stretch, which should be your night stop, eliminating the need to make the old 10 to

11-hour slog from East Ruggedy Bivvy (now a hut) to Little Hellfire Bivvy in a single day.

The south-eastern branch (left fork) at the junction gradually sidles off the range to a hut located on the eastern side of Benson Peak (360 metres). Upper Freshwater Hut, also known as Benson Peak Hut, has an open fireplace and six bunks. It's about five km (a two to three-hour hike) to Benson Peak, and there is a track from the peak down to the Hellfire Pass Hut.

Stage 6: Hellfire Pass Hut to Mason Bay

Walking Time: seven hours
Accommodation: Mason Bay Hut (20 bunks)

A 15-minute walk through thick bush and over two gullies brings you to an open tussock flat, a side arm of Ruggedy Flat. Follow the poles for three km through the tussock clearing until the track enters bush again and begins a short and steep climb to the top of a pass. From here, you can view Ruggedy Flat to the east and Big Hellfire Beach to the west. You can reach the beach by following the sand dune for 200 metres down towards the ocean.

The track follows the main ridge of the coastal range, providing more views of the western shoreline of Stewart Island, before descending sharply towards Richard Point. It then swings to the south, works through a number of gullies and, two km from the pass, skirts a small beach. From here, you are less than an hour from Little Hellfire Beach, and just after crossing the next footbridge you come to the site of the Hellfire Bivvy.

Follow the beach for a km, to the southern end, to pick up the signposted track. It quickly moves inland to climb a bush and scrub saddle around Mason Head before descending to the northern end of Mason Bay. From here, you follow the hard, sandy beach – one of the most scenic walks on the island. Mussels are abundant, and are excellent when steamed with a clove or two of garlic.

After a 4½-km stroll, you near the mouth of Duck Creek, where a sign points to Mason Bay Hut. Follow the buoys and stream through the sand dunes to pick up the tractor track that leads to the hut, a pleasant facility with three rooms, 16 bunks and a stove. The hut and the scenic wonders of Mason Bay make it hard not to spend a spare day here. During the day, you can explore the sand dunes, or hike the beach another 10 km to the south; at night you can look (or just listen) for kiwis.

Stage 7: Mason Bay to Freshwater Landing
Walking Time: three to four hours
Accommodation: Freshwater Landing (12 bunks)

The final stretch is presented here as a two-day walk, but stronger trampers would probably combine the last two stages into one long day, stopping for lunch at Freshwater Landing Hut.

The track that leaves Mason Bay is a tractor track. It quickly passes the Island Hill Homestead, one of two on the west coast, and continues as a tractor path around Island Hill and down Scott Burn – it's surprisingly dry, with boardwalks for the wettest parts. After a walk of about three hours through manuka, tussock and scrub, the track reaches Freshwater River and a track junction. From this junction, a track heads off to the north-west (the left fork) onto Ruggedy Flat and eventually to the Upper Freshwater Hut (five

hours). A track also heads down the river along its true right (south) side to Fred's Camp, a hut on the entrance of the South West Arm (four hours) and part of the Southern Circuit. The main track crosses the swing bridge over Freshwater River to arrive at the 12-bunk Freshwater Landing Hut.

Stage 8: Freshwater Landing to North Arm Hut
Walking Time: five to six hours
Accommodation: North Arm Hut (30 bunks)

Avoid the side track to Rocky Mountain (five km, three hours return) and continue along the main track, which begins with a gradual climb from the hut up Thomson Ridge. After 2½ km, the climb becomes considerably steeper, wetter and more slippery. Once above the scrub-line, much of the ridge is boardwalked to avoid boggy areas.

The descent off the ridge is also steep, but in an hour the track sidles above the end of the North Arm and in 2½ km reaches North Arm Hut (30 bunks), overlooking the inlet. Plan on five hours to reach the hut from Freshwater Landing if conditions are good, even longer if it has been raining all day.

It's a five-hour trek from North Arm to Halfmoon Bay. For details of this walk, see Stage 3 of the Rakiura Track (described earlier in this chapter).

Glossary

adit – a horizontal mining tunnel

argillite – hard sedimentary rock composed of mud-sized particles, occurs as bands in greywacke

benched – the gradual nature of a track which eases up or down a slope

bivvy – a crude shelter; also used as a verb meaning to camp, usually without a tent

bridle – a track which was prepared so that it could accommodate horses

cairn – a pile of rocks used to mark a route

circuit – a loop track that brings the tramper back to where they started without covering the same ground

cirque – an alpine basin carved by a glacier, usually at the head of a valley

contouring – to sidle around a hill at approximately the same altitude (or contour interval)

DOC – Department of Conservation, the department which manages the national outdoor estate

DOSLI Department of Survey & Land Information, the department that produces and sells topographical maps, including Topomaps, Parkmaps and Trackmaps

endemic – found in a certain area, eg species of bird

fork – an alternative track leading off from a track junction

4WD track – a track used by a 4WD vehicle such as a Toyota Landcruiser or Land Rover

Gondwanaland – the supercontinent that broke up to form the southern continents

Great Walk – a walk selected by the DOC as being representative of outdoor New Zealand, though not necessarily the best

greywacke – crumbly, dark-grey, sedimentary rock which makes up much of the Southern Alps

moraine – an accumulation of debris pushed into a mound by a glacier; it can be terminal, lateral or medial, depending on its position within the glacial valley

pakihi – the reedy swamp which is peculiar to the West Coast, dominated by manuka and rushes

papa – blue-grey mudstone, from the Maori for Earth Mother

Parkmaps – maps of national parks or forest parks produced by DOSLI

podocarps – native conifers (*Podocarpaceae*), such as miro, rimu, totara, kahikatea and matai

poles – a series of distinctive coloured markers enabling a route to be found even in difficult conditions

SAR – search and rescue

scree steep slopes covered in rock, found in alpine areas

sidle – to walk around or along the side of a hill (see contouring)

slips – areas where huge volumes of earth and rocks have 'slipped' from the hillside obliterating parts of a track; also called a landslide

spur – a small ridge that leads up from a valley to the main ridge

switchbacks – a zigzag pattern of tracks designed to reduce the steepness of a climb or descent

tarn – a small alpine lake, often nestled in flat ridges

Topomaps – those maps of 1:50,000 scale produced as quads (squares) to cover the whole country (those not produced in metric are available as 1:63,360 or one inch to the mile)

traverse – to move horizontally across a slope

true left – the left side of a river when facing downstream

true right – the right side of a river when facing downstream

tuff – volcanic ash

walkwire – a rather flimsy (but nevertheless adequate) set-up for crossing streams and rivers.

Index

MAPS

TEXT

PLANET TALK
Lonely Planet's FREE quarterly newsletter

We love hearing from you and think you'd like to hear from us.

When...is the right time to see reindeer in Finland?
Where...can you hear the best palm-wine music in Ghana?
How...do you get from Asunción to Areguá by steam train?
What...is the best way to see India?

For the answer to these and many other questions read PLANET TALK.

Every issue is packed with up-to-date travel news and advice including:

- *a letter from Lonely Planet founders Tony and Maureen Wheeler*
- *travel diary from a Lonely Planet author - find out what it's really like out on the road*
- *feature article on an important and topical travel issue*
- *a selection of recent letters from our readers*
- *the latest travel news from all over the world*
- *details on Lonely Planet's new and forthcoming releases*

To join our mailing list contact any Lonely Planet office (address below).

LONELY PLANET PUBLICATIONS
Australia: PO Box 617, Hawthorn 3122, Victoria (tel: 03-819 1877)
USA: Embarcadero West, 155 Filbert St, Suite 251, Oakland, CA 94607 (tel: 510-893 8555)
TOLL FREE: (800) 275-8555
UK: 10 Barley Mow Passage, Chiswick, London W4 4PH (tel: 081-742 3161)
France: 71 bis rue du Cardinal Lemoine – 75005 Paris (tel: 1-46 34 00 58)

Also available: Lonely Planet T-shirts. 100% heavyweight cotton (S, M, L, XL)

Guides to the Pacific

Australia – a travel survival kit
The complete low-down on Down Under – home of Ayers Rock, the Great Barrier Reef, extraordinary animals, cosmopolitan cities, rainforests, beaches ... and Lonely Planet!

Bushwalking in Australia
Two experienced and respected walkers give details of the best walks in every state, covering many different terrains and climates.

Bushwalking in Papua New Guinea
The best way to get to know Papua New Guinea is from the ground up – and bushwalking is the best way to travel around the rugged and varied landscape of this island.

Islands of Australia's Great Barrier Reef – Australia guide
The Great Barrier Reef is one of the wonders of the world – and one of the great travel destinations! Whether you're looking for the best snorkelling, the liveliest nightlife or a secluded island hideaway, this guide has all the facts you'll need.

Melbourne – city guide
From historic houses to fascinating churches and from glorious parks to tapas bars, cafés and bistros, Melbourne is a dream for gourmets and a paradise for sightseers.

New South Wales & the ACT
Ancient aboriginal sites, pristine surf beaches, kangaroos bounding across desert dunes, lyre-birds dancing in rainforest, picturesque country pubs, weather-beaten drovers and friendly small-town people, along with Australia's largest and liveliest metropolis (and the host city of the year 2000 Olympic Games) – all this and more can be found in New South Wales and the ACT.

Sydney – city guide
From the Opera House to the surf; all you need to know in a handy pocket-sized format.

Outback Australia
The outback conjures up images of endless stretches of dead straight roads, the rich red of the desert, and the resourcefulness and resilience of the inhabitants. A visit to Australia would not be complete without visiting the outback to see the beauty and vastness of this ancient country.

Victoria – Australia guide
From old gold rush towns to cosmopolitan Melbourne and from remote mountains to the most popular surf beaches, Victoria is packed with attractions and activities for everyone.

Fiji – a travel survival kit
Whether you prefer to stay in camping grounds, international hotels, or something in-between, this comprehensive guide will help you to enjoy the beautiful Fijian archipelago.

Hawaii – a travel survival kit
Share in the delights of this island paradise – and avoid some of its high

prices – with this practical guide. It covers ìall of Hawaii's well-known attractions, plus plenty of uncrowded sights ìand activities.

Micronesia – a travel survival kit
The glorious beaches, lagoons and reefs of these 2100 islands ìwould dazzle even the most jaded traveller. This guide has all the ìdetails on island-hopping across the Micronesian archipelago.

New Caledonia – a travel survival kit
This guide shows how to discover all that the idyllic islands ìof New Caledonia have to offer – from French colonial culture ìto traditional Melanesian life.

New Zealand – a travel survival kit
This practical guide will help you discover the very best New ìZealand has to offer: Maori dances and feasts, some of the most spectacular ìscenery in the world, and every outdoor activity imaginable.

Papua New Guinea – a travel survival kit
With its coastal cities, villages perched beside mighty rivers, ìpalm-fringed beaches and rushing mountain streams, Papua New Guinea ìpromises memorable travel.

Rarotonga & the Cook Islands – a travel survival kit
Rarotonga and the Cook Islands have history, beauty and magic ìto rival the better-known islands of Hawaii and Tahiti, but the world ìhas virtually passed them by.

Samoa – a travel survival kit
Two remarkably different countries, Western Samoa and American ìSamoa offer some wonderful island escapes, and Polynesian culture ìat its best.

Solomon Islands – a travel survival kit
The Solomon Islands are the best-kept secret of the Pacific. ìDiscover remote tropical islands, jungle-covered volcanoes and traditional ìMelanesian villages with this detailed guide.

Tahiti & French Polynesia – a travel survival kit
Tahiti's idyllic beauty has seduced sailors, artists and travellers ìfor generations. The latest edition of this book provides full details ìon the main island of Tahiti, the Tuamotos, Marquesas and other island ìgroups. Invaluable information for independent travellers and package ìtourists alike.

Tonga – a travel survival kit
The only South Pacific country never to be colonised by Europeans, ìTonga has also been ignored by tourists. The people of this far-flung ìisland group offer some of the most sincere and unconditional hospitality ìin the world.

Vanuatu – a travel survival kit
Discover superb beaches, lush rainforests, dazzling coral reefs ìand traditional Melanesian customs in this glorious Pacific Ocean ìarchipelago.

Also available:
Pidgin phrasebook.

Lonely Planet Guidebooks

Lonely Planet guidebooks cover every accessible part of Asia as well as Australia, the Pacific, South America, Africa, the Middle East, Europe and parts of North America. There are five series: *travel survival kits*, covering a country for a range of budgets; *shoestring guides* with compact information for low-budget travel in a major region; *walking guides*; *city guides* and *phrasebooks*.

Australia & the Pacific
Australia
Australian phrasebook
Bushwalking in Australia
Islands of Australia's Great Barrier Reef
Outback Australia
Fiji
Fijian phrasebook
Melbourne city guide
Micronesia
New Caledonia
New South Wales
New Zealand
Tramping in New Zealand
Papua New Guinea
Bushwalking in Papua New Guinea
Papua New Guinea phrasebook
Rarotonga & the Cook Islands
Samoa
Solomon Islands
Sydney city guide
Tahiti & French Polynesia
Tonga
Vanuatu
Victoria

South-East Asia
Bali & Lombok
Bangkok city guide
Cambodia
Indonesia
Indonesia phrasebook
Laos
Malaysia, Singapore & Brunei
Myanmar (Burma)
Burmese phrasebook
Philippines
Pilipino phrasebook
Singapore city guide
South-East Asia on a shoestring
Thailand
Thai phrasebook
Vietnam
Vietnamese phrasebook

Middle East
Arab Gulf States
Egypt & the Sudan
Arabic (Egyptian) phrasebook
Iran
Israel
Jordan & Syria
Middle East
Turkey
Turkish phrasebook
Trekking in Turkey
Yemen

North-East Asia
China
Beijing city guide
Cantonese phrasebook
Mandarin Chinese phrasebook
Hong Kong, Macau & Canton
Japan
Japanese phrasebook
Korea
Korean phrasebook
Mongolia
North-East Asia on a shoestring
Seoul city guide
Taiwan
Tibet
Tibet phrasebook
Tokyo city guide

Indian Ocean
Madagascar & Comoros
Maldives & Islands of the East Indian Ocean
Mauritius, Réunion & Seychelles

Mail Order

Lonely Planet guidebooks are distributed worldwide.They are also available by mail order from Lonely Planet, so if you have difficulty finding a title please write to us. US and Canadian residents should write to Embarcadero West, 155 Filbert St, Suite 251, Oakland CA 94607, USA ; European residents should write to 10 Barley Mow Passage, Chiswick, London W4 4PH; and residents of other countries to PO Box 617, Hawthorn, Victoria 3122, Australia.

Indian Subcontinent
Bangladesh
India
Hindi/Urdu phrasebook
Trekking in the Indian Himalaya
Karakoram Highway
Kashmir, Ladakh & Zanskar
Nepal
Trekking in the Nepal Himalaya
Nepali phrasebook
Pakistan
Sri Lanka
Sri Lanka phrasebook

Africa
Africa on a shoestring
Central Africa
East Africa
Trekking in East Africa
Kenya
Swahili phrasebook
Morocco, Algeria & Tunisia
Arabic (Moroccan) phrasebook
South Africa, Lesotho & Swaziland
Zimbabwe, Botswana & Namibia
West Africa

Central America & the Caribbean
Baja California
Central America on a shoestring
Costa Rica
Eastern Caribbean
Guatemala, Belize & Yucatán: La Ruta Maya
Mexico

North America
Alaska
Canada
Hawaii

South America
Argentina, Uruguay & Paraguay
Bolivia
Brazil
Brazilian phrasebook
Chile & Easter Island
Colombia
Ecuador & the Galápagos Islands
Latin American Spanish phrasebook
Peru
Quechua phrasebook
South America on a shoestring
Trekking in the Patagonian Andes
Venezuela

Europe
Baltic States & Kaliningrad
Central Europe on a shoestring
Central Europe phrasebook
Dublin city guide
Eastern Europe on a shoestring
Eastern Europe phrasebook
Finland
France
Greece
Hungary
Iceland, Greenland & the Faroe Islands
Ireland
Italy
Mediterranean Europe on a shoestring
Mediterranean Europe phrasebook
Poland
Scandinavian & Baltic Europe on a shoestring
Scandinavian Europe phrasebook
Switzerland
Trekking in Spain
Trekking in Greece
USSR
Russian phrasebook
Western Europe on a shoestring
Western Europe phrasebook

The Lonely Planet Story

Lonely Planet published its first book in 1973 in response to the numerous 'How did you do it?' questions Maureen and Tony Wheeler were asked after driving, bussing, hitching, sailing and railing their way from England to Australia.

Written at a kitchen table and hand collated, trimmed and stapled, *Across Asia on the Cheap* became an instant local bestseller, inspiring thoughts of another book.

Eighteen months in South-East Asia resulted in their second guide, *South-East Asia on a shoestring*, which they put together in a backstreet Chinese hotel in Singapore in 1975. The 'yellow bible' as it quickly became known to backpackers around the world, soon became *the* guide to the region. It has sold well over half a million copies and is now in its 8th edition, still retaining its familiar yellow cover.

Today there are over 140 Lonely Planet titles in print – books that have that same adventurous approach to travel as those early guides; books that 'assume you know how to get your luggage off the carousel' as one reviewer put it.

Although Lonely Planet initially specialised in guides to Asia, they now cover most regions of the world, including the Pacific, South America, Africa, the Middle East and Europe. The list of *walking guides* and *phrasebooks* (for 'unusual' languages such as Quechua, Swahili, Nepali and Egyptian Arabic) is also growing rapidly.

The emphasis continues to be on travel for independent travellers. Tony and Maureen still travel for several months of each year and play an active part in the writing, updating and quality control of Lonely Planet's guides.

They have been joined by over 50 authors, 90 staff – mainly editors, cartographers & designers – at our office in Melbourne, Australia, at our US office in Oakland, California and at our European office in Paris; another five at our office in London handle sales for Britain, Europe and Africa. Travellers themselves also make a valuable contribution to the guides through the feedback we receive in thousands of letters each year.

The people at Lonely Planet strongly believe that travellers can make a positive contribution to the countries they visit, both through their appreciation of the countries' culture, wildlife and natural features, and through the money they spend. In addition, the company makes a direct contribution to the countries and regions it covers. Since 1986 a percentage of the income from each book has been donated to ventures such as famine relief in Africa; aid projects in India; agricultural projects in Central America; Greenpeace's efforts to halt French nuclear testing in the Pacific and Amnesty International. In 1993 $100,000 was donated to such causes.

Lonely Planet's basic travel philosophy is summed up in Tony Wheeler's comment, 'Don't worry about whether your trip will work out. Just go!'.